PRAISE FOR JONATHAN SHAW

"Finally, after twenty-plus years of coaxing, cajoling, pleading and basic needling on my part, my ol' scallywag brother, Jonathan Shaw has put his pen to paper, dragging and drudging up virulent and violent hallucinations from his not-so-cute brainscape. Been waiting too long for this. So have you, whoever you are, believe me.

"If you don't yet know him, you will. If you didn't want to, too bad. Once he's in, he's in. Jonathan Shaw's words, work, life, lives, deaths, rants, rage, hilarity and taste rank with the best of 'em.

"If Hubert Selby Jr., Charles Bukowski, Ernest Hemingway, Jack Kerouac, William Burroughs, Neil Cassidy, Dr. Hunter S. Thompson, the Marquis de Sade, Antonio Carlos Jobim, Joao Gilberto, Edward Teach, Charley Parker, Iggy Pop, Louis-Ferdinand Celine, R. Crumb, Robert Williams, Joe Coleman, Dashiell Hammett, E.M. Cioran and all of the Three Stooges had all been involved in some greasy, shameful whorehouse orgy, Jonathan Shaw would surely be its diabolical reprobate spawn."—**Johnny Depp**

"Although known primarily for his work as a famed tattoo artist, Shaw is also a talented writer whose latest book, *Scab Vendor*, draws on his own life, vacillating between first person and third person to tell his story in this sprawling, experimental autobiography... The comparisons to Charles Bukowski are obvious, but *Scab Vendor* reminded me more of Hubert Selby Jr. and Henry Miller in terms of tone and style... Interspersed with vignettes from Shaw's life (and foggy memories of a chaotic childhood ("other kids got [the] Hardy Boys... I got Hieronymus Bosch"), *Scab Vendor* [is] a whirlpool of drugs and alcohol. The gritty, gutter prose is sharpened by Shaw's gift for dialogue and sharp insight. This tale is one of shame, humility, and wonder at how it all happened."—***Publishers Weekly***

"The grunge of Bukowski... The teeth-grinding momentum of the Beats."—***Kirkus Reviews***

"Jonathan Shaw is the next Bukowski."—***Rolling Stone***

"{Shaw is} a hunk of shit fish-asshole cunt-sucker!"—**Charles Bukowski**

"Is he bitter? Oh, just a tad."—**R. Crumb**

"Compelling and hot as a sticky summer night that won't let you sleep."—*New York Times Book Review*

"Jonathan Shaw's writing is one hell of a wild ride through the bizarre netherworld of his own damaged consciousness. His experiences are real and his language and insights kinetic and brutal. This is what the French would call "littérature maudit," and Shaw's writing certifies him as a subversive and criminal inhabitant of the world of human expression."—**Jim Jarmusch**

"Jonathan Shaw is a decorated veteran of the drug war whose deviance is only exceeded by his clever ability to weave his own sickness into a true classic of American literature. He is Oscar Wilde and Charlie Manson tattooing a portrait of Dorian Gray on the white underbelly of a society desperately in need of this type of fearless storytelling."—**Marilyn Manson**

"Jonathan Shaw has been a Zelig-like figure in American underground culture for the past forty years."—*Esquire*

"...{Jonathan Shaw is} a real writer..."—**Henry Rollins**

"Jonathan Shaw has made it through the eye-of-the-needle into our lives. This kind of rite of passage gives his perspectives a sense of the physical world that he creates for us. To immerse ourselves in this bare bones-attitude is what a novel is supposed to do for the reader. Lucky us."—**Debbie Harry**

"Jonathan Shaw's passionate descriptions of the surreal, paranoid jungle he inhabits capture the haunting poetry of his soul."—**Hubert Selby Jr., author of *Requiem for a Dream* and *Last Exit to Brooklyn***

"Shaw's writing reinvents and promotes life. Be prepared to see yourself in the pages of *Narcisa*, the essence of your own poor humanity, weak and vulnerable and unprepared - and to see at the same time your own strengths, whatever your circumstances."—**Paulo Lins, author of *City of God***

"Required reading. One of my favorite writers."—**Lydia Lunch, author of *Paradoxia***

"Jonathan Shaw has had his passport stamped in hell so many times he could get his mail there… Written in blood, his writing takes us places most people never come back from… Vile as junkie-cum, beautiful as a dead drunk's bible, Scab Vendor will keep you clawing at the pages…"—**Jerry Stahl, author of *Permanent Midnight***

"{Jonathan Shaw's *Narcisa* is a} compelling novel that grips you right from the beginning."—***VICE***

"Shaw's poetic collage lays bare the poetry of the streets and probes the shadowy corners of the soul with fearless candor."—**Jillian Lauren, *New York Times* bestselling author of *Some Girls***

"Literate and compelling…"—**Harlan Ellison, Grammy Award-winning author of *Strange Wine***

"Jonathan Shaw has blazed a new literary trail, and ripped a new asshole in consensus reality along the way."—**Carlo McCormick, author of *Trespass***

"Jonathan Shaw is a revelation. The pen may be mightier than the sword, but Shaw's work is an IED on paper."—**Dan Fante, author of *Chump Change* and *86'd***

"Dazzling!"—**Harold Schechter, author of *Deviant* and *Man-Eater***

"Amazing writing."—**Kat Von D.**

"An example of human indestructibility that is hard to surpass."—**Eugene Hutz, Gogol Bordello**

"A writer of immense passion and soul, Jonathan Shaw has the courage to vivisect his own soul."—**Joe Coleman, author of *Cosmic Retribution***

"Few have dipped so deeply or functioned so extensively in the cultural underbelly of our world than Jonathan Shaw… He is a virtuoso."—**Robert Williams, author of *Slang Aesthetics***

"Jonathan Shaw is a true old-school storyteller with a criminal mind and heart who's lived what he writes. Welcome to Hell."—**Bonge, Hells Angels**

"Jonathan Shaw is a Renaissance Lowlife. Openhearted prose... Pure magic."—**Larry "Ratso" Sloman, author of** *The Secret Life of Houdini*

"An agonized cri de coeur ... Shades of Dante, of Baudelaire, of Bukowski, of Celine..."—**Tom Nolan, author of** *Three Chords for Beauty's Sake*

"Nightmarish talent... wedged between outlaw and genius... serious street cred."—*N.Y. Press*

"Jonathan Shaw is a myth: an American anti-hero whose wild exploits are folklore in underground circles the world over."—*Huck* **magazine**

"Bruised, brilliant and unapologetically raw."—*Gonzo Today*

"Jonathan Shaw is an American classic... a barbarian intellectual and optimistic cynic..."—*Juxtapoz*

"{Shaw's Narcisa follows} in the great tradition of cultural criminals like Genet, Rimbaud, Artaud through the Beats."—*Paper*

"Shaw is an acknowledged master craftsman."—*Seconds*

"Narcisa reads like a long-lost literary classic by Kerouac, Burroughs, Miller, Fante, Bukowski."—*CVLT Nation*

"A cult classic... Oozes delicious dysfunction... Gritty and raw as an open wound... Never before has an author explored {co-dependency} with such honest integrity ..."—*Beverly Hills Courier*

"In line with the best of Fante, Bukowski and Kerouac...Uppercuts for each sentence... Powerful, furious, brilliant." —*Librairie Quai des Brumes,* **France**

"Magnificently narrated by Shaw, *Narcisa* presents a violent and dazzling Rio de Janeiro as its ghostly, otherworldly stage."—*El Fanzine,* **Mexico**

"Intense as hallucinations from the flames of Hell, Shaw's writing transcends the dark melancholy of a devastated Paradise."—*Reporte Indigo,* **Mexico**

"{*Narcisa*} will bring tears to reader's eyes."—*Folha de São Paulo,* **Brazil**

"*Narcisa*' is the confession of a hungry ghost, the insatiable, the unloved core of humanity's deepest sorrow. This beautifully written, brutally honest tale speaks to the wounded and weary child within each of us. "—**Noah Levine, author of *Dharma Punx* and *Against the Stream***

"An intoxicating classic of subversive writing. Stains your soul with pitch black tar."—*Dengue Magazine,* **Brazil**

"Shaw is an iconoclastic stranger in the literary nest."—*Life and Style*

"Very vibrant, very important art."—*Men's Journal*

"Jonathan Shaw is a notorious innovator and creator."—*Ponyboy* **magazine**

"… A resoundingly successful debut {by a} counter-culture icon… "—*Inquisitr*

"Shaw is a true philosophical, transcendent soul."—*Citizine*

"Absolutely intoxicating… Bukowski on acid… Dark and hypnotic."—**Powell's Books**

"Your jaw will drop, your mind will be blown, and you might even want to jerk off a few times."—*Crusher* **magazine**

"A sordid tale… Fascinating and toxic..."—*Grazia,* **France**

"… An explosive, intoxicating novel. Oral, electric, crazy. *Narcisa* seduces."—*Hall des Livres,* **France**

"Jonathan Shaw is an authentic 'beatnik'… The real-life model for Johnny Depp's Captain Jack the Pirate… Heir to Kerouac and Bukowski, with a strong Brazilian cultural orientation."—*O Globo* **magazine, Brazil**

"Written in a frenetic, addictive style not suitable for all audiences, *Narcisa* is either loved or hated, but never ignored."—*Revista Semana,* **Colombia**

SCAB VENDOR

SCAB VENDOR

CONFESSIONS OF A TATTOO ARTIST

A self-portrait by **Jonathan Shaw**

TURNER

Turner Publishing Company
Nashville, Tennessee
New York, New York

www.turnerpublishing.com

Scab Vendor: Confessions of a Tattoo Artist

Cover artwork: R. Crumb
Back cover artwork: Jorge Flores-Oliver
Cover design: Maddie Cothren
Book design: Glen Edelstein

Library of Congress Cataloging-in-Publication Data

Names: Shaw, Jonathan, 1954- author.
Title: Scab vendor : confessions of a tattoo artist / a self-portrait by
  Jonathan Shaw.
Description: Nashville, Tennessee : Turner Publishing Company, [2017]
Identifiers: LCCN 2016050530 | ISBN 9781681629155 (pbk. : alk. paper)
Subjects: LCSH: Shaw, Jonathan. | Tattoo artists--United States--Biography.
Classification: LCC GT5960.T36 S53 2017 | DDC 818/.603 [B] --dc23
LC record available at https://lccn.loc.gov/2016050530
9781681629155

Printed in the United States of America
16 17 18 19 20 9 8 7 6 5 4 3 2 1

FOR GENEVIEVE, WITH GRATITUDE AND LOVE.

PREFACE

You might know the name Jonathan Shaw as belonging to the first tattoo artist to ever appear on *The Tonight Show with David Letterman*. Or maybe you've seen my unlikely likeness depicted by Pulitzer Prize-winning artist Art Spiegelman on the cover of the stately old *The New Yorker*. You might know me as the son of legendary Swing-era bandleader Artie Shaw—or maybe the tattooed thug giving Clint Eastwood beef in the movie *Tightrope*.

You may have seen the magazine I founded back in the early '90s, *International Tattoo Art*, at your local newsstand. Or you might have read my novel, *Narcisa: Our Lady of Ashes*, published by Johnny Depp's HarperCollins imprint, or my recent visual archeological dig into the history of tattoo art, *Vintage Tattoo Flash*, on Powerhouse Books.

You may have read random excerpts from my ongoing Scab Vendor memoir series online. Or maybe you only remember the name Jonathan Shaw as the infamous "Tattoo Artist to the Stars" who made headline news for being indicted by a New York City Grand Jury and charged with 89 felony counts of illegal weapons possession.

Or . . . maybe you've never heard of me at all. I'm going to assume that's the case and - at my publisher's suggestion - write a few short words of introduction about myself, and this book:

For decades, I was a world-famous "celebrity tattoo artist." Over the course of a long, surreal career, I became one of the most infamous and influential tattoo men on the planet. My client list included cops, criminals and captains of Industry, along with many famous names. Names like Johnny Depp, The Cure, The Velvet Underground, The Pogues, The Ramones, Marilyn Manson, Jim Jarmusch, Joe Coleman, Johnny Winter, Kate Moss, and the notorious Great Train Robber, Ronald Biggs—not to mention Tupac Shakur and all his bitches. Even Vanilla Ice was lining up for an appointment - much to my embarrassment - but hey, it was the 90s, right?

Strangely, I'm still one of the most respected names in the tattoo profession today—despite having officially retired over 15 years ago from an industry with an absurdly short memory—an industry I was unwittingly instrumental in pioneering.

So, what to say about this book?

The long, cockeyed evolution of this opening installment my multi-volume *Scab Vendor* memoir saga has more to do with the long, cockeyed evolution of the long, cockeyed life that spawned it than with any high-falutin literary aspirations. All of the crazy shit contained herein is basically fertilizer for this humble chronicle of a life. My life. The good, the bad, and the ugly. This initial volume spans roughly the first twenty-something years of this bizarre, stranger-than-fiction existence – what is commonly known as my "formative years." The rest, as they say, is history. History, which will be covered in subsequent volumes, God willing.

That said, I believe that, as human beings, we all come hard-wired with an inherent need to share our strength, weakness, pain, passion, despair, hope, love, hate and general personal stories with those of our kind, in order to help one another navigate our common human experience. In that sense, storytelling can be seen as a powerful evolutionary tool. And, like tattooing, it seems to be one of the most ancient compulsions of the human psyche. So, dear reader, without further introduction I invite you to dig in and read all about it. In the words of my esteemed predecessor, Hunter S. Thompson, "buy the ticket, take the ride."

So, I thank you for buying the ticket. And I sincerely hope you will enjoy taking the ride half as much as I've enjoyed surviving it.

Jonathan Shaw
Cartagena, Colombia, 2017

SCAB VENDOR

BOOK ONE

'Twas brillig, and the slithy toves
Did gyre and gimble in the wabe:
All mimsy were the borogoves,
And the mome raths outgrabe.

"Beware the Jabberwock, my son!
The jaws that bite, the claws that catch!
Beware the Jubjub bird, and shun
The frumious Bandersnatch!"

He took his vorpal sword in hand:
Long time the manxome foe he sought —
So rested he by the Tumtum tree,
And stood awhile in thought.

And, as in uffish thought he stood,
The Jabberwock, with eyes of flame,
Came whiffling through the tulgey wood,
And burbled as it came!

One, two! One, two! And through and through
The vorpal blade went snicker-snack!
He left it dead, and with its head
He went galumphing back.

"And, has thou slain the Jabberwock?
Come to my arms, my beamish boy!
O frabjous day! Callooh! Callay!"
He chortled in his joy.

— *Lewis Carroll*

1. A DREAM OF LIFE

"THE WORD 'HERO' NEVER SEEMS TO FIT THE NOIR
PROTAGONIST, FOR HIS WORLD IS DEVOID OF THE MORAL
FRAMEWORK NECESSARY TO PRODUCE THE
TRADITIONAL HERO."

—ROBERT G. PORFIRIO

HOTEL blink *HOTEL* blink *HOTEL* blink *HOTEL* blink *HOTEL* blink
HOTEL blink *HOTEL* blink . . .

Dusk. Drawn to a hypnotic red neon flicker, a heavily tattooed leather-clad figure eases his battered black motorcycle to the edge of the apocalyptic Mexican highway. Lured like a giant metallic insect to another downbeat oasis, the road-weary Gypsy brings the big bike to a stop, surrendering to the night.

They say the months before you die are the most relieving and joyful, the most magical of your life. They say the magic is in an unconscious surrender to death. That's what they say.

Late winter, 2002. Still alive. It's been over a year since the Curse caught up with Cigano and almost snuffed out his life; just months now since the gates of Hell opened wide in New York City on September 11; and a decade to go—according to the ancient Mayan Calendar—until 2012 and the long-prophesied "Death of Illusion."

For Cigano, the Death has already happened. There's nothing left to lose. But he's not tripping on any of that shit. He's too shot after another hard day's ride to be tripping on anything. His body aches. Road dust fills his nostrils, clotting up his rusty old DNA. Dust and bones. Calcified larynx. He feels like he's been waiting forever for a glass of water at the bottom of a dried-out well. The big trucks rumble past as he pries his ass from the bike and limps over to a hut marked *OFICINA*. Another darkened city of the Mexican night; another faceless urban landscape whose name eludes him, like all the others. He'll find out where he is in the morning, should he live another day. Not that he'd give two pinches of shit to know. Like all the other anonymous piss-stops along the road to hell, Cigano knows he'll never see this place again.

As he stretches his pained-out arms and hands above his head, his limbs seem to vibrate still with the steady hum of the throttle and the pounding motor that's as much a part of him now as whatever's left of his liver, his kidneys, his overloaded, heat-maddened brain. Cigano is well accustomed to the solitary motorized pull of constant motion, momentum, concentration and speed. Off the bike, though, he feels unsteady, like a drunken sailor. With a weary grimace, he reaches into his pocket and fishes out a handful of crumpled peso notes. He hands the cash to a faceless man, takes the room key and parks the bike by a row of colorful low cement bungalows. He finds his cell-like cubicle at the end of a dirt path littered with dusty cactus plants. He limps back to un-strap a worn leather valise from the seat, then steps into another neat little room and the familiar scent of cheap hotel soap, roach spray and eucalyptus floor-wash.

Minutes later, he's passed out on the hard single mattress. Falling like a helmeted Jules Verne deep-sea diver into chambers of golden sleep, down, down, down he sinks, emerging in another time, another dimension, another life, where he is a disincarnate camera of mind.Images appear like in an old movie: vague outlines of a group of boys emerging from the watery dreamscape, American kids marching along a tree-lined suburban street, past rows of orderly homes with neatly trimmed green lawns. The boys are all talking at once, gesturing in slow motion, pushing and shoving each other down a sprinkler-hissing summer sidewalk. The dreamer can make out an intense brooding eight-year-old named Jono, walking out of step with the others. As the boy breaks away from the group, the dreamer's vision follows him through a vacant lot and past a row of tall eucalyptus trees. Leaves writhe in the wind like tiny puppets. The camera eye halts at the tree's surface, where bark is peeled away, exposing a flesh as white as the boy's tight young skin. The eye moves on, scanning down the trunk, past crawling ants, over knotholes and bumps, down, down, to where the wood is littered with names and initials. The graffiti grow denser at the bottom, jumbled together like angry hieroglyphics, competing for space where generations of kids and lovers have carved their memories.

The other boys crowd around in an excited cluster as an alien reptilian eye watches from another chamber of the dreamer's vision. The brooding boy stands slightly apart from the group, observing a lizard on a branch. The creature seems to be watching him too as he squints, whittling its crude likeness into the tall shimmering eucalyptus's sappy green flesh. The boy's concentration is focused only on the lizard, taking its shape and detail into his eye as his hand reproduces its image. The other boys move closer. They seem to be taunting the carver. Ignoring their jeers, he remains transfixed by the reptile, obsessed with its essence and form.

A sudden streak of gray startles his eye as a rock bounces off the tree and the lizard scampers off. The others are laughing out loud. A red-headed kid picks up a rock and takes aim again. Jono stops, penknife in hand. Quick as a rattlesnake strike, he turns and stabs the rock-thrower in his freckled arm.

Gawking, frozen faces. Blood. The dreamer watches the shadowy silent movie unfolding as Jono stands in the center of his vision, brandishing the knife with a feral grimace, a silent rage of pristine hate. Scrambling feet trample over dirt, and then the carver's tormenters are gone. Alone now, he completes his first tattoo on living tissue. He stands back, regarding his handiwork with a sly grin. It feels significant to him, like one of those old-time cave paintings in history class.

Wood chips fall like snowflakes, covering the cracked yellowed dreamscape and landing around the roots as the wood begins to bleed in dark red weeping pools. With a freeze-frame flicker, the roots start to move, entwining themselves around the boy's legs.

The dream, the dreamer, and Jono are one. Jono. Jonathan Shaw. Cigano.

He stands rooted to the trembling ground, surrounded by a surreal landscape of pounding fevered shadows, trapped, paralyzed, as the old nightmare engulfs him; and once again, he is unable to scream or run or awaken.

2. VERACRUZ

"FATE HOLDS THE STRINGS, AND MEN LIKE
CHILDREN MOVE."

–SIR HENRY LANSDOWNE

Siesta time in the port of Veracruz. Built by unsmiling Spanish invaders on the malarial Gulf Coast of Mexico, the antique hurricane-beaten time warp of Cuban-style buildings lingers like a watery fragment of forgotten memory. Rusty freighters bask at anchor in the old port's dirty green waters. Time moves slowly under the indifferent gazes of blinking Chinamen and lethargic sailors. Enormous winches strain at the docks. In a ceaseless din of pounding machinery, they extract their mysterious cargos from the musty bowels of hulking phantom shadows.

In a disheveled plaza, a rusty iron anchor sits in tall weeds. An Indian boy with hair black as crow's wings stares up into the sky where a red balloon, slipped from his grasp like a lizard's tail, rises in the stagnant air. Tears form in obsidian eyes beneath the humid blanket of low-lying clouds. Stifling a brave little sniffle, impotent as a bedbug, he squints into the steely heavens where his lonesome red balloon bounces off into the distance.

Families stroll the whitewashed seawall like flocks of colorful birds in a scruffy zoo, mingling with the port's timeless whores and sailors. Distant marimba music glides across muggy air currents as white scavenger seabirds circle above. A transistor radio's tinny Salsa beat cuts through the fading afternoon air like a straight razor flashing in a dark cantina. Old men sit in long shadows near the docks, playing dominoes at cock-eyed wooden tables. Sailors in sun-faded blue shirts loiter on the decks of small boats, passing marijuana cigarettes and drinking. Tattered Indian children hawk bright scraps of nothing to passersby, playful ghosts of the long Mexican afternoon.

Veracruz, the eternal puppeteer, ebbing and flowing to her own sensuous tropical rhythm. And all who touch upon her ancient soil stumble like actors in a trance across the stage of her shabby dreamlike spell.

3. CIGANO

Cigano leans the scarred black-iron wasp into another graceful green curve. Another perfect moment, free from the burden of mass and matter and self. Hurtling through sunlit time and space, weightless and free, motorcycle and rider are at one with the ride, a total focus in the One, the Holy presence of Now. The humid air seems to flow right through him, filling his beat-up Gypsy soul like a red balloon with a feast of smells, sights, and sounds of the eternal Mexican road. This is the only place Cigano has ever really wanted to be, the blessed intersection of Here and Now. No past, no future; nothing but the caressing tropical winds of motion and momentum cooling the sweat of his body. Navigating the highway's narrow black typewriter ribbon, his mind wanders over the pages of the book he'd read after awakening from the nightmares. Liberated from their greasy weight, he smiles as the words run through his head like ticker tape.

"The human brain is divided into two distinct 'halves,' the left and right sides. These two separate brain hemispheres see reality in different ways, and this is expressed in different perspectives. The left side is the 'material world' reality of language and structure, what passes for 'logic' and the general 'physical' world perspective. It decodes information encoded in the energetic fabric of our reality into sequence, to give us the

illusion of 'time' passing from 'past' to 'future.' The right brain knows that there is no time, only the eternal 'Now' . . ."

Only the eternal Now. Cigano knows this is the only truth for him today; that everything he once believed to be real and important was but a parade of persistent, dangerous illusions, phantoms of his own dangerous, damaged mind. The insidious, lying bondage of Self.

He glances at the bike's oblong mirror. Seeing his image floating before him like a caricature, his devilish goateed grin, gold teeth sparkling in the afternoon light, he starts to laugh, cackling like the crazy little yellow-green parrots darting through the riotous roadside carnival of blurry details and jumbled *chingaderas*, all winking and whirring in a speeding streamlined cacophony of the senses; a mad carnival of sounds, sights, and colors, flashing details of impossible nameless contraptions and fascinating holy configurations, fabulous bursts of speed and freeze-frame stillness, light, shadow, and motion. Life. For Cigano, God is in the details.

"Thank you, Lord!" He hears his voice shouting over the engine's rumble. Feeling tears running along his face and drying in the warm rushing wind, he prays in a loud stream of gratitude, verbalizing his thanks to whatever angels or gods or spirits have delivered him into this blessed moment of merciful peace and surrender. Leaning the big machine into another quintessential curve, the powerful motor beneath his crotch unwinds, an extension of his next expansive breath.

"*Obrigado, Senhor!*" he shouts in Portuguese, as he long ago learned to give thanks in another language, another country, another life. He squeezes the throttle and blasts around a lumbering truck that's spitting a jagged column of black smoke into the sparkling green moment. As he speeds past the truck and its human cargo of landless migrant *campesinos*, his skin senses the flash of a dozen dark eyes watching him like cats.

"*Adios, pendejos!*" he laughs into the wind's rushing spirits. Up ahead on a long stretch of open road, Cigano puts pen to paper in his mind and begins to write of long-forgotten memories and lives.

○   ○   ○

My brain is a rumbling washing machine of colors, darks and whites, all swishing around in a foamy fog of abstract thoughts and dreams; a churning psychic stew. I'm swarmed by an incessant stream of recollections: mostly of missteps, regrets, and failures, desperate spastic strategies and plans; schemes and plots that ultimately led to self-condemnation and ruin. I sure left my mark on the world, though. More like a greasy, indistinct little smudge, punctuated by faint traces of blood, vomit, tears, and sperm, all splattered about like some angry, fevered Jackson Pollock nightmare.

My earliest memories are especially vague, covered in dust and cobwebs, like ghostly scraps of furniture in abandoned houses. Long inaccessible to my conscious thought, these fuzzy images have been moldering in shadows forever, forgotten by sunlight and air. But one thing always stands out in the darkness: a faded black-and-white photo of an old New York skyline, an image of the city of my birth, with a mysterious caption: *A LONG TIME AGO.* That's all. I don't know what it portends. I wonder if it might be like a link to a past lifetime, another incarnation or something, but I really don't know. It's always just been there, lurking like a bothersome stranger at my mind's back door, holding fast and steady as one of my very first memories. Other weird fragments are floating around in the past's stagnant air, but for the most part it's dusty in these old rooms; foggy and dark behind locked doors. They have remained shut for so long now, they seem to be frozen by the rust of fear, warped by a lifetime of fevered delirious visions.

As I stumble around in the shadows searching for clues, I conjure another vague recollection: a big glass water bottle in a Tijuana hotel room. It was a long time ago. I was only four or five years old, I think. I was probably hallucinating, even then, my little brain stewing in nightmare juices of pounding fevers . . . *"Row, row, row your boat"* . . . Later, my mother would tell me how I'd almost died of typhoid fever. My mother, whose memory is probably no more reliable than my own, used to talk of sitting with me in a Mexican hospital. I can picture her there, begging, pleading, bargaining with a God she feared and hated to spare the life of her only child. And I remember the grinding, whirring machines of delirium, an overwhelming web of wild hallucinations; terrible visions that would follow me for the rest of my life. It is those hellish apparitions that will always stand firm as my first deep impressions of this life, the painful sickly images that first shaped and colored my perceptions.

Perhaps that's where it all began for me—the certainty that the world I inhabited was not really "real" at all, but a big complex web of hallucination; a million uncontrollable, thundering machines raging all around me. Maybe that's when I first came to see life as an unfriendly condition, a disease; a vivid nightmare that could snatch you away from loving arms of comfort and security, and throw you kicking and screaming into those mad unstoppable gears of chaos.

Brain damage likely occurred after days and nights of dehydration and organ-scorching fevers. My childhood hallucinations would later become habitual, recurring throughout my life like some noxious Mexican jumping bean of insanity, placed in my being by the stealthy unseen fingers of an ancient Curse. Yeah, maybe that was the exact time and place where the wild seed of a lifelong mental dis-ease first entered my psyche, causing me to grow up never quite trusting what my eyes saw or my senses perceived. Life was but a dream—a pounding, spinning washing-machine cycle of delirious spook-house visions, rocking me down, down, down the stream, into the clanging banging bowels of madness. And so I will always remember a hotel room and a big glass bottle of poisonous roach-shit bacteria water. I can see it now as vividly as one remembers a red-lipped, toothy demon hovering over the bed where the child he once was lay paralyzed, sick and dying.

◯   ◯   ◯

Approaching another hairpin curve, Cigano snaps out of it and guns the throttle, passing another slow-moving truck. He knows the words he's been playing with are now engraved on his consciousness. Soon as he gets to Veracruz, he will have to sit again and write them in his notebooks, along with all the other words. *Words, words and memories. A long time ago. A long time ago.* The words play in his head as he speeds on, keeping pace with a rust-colored freight train rumbling in the distance, *clackclackclack*. Up ahead, a volcano looms over the steamy black snake of highway as another blinking image registers in his brain's hungry camera; a faded pastel-blue roadside shrine to Guadalupe, the Holy Virgin Mother. A sudden burst of black feathers flashes in his peripheral vision. *What's that? A vulture, an evil spirit? Whatever, it's gone, speed, wind, keep going, almost there now.*

An hour later, cruising along a palm-studded tropical shoreline, Cigano thinks of the sad-faced little whore he'd spent the night with. Last night? Or was it the night before? He can't remember. It doesn't matter. He remembers her name, though. Of course. *Como no?* Lupe. Guadalupe. But that one was no virgin. He grins, replaying the vision of her clinging to his body like a greedy spider monkey. A shy Indian *chamaca* from the dusty illiterate backlands of nowhere. As he conjures the image of her face, details of the night emerge in memory's yellowed chambers. A dingy cantina shaking with fuzzy strains of boisterous *Norteña* music that made the tequila turn ugly and made the men need to fight. Sudden chaos, cowboy hats flying, blood and angry curses, a crowd of dull-faced olive-clad teenage soldiers gripping oily black machine guns like evil metallic alien pets. He recalls how when he took the girl back to his hotel she'd become awkward, standing stalled before the ancient elevator door, whispering; dark bovine almond-shaped eyes wide, gawking like a frightened child as she breathed. *"This is where you stay? Pero como? What a strange little room, no place even for a bed! You must sleep standing up, pobrecito!"* Up in the room, he'd teased her for her barefooted ignorance and she'd kissed him with hungry rotten peasant teeth and fucked him to sleep. Then she'd slipped away to join the unformed shadows of insect-twilling dawn in that muddy little piss-hole with no name.

When he departed in the morning, he found she'd left a sad little red hair-ribbon tied to his doorknob. There it was as he opened the door, like some ancient tribal love code. Now, tied to the handlebar, it wiggles in the heat, a bright little red flash flapping in indifferent Gypsy winds of distance and movement, a dancing vision of red lust memory against a dizzy sea of humid green speed. It's another random memento of another Holy One he will never see again—but whose spirit he knows he'll carry with him, like another faded tattoo mark on his battle-scarred soul.

He breathes deep and exhales as he shifts gears, opening the throttle, reveling again in the sights, sounds, and smells of the road. And again he ponders the book he's been reading, the concept that his entire physical being, left brain and right, is an infinite webwork of roving cameras, a complex, integrated recording device. He knows it's always been like this for him: seeing, observing, memorizing, storing it all away in the archival vaults of his earthly experience. Riding along, he pores over details of his life in another hurried avalanche of recollections, a confusing matrix of sights and impressions, memories, visions, shouts and curses, kisses, sighs, and long-lost ghostly whimpers; lives and deaths; people, places, and events. Millions of snapshots to sort through and remember, to write about.

A road sign flashes by and is gone. The shutter of his eye's lens snaps open and shut, tattooing another indelible image onto the walls of his brain. *VERACRUZ 190 KM.* Only two hours to go. He grins, gulping in another deep breath of humid salty Gulf air. He can sense a nearness to the place where, soon, many more memories will be revealed. Wondering how he'll find it changed after so many years, he dodges around a boy on a donkey, and then there is nothing but the long empty highway stretching out before him.

The setting sun rides low behind his lengthening cowboy shadow, which precedes him down the straight black asphalt ribbon unfolding ahead into shimmering, chattering nonsense realms of unformed, unwritten memories, visions, and dreams.

4. THE KID

"THE GROUND THAT A GOOD MAN TREADS IS HALLOWED."

—GOETHE

In the Port of Veracruz, a group of seamen is standing at the rail of the recently docked Brazilian freighter M/V *Destino*. Jaco, a lean handsome youth, wears an awkward smile as he finds himself the center of attention, bombarded by hugs and handshakes from his shipmates. A round-faced black-skinned sailor with a smile wide as Africa messes the kid's longish brown hair. Jaco grins, his lively brown eyes bright with the life of a young man's soul. He turns from his companions. Hoisting a small brown duffel bag over his shoulder, he starts down the long bobbing ramp to the wharf.

One of the sailors shouts out after him in Portuguese. Jaco raises a thumbs-up above his head. But he doesn't turn around. He is already gone as his feet reach the dock. He strides toward the port gate, taking in details. Mexico. Lazy musical patterns tremble in his ear, blending with the sound of rapid-fire *Castilhano*, a language he sort of understands.

He breathes in the Gulf's pungent air, laden with smells of a new land: chili peppers, garlic, and roasting meat; diesel fumes and dried fish—and something indefinable. Jaco feels good. He likes the lethargic feel of this place. Sort of like his home in Rio de Janeiro, but different. It feels as if he's been here before, a long time ago, but he can't place it. Humming an old tune that's popped into his head, he passes a stack of wooden crates with Chinese lettering. Near the street exit, he's bombarded by a gang of children with dark Oriental faces. *"Chiclets, señor, Chiclets!!"* As their birdlike cries surround him, he wags a smiling finger at the diminutive *caboclos* and they fall behind.

Approaching the big iron gate, Jaco reaches into his jacket pocket, extracting a pack of Hollywood cigarettes and a bottle of cheap Brazilian *cachaça*. With a shy smile, the young sailor hands his unofficial tribute to a beefy uniformed mustache standing at the guard post. He remembers being told by one of his shipmates that this is the way to get around red tape in Mexico, just like back home. Sure enough, he is waved through with a flash of gold teeth. On the street, he sees a weatherbeaten sign dominating the high cement wall between the port and the outside world. The words are written in many languages, all saying the same thing: *WELCOME TO VERACRUZ, MEXICO.*

He passes a ragged gathering of swarthy stevedores in dirty sun-bleached shirts and straw hats. Lounging in the shade, they look as if they've been sitting by that wall in a perpetual *siesta* forever. A stocky round-faced Indian woman with long black braids and a colorful flowing skirt like a *Cigana*, a Gypsy, stands beside a food cart shouting out her wares. *"Tacos; tacos a dos pesos, tacos de assado, carnitas, tripitas, tacos, tacos!"* Her mechanical drone is a song to Jaco, welcoming him. He stops and eats the food of this new land, bonding with the scenery. He watches antique buses festooned with colorful hand-painted lettering rumble past. His eyes wander across the road and stop at a ramshackle two-story colonial building under a big faded powder-blue sign: *HOTEL BUENOS AIRES.*

Jaco nods to an old man who's feeding scraps of spicy *carnitas* to a child standing at his side like a hungry midget, and at once he knows this place; knows it in his heart. He thinks again of why he has come here, and a nervous wind of excitement stirs in his center.

5. ANOTHER LIFE

"THE CAUSES OF HUMAN ACTIONS ARE USUALLY
IMMEASURABLY MORE COMPLEX AND VARIED THAN OUR
SUBSEQUENT EXPLANATIONS OF THEM."

–DOSTOYEVSKY

A stark empty stretch of road greets Cigano as he navigates a minefield of potholes, bouncing over the port's ancient cobblestone outskirts. The weedy railroad tracks and freight yards are familiar relics of the place he once knew so well. A septic shantytown vision clicks past his eye as a sickly-sweet stench of sewage invades his senses, conjuring vague graffitied images on his mind's haunted back walls. With a flash of excitement, he thinks of the words he will use to describe his impressions on the day he first arrived here in *Veracruz Puerto* over thirty years ago.

Flickering bat wings of menace and promise stir on rain-slick street corners of night as a young traveler emerges from a deserted train station. In a dreamlike trance, he passes a booming shipyard, his dusty boots trudging unknown streets past sleeping colonial buildings. Under a hazy amber glow of insect-buzzing street lamps, the ghostly pirate wail of marimba music moans from unseen cantinas. He moves through shadows of ramshackle structures stained with the humid mildew of the tropics and the sea. The sea, always the sea. Weathered sailors slouch like phantom sentries on hurricane-beaten corners; old men in straw hats and faded *guayabera* shirts sit drinking at crooked tables in the ragged plazas around the *Mercado Central de Veracruz*.

○　　○　　○

Up ahead, Cigano spies the old whitewashed bridge he used to cross every day. And then, there it is: the dilapidated high-ceilinged train station by the port. Nothing has changed! Breathless with anticipation, he sees a familiar dreamscape emerging in the distance. His old home, the Hotel Buenos Aires, still standing on the same dusty corner, suspended in time like a sun-faded snapshot. Distant lightning crackles, awakening a nostalgic stir in his gut. He knows he's riding into another life as he crosses the narrow bridge into his past. Memories spatter in his head like big pregnant drops of tropical rain as he plays with the words he needs to write. His mind strains like a hand reaching underwater into rocks at high tide, searching for some ancient crustacean, and—"Fuck!! *Hijo de puta!*" He hits the brakes and swerves, dodging around a deadly brown flash. It's a rusty baby carriage that has jumped off a garbage-laden old pickup, landing right in his path.

Jaco steps off the curb as Cigano cuts around the obstacle, almost slamming into the young sailor. Startled, Jaco drops his duffel and hops back onto the sidewalk. He curses the speeding bike as it weaves around the pickup and disappears into the flow of traffic. Jaco's eyes fix on the broken carriage lying in the road like a crippled cockroach. He shakes his head, bends, and scoops up his bag. Looking both ways, he sprints across the street.

He crosses some overgrown railroad tracks and walks through a scruffy plaza. An Indian child stands beside a rusty anchor, peering up to where a red balloon has disappeared into the marbled cloud cover. Their shadows merge on the cracked pavement, shimmering like a murky mirage: a pair of ghostly images meeting in the afternoon heat, then separating again as a spirit of purpose pushes Jaco toward the old hotel.

6. HOTEL BUENOS AIRES

"I WAS LIKE A SCREAM LOOKING FOR A MOUTH."

—HUBERT SELBY JR.

Room 27 sits at the corner of the secondfloor hallway, its windows facing the port. The timeworn door stands ajar, inviting in a soft midday cross-breeze. A steady buzzing sound mixes with Cuban music from a radio as an electric tattoo needle pushes ink into brown skin.

Forty-nine-year-old tattoo artist Jonathan Shaw—aka Cigano—sits in a shiny powder-blue wooden chair, etching an anchor onto a chubby-faced Mexican sailor's upper arm. A maze of faded blue-green designs covers the tattooer's torso. Sweat glistens on the weathered tapestry of his skin beneath a necklace of red crystal *Santeria* beads and a gold-and-silver medallion: Saint George slaying the dragon. *Bzzzzzz bzzzzzzzzz gzzzzzzzz.* Lost in an intricate microcosm of imagery only he can see, his dark brown eyes lurk behind blue-tinted glasses, longish dark hair slicked back above an imposing, lived-in profile. Gold jewelry glitters in the light and shadows of Cigano's makeshift tattoo parlor. The shabby room is clean and tidy; a humble workshop where the order of things glows with an odd dignity. Dusty Mexican sunlight bounces off the tattoo man's gold teeth and onto his goatee. As he squints into a void of practiced concentration, like a Buddhist monk in deep meditation, Cigano is writing in his mind again. Time-traveling. Piecing together the story he has returned to Veracruz to tell.

○   ○   ○

I will always remember the nightmares. I can still see myself as an unfortunate five-year-old lying paralyzed in a bed, frightened, unable to move or scream or awaken. I struggled and fought like a wildcat, but I was powerless to escape. The Jabberwock had me! What scared me most was that I *knew* I was dreaming, and still I couldn't open my eyes or cry out. I was trapped underwater and couldn't find the surface. Finally, I'd fight my way up from the bed. Shot from a cannon of terror, I ran down the endless cold white hallway, the dreaded beast closing in fast behind me.

"Mommy! Mommy!" I cried, trembling as I scampered into the warm comfort of her heavy silk quilt. Sometimes she'd let me stay and sleep with her there, safe from the monster's jaws.

I remember one man she used to bring home a lot. His name was Bob and I think they were married or something. He wasn't my father, but he was nice. I liked Bob. He'd let me snuggle between them when I had the bad dreams. Then one day he was gone. I remember waking up late at night to a sound of angry quarreling voices: high-pitched and terrible like the rumble of those pounding fever delirium machines, but shriller, closer, scarier. There was a big fight outside my window. I could hear coins bouncing off the pavement. I looked down and watched her hitting him in the face with her shiny black purse. I remember thinking I'd go down and collect all those coins in the morning and use the money to run away forever.

Later, Grandma would tell me my mother was drunk, and how she shouldn't drink, how she had this "demon" thing inside her that came out when she drank, *"just like her poor father."* Maybe I shouldn't drink either, I thought, remembering a water bottle full of thundering demons pounding away in angry delirious shadows in a yellow Mexican hotel room. Or maybe that part comes later. Yeah. Maybe that was the time we went back to Tijuana to get her divorce from Bob after another fight. I don't know. There were so many fights, it all kind of jumbles together in those musty old rooms. I can remember all sorts of other little things, though, like buying firecrackers and switchblades in Tijuana to sell to the big kids at school. I remember getting in trouble for selling these garden pebbles I'd spray-painted gold to the little kids, telling them they were gold nuggets. I was always conning those kids out of their lunch money.

My mother said I had "larceny in my heart," just like her father, my grandfather, the *"no-good Gypsy bum,"* who Grandma said was a drunk and a crook and went away to jail. I just wanted to get enough money to run away. That was my big dream, far back as I can remember. I even sold those dumb kids dirty pictures of naked ladies I cut out of the girlie magazines I swiped out of Bob's dresser drawer. That's when I got kicked out of their fruity goody-two-shoes rich-kid school and had to go to some other retard place way out in the Valley. Or maybe that comes later. I'm not sure. I can't remember the timing of things so good. It all runs together in a dark sea of memories, deep and scary as the gulf between me and the fuzzy gray skyline in that old black-and-white picture. In my mind, there's a big drawer full of snapshots like that, going back farther and farther, all the way back past the beginning of time.

I don't know if it was after that fight or another one when they came and took Bob away in the ambulance. I mostly just remember the angry voices, yelling and cussing. And they buzzed and pounded in my head like echoes for a long, long time, especially when there was nobody around and the thin veil of reality would slip away to expose a trembling web of pounding booming delirium machinery. And blood, I remember. Yeah, there was lots of blood on the living room's white, white carpet; a stain of dried blood gone brown like the shadow of some dirty little secret. I went out to the driveway the next morning and started picking up all the quarters, nickels, and dimes strewn across the pavement, even the pennies. I knew I was going to need plenty of money to run so far away from there that they'd never be able to find me.

Grandma told me that Mommy had bopped poor Bob on the head with a marble table lamp and darn near killed him, and that's why the big white car came screaming like an angry Christmas tree, red lights flashing in the night like icepicks. That was the last time I ever saw Bob. My mother never mentioned him again and I never asked. But those voices would echo in my head like pissed-off ghosts for many years to come.

Still assembling words in his mind, Cigano tattoos on. A faint movement in his peripheral vision pulls him back from memory's fuzzy underwater realms. Like a pair of skittish fish, his eyes dart across the room, then stop at the door where a young figure is hovering, half in, half out. With a glance, the tattoo man takes it all in. The kid seems out of place, just standing there, as if his intentions are too big for the little space. Wearing faded jeans and a black-and-red Brazilian soccer jersey, he's shifting from one foot to the other in worn black Converse sneakers.

Raising one eye, Cigano nods at his visitor, then sinks back into his hand's steady ritual. Silence, but for the tattoo machine's hypnotic buzzing and the radio's clacking rhythms. Jaco stands watching from the door. Frozen in evident fascination, he maintains his distance; he hasn't been invited in. His awkwardness crawls through the air behind the tattoo machine's steady hum. Cigano, still ignoring his visitor, nods to his customer. The tattoo is done. With a practiced flair, he reaches across the table and hands the sailor a tiny mirror with an orange wooden frame, the kind they sell at roadside *mercados* for five pesos.

The Mexican scrutinizes his new tattoo intensely, then looks up at the tattoo man. *"Muchas gracias, maestro!"*

"Orale pues, para servirle." Cigano nods with a wink as the sailor puts two crisp hundred-peso notes into his hand.

"Adios, jefe. Con su permisso." The sailor smiles. Nodding to Jaco, he heads for the door and then he is gone, the footsteps of another tattoo echoing down the long hotel corridor's polished Spanish tiles.

The tattooer leans back in his chair, conjuring an unfiltered cigarette from behind his ear. He lights up, stretches his arms and exhales. A long cloud of gray smoke dances in the kid's direction. Eye contact. Silence. Cigano nods an invitation. Without a word, Jaco steps into the room like a nervous actor taking a cue. The young man pulls a glossy American tattoo magazine from his back pocket—a picture of his host on the cover—and offers it to him.

Cigano raises a cool Dirty Harry eyebrow.

"Jonathan Shaw . . ." Jaco speaks in a voice that seems not to be his own, intoning the name in a soft accented hush, as if pronouncing some important, well-rehearsed line.

7. QUESTIONS

"MY WORK WAS SO LONG SO LITTLE APPRECIATED THAT I LEARNED NOT TO CARE A SCRAP FOR EITHER BLAME OR PRAISE."

—JAMES MURRAY

Cigano takes in the frozen moment from behind a cloud of smoke, but his eyes stay neutral, giving nothing away.

The kid shifts on his feet, stammering in a voice that sounds stiff, nervous, disembodied, rehearsed. "It is an honor to meet you."

Cigano takes the magazine from Jaco's hand and gestures him to sit. The tattoo man flips through the pages as his young visitor takes a seat.

"Jonathan Shaw . . ." Jaco speaks again with an air of awkward reverence. "I have followed you, followed your, your work that is, for a long time . . ." With a shy smile, he holds out his hand. "I am Jaco. I'm from Brazil."

The tattoo man says nothing, eyeing the kid with an air of suspicion. Jaco keeps the hand out. Cigano hesitates, then reaches for it. Despite the kid's nervous demeanor, Cigano feels a firm, confident grip.

"I read that you lived in Rio de Janeiro." Jaco smiles. *"Fala Portugues?"*

"Falo." Cigano drawls without expression.

Silence. A ship's horn blows. The tattoo man glances toward the window. A radio announcer vomits a wild avalanche of advertising that flies around the room like wood chips. Cigano leafs through the tattoo magazine and stops at an article. "JONATHAN SHAW—THE TRAVELING

Tattoo Gypsy." He stares at a full-page photograph of himself tattooing an American movie star back in another incarnation, another life. Finally, he looks up. "Son of a bitch. Ya just can't get away from this shit!" Closing the magazine like a coffin, he hands it back to the kid with a sigh. "Okay, so ya found me. Whaddya want, my fuggin' autograph?"

Jaco looks at him. The look says nothing.

Now, Cigano is puzzled. He raises an eyebrow. "What's the deal, man? Spill it."

"I want to get some tattoo work done . . ."

"Ye-ah?" Cigano breathes. "Well, okay . . . So, uh, ya got any tattoos?"

Jaco shakes his head.

"Still a virgin, eh? That's cool. Whaddya got in mind?" He smiles, all business now. As if he could give a shit.

"I'm not quite sure. But I'd like to have you do a full body tattoo on me."

Cigano cocks his head. "Body suit? Ya gotta be shittin' me, bro!"

"No. I'm serious."

"Yeah, well, that's a serious fuggin' project for a guy with no tattoos."

"Yes, I know it is. But I, I've been . . ." Jaco stands and reaches into his pocket, pulling out a stack of hundred-dollar bills. He separates a couple and hands them to Cigano. "Do you think, would this be enough for a, a consultation?"

Cigano grins. "Sure." He puts out his hand, revealing a faded dollar sign tattooed on his palm. "Money talks, baby."

Jaco puts the cash into his hand and Cigano pockets it.

The young man sits down again, facing him.

8. ANSWERS

"DON'T DO NOTHING YOU CAN'T SHARE, AND BE PREPARED
TO DISCUSS EVERYTHING THAT YOU DO."

—MARTIN SHEPARD, M.D.

"So, why are you tattooing here?" Jaco smiles.

Silence. Cigano looks at his visitor, saying nothing.

"Why Mexico?" the kid insists. "I mean to say, what are you doing in this place? Why are you working in Veracruz?"

After a moment's hesitation, the tattoo man looks up and sighs. "Lissen, Jaco. It's Jaco, right? Ya already paid me for my time, so the time's yours, for now." He glances at a battered stainless and gold Rolex on his wrist. "So are ya gonna waste yer consultation time asking me twenty questions about my personal life, or ya wanna talk about this tattoo?"

"I was just curious, Mr. Shaw."

Cigano winces. "Plee-eeze, don't call me that . . . Jonathan's the name, Jonathan Shaw, all right?"

"Sorry, er, Jonathan. Jonathan Shaw. Yes. Well, I, I'm very familiar with your work, you know. You're a well-known artist, of course . . ." The kid hesitates for another uncomfortable heartbeat, a stupid, embarrassed look on his face, then smiles. "So, what are you doing here working in this place, in Veracruz, um, Jonathan Shaw . . . if you don't mind too much the question?"

Cigano looks at his feet. He's never liked questions much, or the people who ask them, for that matter. But this kid seems all right. The tattoo man looks up with a sigh. "We–ell . . . I guess I'm kinda just hanging out here for a while, y'know, doin' a little tattooing. Mostly, though, I'm trying to get some work done on this book I been trying to write . . ."

"Oh, really? You're writing a book? What about? Your tattoo career?"

If this kid had a fucking tail he'd be wagging it. Now, it's the tattoo man's turn to shift in his seat. He reaches across his work gear and grabs a thin pack of cheap Mexican cigarettes. He lights up, licking the sugary-sweet paper taste from his lip. Exhaling a long gray stream of smoke, he looks at the kid. "How the hell didja find me here, anyway?"

"Easy to find you, Jonathan Shaw. I called your tattoo studio in New York City. From Brazil. Before I came here. Somebody named Elvis, one of your tattoo artists . . . ? He said I could find you in this pl—"

"Fuck!" Cigano's gut churns. "Those fuggin' mooks! I *told* 'em not to talk about where I go! Nobody's fuggin' business! Fuck me! Why don't they just announce it to the whole fuggin' world? I may as well have some fuggin' LoJack-bar-code-micro-chip-tattoo-detector-radio-transmitter shoved up my fuggin' ass here." He spits tobacco flakes onto the floor and stubs out the smoke, then digs through his tattoo kit in a beat-up metal toolbox. Muttering, he pulls out an ink-stained cell phone. "Jee-sus!" He dials and puts the phone to his ear, getting ready to tear someone a new rectum. He listens to a recording in robotic Spanish, "*No se puede completar su llamada*," then slams the phone down on the table.

Jaco watches as Cigano takes off his glasses and pinches his nose between his eyes. The tattoo man takes a deep breath, then another. He puts his head down and sighs, silently reciting the familiar words in his head. *God, grant me the serenity to accept the things I cannot change.* Over and over, he repeats the comforting mantra, breathing slowly, consciously, in and out, in and out. Finally, he runs his hand through his hair and looks up. As if coming up from underwater, he sees the kid staring at him. Cigano lets out a peal of nervous laughter, surrendering to the spell till he's cackling uncontrollably. It feels good as he gives in to the tidal wave of merriment rising up from his belly. Every time he tries to stop, he looks at the kid's bewildered expression and laughs some more.

"Are, are you all right?" Jaco looks at him.

This brings on a new wave of giddiness. Cigano laughs till tears fill his eyes. "Oh, yeah, I'm fine. Sorry, man." He reaches over and lights another cigarette, looking up with a sheepish grin. "I guess I just got kinda freaked out, y'know, just thinking about New York, the whole stupid tattoo world up there. Ugh! I dunno, man, I s'pose I expected to find some anonymity or something down here, y'know? A little privacy." He guffaws. "I guess I thought I'd gotten away from all that shit, being here . . ."

Jaco keeps looking at him, but says nothing.

"Hah!" Cigano snorts. "Shoulda known better, right? Nowhere's safe anymore with these fuggin' things!" He shoves the cell phone back across the table. "Fuggin' global tracking devices, what a crocka shit . . . Hey, sorry, bro." He grins at the confused face watching him. "I didn't mean to freak ya out or anything. It's all good . . ." He laughs again, lightly now. *Shit, what am I getting all bent outta shape for? Just lucky to be alive. What do I care? Every day above ground's a good day. One day at a fucking time. Easy does it. Live and let live. Just lighten up, man. The war's over, and you lost! No fucking big deals anymore. Always gotta remember that. No more big deals.*

9. TRUE CONFESSIONS

"EVERY TIME A MAN UNBURDENS HIMSELF TO A STRANGER,
HE REAFFIRMS THE LOVE THAT UNITES HUMANITY."

—GERMAINE GREER

"So what's it about, Jonathan Shaw?"

"What's what about, kid?" The tattoo man scratches his head, wondering if this fanboy's waiting for him to reveal Secrets of the Universe or some shit.

"The book you told me you're writing. What's it going to be about?"

Cigano smiles. "The book." He stumbles over the word.

"What is it about?"

"Good question, man. I dunno. I guess it's sorta like a . . . confession."

"Like in the church?"

"Ye–eh, kinda. Something along those lines." He coughs. "I mean, I don't really do churches, y'know, but the principle's basically the same. A mental inventory. Cleaning house, clearing the air, whatever . . . I dunno, man, they say confession's s'posed to be good for th' soul, right? God only knows my shit could do with a good fuggin' overhaul." He grins.

"But, what is the story about? It's a novel? A memoir?"

"Jesus! Ya don't give up, kid!" He takes a deep breath and tells the closest thing he can to the truth. "Whatever ya wanna call it, it's basically just a kinda stock-taking of my life. *Mi vida loca,* y'know? Dubious childhood. Fucked-up family. Checkered career, travels, chicks, a lotta stuff about the past. But it's mostly about the road . . ."

"The road?"

"The road, yeah . . . How can I explain?" He strokes his goatee. "I read this great book when I was a kid, maybe fifteen, sixteen years old? Kerouac's *On the Road*. Swiped it from this all-night newsstand in Los Angeles."

Jaco nods. "A great book."

"Yeah, but I had no idea what it was about. The title just called out to me, so I grabbed it off the shelf and stuffed it in my pocket. I took it home and started reading, and, well, I couldn't put the fuggin' thing down. So that was a big moment for me, even though I didn't know it at the time."

"How was it a big moment?"

"'Cuz after reading that book, man, I was never the same. I guess that's what makes a really great book, right?" He falls silent for a moment. "Strange . . ." He goes on. "The last chapters ended him up in Mexico. Weird. I just remembered that. It's funny sometimes, the way things turn out . . ."

A cross-breeze dances in through the open window, stirring up a familiar scent of eucalyptus floor wash from the hallway. Cigano goes quiet again. He closes his eyes and begins chasing the words like translucent moths, writing down the memories in his mind again.

○   ○   ○

There was this big eucalyptus outside my window when I was a kid. On winter afternoons, I'd lie in bed, watching it, hypnotized by the dancing figures of the leaves twirling around in the cool Pacific wind. I used to see so many things in those leaves, shows and stories and ballets. I'd get lost in the secret world of that old tree. Its smell would fill my room when it rained. Sometimes I'd hear my grandma's voice in the hall, talking to my mother.

"Dah-ris. I'm worried about th' boy. He sits up there in his room fa' hours at a time, just starin' off inta space. That's not normal . . ."

"Oh, hush, Mother. Jono just has a vivid imagination."

"Call it whatever ya wanna, th' boy's broodin' in there. Fa' hours. Every day. He don't wanna go out an' play wit' th' other kids. That's *morbid* . . ."

"Mother, will you *please* get off my back about my son?"

"Well, excuse me fa' livin'! I was just tryin' t' help! After all, I did raise four children myself, y'know . . ."

"Oh, and a *splendid* job you did with us! Jesus! You and those lousy, sadistic penguins . . ."

"Well, that's a fine thing ta say about a decent Catholic school ejacation! An' me slavin' away . . ."

I could hear my grandma's voice rising, becoming shrill, then my mother growling back.

"Jesus Christ! I need a drink! I can't listen to this crap . . ."

"Yeah, that's right! Go get good an' soused, just like ya' no-good fatha'."

I'd tune out the voices, losing myself in the leaves' languid fantasy dance, whirling in the wind outside my window.

○   ○   ○

Cigano is staring into space when he hears the kid saying something. He looks up, scratching his head.

"How do you mean?" Jaco is staring at his host.

"Wha' . . . ?" The tattoo man snaps out of it. "Oh, shit. Sorry, man . . . I kinda lost my train of thought there. What was I talking about?" He furrows his brow and rests a hand on his cheek.

"You were talking about Jack Kerouac's *On the Road*? How your book was about the road, too . . ."

"Yeah, right. Well, the road became like my home real early in life, see? The Gypsies call it *o lungo drom*. Means something like 'the long road to nowhere.' I'm Gypsy on my mother's side, y'know, so I dunno, maybe that had something to do with it. Anyway, the road was always real important. It became like my mother and my father, my family, school, home, the whole world for me. So this book's got a lotta travels and weird adventures, people, places. And it all started when I read that Kerouac book and it made such an impression. Sometimes I feel like I sorta been living in it ever since . . ."

"Living in it?"

"Well, I did a lotta moving around over the years, traveling all over the planet. So I've got all these random memories and stories backed up in my brain, a lotta stuff to sort out and take stock of. Get it?"

Jaco nods. "So why did you decide to come to Veracruz to write? Why this place? This cheap hotel? You could go anywhere in the world to write a book, Jonathan Shaw. Why did you want to do it here?"

"I dunno, man . . ." Cigano runs a hand through his hair. "Different reasons, I guess. On some level, I think it's 'cause this is where I first started out as a tattooer, y'know? And I always felt real comfortable here back in the day. I still like it a lot. I just feel at home here. I dunno, I guess what I mostly like is that it hasn't changed much over the years. Not like New York . . ."

"New York has changed for you? But you're still respected there, no?"

"Respected?" The tattoo man guffaws. "I dunno about that. Feared, envied, hated maybe. I dunno about respect."

Jaco nods, waiting for him to go on.

"Man, I really used to love New York City . . ." Cigano continues, reminiscing, remembering all the times he'd been interviewed in the press, how well he used to be able to express himself with words, suddenly realizing how long it's been since he's really talked to another human being. "I was born there, y'know." He shrugs with a sad little grin. "Moved to California with my mother when I was just a little kid. Then I went back to New York in the '80s after hopping around South America most of my life. And I just totally fell in synch with the place." He pauses. "Well, I *thought* I loved it, even though I know now I probably mostly hated it. Anyway, I built a whole empire for myself there. But then it all started changing. Really changing. Fast. And then everything just sorta went lopsided."

He stops talking and looks at Jaco. From the look on the kid's face, he realizes he's not getting his meaning across, not expressing himself very well. He takes a deep breath, reaches over for another smoke, and tries again. "The whole New York underground art scene I was a part of is dead now. Gone. Wiped out and swept away. Gentrified, homogenized, globalized, whatever th' fuck ya wanna call it. It's been sad to see. I mean, for better or worse, New York always had a character, a special sorta creative soul about it. That's what first drew so many of us to the place, back in the day. There was nowhere else like it, man. But now . . ." He sucks his teeth. "It's all gone to hell in a fuggin' hipster basket. The whole thing's been turned into this big horrible American Dream shit heap, just another cookie-cutter corporate yuppie playground for greedy shit-brained college-indoctrinated frat boys. Starbucks-slurping, money-grubbing bleating sheeple . . ."

He stops, not wanting to go on another hateful rant, not daring to give his deep resentments too much expression. But he's thinking, feeling, tasting the bitter poison rising up in his gut again as he remembers his last months in New York, those terrible times right after 9/11. The unforgettable stench of death and fear; that obscene black cloud trailing from the buildings he'd lived and worked in the shadow of for so many years. He can see it like a movie playing across the screen of his mind: he and his girlfriend Amy watching in mute horror from their Chinatown loft window as a grotesque black portal cranked open the gates of Hell right before their eyes, splitting that impossible blue morning sky and wafting across the East River, raping his mind, tattooing his soul with a dull and final dread. God is in the details, he thinks; as is the devil, the very face of Evil. He begins writing in his mind again, remembering, reconstructing the faded words from the journal pages of his final weeks in New York.

JOURNAL ENTRY – SEPTEMBER 14, 2001:

NEW YORK. *The day faded into awful night yesterday and I didn't even see it go or come or exist. Like a death whimper in an empty hospital corridor reeking in the dead of night, it just disappeared, unheard, unknown. And feeling alone, so very alone, like a dying patient in vast, sterile starless sick wards of eternity, I looked up by chance and peered out the bedroom window. The sky was a silent riot of suffering spirits, like a forest fire raging over lower Manhattan, fading gray and still in my thoughts, irrefutable, teasing me into some kind of dismal final conclusion. I gotta get out. This sky haunts me, the building I live in, ghostly chains rattling in the night, taunting me, torturing me like a parade of angry phantoms in abandoned houses ringing with a thousand stifled cries of madness. All is still and quiet as the grave on these forlorn empty streets behind the fragile ribbons of sanity. A bloody September sunset fades, and our lives fade and all is desperation and sadness and stillness. The Lizard People stalk the moving shadows of our times, and I'm afraid beyond the empty pit in my middle; scared beyond words, beyond this terrible fucking doomsday sky. This must be Hell, I think—but why can I still think if I'm supposed to be dead? Isn't Hell a place beyond thought? No! Hell is thought itself! And I think and think and think, thinking my way down into the angry prodding pitchforks and red-hot points of some mad loony-bin Hell-spawned dream-arcade from a long time ago. Days spent lost and alive as the restless spirits go plodding past like sad silent-movie images on the fetid, decaying winds of time. Time is my Master and the gun lies black and silent in the drawer. Suicide? No! Not ready to end this hellish decrepit horror movie yet. Not just yet. The lemons turn brown on the kitchen counter, hard and foul like dinosaur turds, as my woman and I wander these dead city streets with other lost hollow-eyed children of the damned and I struggle the words along, dragging lines of hot sickly horror across a hopeless page, like a tiny trail of defeated worker ants.*

10. THEN AND NOW

"MY LIFE IS A CONFUSING SYMPHONY OF MY OWN
THOUGHT PATTERNS."

– ANONYMOUS

The tattoo man stubs out his cigarette in the ashtray. Forgetting the kid sitting across from him, he sinks back into a sea of memory, reliving the day, the indelible nightmare image of tragedy carved into the race mind again and again in a terrible unholy unforgettable mantra: *"Holy shit! Holy shit! Holy shit! Holy shit!"* Censored, sanitized, and then mercilessly magnified by the television screens of the world, the words play over and over and over.

> **JOURNAL ENTRY – SEPTEMBER 20, 2001,**
> **NEW YORK:** *Can't stop thinking about that horrible moment*
> *where everything changed and turned to shit forever. "Holy shit!"*
> *was the vision that escaped a man's soul and flew across the world*
> *in a flash as those planes hit the hellish twin towers of history again*
> *and again, destroying the towering shadows like a first perception of*
> *Mommy and Daddy being massacred in a child's nightmare. And*
> *then the great human wave of terminal sadness, and the television*
> *lies, and the big bloodthirsty patriotic fury rising up like a storm*
> *of the most unholy shit. "Holy shit! Shit shit shit." The stinking*
> *shit of deception. Giuliani and Bush hamming it up for the TV*

cameras like a pair of twin talking lizards, standing in the stench of those smoldering ruins of death and human despair, talking shit on the shit-talking TV news. Shit! Lies! Fucking inside job! They finally did it! Bastards! Fuck! This was our home. Those people were our friends, our neighbors and customers. Firemen and cops and regular guys, all dead for stinking puddles of lying politicians' oil! Then all the fucking mind-controlled TV-watchers getting out their flags and waving them around, right on cue, whipping it up into a big slobbering frenzy of hate. Morons! War on Terror! Send in the troops! Go get the oil! Big business! Money! Power! World domination! Nobody could see the flimflam man's sneaky sleight of hand, and then it was on, just the way those fat petrol-slurping slithering snakes had it all planned right from the start! Patriot Act. Homeland Security. Police state. Apocalypse. Kali Yuga! Hula hula! Rah-rah, sis-boom-bah! Holy shit! Holy shit! Holy shit! God's voice ringing on deaf ears again and again as the shitty wars of shit rage on and on in this big end-of-days war of time and the raging river of holy shit forever.

Spinning in a churning whirlpool of memories, Cigano begins talking to his visitor again, detailing how after the tragedy he'd needed to get out of New York, had to get the fuck away from the whole decaying dying American Empire; had to go somewhere else, far away. But it had been long overdue anyway, he says. Nine-eleven was just the last nail in the coffin of his world. He was already long fed up being a Registered Trademark, a "World-Famous Tattoo Artist." His hands jump around as he talks of how, after years of restless, irritable white-knuckle sobriety, he'd started drinking again, then hit a hellacious bottom and almost bought the farm from a speedball overdose.

In desperation, he'd gotten clean and sober again, this time for keeps, God willing. He explains how, in a rare moment of clarity, he'd decided New York was no place to live anymore. He was done with the dark dangerous scene he'd lived in all those miserable dry-drunk years before his relapse. So he'd decided to give up tattooing. That's when he'd started to write again. He'd given all his appointments to his assistants and handed his woman the keys to his pathetic moribund little kingdom; and then he got the hell out of town, searching for memories of his long, confusing life's path. The time had finally come to start working on the book full-time, no matter what. Time to begin putting together all the weird, confusing little jigsaw-puzzle pieces of his life.

JOURNAL ENTRY – New York, October 2001: *Nine months clean and sober. Sitting up in the loft bed again. The scent of freshly laundered bedclothes, crisp and clean, but they don't smell like they used to from the old laundry ever since Amy's been taking them to the Chinese down the block. The old place washed them with this stuff that made everything smell like a storybook childhood—the kind I never had. Now they smell sort of like the childhood I did have. Dull and sterile. But they still feel okay, nice and fluffy, soft and fresh. Ah, the look and feel of clean, worn cotton! It's calm and quiet up here now, just sitting up on the bed writing, far from that shit-hole nightmare-factory tattoo shop, thank God. And so I spend my days writing, digging, looking deep and microscopic into the mysterious weave and pattern of things that just went blank a long time ago—the childhood I could never remember. It's ironic how I've been spending my time in bed these days, pen in hand, trying to unlock the mysteries of a long-forgotten past, while across the continent my mother spends her life in a bed too, drinking in a desperate effort to erase hers. It's tragic how the old lady's living out the last days of her life on earth. She lived the years I witnessed and endured in a rage of restless, angry abstinence, alternating with incoherent drunken rages, possessed by the demons of old unresolved resentments, choking on self-pity, interspersed by horrible outbursts of violence. Yeah, she was a raging bull, and like a bull she trampled everything in her path— well, not everything, but not for lack of raging. That bull quality was a good part of the source of her wrath, at least the mindless ways in which she expressed it. But that blind, destructive fury was only the surface expression of a deep dark relentless alcoholic anguish I myself would come to know too well. This was a hard life for the old lady, God knows. She suffered even more than those who she caused so much pain, poor thing. But we all suffered from it. Well, the strongest ones survived, the only way there was to survive—by getting out. First my father, then me, soon as I was old enough to get away from her insane frequency on my own propulsion. It's ironic that she came from the same childhood violence and insanity she eventually inflicted on me.*

And like me, she ran as far and fast as she could from where she came from. It's amazing, really, because my father came from a mess he had to run from, as well. And even though his childhood made him bitter, what fucked him up the most weren't so much the betrayals of his past as the disappointments of the cockeyed world of fame and fortune he created trying to escape it. Like Nietzsche said, whatever doesn't kill you makes you stronger, and so the whole concept of running from pain is ultimately weakening to the spirit, futile, self-defeating and self-destructive. Yeah, my father's big disillusion was with the Beast of the Public. Ironically, I wound up being disillusioned in much the same way as a tattoo artist. Funny how things work out. But that's another story, and a real long one. God help me to find clarity, should I live to tell it.

Cigano talks on, describing how he finally split New York and took to the road again, all alone. But this time, he says, maybe for the first time in all his travels, he wasn't running from his past. This time he was running right into it, headlong. Carl Jung said it best, he explains: that God enters through the wound. So he decided he was going to dive straight into the old festering wounds of his existence, the roots of his madness. No matter how scary or painful, he needed to go back, seeking answers to all the weird fucked-up confusion of his life, his memories, his scars. Time for a psychic change. Time to go to any lengths to get it. Time to change, or time to take that gun out of the drawer and put it into his mouth and pull the fucking trigger.

JOURNAL ENTRY – NEW YORK, OCTOBER 2001: *The bottom line is that I come from a long line of runners and madmen. So did my parents, and their parents, all the way down the line, the cycle of this big crazy karma wheel of fortune and misfortune, and that's okay today. Some people are born to be farmers and some are born for the military or for the priesthood or whatever. Me, I was born for the run. Fame and fortune, self-sufficiency, defiance, drugs, alcohol, and rebellion: they were all just a means to an end for me. But ultimately, a quest for redemption through art has been the only thing I ever did that didn't end up in the toilet. At least I feel like I'm fulfilling some kind of destiny today, one baby step, one memory, one little day at a time. And I feel fortunate to have made* *it this far, even as my mother sits in her bed with her bottles of pills and booze, and my father hides away in his isolated suburban bunker, struggling all alone with his past, moldering away in his selfish little zone of seclusion, buried in a self-imposed exile from humanity, living the lonely, obsessive, introspective life of a writer. Just like me.*

So he'd gotten on his bike. He'd gone back out on the road, his only real home, searching for the key to his everlasting existential dilemma, seeking a way to find some fucking peace of mind.

JOURNAL ENTRY – NEW YORK, NOVEMBER 2001: *I've got to make the jump. Time to go back to California and see who the fuck my father is. But I gotta tread lightly with the old bastard. That's another Jabberwock to battle, but today I'm looking out for little Jono first; looking out for what's left of the kid locked away and buried inside me. Easy does it, but DO IT. Go and face them both now, before it's too late to ever know the two unfortunate old freaks that made me. I honestly believe that some higher purpose has finally prepared me for this contact. And at the ripe old age of forty-eight and ten whole months clean and sober, it's looking like the only path left. They're old now, and even though Artie's older, I'm pretty sure he'll outlive the old lady. It almost defies medical science that she's still alive after all the damage she's done to herself—as if she's just staying around as long as that old body can hold up to be of loving service to me somehow. And if she needs to make amends to the boy Jono who's not dead and who kept coming back, galumphing triumphant, Jabberwock head in hand, then this could be the moment of loving redemption for us both, God willing. That's as good a reason as any for me to have survived this long, to finally try and do something right for the sake of us all.*

First, he'd saddled the bike and ridden out to California, he explains. But even with the best of intentions, it had been an emotional overload; too much pent-up trauma and discomfort there to write about all the fucked-up memories and family histories he unearthed; too many creepy old shadows and clamoring ghosts lurking in Los Angeles; too close to the festering wounds that had driven him to drink and drug his way to near-extinction in the first place. So, after almost a year spent with his people there, examining the scenes of the crimes of his childhood and adolescence, taking notes, getting ready to delve deeper, he knew he needed to get some distance, find some kind of larger perspective. He just wanted to go somewhere simpler, he says, someplace peaceful and neutral, where he could get quiet and sit all alone to write.

He searched the back closets of his memory for a cheap, comfortable spot where he'd feel secure and at home, someplace safe from the phantoms. And that's when he'd jumped back on the bike and headed south into Mexico, just as he'd done the first time he left home, back when he'd been a shell-shocked kid, running, minus the bike, for his life.

11. SIGNIFICANT EVENTS

"ALL MEN DREAM, BUT NOT EQUALLY. THOSE WHO DREAM
BY NIGHT IN THE DUSTY RECESSES OF THEIR MINDS WILL
WAKE IN THE DAY TO FIND THAT IT WAS VANITY - BUT THE
DREAMERS OF THE DAY ARE DANGEROUS MEN, FOR THEY
MAY ACT THEIR DREAM WITH OPEN EYES, TO MAKE IT
POSSIBLE."

-T. E. LAWRENCE

"And then, boom, here I was." He snaps his fingers and grins, feeling lighter. "Back in good old Veracruz Puerto after all these years. So there ya go, man." He shrugs. "That's how I ended up here. Any more questions?"

Jaco shakes his head, still reeling from his unpredictable host's unexpected onslaught of openness.

"No?" Cigano shifts gears. "Okay, then. Cool. Next. So you're really serious about getting this big tattoo work done, huh?"

Jaco looks at him for a moment, then nods.

"Okay. Well, lissen, man. I'm gonna tell ya again, a body suit is a real serious deal, y'know? A huge undertaking. Seriously. A lotta pain and stress and time goes into something like that, on both ends, believe me. It's a real commitment—not to mention a considerable cash expenditure on your part, like I told ya before." Cigano scans the kid's face and nods. "Just thought I should make it real clear, before you get into something yer not ready for."

"Thank you, Jonathan Shaw." Jaco smiles. "Just so you know, I've traveled all the way from Brazil by ship for this. I've been wanting to get tattooed for a long time, ever since I was a child, really. But it's only now I have the money and the time, if you agree to make it for me."

The kid's eyes are lit up like Times Square. Cigano recalls when tattooing used to make him feel that way, too. He nods. He gets it. This guy doesn't just want some big tattoo; he needs it. The tattoo man smiles, letting out another cloud of smoke as he snatches the magazine out of Jaco's hand and waves it in the air like an orchestra conductor. He gets up and starts pacing the room, searching for some new point to make. "I got real specific ideas how tattoos oughta be designed, so it's pretty much artist's choice if I take on a project like this. No art directing from the customer, y'know. I had my fill of that shit, man, working in walk-in tattoo shops. It's my way or the highway now, if you wanna get big work from me."

The tattoo man stops pacing and looks the kid square in the eyes. "Just thought I oughta warn ya, in case you're not down with it." He shrugs. "Lissen, I know it's not for everyone, that kinda trust. I mean, there's plenty of good tattooers who'll do whatever you want, y'know . . ."

"I know all this, Jonathan Shaw. I've read interviews you've done and I appreciate your views. That's why I want only you to do my work."

Cigano moves to the window and rests his elbows on the windowsill. Leaning back, he stares at his odd visitor with a new interest.

"I have enough money to see it through to completion, Jonathan Shaw, if that's your concern. And I'm very serious about it. I just want to wear your best artwork, something *you* can feel proud of."

Cigano nods, then turns and stares out the window. A ship's horn blows as he looks out over the old port, thinking, recalling. He can feel his gut slinking south. He tries to place the feeling. Excitement? Fear? Awkward memories bubble up like sharks in a placid sea. He feels overwhelmed, confused. Then a soft inner voice seems to speak to him. *When in doubt, do nothing.* He turns and faces his visitor again. "Listen, lemme sleep on this, man. I'll give it some thought. Howzabout I letcha know tomorrow? Is that cool?"

Jaco nods and stands. They shake hands. Cigano feels a vague sense of accomplishment as the kid turns to go.

He calls out. "Hey, kid . . ."

Jaco stops by the door. Cigano looks him right in the eyes again, making a conscious effort to do so. The time for treating his fellow man as an irritating inconvenience is a thing of his ugly self-centered past.

"There's a quote from a writer that I like." Cigano is smiling. "It goes like this: 'When the most significant events in life happen, we usually don't know what's going on.' So to answer yer question, I guess I'm kinda hanging around here trying to remember the 'significant events' in my life, y'know?"

Jaco nods. "Maybe tattooing something significant while you're here will help you to remember more."

"Yeah, maybe. Could be. Anyway, I'll letcha know tomorrow, bro . . ."

Cigano turns his back to the door and listens to the young man's footsteps as they fade off down the hall. He can hear the little voice in his head again, repeating a familiar phrase, over and over. *No matter what your present circumstances, from now on you must make your creative expression the most important focus in your life.*

He smiles, remembering when he first heard those odd words, right after he'd crashed and burned in New York. After getting sober, he'd come to believe the voice wasn't coming from his own thoughts, but from somewhere else: a download from the gods, guardian angels, higher self, inner child, whatever; some kind, wise, compassionate presence, gently and firmly urging him to quit living like a miserable old whore, to give up tattooing and forget all the cash and prizes; to move on from all the insecurities and ambitions that had driven him so hard for so long. Somewhere deep inside, he knew he had to get out and spend the rest of his days traveling, seeking his truth, looking inward, remembering, writing, learning to speak the language of his own heart.

With a long, deep sigh, he breaks down his tattoo gear. He stops and looks around the room. He opens his journal and stares at the next empty page. It's time. There's something about a hotel room, he muses, that makes him feel lighter somehow, clear and unfettered from the burdens attached to his memories. It all seems less threatening here. How ironic, he thinks, that he's finally ended up in a Mexican hotel room, of all fucking places. The perfect setting for prying open those dusty old vaults of memories and hallucinations that had all started in a Mexican hotel room a long time ago.

The radio drones on as he limps across the room and flops onto the bed, bolstering himself up with the hard little pillow at his back. He opens the speckled black-and-white notebook. As his pen rushes across the page like a frantic little dancer, the words pour from his hand in a furious childlike scribble, possessed by the spirit of a long-forgotten little boy named Jono.

○   ○   ○

I remember when I was around five, playing by myself in the big empty yard behind the old Beverly Hills house. I was alone a lot when I was little, except for my dog Princess. She was a boxer. She always tried to lick my face. I thought it was gross after I saw her licking another dog's butthole at the park. I loved Princess, but I liked to explore the yard alone. Princess would stay away from that big old backyard anyway. She wasn't much of a watchdog; didn't even bark. Maybe she was scared. That was okay. I was scared of lots of stuff, too.

One day I was out back trudging through this big forest of overgrown ivy when I came to the wooden fence at the end of the property. Looking closer, I could see the gray unpainted wood moving and shimmering like jewels in the afternoon sunlight. I plodded through the ivy to look closer. When I got right up there and put my hand on the fence, it was all covered in little crawling things I'd never seen before. Spiders! They started creeping up my arm, a hundred gray particles of terror! "Arrrggghhh!!" I screamed as I swatted at them, running fast as my legs could go. Nobody was around to hear me crying as I tore back through the ivy and into the big empty white house, my little lungs pounding with the bitter acid of fear. I never went in that stupid old yard again. I always stayed away from ivy and wooden fences, too.

Coming home after school one day, I could hear the classical music blasting from the den. The door was vibrating with pounding, dark, gloomy thunder. I'd heard that music before and I didn't like it. It was creepy and scary. Monster music. Jabberwock music, an ugly backdrop to the angry voices in my head. I hurried past into the pantry. The kitchen was empty, the refrigerator breathing in the corner. "Grandma . . . ?" I walked over to the icebox and stood with my hand on the cool white door, reading the note under the flowery little magnet thing.

DEAR JONO– *I'm taking the bus downtown to go shopping. There's some stew on the stove for you. I'll be back in time for supper. Love, Grandma.*

That's all it said. Nothing about the booming, trembling door of the den, where Bob used to play with me and we would sit around and laugh. But that was a long time ago, before Bob went away and never came back. Now there was just the sound of creepy music from dark mad Russians. It was early. My mother's new husband was still at the office, doing whatever stupid old guys in suits did in offices. I stood outside the den, feeling kind of confused. I knew she was in there, sitting all alone in the dark. I could hear muffled wails and curses mingling with the big waves of musical gloom. She was drunk again. "Dancing with the demons." That's what Grandma called it when my mother locked herself in the den. I wanted to knock. But I knew better.

I slipped out the kitchen door, turned on the garden hose and drank from the nozzle. It tasted rubbery and warm from the late afternoon sun. I could hear a big crazy blue jay call as I sat on the cool cement step in the shade with my cat Swifty. He looked up at the angry bird, arching his back and purring as I petted him. I loved Swifty. He was a Siamese and he was real old. My mother got him from Marilyn Monroe, who was friends with Shelley Winters. Shelley was my mother's best friend. My mother always said she was my "godmother." Shelley was nice. She used to come around a lot. That was before my mother started locking herself in the den. After that, Shelley stopped coming. Nobody came around anymore, except my grandma, and Aunt Connie sometimes. And Swifty was still around. When I was sick he would sit on the quilt pulled up over my chest and drool and purr. Those were the cloudy days when the fevers kept me home from school. I didn't mind being sick, 'cause I got to stay in bed with Swifty and my picture books. And Mommy would come and fuss over me and bring me peanut butter and jelly sandwiches she made herself, and I could just lie around all day. That was the best. Poor old Swifty. He wasn't too swift anymore. And that mean old blue jay was sitting up on the wire teasing him. I was only five, not as old as Swifty, but I felt kind of old, too.

I had this toy gun I'd gotten from Bob. One day when my mother was sitting in the den, my grandma came out and saw me aiming at her through the window. When she scolded me, I told her, "I'm not shooting Mommy. I'm just trying to kill her sadness." Even as a little kid, I was always doing battle with the Curse. After that, my mother took away all the stuff Bob had given me. She told me guns were bad, even toy ones, and that was that. I guessed she must have known, after trying to shoot my father and all. But that was a long time ago and it was kind of hard to tell if it was real or just another nightmare. I had a lot of bad nightmares as a kid.

Life was pretty creepy in the big sterile white house on the big empty street. Most days after school, I'd find the door to the den shut tight and the rest of the house quiet; only those booming strains of trouble and my mother's angry sobs and wails behind the big white door. One time I came home and found her lying naked on the kitchen floor, all covered in blood from where she'd cut herself up with a big knife. I ran over to the neighbors and they called the ambulance people. After that, I knew all the guns in the world would never be enough to kill my mommy's sadness.

As I got older, I'd just stay away after school. I'd ride around on my bike alone, exploring the neighborhood. Day by day, week by week, I rode farther from home. One time, when I was around eight or nine, I crossed the railroad tracks and a gang of tough Mexican kids chased me on their bikes. My heart was pounding all the way home. After that, I mostly just rode down to the corner liquor store. That's when I started hanging out there. I really liked that corner. There was always lots of activity there. People and cars and movement, everybody coming and going down on Santa Monica Boulevard, the big busy street where the buses ran all the way to downtown.

I'd ride downtown on the bus with Grandma when I was little. It was like another country, like New York City where I was born. I couldn't remember New York because it had been a long time ago, but there were crowds and lots of traffic and noise downtown, the way I always pictured New York. There were lots of store windows filled with rows and rows of magical mysterious stuff: colorful shapes and textures all piled up to the ceilings—nothing like the empty white walls at home. I'd stand gawking like a farmer on his first time in the big city till I felt Grandma tugging on my shirt. "C'mawn, Jono. We ain't got all day to stand around. Edith's waitin' for us at th' cafeteria. C'm-awn!"

I liked going to the cafeteria with Grandma. We'd pick up brown plastic trays and plates from a big pile by the door and push them down a long shiny metal rail. You could see all the different stuff steaming under the big glass covers. And you got to pick out whatever looked good instead of being told to eat a bunch of stuff you didn't like. The best part was that I never had to get meatloaf. And you could even get two desserts if you wanted. We'd go sit at a table by the window, looking out on the busy street and eating right off the trays. I'd always eat my dessert before my lunch, and Grandma wouldn't yell at me. Grandma and Edith would just sit there for hours, talking about Florida and tenements and dead relatives and old-lady things.

We went downtown like that for years. One time, I must've been around eleven or twelve, and we were at the cafeteria. I'd already finished my custard and Grandma was still yacking away with her friend, like those old magpies Heckle and Jeckle on the teevee. I slipped away from the table, and then I was out on the hot summer sidewalk, wandering around in the hot, bustling old downtown Los Angeles streets. I could feel a special rush of excitement like in a dream, like I was being pulled through all that colorful busy stuff by strong invisible hands. It felt good, getting all jostled around like that, the first time I can remember feeling real happy as I looked into the shop windows. I loved all the rows of colorful things vibrating with life. That's when I saw it. A tattoo place.

I stopped and stared in the window. The little pictures on the walls were calling out to me like hieroglyphics in a strange new language. They made my cells twitch and jump and sparkle like the shiny glass and metal stuff in my mother's jewelry box that I used to play with when I was a little kid. My eyes fastened on a drawing of this big sailing ship with the words "Homeward Bound" in a banner. It seemed like the most beautiful thing I'd ever seen. I was about to go inside for a closer look when I heard a voice.

"Jono! There you are!" Grandma was standing beside me, huffing and puffing. "Ya had me worried sick, boy. I been lookin' all over th' place fa' ya." She muttered and sputtered like an old jalopy as we made our way through the busy crowds back to the bus stop.

When we got home, Auntie Connie's station wagon with the fake wood paneling on the side was parked in the driveway. That made me happy. I liked it when Auntie Connie came to visit. Her two kids, my younger cousins Peter and Stevie, were there too. They were my only friends.

"Hello-o-o . . . ?" Grandma's voice echoed in the big white entryway as we walked in the front door. We usually came around back and went in through the kitchen, never knowing what to expect at home. But today there were Auntie Connie and her kids, and I guess Grandma was just as happy as I was for company. I could hear my mother's and Connie's voices from the living room and the buzz of Peter and Stevie yelling and playing in the backyard.

"We're down here, Mother. Is Jono with you?" She sounded pretty normal. That was good. I ran into the living room. "There you are!" My mother was sitting in the big white armchair, beaming. She was in a good mood, putting on a show for her big sister. Auntie Connie was tall and blonde and cheery, with eyes that sparkled and laughed. I gave her a hug, and she stood there smiling at me, glowing like an angel in the late afternoon sunlight. "You're growing up so fast I can't keep up with you, Jono."

I loved Auntie Connie. Why couldn't my mother be like her? My mother used to tell me how when I was a baby they'd take turns pushing my stroller down the street in New York City, and people would peer in and say, "What a cute baby! How old is he?" Auntie Connie would answer with a proud smile, pretending I was hers. That was before she had kids of her own. My mother and her big sister had always been real close, my mother always said. She told me I really had two mothers. More like three, I'd think, remembering the dark one with the demon that came out when she drank. Why couldn't the good ones be around more?

"Hey, Jono! What's happ'nin', man?" Steve, who was two years younger than me, ran in from the yard, smiling like a shaggy dog.

Peter, a year younger than Steve, stood behind him, grinning. The three of us shook hands. I'd taught them that, like the gangsters on teevee. Aunt Connie didn't let her kids watch teevee. She said it was bad for their brains and would turn them into "morons," so Steve and Pete didn't know about stuff like *The Naked City*. But they sure wanted to. My mother called me the Ringleader, 'cause they always followed me around. I liked them both, but little Pete was my favorite. He was the troublemaker, the Bad Seed. Like me.

"I swear, that boy's got th' Curse on him, Constance," Grandma warned. "Just like ya poor fatha' . . ."

"Oh, shush, Mother!" Auntie Connie threw back her blond hair, guffawing. "The only curse is that those two want to eat us out of house and home!"

Auntie Connie and my mother laughed and sipped their cocktails, talking about whatever grownup sisters talked about. Even though my mother drank with Auntie Connie, she never seemed to act drunk. For some reason the demons stayed away when Auntie Connie was there. I wished she could stay with us forever. But she had her own family and they lived up in Bel Air in their own big house a few miles away.

My cousins and I stood shifting in our sneakers and grinning. I'd told them I'd take them down to the busy corner with the pizza parlor and the liquor store. We looked at each other. It was time. "Well, uh, see ya," I mumbled, edging toward the back door, my cousins following in silence.

"And where are you three hooligans off to now?" My mother smiled, sounding all normal.

"Just gonna go mess around." I shrugged. Peter and Stevie nodded.

"Just look at the three of you." My mother smirked. "Butter wouldn't melt in your mouths, would it?" She and Auntie Connie laughed again.

As we slipped out the back I could hear my mother, the dark one, talking. "Can I freshen that up for you, Con?"

Grandma's voice called behind us in the warm afternoon. "Hey, you boys don't go too far now. There's a chill in th' air, you'll catch ya deaths!"

○   ○   ○

Feeling restless and tired, Cigano gets up and lights a cigarette. He reaches over and reads what he's written, scanning the pages as if trying to decipher a stranger's words. Closing the notebook, he lies down and clamps his eyes shut, saying a silent prayer to stop the avalanche of memories. He can still hear his grandmother's voice calling out, *"You'll catch ya deaths!"*

Taking a drag, he mutters, "Yeah, we'd catch our fuggin' deaths, all right!"

He lies back again, listening to the sound of mariachi music from his little radio on the bedside table. The steady afternoon rush of mufflerless cars and trucks rumbling outside the window blends with the sound of booming machinery from the port. *What the fuck am I doing in this dump?* As he drifts off to sleep, another thought comes wandering up to his pillow like a ragged beggar. *Yeah, well, the one thing worse than this would be going back to New York. Fuck that! You're here now, so just suck it up and keep writing. No other way out. Only way out now is in.*

12. GOING DEEPER

"A MAN WHO SAYS HE'S NEVER BEEN SCARED IS EITHER
LYING OR ELSE HE'S NEVER BEEN ANYPLACE OR
DONE ANYTHING."

—LOUIS L'AMOUR

After a longer-than-usual afternoon siesta, Cigano is jolted awake by blaring horns outside the window. Sweaty, tormented by vague ghostly visions, feeling confused and disoriented, he looks around the room, trying to get his bearings as shadowy wings of impending doom swarm him like attacking birds of prey.

"Fuck!" He jumps up from the bed and stands in his underwear, looking around. His surroundings seem shabbier than before, somehow. Bleak. Hopeless. He limps over and sits at the table, feeling heavy and dull, hung over. Siesta time. Silence on the street. Silence in the room but for the constant babble of his little radio. Then he remembers that odd Brazilian kid and his big tattoo project. *Where did that shit come from? It just keeps getting weirder.* He picks up one of his journals and leafs through pages of dense writing. A letter falls out. He picks it up and reads.

HEY JONATHAN, I was going through some boxes of old magazines I had in storage, and re-realized just how important, what a key figure you played in tattooing. You steered a whole generation of tattooists in the right direction. If this was the Mafia, man, you'd be getting envelopes from a hundred people a week. I had the fortune of

*working at your shop for about nine months in 1999. I still cite it as
the most real-deal tattoo studio I've ever had the privilege of working. I
don't know if you hear it enough, but thanks for all you did for me and
for this business. With respect and gratitude, Phil Luck*

Shaking his head, the tattoo man smiles. He folds the letter with care
and tucks it into the back of the notebook. He picks up a ballpoint and
draws the outline of a man's body, then stops. Staring at the page, he feels
haunted, apprehensive and uncertain. He scans his brain-files, trying to
remember an idea he'd had for a full-body tattoo back when he was
working in Japan. After sketching out a few more tentative lines, his hand
falters again. *It's no good. Shit!* He looks around the room and curses under
his breath. "Shit shit shit!" Tears cloud his vision as he rips the page from
the notebook and tears it into tiny scraps. They fall from his hands like
murdered moths. He snatches his old brass tattoo machine off the table
and flings it across the room. It bounces off the thick plaster wall with an
ugly **thunk**, leaving a dull scar and landing on the bed, where it lies like
a dead sparrow.

As quickly as it came over him, the rage subsides, drowning itself in a
deeper well of sadness. Cigano sinks from the chair to his knees, weeping.

"God, whoever's out there, please show me a way outta this mess.
How do I ever write it all down? How can I live with all the noise in my
head if I don't keep going? Help me let go of this shit! Please, God, show
me the way. Help me forgive th' bastards. Help me find some meaning
here, *please!*"

Tears flow, washing over him in waves of frustration and sorrow. His
brain is crumbling under an unbearable psychic weight. He can sense
a thousand dark slimy slugs slithering over his soul as he feels the sweat
of his bare skin against the cool floor tiles. He prays on, silent words
of supplication emerging from a raging sea of confusion. "Thy will be
done," he moans. "How can I best serve you? Whaddya *want* from me,
man? Just *show* me! Gimme a fuggin' sign, something! Please, God, show
me how to do this shit. I'm so fucking scared! Please, guide me, teach me,
show me the way."

Finally, he rolls over on his back and sleeps. This time he doesn't dream.

Hours later, he awakens on the floor. His consciousness merges into the muddy depths of night. Time has stopped. It's dark; only the yellow glow from a streetlight outside the window. He sits up and looks around the room. The shadows seem heavy, cumbersome, malevolent. He pulls himself to his feet and limps to the table. Eyes adjusting to the dim light, he looks at his notebooks: thirty years of writing, all his old journals, poems, and stories.

Rubbing his face to confirm he's still alive, he picks up a worn paperback and stares at the cover: *The Trouble with Cinderella*, by Artie Shaw. He cracks it and studies a hastily scrawled inscription on the title page. "Best wishes, Artie Shaw." He purses his lips, fighting an urge to spit on the floor.

"Best wishes my *dick*, ya selfish old bastard!" He drops the book onto the tabletop like an ancient curse and stands staring into the shabby yellow shadows, whispering the word over and over like some weird, involuntary mantra. "Bastard, bastard, bastard, bastard . . ."

He snatches his denim jacket off the chair and hurries out the door, muttering under his breath, "Gotta get th' fuck outta here." And then he's walking the streets of night again, accompanied only by a familiar chill in his heart and the ghost of a restless young traveler named Jonathan.

He trudges the port's ancient walls like a soldier, mingling with the muted lights and shadows. He can feel unseen shapes dancing around him, flickering, following. His steps seem to be taking him nowhere, and still he moves forward, prodded by an inner desperation; a haunted ghost stumbling through a cold surreal limbo, somewhere between memory and a long-nameless dread. Even the gaudy transvestite whores manning the port wall avoid eye contact, as if the specter of *Santissima Muerte* were attached to his shadow. There's a big rat scrambling around in the pit of his gut, running his feelings through an unfathomable emotional maze. He knows in his bones that he is truly untouchable, unclean and cursed beyond redemption. Never before has he felt so alone, so lost, so damned; worse than kicking dope. He knows this horrible desolate sober feeling clawing at his gut is the reason he got strung out again in the first place. There's nowhere left to hide, and he knows it. Nowhere to run. Now he must finally learn to embrace the pain.

On a deserted side street near the port, he comes upon a weatherbeaten statue of the *Virgin de Guadalupe* in a little shrine between two crumbling buildings. The comforting glowing icon beckons to his weary faith in the trembling light of a dozen tall glass votive candles. The tattoo man stops and stands transfixed, quiet as a ghost, gazing at the familiar effigy as the flickering candlelight pulls him into a trancelike daze. A smell of crackling lightning descends over the Gulf, and he falls to his knees, praying.

A wave of inner warmth engulfs him. Forms take shape in the candle-light, drawing him deeper into the vision. An amber glow surrounds him. Tears fall from his burning eyes as he feels himself enfolded in a shining golden bubble of relief. The bubble expands, widening, becoming clearer, carrying him back to another time, another life, another dream; and then he is gone, falling into a cosmic wormhole that's sucking him through invisible portals into a past that feels as real and present as anywhere he has ever been.

Going deeper, Cigano emerges into a state of pure awareness where this feeling, this place, this *knowing* is all there is, all there ever was. He's in a continuous loop of the dream of his life, of all the drugs he took in another time, another world, another dream that is now and real and forever. Past, present, and future all merge as one, without question or answer or meaning, free of time and space. And he is there, arriving in Veracruz for the very first time, walking these same shabby old streets. A long time ago.

13. FLASHBACK

"IT IS GOOD TO HAVE AN END; BUT IT IS THE JOURNEY THAT MATTERS."

-URSULA K. LE GUIN

Veracruz, 1977. Dust kicks up around the boots of a road-weary young traveler. Cigano's mind's eye watches the hazy figure walking along, carrying a little satchel. He recognizes the bag. He is that traveler, awake in a vision without beginning or end.

"Decades gone by like an elephant's dream." He sighs, surrendering to the relentless movie of his life as he sees the shadowy figure skirting the familiar port wall. The sound of giant machines crashing and banging blends with the straining winches' steady whine. The noises echo into a humid night of the senses, where shadows of ships loom like sleeping dinosaurs under sultry skies. Distant lightning crackles over a steely horizon. A rooster is crowing. The young traveler crosses a deserted plaza where a big rusty anchor sits in the tall weeds. He stops and stares at it, rubbing his eyes. He has seen it before somewhere, maybe in a dream. He looks down at his dusty boots and remembers. This is real. This is now. Thunder rumbles from afar as a twenty-something-year-old Jonathan Shaw's eyes focus in on a weather-battered building. *Click*. Another snapshot. *HOTEL BUENOS AIRES.*

The phantom traveler drifts across the street like a sleepwalker. On the corner outside a shabby cantina, a one-shoed drunk lies face up, spread-eagled on the pavement in a puddle of vomit, a piss stain widening at his wrinkled crotch. Blaring mariachi music fills his ears. Cigano knows he is not dreaming as he watches the molecules of his vision taking form. He *is* the dream; the movie, a sliver of the sleepless infinite All. Down the street, a pack of stray dogs barks in the night. A salty breeze is blowing in from the Gulf as his feet lead him forward. He rounds a corner where old men sit at a wooden table on the sidewalk, playing lazy dominoes by a hotel's crumbling entryway. The vision is cluttered with wild chaotic patterns of bougainvillea and spindly cactus. Warm lights of life beckon him toward lethargic rhumba rhythms hanging in the muggy air.

He steps inside and stands before a timeworn reception desk by a crumbling stairway. A faded image of the *Virgin de Guadalupe* hangs on a peeling plaster wall. A dusty wooden ship sits on a shelf amidst the clutter of memory. Through a wide archway he sees three black-haired rag-doll children kicking a deflated green-gray ball around a shabby courtyard. Laundry hangs under an ancient mango tree. Scruffy parrots watch from their perches, tiny dreamscape pirate spies. A stout, stoic-faced Indian woman follows a plodding broom across the worn rain-slicked Spanish tiles. Cigano can hear the sound inside the expanding sepia balloon, ***sssssskkk sssskkk sssskkk,*** drawing him deeper, deeper. A playful smile emerges under a pencil-thin mustache from behind a faded floral curtain as *Señor* Ramón appears like an old-time vaudeville magician, a wide-faced childlike grin floating above his threadbare guayabera shirt; a religious medallion hanging from a thin gold chain. The dreamer sees the crude homemade tattoos on the smiling hotel man's arm, a headless naked pinup and a fuzzy old blue/green anchor. The traveler likes him. He likes this place. From the debris of his memory, Cigano watches as the traveler bonds with the man in easy banter as a waif-like girl with rough indigenous features flitters in from the courtyard. Gliding around *Señor* Ramón like a fairy shadow, she disappears behind the magic curtain. Ramón hands the traveler a brass key on a big wooden anchor with the number "27." The girl emerges again and places a towel and a small pink bar of soap on the counter.

Cigano sees himself as he was a long time ago, walking up the same timeworn stairs. He can smell the soap and clean towel in his hand. A familiar scent of Lysol and eucalyptus wafts up from the tiles as the young traveler measures his steps to the end of a hallway. He fits his key in the lock. In slow, dreamlike motion he opens the door and surveys his new home. Stepping inside, he feels for a light switch and finds it, as if he already knew where it was. He strides across the room and opens a window overlooking the port. As the trembling old ceiling fan begins to stir, he sets down his bag, strips to his shorts, and lies down on the bed. He relishes the comfort of cool starched sheets against his skin. End of the day, end of the road. The spinning overhead fan lulls the young traveler like a hypnotist's wheel. He drifts away, falling deeper into another dream within a dream within a dream.

O   O   O

Images of Rio de Janeiro form on an old movie screen, dancing black-skinned bodies reminiscent of *Orfeu Negro*, his favorite film; sparkling blue ocean vista dotted with islands. Green mountains and crumbling colonial buildings. He is there, in another life, another film, another dream, a long time ago . . . *A long time ago* . . . The dreamer strains to remember as his thoughts weave through rows of clotheslines crisscrossing the vision like pieces in a complex jigsaw puzzle, and he is walking down a familiar dirt path with his old girlfriend Suzanne. She's wearing a red *guayabera*, yellow shorts, and flip-flops, like the hotel girl. She reaches out to take his hand and he pushes it away, demanding to know where his cousin Malcolm is.

She morphs into his mother, a drawling, annoying phantom. "Oh, Malcolm, yes, dah-ling. I believe he's, let me see, oh yes, he's in East Los Angeles, poor boy. He's dying, you know. Arsenic poisoning."

"How can you act so casual?" the dreamer shouts back. "Aren't you gonna go to him? Ya can't just leave him to die all alone like a rat!"

"Don't worry, dah-ling." His mother's voice hisses like a thousand snakes. He feels a bloody vomiting skull of rage rising into his chest as she strokes his head. "He'll be fine, dah-ling. It's only rat poison. And every-body dies alone, silly child . . . Oh, my beamish boy! My beamish boy! Come to my arms, my beamish boy!"

His mother shape-shifts into Medusa. The serpents in her hair are hissing with her whispers as she repeats the familiar phrase over and over. "Come to my arms, my beamish boy!" As she moves forward to embrace him, her hands sprout into bouquets of writhing snakes, hissing, spitting, flicking evil black tongues. He tries to scream, but his lips are sewn shut like a shrunken head's. His face is a hard leather mask. The word "lockjaw" flashes across his mind, and then something shifts.

He's walking alone down an empty street somewhere in Mexico. He comes to a cul-de-sac where a mariachi band is playing. The musicians are wearing papier-mâché skull masks; a *Dia de Los Muertos* celebration. In the shade of a dusty eucalyptus, the mariachis play a languid funeral dirge over a body. Approaching the corpse, he strains to remember who has died. Laid out in the dirt, he sees the cold, pasty, gray-blue skin of death. The face has no eyes, only two gaping black pits that seem to go down forever to a dark nightmare place. He hears a rude catcall whistle from above and he looks up into the tree. The branches are clustered with dozens of jittery little blackbirds, cackling, calling, whistling, singing. Each one is holding an eyeball in its long shiny black beak. He watches spellbound as they fly off in a great thundering roar, like the big muffler-less trucks that shake the building from the street below while his body sleeps. From above, the dreamer can see himself tossing around on the starched white sheets. Beneath a wobbly ceiling fan, he sees lazy flies alighting on his sweaty chest. But he stays where he is, walking along in the same weird dreamscape. Making his way through the maria-chis, he realizes the body lying on the ground is his cousin Malcolm. Maggots squirm in the dark bloody cavities of his eye sockets. Malcolm's body doesn't have any legs, only a pair of stumps protruding from his shorts. Someone calls out, "We must bury the dead!" and then they are all standing in a cemetery on the outskirts of Veracruz. The dreamer sees that the skull-faced revelers are people he has known in his travels: truck drivers, hobos, and drinking companions. Everyone is standing around joking and laughing. His friends prompt him forward, shouting encouragement as he sweats and struggles to shove his cousin's body back into the open slot of the raised grave. But the tomb is shallow and he has to climb inside with the body, hauling Malcolm in by his belt-loops. Sweating and breathing hard, he can hear somebody commenting from outside. "It is good the dead one has no legs, only a pair of tamales . . ." Above the others, he hears a woman's voice shouting, "*Tamales! Tamales!*"

Jolted from the dream, sweating and confused, young Jonathan sits up on the bed. Dizzy and disoriented, he staggers over to the window. Wide awake now, he can still hear that strange dreamlike call crying the words again and again. "*Tamales! Tamales!*" He looks down onto the street and watches a horse round the corner, like in a surreal slow-motion funeral procession. Behind the scrawny gray nag, an old woman sits on a beat-up wagon with threadbare truck tires. She looks like one of the Day of the Dead skeletons. Beside her sit three large aluminum pots draped with white towels. The woman drones into a microphone attached to a car battery and a battered loudspeaker, *"Tamales! Tamales!"* repeating the word in a monotonous mechanical tone as the wagon disappears into the distance, jolting off over the crooked cobblestone street. *"Tamales! Tamales!"*

Looking around the room, Jonathan can still hear the words. *"Tamales, tamales!"* But somehow that is not what he is hearing. What he hears are the real words behind the other words, as if listening with some other, more perceptive, inner ear. *"Flores! Flores! Flores para los muertos!"* The voice drones on. *"Flo-wers! Flo-wers! Flowers for the dead!"*

Shaking off the dream like a layer of dust, the young traveler picks up a thin cotton towel with faded blue-stenciled letters: *HOTEL BUENOS AIRES.* Groggy and covered in sweat, he wanders down the hall and into the cool, dark solace of a green-tiled shower stall.

The water feels good on his head as he breathes in a comfortable scent of disinfectant and mildew. He towels off and goes back to his room, where he stands beneath the ceiling fan. He lights a cigarette, moves to the window, and stares out over the port, listening to the booming sounds from outside—and from within.

14. A FRIEND

"EACH FRIEND REPRESENTS A WORLD IN US, A WORLD
POSSIBLY NOT BORN UNTIL THEY ARRIVE, AND IT IS ONLY
BY THIS MEETING THAT A NEW WORLD IS BORN."

—ANAÏS NIN

Veracruz, 2002. Kneeling on the sidewalk before the glowing shrine with his eyes closed, the tattoo man is deep in time travel, shuttling through his past: seeing, dreaming, remembering, living it all again. In the warm amber vision of his mind's eye, he watches the kid he once was bouncing down a flight of stairs and out into the soft early-evening light.

Veracruz, 1977. In the hotel lobby, the young traveler is greeted by smells of the tropics: a vital scent of soap, garlic, smoke, eucalyptus, and the churning waters of the Gulf. His gut stirs with the promise of new adventures in a new place for a new man: a restless vagabond soul, hungry to live and be alive again at the end of a long weary road. He drifts past the reception desk and out onto the sidewalk. Ramón and some men stand around drinking beer. Someone hands him a cool brown bottle of Superior. He upends it and lingers with them, listening to their easy Mexican banter, the lyrical rhythm of their animated singsong talk. The brew lubricates his tongue, teeth, eyes, ears, blood, bringing life back into focus. Jonathan feels good.

A dilapidated aging hooker stumbles past in bright evening colors, and the men launch a barrage of playful whistles and catcalls. The young traveler whistles too, just for the hell of it. When in Rome. She smiles with a grateful little wave as her heels click off down the sidewalk like a worn-out old burro. A young guy named Pepe has the best whistle, cool and sharp like one of those shiny little tropical blackbirds. Pepe is a frenetic vision of homemade tattoos, gold teeth, and a gold cross. Sparks of kinetic energy seem to fly from his face as it crystallizes in the yellowed air of Cigano's memory. Like a grubby magician, Pepe winks, takes a pull on a crooked joint, and passes it to the newcomer, exhaling a smoky barrage of smiling words and questions. *"¿Tu eres extranjero, guero?"* "Ju foreigner?"

Jonathan takes the joint from his callused brown fingers. He forces a long, deep breath of pungent green jungle smoke deep into his chest. Holding it in, the young traveler nods back with bulging eyes.

"Orale . . ." Pepe grins, hands dancing in the air like a fiery delinquent scarecrow. "Ju e'peekie Eeen-glee?"

Jonathan nods again, then exhales into the humid night. *"Marineiro? Ju e'sailor?"* Pepe stares at him, a wide-eyed child. "Ju come on de sheep to Veracruz Puerto, *no?*"

"No, hombre." Jonathan shrugs, feeling his way into the conversation like a blind man entering a room. *"Por tierra, pues."*

"Orale . . . I wan' get de work, how e'sey it, *abordo,* on de e'sheep . . . *pero,* me no e'peekee *Miami, ju know? Oye, mucho gusto!"*

The two young men shake hands and wander off down the street, talking. Jonathan is glad to be in this soulful old port, which all along the long dusty road had been but a dream, a little red star on a tattered roadmap in his pocket. Now he's finally walking its rain-slick streets with a new friend, an oddball charismatic native of dreamlike tropical nights.

Soft footsteps glide along dark cobblestones, echoing down the hallways of Cigano's memory as the two young men pass a faded shrine to the Virgin of Guadalupe. Cigano watches it all clicking into focus from the same spot where, in a parallel dimension some twenty-five years hence, the tattoo man kneels praying before the same shimmering candlelit icon. Waves of emotion collide in the shadows of his mind. Time, shape, image, and sound emerge as he surrenders to the spell. His eyes closed tight, he can hear singing and bottles breaking in the trembling air of the past. A long steady tone echoes from a ship's horn above a gay cacophony of harps and marimbas, and Cigano is there again. A long time ago; a rum-soaked tropical night in the lively open-aired cantinas of the old port. Familiar images expand in colorful waves of memory as the tattoo man falls back into the spinning funhouse ride.

○   ○   ○

Veracruz, 1977. Under looming archways of the weathered colonial buildings in the old city's nocturnal hub, nightlife is in session. An aging hooker's face blinks into focus. Like a sleepwalker wandering into Cigano's vision, she gestures tipsily across a table cluttered with bottles. Three whores, two Greek sailors in colorful silk shirts, Pepe, and Jonathan are drinking, talking, laughing. All around them the plaza is a living tapestry of flowers. Giant souvenir wooden ships sail the bony shoulders of roving peddlers, across a sea of bottles, glasses, and trays of food, in a sparkling carnival of sound and motion. An army of shoeshine boys, Gypsy fortunetellers, and stone-faced Indian women in long colorful hand-embroidered skirts moves between the crowded tables, hawking cigarettes, Chiclets, and spiced peanuts; a rum-soaked blur of baskets, hands, faces, laughter, and song. White-jacketed waiters navigate the jangling chaos as dirty-faced children peddling trinkets weave among the drinkers, blinking their shiny eyes like feral cats.

Pepe leans forward, struggling with a joke. Drunk enough to brave the choppy currents of his own bad English, the bright-eyed young hustler drags each word along like a rum-soaked sailor stumbling home. "So, thees one maing, he go see de ladies, okey?" He winks to his smiling audience. "He take de girl an' they go hotel for mek de boom boom . . ." He makes a crude gesture, provoking peals of drunken laughter. As the giggles subside, he goes on. "Okey, so de nex' day he, how e'say it, *huevos*, he *balls* so-oo e'scratchy, ju know?"

More howls of merriment as Pepe grabs at his crotch in a frantic movement. "Okey, okey." He holds his hand up. "So he go back an' see de e'same *chamaca*, an' he e'say her, 'Hey, ju! Ju gimme de crabs!'"

More laughter as he delivers the punchline. "She look him an' e'say 'Pues si, cabrón. Wha' ju wan' me give to ju for only fifty peso, de *lobsters*?'"

The table explodes in riotous cackling as the sailors call for more drinks. Machine-gun–toting soldiers wind their way through the vendors, strolling mariachis, and dueling marimba bands as a grizzled sailor flexes a weathered forearm, making his tattooed hula girl dance, to the whores' delight, carving the moment forever into Jonathan's brain.

○   ○   ○

Hours later, distant strains of music mix with a splash of lazy waves lapping at the deserted seawall. Under a flickering streetlight's yellow glow, Pepe glances down, frowning at the crude handmade anchor on his forearm. "*Oye*, Joni, ju look de tattoos on thees sailor? *Que bonito!*" He grimaces at his own tattoo again, shaking his head. "No like thees e'sheet."

Jonathan squints at his new friend's coffee-colored skin, trying to decipher the blurry chicken-scratch markings.

Pepe looks up. "*Oye*, Joni. Ju got any de good gringo tattoo?"

"Nah." Jonathan shrugs, raising his sleeve to reveal a crooked little jailhouse star on his biceps. "Unless ya call this little shit a tattoo."

The two young friends laugh at each other's crappy ink, then fall quiet. The dark water splashes at the rocks. Silent lightning flashes over the Gulf.

Jonathan breaks the spell. "Where ya wanna get to from here, Pepe?"

He shrugs. "I donno, maing. Anyplace more better for me than de home."

"Where's that? Where's home?"

"Nicaragua. Managua. *Conoces?*"

"Nah, I never been there, not yet. I know what ya mean about home, though, 'mano. Anywhere I end up's better'n where I come from, too."

"*Pero porque?*" Pepe looks at him with wide eyes. "Ju no come from Junite Stase? All de peoples wan' go over there. Is no *bueno* thees place?"

"Not for me." Jonathan sucks his teeth, picturing a little boy shifting from foot to foot on the cold linoleum floor of a bright American class-room, children reciting in unison, "*I pledge allegiance to the flag.*" He feels an old toxic hatred rising in his gut as he hawks a big ball of phlegm into the water.

Silence, lapping waves. They light cigarettes and stand smoking, looking out at the distant lightning flashes riding the horizon like horses of the Apocalypse. Two figures appear from a dark side street. They amble along the deserted seawall like a pair of scruffy ghosts. As they approach beneath the streetlight's glow, Jonathan can make out rotten teeth on one and a brutal ear-to-chin scar on the other.

"*Tienes fuego?*" The young guy with bad teeth studies Jonathan with a crooked grin, holding up a joint.

Jonathan nods, leans over and strikes a wooden match, cupping his hands against the wind. The kid lights up, takes a big hit, and passes it over. Jonathan is taking a long hungry pull when, quick as a rattlesnake, snaggle-tooth presses a long deadly screwdriver to his throat, growling "*Dame la pinche feria, puto!*" "Ju fucking money, faggot!" The rotten black stubs snap at his face like an ugly reptilian curse. He can smell the sour chemical stench of a glue-sniffing soul, stirring up angry shadows in his gut.

Pepe starts to move toward them, but the scar-faced kid steps up behind him, thrusting a big rusty blade against his Adam's apple. Jonathan grimaces as the black stubs bark with a poisonous urgency. "*Andele, putito!* **Vamos!**"

"*Okey, okey, calma, tranquilo.*" Jonathan reaches into his pocket for a crumpled wad of pesos. Accidentally-on-purpose, the bills slip from his hand and flutter to the pavement, and the biting metallic pressure subsides from his throat. As the stoned adolescent bends to grab the cash, Jonathan takes a quick step back. With all the rage in his heart, he kicks him in the face, hard. **SPLAT!!** Snaggletooth falls back, his head striking the pavement with the hollow *thunk* of a green coconut falling from a tree. A mindless surge of adrenaline floods Jonathan's body as he begins kicking the half-unconscious head. Drunk, spitting, he kicks and shouts. "Die! Die! *Te mato, hijo de puta!*"

As Jonathan rages on, the other punk turns from Pepe and steps forward with the knife. In a flash, Pepe pulls a big revolver from under his *guayabera*. Cool as a cat, he puts it to the kid's head, cocking the hammer with a sinister **C-rrrck**. "*Pa'bajo, come mierda!*" "Down, shit-eater!" Pepe growls the order in a tone as soft as a lover's whisper and final as the grave. Scarface freezes into a comical slow-motion cringe as Pepe nudges him to the ground with the long steely black barrel. Compliant as a schoolboy now, the scruffy teenage thug lies facedown beside his unconscious partner.

Pepe winks at Jonathan, who bends over and starts going through their pockets. Pepe flashes a wide grin. "Ju know, Joni, back in my country de peoples e'say, 'when de tif tif de tif, hah, God laugh!'"

Still kneeling before the shimmering candles, Cigano looks up and glances around. Slowly, carefully, silently, he constructs the words in his mind, words he knows he will soon have to add to his confession.

○   ○   ○

I bent down and snatched my cash from the ground, then picked up the screwdriver. I tucked the long evil rod into my belt and turned back to my aggressor. His mouth hung open like a grave, his ugly rotten teeth smeared with blood. As Pepe held the gun to his partner's head, I pulled a few rumpled banknotes and coins from both their pockets. There was a folded scrap of newspaper filled with dirty-brown powder: Mexican heroin. My old friend. I glared at scarface lying on the ground with the muzzle resting on his greasy hair. As I held his dope over the seawall, watching the wind take it back to Hell, the look of despair on his face filled me with a deep surge of triumph. That shit had ruined enough of my short life, killed enough of my friends.

Feeling another sudden wave of fury, I turned to where his partner lay passed out on his back. I lunged back and kicked him in the side, hard as I could. I could feel his ribs cracking and it felt good. He didn't move, just groaned a little. I was sort of hoping he'd try to get up. He didn't. As scarface looked on in sullen terror, I dragged his partner's limp body over and propped his back against the seawall. I stepped up onto the ledge and jumped, landing my boots above one of his kneecaps. This time he groaned louder. My blood still pumping with rage, I heard myself cursing *"Hijo de puta!"* I could hear my mother's angry screams echoing behind my curses, and then there was nothing but the old pounding nightmare voices clamoring in my head. I didn't even hear Pepe telling me to stop as the other kid scrambled to his feet and ran off down the road like Satan was chasing him with a red-hot pitchfork. I took one more kick at the side of that ugly unconscious snaggletoothed head. As I stepped back to put the boot to him again, Pepe pulled me away.

I snapped out of it, breathing hard. The red spell of rage was spent.

My friend and I walked back toward the plaza. As we approached the bar where we'd been drinking before, all I wanted was to get good and drunk.

15. VAGABOND HEART

"WHEN THE MOST IMPORTANT THINGS IN OUR LIFE HAPPEN WE QUITE OFTEN DO NOT KNOW, AT THE MOMENT, WHAT IS GOING ON."

−C.S. LEWIS

Veracruz, 1977. Afternoon emerges from a long dreamless sleep. Jonathan awakens with a start. Covered in sweat, the young man looks around the room, his fuzzy vision adjusting to the hazy afternoon light. He doesn't dare move yet. His head is pounding. His mouth is dry and bitter. A quiet pit of dread lingers in his gut. He's become used to it over the hard-drinking months of his travels. Soon, he knows, the waking jitters will pass.

Finally, he rises up and stumbles down the hall, still feeling groggy. With a trembling hand he opens the shower tap above the toilet. He pisses long and hard into the seatless bowl as a stream of lukewarm water trickles over his head, waking him fully to another pounding hangover. He winces as he pieces together jagged-edged details of the night before. Longing for a wake-up beer, he towels off and trudges back to his room. He knows that after a big cold *caguama* he'll feel a lot better. He steps into his faded gym shorts and flip-flops and wanders down the hall toward Pepe's room. Maybe Pepe would like a *cerveza* too.

He taps lightly at his new friend's door, as if his own ears couldn't bear the noise of a real knock. As he pokes his head in, cool afternoon shadows stir like underwater plants beneath a table fan. A poster of Che

Guevara is tacked to the wall. Beside it, a calendar with a pinup girl, a framed picture of Jesus, and a poster of a Mexican soccer team. A radio plays a shuffling *cumbia*. Pepe is sitting propped up on the bed in his underwear. Looking up from a pocket-sized comic book, he grins, gesturing his visitor in. Half a bottle of rum and two empty glasses sit on the bedside table. The Indian girl from the day before lies passed out in a tangled sheet, snoring.

Jonathan's eyes focus on the chick. Pepe winks and lifts the sheet, exposing her sleeping naked coffee-colored ass. The two friends snicker like schoolboys. Without a word, Pepe reaches over for a scrap of paper on the table. His eyes light up like whorehouse neon as he hands it to his visitor.

Jonathan raises a quizzical eyebrow as he scans the paper: a rough sketch of a crude lopsided heart and anchor with the words: *VAGABUNDO CORAZÓN.* "Vagabond Heart. Yeah . . ." Jonathan nods.

"Ju like thees for de tattoo?" Pepe grins. "Is pretty good, no?"

"Ye-ah . . ." Jonathan smiles, remembering their talk the night before. "This would make a good one, 'mano. Got a pen?"

Pepe reaches over the girl again and hands him a ballpoint. Jonathan pulls a small notebook from his back pocket and leafs through his dense writing till he comes to a blank page. He sits down on the edge of the bed, studying the sketch. Forehead crinkled in concentration, his tongue plays at the corner of his mouth as he draws. Finally, he holds up his version of the design.

Pepe grins. A snappy blackbird-whistle emerges between his gold teeth. "*Joni, mi amigo, mi hermano!!* I wang ju mek it to me thees tattoo!"

"*Orale!*" Jonathan nods. "Shit, man, how hard could it be?"

"*Andale, chignon!*" Pepe's hand comes down with a hard *SMACK!!* on the sleeping girl's naked backside.

"*Aiiiiii!*" she cries as the two young would-be tattooists explode in laughter.

16. ON THE WATERFRONT

"O MY HATRED, MY MAJESTIC MALICE, MY SACRED PURE
AND BENIGN MALEVOLENCE, ANOINT MY FOREHEAD WITH
YOUR PURE KISS SO THAT I MAY BE BOTH PROUD
AND HUMBLE."

—CRUZ E SOUZA

All at once, Cigano is back in his body. Echoes of ghostly laughter
still ring in his brain, blending with the pounding industrial sounds from
the port. He rises up from his knees. Dusting off his trousers, he stands
squinting at the shimmering candlelit image of Guadalupe. He rubs his
eyes and shakes the spell of the past off himself like a wet dog; and then
he is walking again, wandering onward through the dark, empty streets
of Veracruz.

JOURNAL ENTRY – VERACRUZ, MARCH 2002:

*unable to sleep. Living in rooms of haunted memories, long heartless
nights spent rotting away in a wretched black bubble of solitude, hating
and hurting in eternal echo-chamber of pounding delirium yesterdays.
This must be what madness smells like; a stench, a filthy little stain, a
vague recollection of burning rubber. After all these years seeking relief
in the bottle, the pill, the needle and spoon, the memories are louder, more
obnoxious than ever today, more unresolved. Tedium and rot, my brain
burning a steady hole in faded roadmaps of nowhere. The death of all
romantic notions, a half-century-long funeral procession, a day, a minute,
a second at a time, suffering a Chinese water torture of rat-poison*

angst dripping into an empty dry pit of nothingness. Drip drip. Down down. Some are born blind, legless or bombed out, suffocated by poverty, ignorance, lack, limitation, and self-doubt. But this sort of madness is another realm of agony, which only the initiated can call by name. Soul rot. Here now to meet and face down the foul breath of King Jabberwock as his acid stench invades the crumbling sand castles of my world, my life, my mind. Powerless and impotent before the hot winds of death, I pray to whatever gods or demons guard the gates of this place where I sit writing in madness letters, bug scrawl crawling across sickly green pages of crippled dementia. I wanna run amok and go tearing back across the Pac-Man paths of my life. I want all the wasted years back, all the dead friends and lovers gone forever. I crave the warm lustful bleeding slobbering relief of needles stabbing into yearning veins, promising a Special Delivery rush of oblivion and relief from this nightmare horror- show hell raging behind my eyes. Come to me, please, kind spirits of annihilation, come and dribble your insane babbling currency of salvation on my shoulders, my feet, my dick, my balls, my brain, my aching liver. Take me and wake me and lift me like a shiny new red balloon far away from this pounding place of gaping senseless fevered Want. Amen.

JOURNAL ENTRY – VERACRUZ, MARCH 2002:

Woke up to the horrors again, that sick sinking dread of existential disappointment. Sitting amidst the dusty rusty decaying scraps of youth's broken ruin, it disturbs me greatly, this incessant insistent maddening awareness that the world is nothing but a persistent illusion of time and space and matter. And still I cannot stop this demented entity that runs me like a rat on a wheel, chasing the absurd notion that I might somehow someday wrest satisfaction from this ridiculous house of lies and broken mirrors called My Life. This must be the true meaning of the word "powerless," I think as I sit writing, creating my own little myths revolving around this absurd tragic-comic little cartoon character called "Me": a heroic personage that doesn't even exist, but nonetheless strives and battles against all that is and ever was in a desperate effort to take on an identity. Oh, Lord, and that's where the fun begins. Because this craving little "Me" knows it is some sort of mad genius—much smarter and infinitely more resourceful than the other "me," who sits here writing under its double-barreled shotgun gaze. God, have mercy on this tragic dying planet and everybody on it. Bugs crawl across the cluttered table of my physical reality as I stand by the window looking down on a frantic anthill of fellow prisoners. Nine in the morning and they're all running amok down there as I sit listening to the constant sound of gunfire from the firing squad of my brain, blessed and cursed by a lingering disturbing inconvenient awareness of my own madness. And it doesn't even matter whether I'm in Madagascar or Madison Avenue or the madhouse, because the whole fucking planet is the madhouse, a science-fiction hell that has become fact, the lie that tells the Truth, which reminds us that we live in a war-zone horror-show here. Why, oh, why the fuck did my spirit ever elect to be born into this second-rate slapstick-tragedy? Why did I want to be brought into this insane apocalyptic junkyard, hurtled down here through the bloody chute of my poor mad mother's accursed womb, hatched like a befuddled scorpion from the tortured seed of my father? And how did this insidious collection of circumstances weave together to create the weird discordant symphony of my life?

Memories roll across Cigano's consciousness, crashing together like waves on a dark, troubled sea. He digs still deeper into the shadowed recesses of himself as he walks on, a weary archeologist piecing together details, dusting off the image of a long-lost buried child, hearing its voice and writing, dictating its stories into his mind's battered notebooks.

My mother used to give these big "cocktail parties" when I was little. There'd always be a lot of noise downstairs at night, like mooing cows and tweeting birds, a tinkling of glasses and loud voices laughing like crazy people. As I lay in bed, the moos and tweets gave me the feeling they were all talking about me. And the louder the voices got, the farther I went away into the secret world of dancing eucalyptus leaves spinning in the wind outside my window, until I couldn't hear them at all anymore.

One night, the clumsy chatter was humming away downstairs as I drifted off to sleep; people talking, men making muffled cow sounds, the tipsy bird chirps from women. The noises all mixed together with the shouts in my head like a muddled angry lullaby till it was a steady drone, putting me to sleep. I dreamt my fingers were clutching a string tied to a big bunch of balloons. I could feel my feet lifting up off the ground and floating away. I looked down and saw the house, the neighborhood, the city getting smaller and smaller. I held tight as I rose far up into the clouds under layers of sleep, deeper and deeper, higher and higher, till I couldn't see down below anymore. My hands started to hurt and I couldn't hold on. As the strings burned and slid through my fingers, I let go and fell, down, down, into a dark nightmare place where I couldn't breathe! I struggled, but I couldn't move. When I tried to yell out there was no voice, not even a little squeak. I'd been turned to stone by Medusa, the snake lady, like that ugly statue my mother kept on the table she put in the corner to hide the big brown bloodstain on her white wall-to-wall carpet. Angry shouts banged and pounded in my head, mixing with the mooing and tweeting and cocktail glasses clinking downstairs.

Just when I was about to sink underwater for good, I shot to the surface and hollered till my lungs hurt. I bolted from bed and ran for the door, the slobbering Jabberwock coming up fast behind me. *"Mommy, Mommy!"* I struggled with the big diamond doorknob, then ran down the hall. Breathing hard, I stopped, frozen at the top of the stairs.

"Jono? Dah-ling . . . ?" Her voice floated up from the cold whiteness below. I peered down and saw her staggering to the stairway. "Is that you, dah-ling?" Her tone was different. It was that other Mommy, the dark one. "Come down, dah-ling." Her words were slurred, blurry. "Come and meet my friends . . ."

Cigano walks past a row of scruffy eucalyptus trees lining a deserted stretch of beach. The memories stir in his gut as he trudges on, listening for the voice of that long-neglected abandoned child. The little ghost's dialogue fights its way out of the darkness, laden with unfamiliar unnamed emotions, a tangled rush of words struggling to be vomited out into the dull tepid awareness of another endless, restless, drinkless night.

I didn't want to go down there. I wanted my mommy to come upstairs and hug me and tuck me in like she used to. But this one wasn't that mommy. It was the other lady. The mean one. She again ordered me to come down, and I began descending the stairs, holding the rail, one big step at a time.

"That's my good boy!" She stood there smiling, a cigarette slashing across her shiny red lips like a scowl. When I got to the bottom a whole bunch of big ugly cow-people gathered around. I didn't know any of them. They stood around holding their stupid cocktail glasses, and they were all laughing at me! My mother said something I couldn't understand and they all tweeted and mooed and laughed some more. Then she took me by the hand and paraded me around the big living room in my pajamas like a trained monkey. An old bald guy in a gray suit picked me up and held me for them all to inspect. He had cold hands and his hot breath smelled like cigars and martini drinks. Stinky. I went limp like my cat Swifty, waiting for him to set me down. They all laughed and mooed and tweeted and said dumb things I couldn't understand. I hated them and I wished they'd all go home.

"Please excuse me for a minute, will you?" My mother smirked. There was a murmur from the people and more stupid laughter, like she had said something real funny. "Let's get you back into bed, mister." She lifted me from the floor and carried me up to my room.

"Why don't *you* go to bed, Mommy?"

"Later, dah-ling. I'm entertaining my friends. Now you be a good boy."

I could tell by the tone of her voice that I'd better not say any more. This was that other mommy. The dark one.

Caught in a toxic whirlwind of somber recollections, Cigano walks on, the visions oozing from his brain like bleeding pus from a throbbing infected wound. Restless as a ghost, he marches forward, navigating the shadows. Coming to a place where a deserted beach stretches to his left, he stops and looks out over the Gulf. He can feel spirits of the dead howling at his back, their cold weight settling on his soul as tears begin to cloud his eyes. Desperate for relief, he hurries toward the water's edge. Seeing no nocturnal predators, he strips, folds his clothes, sets them at his feet, and stands naked as an alligator, staring out to sea. His head is pounding as a crab scuttles over his bare feet. The dark waters undulate before him, an endless cemetery of howling tormented souls. He crosses himself, then wades in, reciting the Lord's Prayer in Portuguese: *"Pai nosso, que estais no Ceu, Santificado seja o Vosso Nome . . ."* Repeating the words again and again, he disappears beneath the surface, his tears mixing with the tepid salt water.

After staying underwater a long time, he shoots to the surface like a crazed Jack-in-the-box, raging, shouting, spitting; cursing the living, the dead, the monstrous, unbearable evil entity sitting on his spirit, a hungry, nagging black vulture eating him alive from within. "*Filhos da puta!* Bastards!" he shouts into the night, punching his clenched fists at the water again and again till he's dizzy and out of breath. Crumbling under the foul weight of blackness pulling at his heart, he starts to pray again, spitting the words out in English this time, wailing into the darkness, an urgent desperation prayer, crying, yelling, demanding, begging, "Forgive me my fucking trespasses, goddammit, as I forgive those miserable sons of bitches' bastards' whores who trespassed against me . . . *perdoaí a porra das minhas ofenças, porra, assim como eu perdou aquéles filhos das mil putas que me ofendéram . . .*"

He shouts the words out again and again, first in English, then Portuguese, then English again, the language of his past, his father, his mother, his country; those he hates, those he knows he must forgive somehow; he's like a junkie craving an impossible desperate fix. Then, like a shot of heroin, he feels a blanket of serenity descending over his mind. He goes still as the night, still as the grave. He stands in silence, a ghostly statue in the calm water, listening to the soft *splissh . . . splisssh . . . splassh* of the waves. And, for the first time since arriving back in Veracruz, he can feel his breath moving in and out in waves of peace. Surrender.

Lightning flashes far out at sea, defining the dark horizon like an eerie snapshot of Purgatory. Images dart like fish across the airwaves of time as the trembling yellow glow begins to surround his vision again. Cigano closes his eyes. He can feel the taste and texture of his mustache hairs, his teeth on his tongue, as he sinks back into the past once more.

Room 27, Hotel Buenos Aires. Young Jonathan sits hunched over Pepe, poking a crude hand-made tattoo onto his friend's chest. Sweating in concentration, the young man's tongue plays at the corner of his mouth as he finishes the outline of his first tattoo. Pepe's gold-toothed grimace hovers above his eyes as he sits up, regarding Jonathan's work: ink, blood, skin, and the familiar words: *VAGABUNDO CORAZÓN.* A ghostly caress trembles at Jonathan's back as the hotel girl stands at his side, watching wide-eyed. A warm feeling of ease and comfort fills his chest. Like a cat, the novice tattooist delights at the touch of the young girl's hands running over his shoulder.

O   O   O

As the warm waves lap at Cigano's body, his baffled senses long for a soft female touch. Thunder booms out behind him as he steps out of the water, brushes the sand from his feet, and dresses in a hurry. He doesn't want to be alone.

17. RESTLESS GHOSTS

"THE HUMAN WORD IS LIKE AN OUTWORN, BATTERED TIMBAL UPON WHICH WE BEAT OUR MELODIES FIT FOR MAKING BEARS DANCE WHEN WE ARE TRYING TO MOVE THE STARS TO PITY."

—FLAUBERT

JOURNAL ENTRY – VERACRUZ, 2002: Is there ever any relief, or is this the price I gotta pay for my fucking sobriety? A lonely wandering penis out on the prowl, I got tangled up with a coked-up old hooker who was too spun-out to fuck. Went back to the plaza looking for another one. Nothing. Gave up. Walking back to the hotel in dreary defeat, I ran into a bright-eyed teenage drag queen and gave her thirty pesos for a blowjob on a park bench. Just as I'm about to get off, I hear this loud pop, like a gunshot. I push the fag off and jump up. Turns out it was a balloon stuffed in her bra breaking against my knee. Jesus! Ya can't make this shit up! I sat back down for the rest. Afterwards, she adjusted her lopsided brassiere with that comical Mexican "whatever" look, then slunk off into the night with my thirty pesos. God help me.

Cigano is sitting on the bed, writing. He feels oppressed and hungover, even though he still hasn't taken that deadly first drink. Almost two years now, clean and fucking sober. "Shit!" He curses under his breath as his hand skitters across the page, as if by its own device.

O   O   O

I could hear Auntie Connie's and my mother's voices back in the living room as my cousins and I hurried down the hall toward the kitchen. The clinking of martini glasses echoed behind us as we slipped out the back door, single file. Shaking the stifling white patina of the house off us like a layer of dust, we pushed and shoved each other down the big empty street. It didn't seem so big and empty anymore. We were just boys again, laughing and goofing around like three regular kids. And I was the ringleader.

"Awright, you guys, nobody tells, okay?" I gave them a serious look and they both nodded. "Okay. We're gonna go down to th' liquor store I told ya about. C'mon." We all shook hands like gangsters on *The Naked City*.

The liquor store. I'd been going there for a long time. Now that I was almost a teenager, I practically lived there. It was my school and my home after school. Jerry, the guy behind the counter, was big brother, father, favorite teacher, and best friend, all rolled into one. The place sat on the corner where the big buses rumbled by on their way to downtown, with its crowded busy streets, shops, people, and life. The liquor store was a gateway to a real life in a real world far from home and its sterile white silence and angry secretive chatter. Jerry always let me hang out. He was cool. He would tell me stories about being on the road, hitchhiking out here to "The Coast" to join a rock band. He'd talk a lot about his life back in New York, where he was from. I couldn't wait to get older so I could go there and find my real father and be where I belonged. Maybe me and Jerry would hitchhike to New York together someday.

I never saw many other kids at the liquor store. Once in a while one would wander in and Jerry would look up and say, "Can I help you?" and they'd buy some candy or something, then split. I was proud to be the only kid who got to hang around without having to buy stuff. I'd hang out all afternoon, talking with Jerry and leafing through the comic books, lost in the busy little panels of drawings. What got me about the comics was the feel and look of them; all the fascinating little images, like crazy colorful hieroglyphics. The liquor store was a magical portal of fantasy and escape for me. It was my fun house. It was also where I took most of my meals: potato chips, beef jerky sticks, and all kinds of stuff from the candy rack for dessert after a lunch of Beer Nuts and Vernor's Ginger

Ale. Those were my favorites. They went together good. "Just like it says on the package," Jerry would say. I had my favorite candies too: those big chewy Abba Zabba bars, and the little silvery packages of licorice-flavored Sen Sens. I loved Almond Joy, Payday, Turtles, and especially the Boyer's Peanut Butter Cups with the "Cash Prizes" that I saved in a cigar box under my bed. I had a big collection of those prizes, but I never wrote in to get anything. I just liked the way they looked, as if I could cash them all in someday to get to New York. Like the comics, what I liked most about the candy rack was how the candy bars looked, all stacked up in a colorful jumble on the rack. I liked the promise it held in its own sweet secret language, like the rows of bottles behind the counter where Jerry stood smoking, looking like a Wild West bartender.

"Hey, Jonny boy!" He grinned as I swaggered in the door.

"What's hap'nin', Jerry?" I drawled, showing off for my cousins.

He raised an amused eyebrow as they filed in behind me, gawking like farmers.

"These guys are my cousins. Pete and Steve. They're cool."

"Welp, if they're cool by you, big Jon, they're oh-kay by me."

"Can I show 'em th' magazines?"

Jerry looked around, then nodded, taking a lazy sip from his big yellow coffee mug on the counter as the two blond "galumphs'"—that's what my mother called them—stood there grinning.

"Thanks!" We shot behind the counter, where the *Playboys* were.

"Hey, *mi casa es su casa*. That's what th' beaners say." He reached down and poured some more vodka into his coffee mug.

Jerry had been letting me look at the "dirty" magazines on the "special" rack behind the counter lately. That's when I knew I was really in. I'd tear through the pages, checking out pictures of smiling naked ladies, lost in a guilty thrill. I guessed my cousins had never seen a *Playboy*. I picked one out and showed them my favorite naked-lady pictures. Their response was huge.

"Woah! Lookit 'er *titties!* She's *stacked!*"

"Lookit! Lookit! This one, *this* one! Ya kin almost see 'er *crack!*"

"Where?"

"Right there! *There!*" Pete, the younger one, the troublemaker, prodded the glossy page with his dicky little finger.

Some people came in, so we went over and got three slices of pizza from next door. We stood on the corner like gangsters, eating and watching the cars and buses go by. Finally, Steve said we should get back to the house. On our way home, little Peter poked my arm. I looked down. He was holding a pack of Viceroys. I glared at him, hoping he hadn't swiped them from the liquor store. "Took 'em from my mom's dresser," he whispered, beaming.

Without a word, I led the way to the fence bordering a big empty golf course. I went over first, then Steve, who was a pretty good climber. We crouched down in the bushes, whispering and laughing at little Pete as he struggled at the top where the fence ended in spiky points. "Don't leave yer nuts up there, Petie!" his big brother taunted him. At that he jumped, landing on his butt. He looked like he'd cry for a second, but I knew he wouldn't. Little Pete was a tough kid. We grabbed his wrists and lifted him off the ground. He'd snagged his jeans on the fence and there was a gash with blood showing through. Pete grinned up at me, looking proud.

"Whoa! Those are your new Wranglers!" Steve frowned. "Boy, yer rilly gonna catch it now!"

Peter just kept grinning. He didn't give a shit. He was the trouble-maker. Like me. We hiked through the trees, moving away from the fence. We came to the edge of the wooded area and stopped, looking out at the fairway. That's what they called it, that big wide expanse of grass bigger than all the lawns in the neighborhood together. We had to cross it to get to my secret hiding place on the other side. We hunkered down under cover of the trees and I peered out, making sure there weren't any golfers around.

The golf course was a scary place. It was off limits. It was called the Los Angeles Country Club, and it was a real snooty, uptight organization. Not the kind of place you wanted to get caught. My mother always said the country club was for WASPs only. When I asked Grandma why they kept wasps in there, wondering if I might get stung or something, she said that that meant it was for thoroughbred white folks. She told us they had this big sign hanging up by the entrance that said: "No Niggers, Spics, Wops, or Jews Allowed." I never saw that sign, but it sounded pretty creepy. I was always kind of nervous going in there, since I figured that being part Gypsy on account of my granddad and part Jew 'cause of my father, I was all that stuff put together.

Looking around, I heard a car roll by on the street behind us. I pointed to the clump of bushes we were going to and counted three. Then I whispered the command. "Run!"

We sprinted across the fairway like escaped convicts on the lam in *The Naked City*. Adrenaline shot through my lungs. Halfway across, I spotted a white golf cart at the top of a hill. I slowed down, then not seeing anyone else I ran faster, my cousins right behind me. Coming to the woods, I found the little trail and followed it through a jumble of brush toward my secret place. I'd discovered the little clearing in the bushes while exploring the golf course alone one day. "Rabbit's Roost," I called it. I'd never seen a rabbit there, but I'd been coming for a long time and that's just what I called it. If the liquor store was my other home, Rabbit's Roost was my other room where I could get away from everything—even the angry voices in my head. The closer I got to being a teenager, the quieter those pissed-off creepy voices seemed to get. Sometimes I could hardly hear them at all anymore.

Steve and Peter came up behind me, breathing hard as we hiked up the trail. Steve was whispering. "Didja see that cart back there?"

His little brother frowned, trying to look all serious. "Yeahhh. And there was a buncha guys coming down the hill, Steve!"

"There was not, you retard."

"Was too." Pete grinned. "I saw 'em, and they looked real pissed."

"You turd farmer, shut up!"

"Make me, butt bunny!"

Steve shoved him backwards into the bushes. Pete cursed and struggled. Me and Steve laughed as we each grabbed one of his arms and hauled him out. He was covered with dead leaves and spider webs. After taking a swipe at his brother and missing, Pete calmed down and we trudged on. I led the way as we crawled into my "cave" and sat down on the hard dirt floor, cross-legged like Indians. I had a plastic bag tied in a knot that I kept there with some comics and *Playboys*. We looked at the magazines for a while, then Steve and me unbuckled our jeans and compared boners. Little Peter couldn't get one and his brother said, "You homo!" and called him a fairy and a farmer. That was a big insult for kids. "You farmer!" I heard it at school all the time. I guess city kids thought farmers were stupid, maybe 'cause of that guy on the teevee called Mr. Green Jeans who wore overalls like a farmer. Only little kids watched that stuff. The big kids liked Soupy Sales and *The Naked City*.

"Homo!" Steve said again. Little Pete spat, hanging a big loogie in a graceful arc over his brother's head and into the bushes. Then he pulled the cigarettes from his pocket. Me and Stevie watched as he opened the pack, tapped one out, and placed it in the corner of his mouth like a teevee gangster. With a solemn look, he tapped one out for me, then Steve.

Steve frowned. "Are those from Mom?"

Silence.

"Boy, are you gonna get shit!"

Pete looked at him like he was some retard farmer kneeling in the mud, offering up a shriveled old potato to the heavens. "Whaddya, gonna chicken out now, cockjockey?" Pete lit up and puffed, coughing a little as he tossed the cigarette and matches at his big brother. A challenge.

Steve shrugged, lit up, and took a little puff.

"Not like that, stupid," Peter taunted. "Yer supposed to inhale in and blow it out yer nose."

I'd seen my mother blowing smoke from her nose like a dragon. It would make me laugh when I was little. I'd seen some big kids smoking in the alley behind the liquor store. They looked cool. I held a match to mine. I could see the glowing red point as I puffed up a big gray cloud, not inhaling. I could taste a sour flavor in my nose and mouth. It wasn't very nice, but I felt good anyway, like a tough guy on *The Naked City*. I took another puff. We all sat in silence, puffing on our cigarettes like we were waiting for something to happen. Peter coughed again. I inhaled. Stevie was blowing smoke rings up in the air. I inhaled again. Then I started feeling sort of dizzy. I looked over at my cousins with a stab of panic as the little circle started spinning, real slow. I thought about the "Centrifuge" at Pacific Ocean Park, the big amusement park jutting out over the water on a pier. They had this contraption there like a big round room. About twenty people would go in there and stand against a round wooden wall facing each other. It felt like being in a flying saucer or something, 'cause you didn't know what was going to happen next. Every-body just stood there looking around, staring at each other, waiting. Nobody talked. Then the whole place would start to turn, real slow at first, then faster, faster, till you felt this weird pressure pinning you to the wall. Faster and faster, the room spun around and around till the faces were a big blur and you couldn't lift your arms. Faster. Someone screamed and they all started screaming. It was like the nightmares when I was a little kid. Then the floor dropped out and you were pinned to the wall like a fly. Whatever position you started out in, that's right where you stayed. It was hard to breathe, and I couldn't think of any ride I liked less. Some dumb girl next to me barfed but she just got it all over herself. Nothing could go anywhere, so the puke stuck to her face.

When the Rabbit's Roost finally stopped spinning, Stevie was down on all fours, barfing like that girl on the Centrifuge. Pete was laughing and calling him a barf farmer. I felt kind of like puking too, but it passed. I took another puff of my cigarette, but the place had stopped spinning. The ride was over. Me and Pete sat smoking our butts till they were gone.

Steve stood up, looking kind of gray. "So what do you guys wanna do now?" He had a stupid smile on his face, trying to look cool after barfing.

"I dunno. What you wanna do?" I shrugged, playing along.

"I dunno." Steve shrugged back. There was silence in the growing darkness under the bushes. Rabbit's Roost looked kind of different, like I'd just gotten back from a long trip to somewhere real far away.

Cigano sighs and reaches for a cigarette. He sets his pen down on the bed and closes the notebook. Another day's work, another chapter. He stands and begins to straighten up the room, trying to distract his mind from that old feeling of impending dread. Then he looks at his watch and remembers.

Shit, that kid will be back soon!

He starts arranging his tattoo gear on the table.

18. BURNOUT

"THERE IS NOTHING SO MOVING – NOT EVEN ACTS OF LOVE
AND HATE – AS THE DISCOVERY THAT ONE IS NOT ALONE."
                                    –ROBERT ARDRY

Just after noon, the Brazilian kid is back, standing in the doorway.
They make casual small talk as Cigano puts his stuff in order. Jaco sits
down in a chair by the door, uninvited this time, watching as the tattoo
man putters around.

"So, Jonathan Shaw, you told me it was here in Veracruz that you
first got the idea to become a tattoo artist . . ."

"No, man." Cigano cuts him off, feeling an undertone of irritation in his voice. "That's not what I said. I said this is where I started
tattooing. Not professionally, but I did this little hand-poked thing
on a friend here, and . . ." He pauses, surrendering to the memories.
"Well, it was my first tattoo. Did it in a room right down the hall."
He waves his hand toward the door. He sets a notebook on the table
and sits down facing Jaco. He reaches for an opener and cracks a
lukewarm bottle of Squirt. He offers the first swig to his visitor, who
smiles and shakes his head. Cigano guns the sweet sticky soda down
in one gulp. He sets the empty bottle on the table, burps loudly,
then reaches for his cigarettes. "But the idea of tattooing came *way*
before that. Right from the first time I ever saw that shit, man, I was
gone . . ." He grins with a snap of his fingers. "Just like that, *bang!*

I was obsessed with the whole deal, right from the minute I saw somebody getting one."

"When was that?"

"I dunno, I musta been about twelve, maybe thirteen . . ."

"It sounds like it was your destiny."

Cigano lights up and inhales, nodding as a cloud of smoke frames his face. "Yeah, man. Sometimes I feel like it was all planned out somehow, maybe even before I was born. It's a weird feeling . . ."

"You mean like from another life?"

"Something like that, maybe. Who knows? I used to have all these crazy dreams about tattoos, where there were like these old-time pirates tattooing each other . . ." He gets a faraway look, then snaps back. "So, listen, man, speaking of tattoos, I been thinking about this project of yours, and I gotta tell ya, I'm still feeling sorta ambivalent about the whole deal."

Jaco sits in silence, watching Cigano, waiting for him to go on.

"Don't get me wrong, kid. There's a part of me that would love to do some big work like that, y'know. But, shit, I really didn't come down here to do a bunch of serious tattooing. If anything, I came here to get *away* from it."

Jaco begins to say something, then stops himself as Cigano's eyes wander across the table to his makeshift tattoo setup.

"Sure, I been working a little on locals." He rubs his chin. "Little ones here and there, just keeping my hand in, I guess. Treading water. Dunno why I even bother." He shakes his head with a bitter little chuckle. "Guess it's just in my blood, like some old whore who's still going out every night." He pauses, then goes on. "I guess I'm just not so crazy about it anymore. I used to be, but, I dunno. Things changed. *I've* changed, y'know? I really been planning on phasing tattooing out completely. Been thinking about it for a long time now, and I guess this is kinda like the first step for me, coming back to my old tattoo roots here." He grins. "I'm just keeping it real simple these days while I think about what I'm gonna do next, y'know?"

Jaco looks at him like a kid who's just been told there's no Santa.

Cigano rolls his eyes, feeling a pang of regret. "Look, kid, it's nothing personal. It's just that I been trying to write this fuggin' book. That's my only real priority these days. It's all I wanna do with my time right now, y'know? It's just something I gotta take care of, and I been planning to get a good chunk of work done here while I've got the time, without distractions."

Jaco's face brightens. He tries again. "What about that quote you told me yesterday, Jonathan Shaw? When the most important things in life happen, we don't know it. If you really believe that, then how can you make plans?"

An image flashes before Cigano's mind: a recovered alcoholic, an old-timer in the Program, pointing a stubby finger at him, growling: "Listen, man, if ya wanna get better, you gotta be flexible about things, be open-minded. If ya wanna make God shit his pants laughin', just tell him all yer big plans."

The tattoo man breaks out in a grin, feeling sheepish. "Yeah, well, you do got a point there, bro. Sometimes the best plan is no plan." He picks up the tattoo magazine and flips through the pages as if he's examining a giant turd. "Ya really read all this horseshit?"

"Of course I do," Jaco answers. "I've always read a lot. I'm sort of a big nerd." He grins. "I guess maybe because I never had a father to teach me sports, so I started reading. There were always lots of books around . . ."

Cigano stares at his young visitor with a new curiosity.

"My mother, her parents were quite wealthy when she was young, before they lost all their money. They sent her to the American School in Rio, where the rich kids go. You've heard of it?"

Cigano nods with a faraway look.

"She spoke English to me when I was little, so I learned, and she always told me to read in English, too. I read everything I could. I was reading the classics in English when most of the kids in my neighborhood were learning to read comic books in Portuguese." He grins. "And I read everything I could find about tattooing. I've always been fascinated with the art . . ."

"No shit." Cigano raises an eyebrow. "Well, you're a rare bird there, kid. Most people just buy these fucking tattoo magazines to look at the pictures and rip off other artists' work. That's about the level of the thing nowadays."

"Not me, Jonathan Shaw. I was always a fan. That's why I'm interested to know about your book. It was hard to find anything written about tattooing before you started your tattoo magazine. It was rare to find them in Brazil, but I had a friend who worked on a ship and he brought them back from Europe and America. That's how I got my job onboard and came here. Anyway, I've followed the articles and editorials you wrote, the interviews you did with the old-time tattoo masters about tattoo history and traditions."

Cigano smiles. "Yeah, well, I really dug researching and writing about all that stuff. Till a flock of corporate culture vultures swooped down and took the thing over. For those fuckers it was all about profit margins and advertising. Absolutely no love or concern for the art. Fuck the traditions, the history, the magic of tattooing. That's where my problems started with the publisher. I wanted to keep the thing real old-school, so I put my foot down when it came to selling ad space for tattoo supplies. I knew that shit was gonna be the kiss of death for the tattoo world the old guys taught me."

"So, what happened? Why did you quit the magazine?"

"Well, it's a long story, but basically, I took an unpopular editorial stand. I could see the gates of Hell opening soon as I heard people talking about a 'tattoo industry.' What was *that* all about? I dunno, I felt like I had a responsibility to try and preserve the integrity of the thing, y'know, to show people there was more to tattooing than a bunch of shit-brained fashion victims parading their fancy permanent clown makeup around on MTV. Well, that was the beginning of the end for me as managing editor." He lets out a bitter guffaw. "The bean-counters saw me as a threat to profits. It was just a matter of time before I got the boot. They just walked in one day and canned me." He sucks his teeth. "Fired from the fuggin' magazine I started!"

Jaco frowns. "Couldn't you do anything?"

"Like what?" Cigano snorts. "Call a lawyer? Hah, I didn't even have anything in writing. What did I know? I was from an old-school tattoo world, the kinda deal where ya gave your word and kept it, y'know?" He cracks a wry smile. "I thought I was some kinda player, but I was clueless as a schoolboy in Hollywood, a guppy swimming with sharks and piranhas."

"I'm sorry that happened to you, Jonathan Shaw. I had no idea."

Cigano grins. "Yeah, well, that'll teach a fuggin' Gypsy to make handshake deals with guys in suits." He pauses and rubs his chin. "But I wasn't exactly some poor innocent victim, either. I had my part in it. I mean, there was a good deal of shameless self-promotion and favoritism. I ran that magazine like a banana-republic dictator. I was a real control freak, and that pissed some people off, especially the hacks who sent their shit in by the truckload and never got it published. More sour grapes than a fuggin' French vineyard in that game. And me not wanting to share the spotlight with a bunch of piss-ass hipsters. I wasn't too popular with certain types in the 'tattoo industry.' I had my own crowd of guys I was real loyal to, but for every one of them, there was always a dozen haters. Whatever, by that time it all went to shit; it was a relief to just get out. I was pretty burnt out."

"Burnt out? Really? All the articles you wrote seemed so passionate . . ."

"Yeah, well, I *was* passionate about it, man. But after a while, I dunno, it all just started to get to me. I'm lucky I didn't end up killing someone. I was really bat-shit nuts . . ."

"How were you nuts?"

Prodded by the young man's questions, which only yesterday had seemed so intrusive, Cigano finds himself opening up. He laughs. "Well, that's a *long* fuggin' story, bro! That's basically what I'm trying to figure out by writing this book, taking a long, hard look at my life, y'know. But running a loony-bin tattoo shop in New York City all those years sure didn't help."

He laughs again, feeling lighter. Somehow it feels good, cathartic, to be talking to someone like this. Long-buried memories struggle for expression. With a shrug, he lets the reminiscences flow out loud. "The whole thing grew into a big seven-headed greed monster and drove me right over the edge. I was turning into an egomaniac myself, and I didn't even know it." He grows quiet as he puts his tattoo machines in order on the table, one by one, like little soldiers.

Finally, he looks up and sighs. "I dunno, man, I just started getting real bitter about the whole deal, really cynical. I'd suddenly become a reluctant spokesman for this big horrible money machine I never felt any kinship with. The 'tattoo industry.' *Ugh!* Suddenly it was all about cash and prizes, power, prestige, sex, drugs, and rock 'n' roll, going out partying every night, life in the fast lane. Totally destroyed a good, loving marriage. I wound up in a really violent, self-centered, brutal, workaholic, alcoholic lifestyle in New York. I was like a rat on a fucking treadmill!"

"It sounds like a dream life by what most people aspire to."

Cigano lets out a dark guffaw. "Yeah, well, that's the catch, bro. What most people aspire to is what I'm running away from here. Ah, the good old American Dream! I always had a deep aversion to that shit. Ever since I was a little kid, I knew it was pure pigshit. And then all of a sudden, there I was caught up right in the middle of it, running after it like a chump." He shakes his head. "Like I said, I was never much of a people person. I was turning into a real freak of nature. I came off like some kinda hardass, a real asshole, y'know, but I was a sensitive cat at heart. I just didn't know it or give two shits. In the kinda world I was in, being some poetry-reading, socially conscious do-gooder wasn't exactly an asset. At least I didn't think so. What did I know?" He sighs. "Anyway, I started getting disillusioned, y'know?"

The ceiling fan turns and Jaco remains silent.

Cigano shrugs with a wry little grin. "How could I ever know what I was getting into back when I was starting out with stars in my eyes? I was blind, didn't know any better. After I ended up almost dead from a drug overdose, I knew I had to get sober. That's when I started to change my priorities. Instead of trying to polish up a big old stinking turd, I decided to just get the fuck out. I dunno if it's the right decision or not, but, honestly, I got no regrets. I'm just glad I got outta that fuggin' mouse-trap alive."

He smiles, spreading his hands out. "So there ya have it. I'm just trying to see if I can make some sense of the whole deal now by writing about it."

Jaco smiles. "You must have a lot of interesting stories. Maybe I could give you some feedback after you have some more of your book written."

Cigano gestures to the dresser piled with worn composition books. "Oh, I've got a *lotta* stuff written down, man. I've been half-ass trying to piece this thing together for years now." He hesitates. "But it's still pretty rough. Just a bunch of random disjointed chapters and notes and old journals."

Jaco leans forward. "I understand, Jonathan Shaw. But I'm really curious. If you'd like to read me something, anything you like."

On impulse, the tattoo man gets up, picks up a stack of notebooks, and sets them on the table. He fans through dense handwritten pages, rubbing his chin.

"Shit, I wouldn't even know where to start."

19. BEGINNINGS

"ONE IS EJECTED INTO THE WORLD LIKE A DIRTY LITTLE MUMMY; THE ROADS ARE SLIPPERY WITH BLOOD AND NO ONE KNOWS WHY IT SHOULD BE SO."

—HENRY MILLER

"Well, where does your story begin?" Jaco is looking at him. "Do you have a first chapter written yet?"

"Yeah, sorta." Cigano scratches his head. Lighting a cigarette, he settles back in the chair and clears his throat. It all feels a little awkward, like the first time he was asked to speak into a microphone from the podium at one of those meetings of alcoholics. With a sigh, he opens the notebook and begins to tell his story to another person for the first time in his life.

"My childhood memories are dusty shadows," he reads. "Locked away a long time ago, the details sit before me now, a scattered jigsaw puzzle of dried-out artifacts, buried under miles of crooked road and mountains of powders and pills; drowned in uncharted oceans of booze, all in a futile effort to deny their very existence. As I rummage around, squinting into these ancient mummy chambers, the recollections seem strange and unreliable. I picture my mother and father battling into the night like a pair of savage ghosts. The walls of the house are decorated with colorful paintings, framed gold records and photographs. A burning fireplace illuminates the face of my father. Artie Shaw, the legendary big-band leader, is sitting before a ceiling-high bookshelf in the sprawling white country home into which I was born in the summer of 1953."

As the tattoo man reads on, a familiar circle of glowing yellow light expands behind his eyes, conjuring up images of an expansive farmhouse in upstate New York. Home and hearth. A warm summer evening of insect-buzzing country emerges under a flashing blanket of stars. Warm yellow light glows from a window; the reader's eye wanders into the cozy space crammed with colorful mementos of Artie Shaw's life and career. A hand turns the page as Cigano hears his voice reading, as if from far away.

○   ○   ○

I was a baby. The memory is a pungent mental scent of wood-smoke and pinecones and Artie Shaw. My father is lying back on a plush leather sofa, his sanctuary from the demands of a frantic public life. Over the course of my life I would never really know the man, but in my earliest memory of him he is reading a book. Schopenhauer. How does a baby remember such details? I have no answer, but I will always picture him picking up a stubby yellow pencil from a coffee table and underlining a passage. A handsome man in his early forties, his intense brooding eyes shine like distant fire under a dark mass of hair as he glances at his one-year-old boy-child. The baby watches back from a playpen, a tiny prisoner behind wooden bars.

My jailer speaks. "What a fucking world you came into, kiddo!"

As if on cue, my mother appears in a doorway shouting, raging, drunk. Doris Dowling, the beautiful, glamorous Hollywood starlet—Artie's latest wife in a long string of unsuccessful glamorous marriages—staggers into the room, stumbling into an end table and upsetting a framed picture of herself from *The Lost Weekend*. The picture crashes to the shiny hardwood floor. To this day, cracked glass distorts my first blurry image of my mother. Funny how you remember little things like that for the rest of your life.

"Jesus, Doris. What th' fu—" Artie's tongue freezes like a woodchuck in the crosshairs as he focuses on the dull black gun in her hand.

"Bastard! Ya son of a bitch! I shoulda killed you a long time ago, ya dirty bastard!" My mother slurs her words, hefting the heavy pistol in her elegant porcelain hand with those long red fingernails, pointing it at my father.

Shouting, her face is contorted into an ugly mask of hate, screeching and glowering as a baby watches behind playpen bars. "How does it feel now, ya bastard?"

Bastard, bastard, bastard. The angry words echo in my mind, reminding me of something else, something I can't quite place. Something vague and far away, a long time ago. My mother pulls the trigger. ***POW!*** A sound of thunder. A baby doesn't know what thunder is. He only knows it hurts as his father jumps behind a sofa and his mother fires again. ***POW! POW!***

From behind bars, a baby watches its parents like a pair of actors in an old movie. The baby is a prisoner of war, caught in a raging battle of love and hate and confusion. Its father rises up from behind the sofa like a snarling swamp monster. He grabs the pistol clicking in its mother's hand. He slaps her across the face hard, again and again. ***SWAPP!!*** Again. ***SWAPP!!*** Again. ***SWAPP!***

O   O   O

"The baby's cries are drowned out by its parent's shouts and curses as they rage on into the long murky darkness of my earliest memory." Cigano stops reading and closes the notebook like a coffin lid.

After a long silence, he looks up at the kid with a weary grin. "Years later, after moving to Brazil and adopting Portuguese as my own language, I realized my mother's name, Doris, sounds just like *dores*, Portuguese for 'pains.' And Artie's name is pronounced exactly like the Portuguese word for 'art.' How 'bout that shit?"

The kid stares at him. "That would make you the child of art and pain."

Cigano laughs. "Pretty ironic, right? Ya can't make this shit up."

"Would . . . could you read some more?"

The tattoo man speaks again, his voice trembling slightly as he hears himself verbalizing an unexpected decision. "Maybe later, kid. We got work to do now if we're gonna start this tattoo of yours."

With grim resignation, he begins setting up his tattoo equipment.

20. COSMIC TRUTHS

"FOR I THE LORD THY GOD AM A JEALOUS GOD, VISITING
THE INEQUITIES OF THE FATHERS UPON THE CHILDREN
UNTO THE THIRD AND FOURTH GENERATION OF THEM THAT
HATE ME."

–EXODUS 20:1-22

Late afternoon. Cigano pulls off the rubber gloves and tosses them
into the little trash bucket. He shakes Jaco's hand as the kid leaves for the
day. The tattoo man lights a cigarette and leans back in the chair, smiling
to himself. His first day working on his curious new customer has gone well.
The abstract freehand outline covering the kid's right arm looks pretty tight
so far. He doesn't know where it's all going, but it's a start, and that's good.

Fifteen minutes later, Cigano is sitting at the table, writing. The
memories seem to come into focus more quickly, spilling onto the
page in waves, taking shape as his pen hurries along like a harried
little man who's late for an appointment.

My two cousins and I were playing pinball in the big Mexican game
arcade by the newsstand down on Pico when two big guys stepped up and
grabbed us. One wore a white shirt and thin black tie. The other had a fat
belly and a quacking walkie-talkie. The beefy one with the radio grabbed
Peter by the collar. Little Pete tried to run. As his shirt bunched up in the
man's meaty fist, a *Playboy* fluttered to the ground like a dirty secret.

"Hold still there, junior!" The walkie-talkie man was laughing. "You ain't goin' nowhere." Peter looked at me. "Check the other two, Joe," he grunted as watery black Mexican eyes gathered round us like fish in an aquarium.

"They're clean, partner," I heard the black tie say after patting me down. As he held my arm like a clamp, I could smell his hot breath on my ear. Pastrami and cigars. "Where do ya live, son?"

My voice sounded high-pitched and alien as I said my address. The guy from the newsstand stood watching. Skinny old rat in suspenders and a gray hat. I could hear my heart pounding. My ears felt hot and itchy.

"Whaddya wanna do with these two, Joe?"

"Better take all three of 'em in."

The men's toneless dialogue was cold and inflexible as the ratchet of handcuffs and the dull thud of the car door shutting out the night. A radio squawked as we sat in back like dummies, not talking or looking at each other, prisoners to two dark figures. The car wound along dark unfamiliar streets, then pulled up to a brick building, cop cars lined up in front like sleeping sharks. They led us up cement stairs into a big room full of desks and phones and typewriters. Nobody spoke. A little TV glowed on top of a gray metal file cabinet. A pinup from a *Playboy* flashed her big, taunting ironic tits from the wall. In one corner was a cage. They put us in and told us to sit on a scuffed wooden bench. The guy with the belly turned the key and walked off with the little notepad where he'd written down our names and phone numbers. A shoeless Negro boy was sleeping on the floor. He had a big hole in one sock and he looked dirty. Across the room, the cop with the thin black tie got up from a desk and went out through a door with green glass and black lettering that spelled the word *JUVENILE* backwards.

"Now look what ya got us into!" Steve was whispering at his brother. Pete sat between us, staring down at the floor, trying not to grin. "Now they're gonna call Mom and Auntie Doris! Dad's gonna find out."

A picture of my mother's angry face flashed in my head. The handcuffs bit into my wrists as I shifted on the sticky wooden bench. Nobody talked for a while. The colored boy slept on, sprawled on the floor by my foot. A bulletin board held "Wanted" posters like at the Post Office. I couldn't read them, but the faces looked hard and mean and pissed off. One of the "Wanted" guys had a big eagle tattooed across his chest. I stared at it for a long time.

After a while, the cop in the skinny tie came back and sat at a desk, and there was the dull black clatter of a big gray typewriter. *Tap. Taptap. Tap. Tap* . . .

Steve finally broke the silence again. "Boy, when Dad finds out, we're both gonna get th' belt." Their father, my Uncle Ivan, was a chunky, unsmiling Hungarian, with a thick accent like Boris Badenov. Peter snickered, but Steve couldn't hit him with the handcuffs holding his beefy ten-year-old fists to his back. "Ya think yer pretty funny now. Well, you just wait."

A big brown and white clock on the wall, a cyclops eye like the one at school, told me it was ten minutes after eight. Past dinner time. Grandma would be worried. Around nine, the two cops came back, uncuffed us, and took us out of the cage. They marched us through the green door, down a hall, and into another room where my mother and Aunt Connie sat at a brown Formica table. Connie kept putting a lacy white handkerchief up to one eye. My mother wore a long red coat with a leopard collar I'd never seen before.

"We just need you to sign some papers here, ma'am, and you can go. And thanks for your cooperation."

"Oh, please. Thank you so much! You've all been so wonderful!" my mother chirped in her best "stage" voice. Then she shot me a freezing glance. "Just wait till I get you home, buster!"

I wasn't sure if it was for real or just part of the act. Aunt Connie kept silent, dabbing her eye with the handkerchief. My mother flirted a little more with the cops, then glared at me again. "And you! I should leave you here to teach you a lesson!" She turned to her sister. "Come on, Con!"

We followed the angry *clip clip clip* of high heels on linoleum down the hall and out into the warm summer night.

Jesus! Stop! That's enough for today! Cigano sets the pen down. He closes his notebook and sits on the bed. He lies back and closes his eyes, thinking of the dark resentments that have festered like poison in his heart all his life; the wounds of the Curse that nearly murdered his soul. With a little groan, he picks up a dog-eared paperback. He opens it and begins to read, underlining a sentence here and there. Then he turns to the same well-worn page he's read so many times, and he reads it again.

> *Setting others free means setting yourself free, because resentment is really a form of attachment. It is a Cosmic Truth that it takes two to make a prisoner; the prisoner—and a gaoler. There is no such thing as being a prisoner on one's own account. Every prisoner must have a gaoler, and the gaoler is as much a prisoner as his charge. When you hold resentment against anyone, you are bound to that person by a cosmic link, a real, though mental, chain. You are tied by a cosmic tie to the thing you hate. The one person in the whole world whom you most dislike is the very one to whom you are attaching yourself by a hook that is stronger than steel. Is this what you wish? Is this the condition in which you desire to go on living? Remember, you belong to the thing with which you are linked in thought, and at some time or other, if that tie endures, the object of your resentment will be drawn again into your life, perhaps to work further havoc. Do you think that you can afford this? Of course no one can afford such a thing; and so the way is clear. You must cut all such ties, by a clear and spiritual act of forgiveness. You must loose him and let him go. By forgiveness you set yourself free; you save your soul.*

He stops and picks up another pen. Red this time. He underlines again with the new color. He likes the way it looks; blue, black, yellow, green, red, all the different colors blending together to mark each reading, giving new life to his burning desire to pacify his past's unruly ghosts. He sets the book down and picks up another one. He turns to another underlined page and begins to read the familiar words.

> *Experience has taught us we cannot live alone with our pressing problems and the character defects which cause or aggravate them. If we have swept the searchlight of Step Four back and forth over our careers, and it has revealed in stark relief those experiences we'd rather not remember, if we have come to know how wrong thinking and action have hurt us and others, then the need to quit living by ourselves with those tormenting ghosts of yesterday gets more urgent than ever. We have to talk to somebody about them.*

Cigano closes the book and lies back on the bed. Shutting his eyes tight, he begins to pray.

21. HISTORY LESSONS

"DO NOT HOLD AGAINST US THE SINS OF THE FATHERS;
MAY THY MERCY COME QUICKLY TO MEET US, FOR WE ARE
IN DESPERATE NEED."

—PSALM 79

The next day, the kid is back for his second tattoo session. Right on time, Cigano notes, glancing at his watch. Jaco asks him to read some more from his book before they start.

Cigano winces. A quick battle flashes between his ears. Then a truce. *Aw, why not? There's plenty of time. You're gonna be here tattooing this kid forever now. Anyway, this could be a blessing in disguise. Wasn't I just praying for something like this?* The words he just read echo in his head. *"The need to quit living by ourselves with those tormenting ghosts of yesterday gets more urgent than ever. We have to talk to somebody about them." What the fuck. Maybe God sent this guy to listen to my confession. Stranger things have happened.*

A bus horn blares outside amid a spine-shivering grinding of gears and exhaust pipes, snapping him out of it. "All right, bro." Cigano shrugs, picking up his notebook. "You asked for it."

Turning to where he left off, he begins to read again.

O   O   O

After he and my mother got divorced, Artie Shaw left the music business for good. The legendary jazzman just up and quit at the height of his fame and fortune; dropped it all in the trash and moved to a remote fishing village in Spain to try his hand as a writer. People were shocked by his radical decision. I think he'd just had it up to his neck with being in the public eye. He'd always thought his fans were stupid, beneath contempt. He was sick of the hustle. A true innovative artist, a curious seeker and philosopher at heart, Artie Shaw would write in his memoir of how disappointed he'd become with where his glamorous career had taken him. Fame, fortune, and the American Dream just weren't his bag. He wanted to start over and try something new and challenging; something to express whatever was going on in his soul; his confused, restless quest for knowledge.

As a kid, though, I grew up thinking it was the fights with my mother that drove him away. And on some level, that *was* what drove my father away—away from me, anyway.

Feeling a sudden wave of self-consciousness, Cigano stops. "It's funny." He shakes his head, grinning with a sudden epiphany. "I never thought about it till I just read this part out loud, how much Artie's decision was like what I'm doing now, getting out of tattooing right when it's getting all popular."

Jaco smiles. "It's exactly what you told me yesterday."

"Yeah, right?" Cigano nods, rubbing his chin. "I remember in my first weeks sober, I was having coffee with this reformed alcoholic who worked as a recovery therapist. I was telling him I wanted to find a way to overcome the bad habits of my parents, like all these fucked-up inherited traits. Well, he just laughed and told me, 'Man, don't kid yourself about getting over all that; you're dealing with a hundred generations' worth of fucked-up shit.' As time goes on, I'm starting to get what he meant. Ya just can't fuck with DNA."

He snorts and picks up his notebook, staring at the page, reading to himself and scribbling some notations into the margin. His listener sits back and closes his eyes as Cigano starts to read again.

Before I was born, my mother, Doris Dowling, had been a vivacious young model and chorus girl struggling for work in New York City, like her older sister Constance. The two starry-eyed teens left New York, where they'd grown up in poverty, and headed for the glittering promises of fame and glory in Hollywood. My mother got off to a fortuitous start the minute she hit town, when Billy Wilder spotted her at a Beverly Hills watering hole. The legendary director walked up to her table and introduced himself. He came on strong, offering to put her in a movie right on the spot. Doris responded to the golden offer by looking Wilder up and down like a bug she was thinking of swatting, then lighting a cigarette and blowing smoke in his face. When that failed to get rid of the amorous filmmaker, she growled at him for all to hear: "Why don't ya screw off, ya crumb-bum?"

Still not discouraged, Wilder kept after the stunning young New York firecracker. Eventually, she warmed up and they became entangled in one of the hottest Hollywood romances of the day. Wilder kept his promise, casting his teenage beauty in a supporting role in *The Lost Weekend*—which went on to win several Academy Awards. Doris Dowling's portrayal of a young hooker who falls for a failed alcoholic writer would earn her a place in cinema history. It also opened the doors for her to act in several other hot movie projects of the forties— notably, the classic film noir thriller *The Blue Dahlia*, whose production reportedly drove its disgruntled screenwriter Raymond Chandler, a recovering alcoholic himself, back to the bottle.

Off camera, though, my mother's tempestuous affair with Wilder soon went sour. The great director couldn't keep up with her alcoholic mood swings. The Curse, it seems, was never far from her life. After they split, she went back to New York for a job in the theater. The play she was in flopped, and then she was out of work again, down on her luck and broke in the big city. Her older sister Connie had just ended her own affair with another big director, Elia Kazan. This was right after the war when things had slowed down in the film business and both sisters were looking for work. Connie was making a movie in Italy. My mother, faced with the prospect of going back to California with her tail between her legs, opted to hang around New York. Anything seemed better than returning to Billy Wilder's town with her hat in her hand and her head hung low. "Who needs it, anyway? You know," she wrote in a letter to her sister, "that ridiculous town, where no matter how hot it ever gets in the daytime, there's never anything to do at night."

One evening, Doris met up with a friend, the celebrated photojournalist

Robert Capa, who was out on the prowl with John Steinbeck. The three went to a Broadway play together. Afterwards, the men said they were going to an all-night poker session. Doris nagged them to take her along. They acquiesced, and she sat in on the game. My mother—who'd been taught cards as a kid by her Gypsy con-artist father—cleaned up, taking a bunch of shylocks and gangsters for a good chunk of change. Suddenly the down-and-out actress was flush again. But there was a wild card in the deck. A couple of days later, Capa went to see her. She was in trouble. Some of the mobsters at the game resented being done over by some fast-talking Hollywood floozy. Capa suggested she get out of New York. He urged her to buy a ticket to Italy with the money she'd won and join her sister there till things cooled down.

The next day, Doris Dowling took a flight to Rome, sporting a brand-new pair of calf-high red leather boots stuffed with hundred-dollar bills—a definite upgrade from the cement footwear awaiting her at home. When the plane landed in Italy, the bright-eyed young *Americana* stepped into a new world. The air smelled different. The throng of people milling around the airport looked different. Everything was wonderfully new, chaotic and exciting.

In Rome, Connie introduced her sister to all the right people. My mother soon became a sensation in the emerging post-war New Italian Cinema. The two Dowling Sisters—as they were hailed with great fanfare—had been inseparable all their lives. Now they were the first bona fide Hollywood movie actresses working in Italy. The Italians were captivated by the two vivacious young *artistas*. They saw them as authentic movie stars, and treated them accordingly. The girls were equally fasci-nated by Rome, where they were wined and dined by the cream of the Italian intelligentsia. My mother landed parts in several acclaimed films there, including an important supporting role in Dino De Laurentiis's and Giuseppe De Santis's classic *Bitter Rice*. That led, later, to her pretty young face ending up on an Italian postage stamp for her contribution to the country's cultural heritage in the *Neo-realista* Cinema movement. The sisters were right in the middle of a vibrant new Post-Fascist art renaissance. The toasts of the town, they ran with a chic international crowd of writers, artists, and actors, the creative and intellectual elite of the day. In the ensuing years, they worked and rubbed elbows with the likes of Fellini, Orson Welles, John Houseman, Anna Magnani, Sophia Loren, Gina Lollobrigida, Charlie Chaplin, Jean-Paul Sartre, Alberto

Moravia, Roberto Rossellini, Hemingway, Somerset Maugham, George Bernard Shaw, Cesare Pavese, and Vittorio De Sica. Those were Doris and Constance Dowling's glory days.

DORIS DOWLING FILM MAGAZINE

INTERVIEW: *My sister had gone over with an American company. She had no intention of staying in Italy. But by then, well, Moravia was writing parts for her, De Sica, Rossellini. There was a whole circle of artists around us, and I guess we were as interesting to them as they were to us. Italy was a totally different culture. I loved it! I felt at home there right from the start; everything was so different from anything I'd known before. I asked myself, "Where has this been all my life?" I imagine that Constance and I were a strange couple to the Italians. But our timing was fortuitous. We were the first Americans to go "subito dopo guerra." At the time it was enough just to be American to be welcomed there. I think our army liberated or helped to liberate Italy. By the time I left three years later, the American tourists came and lived in marble palaces and would shout, "Why doesn't the elevator arrive?" and "Why doesn't the maid come?" We were never like that. We were both so fluent in Italian that we were considered Italian and not American actresses. And the Italians were fascinated with our culture, as fascinated as I was with theirs. And we were gorgeous! My God! Connie was as blond as I was dark, and we were like the other side of each other. They loved us! I think we had a certain freedom and a kind of energy that was unlike Italian women. My God, you'd go into a restaurant with all these men, and we were the only women in the place. I suppose on some levels we were considered to be women with loose morals. You know, someone would come to visit us and we'd say, "Would you like a drink?" and they'd think we were alcoholics. In America, you offer a cocktail, not coffee. You can imagine what it was like then. It was right after the war and here come two flashy Americans with a lot of energy. Then I snagged the top picture in Italy at the first crack. That caused some resentment with the local talent. But I resented it when certain envious people saw us as two American floozies, these dumbbells who had failed in our own country and hoped to make a career over there. My God, we fell in love with the* *country. The education I had with all the people I was with there was invaluable!*

Before the two sisters' return to America, Connie had a brief affair with the acclaimed Italian poet Cesare Pavese. Pavese became obsessed with marrying the beautiful young *artista*, but Connie dropped him like a hotel toothbrush to go back home and follow her ambitions. Like my mother, Connie's first priority was the quest for fame and fortune in Hollywood. They say that's the reason Pavese killed himself.

DORIS DOWLING INTERVIEW: *Connie and I were already back in America when Pavese died. Maybe he became despondent when it registered that she was really gone and probably wouldn't be back. When Connie heard the news, well, she was shocked and saddened, of course, but there was no great sobbing and weeping and throwing stones at the window, you know. I was always the closest thing to Constance. My God, I had a boyfriend who would call up and say, "Well, Doris is shooting late and she can't have dinner. What are you doing tonight, Connie?" and she'd tell me and I'd call him and say, "Hey, what is your brother doing tonight?" So that's what it was like to be with a Dowling Sister, and that's the way it was with Cesare. No big deal. No doubt, he was heartbroken over Connie leaving, but I was absolutely shocked when I learned of his suicide. I'd already told him early on to forget it, that she was very different. Don't waste your time crying over her, I said. It won't happen. But I don't think she had any idea what an impact she'd had on the poor man. Connie was incapable of hurting anyone. As hard as I am, my nature, my dark side, well, Constance was absolutely the opposite: gentle, soft-spoken, brilliant. But she didn't have to show it to you. It was just there. She was well educated. But when she was with Pavese, Connie had just come out of a long disastrous relationship she'd been in with Elia Kazan, which had left her very hurt and reluctant to open up again. She was sixteen and Kazan was a married man and he just made things very difficult for her. So Constance went off to Italy to do this picture, and suddenly it was a new life. We were young and we were successful in our field and very much enchanted with Italy. Then she met Pavese and he fell in love with her, but the feeling certainly wasn't mutual. It was more of a fling, if anything, for Connie. Pavese had written a very beautiful,* *very sad poem, I remember, which he sent to her after she left. It was called "Last Blues to Be Read Someday." It went: "Twas only a flirt; you sure did know; someone was hurt; a long time ago; all is the same; time has gone by; someday you came; someday you'll die; Someone has died; a long time ago; someone who tried; but didn't know . . ." and so on. I really don't know if Pavese was talking about himself in that poem, about his own history of rejection and abandonment by women, or whether he was talking specifically about Connie's having been hurt so badly by Kazan.*

One of Cesare Pavese's last poems was dedicated to Constance Dowling—officially bestowing upon poor Aunt Connie the unhappy burden of Angel of Death to Italy's beloved poet laureate. Written just days before his suicide, the poem was entitled: *Death Will Come and She Will Look at Me with Your Eyes.* The American pop singer and movie star Nelson Eddy may have been the first one, though, to notice the glimmer of a Curse in Connie's bewitching eyes; he wouldn't even let her look him in the eyes during a scene together because her stare "made him 'nervous'." But Elia Kazan had a whole different take on her eyes when he wrote in his diary: "I love her eyes when she's being fucked. When I think of those moments, I never want to die. Connie means cunt in old English. The delicate folded flower with its twin petals. Two pink petals and two hungry eyes, that's my obsession!"

After a successful run in Italy, Connie wasn't able to make the grade in the competitive new Hollywood, and the young actress's high-flying dreams of fame ended in disappointment. She wound up marrying and settling down in Los Angeles with a small-time television producer—an uninspired but ambitious Hungarian immigrant by the name of Ivan Tors. Her husband's claim to fame would be a string of crappy TV shows like *Sea Hunt* and *Daktari*. The proud creator of such dubious gifts to American culture as *Flipper* and *Clarence the Cross-Eyed Lion*, Ivan Tors was a real dud. But he was getting rich shoveling shit to the masses, so Connie "settled" for him. Like my mother, my aunt Connie had been traumatized growing up in the Manhattan slums and she never wanted to live like that again. She would give Ivan Tors three strapping blond sons, my cousins Steve, Peter, and David Tors, who all looked just like their father. Connie was never happy again. She hated her new life, my mother claimed; hated being shackled to "that thick-headed macho

Hungarian prick." I think she even kind of hated her own children, seeing my unfortunate younger cousins as living reminders of her disillusionment with the sparkly lures of the American Dream. Her fears of financial insecurity had tricked her into an ignoble dead-end: a loveless marriage to a money-grubbing, talentless buffoon, and a life sentence of suburban angst.

"She should have stayed in Italy and married Pavese." That's what my mother always said, after embarking on a far more successful movie career herself. But my mother's fifteen minutes was soon interrupted when she met my father. Artie Shaw was at the height of his fame, and the world was Doris Dowling's oyster, too. The high-profile Hollywood couple fell head over heels in love and got married, just like in a fairy tale. But Artie—many years my mother's senior—had already been married many times. Among his illustrious exes were Lana Turner and Ava Gardner, not to mention his affairs with the likes of Billie Holiday and Judy Garland. Doris was wife number seven. After she quit working to be with him, reality set in. Doris had a drinking problem. Soon the honeymoon was over and their marriage became a battleground of savage artistic egos. In keeping with my father's lifelong pattern of making the same romantic blunders over and over while expecting different results, they stayed together only long enough to have me. When all else fails, let's have a kid, right? After Doris tried to shoot him, Artie filed for another divorce, and that was the end of the fairy-tale marriage.

Not long after their split, Doris met and married Bob, a top executive at a big Hollywood talent agency. That fortuitous alliance—coupled with Doris's charm, talent, beauty, fame, and a successful track record in the movies—should have guaranteed her an upwardly mobile film career. But there was that old joker in the deck. The Curse. My mother tried to kill her next husband, bashing Bob over the head in another murderous drunken tantrum. After a quick divorce—from which she walked away with a sumptuous Beverly Hills mansion and half of poor Bob's money— Doris Dowling was a single mother again, making the rounds of fancy Hollywood cocktail parties.

Without a partner to nag her about her drinking, she pulled the plug from the jug and began a steady descent into full-blown alcoholism. Between her progressive troubles with the bottle and being stuck with a kid, me, her career soon crashed and turned to shit.

I was just a little boy when my mother tried to kill her first two husbands, a little lost child caught in a living nightmare of booze-befuddled madness. By the time she married the Nowhere Man, she'd pretty much given up on being a movie star. She wasn't getting any younger, so like her sister she decided to settle for safety and security.

Her next husband was a textbook alcoholic enabler who wasn't at all troubled by her drinking, as long as it kept her down on the farm. After that, she mostly stayed home, drinking alone. As her world got smaller, if she worked at all, it was taking bit parts on Ivan Tors's crappy TV shows. Her acting was soon reduced to staggering around on the stage of her spotless suburban home in a prolonged drunken rampage, babbling and moaning melodramatically about her long-gone glory days in Italy. By the time I was six, Doris Dowling, the charismatic diva of Italian Avant-Garde Cinema, had degenerated into a frustrated aging suburban *hausfrau* with a serious drinking problem and a really shitty attitude.

22. NOWHERE MAN

"THE MORAL IS THE OLDEST OF ALL: HUBRIS AND NEMESIS; FAME AS A FAUSTIAN BARGAIN, IN WHICH THE PRICE OF WORLDLY SUCCESS, OF LIVING LIKE GODS, IS SHAME, HORROR AND DEGRADATION."

—MICK BROWN

Cigano folds the old clippings and inserts them back into a big Ziploc bag, then glances up. The kid looks like he's about to jump out of his chair.

"What's up, man?"

"You want some feedback now, Jonathan Shaw?"

"Do I have a choice?" The tattoo man rolls his eyes. "Okay, man, spill it. But go easy, huh? I'm only just starting out with this thing."

"Well, first off, your writing reminds me of some of my favorite authors, like Henry Miller and Garcia Marquez, Bukowski, Céline . . ."

Caught off-guard, expecting harsh criticism, surprised by his young listener's effusive words of praise, Cigano stares at the kid. "Whoa! I'm surprised someone your age has even *read* all that stuff."

Jaco smiles. "I told you, Jonathan Shaw. I've been reading all my life. I know good writing, and this is good. I really want to hear more."

"Well, shit!" Cigano beams at his visitor, feeling a deep wave of gratitude, silently giving thanks to a God he knows nothing about for sending him encouragement at such a hard time. In a silent mental flash, he vows to keep telling his story with truth and courage, as best he can. "Thank you, man. Seriously, I dunno what to say . . . but if ya wanna hear more, I got plenty more of this shit, that's for sure."

Jaco nods, smiling.

Overcome by a rush of enthusiasm, the tattoo man flips to the back of his notebook. "Since you dug the biographical stuff so much, check this part out. I been writing down all these random family histories; I dunno if I'm ever gonna use any of it in this book, but fuck, man, if what you're telling me is right, maybe I oughta think about it. Here, lemme read ya this next bit."

Ironically, my mother's first big break in America was playing the role of a young bar girl who befriends Ray Milland, the protagonist of *The Lost Weekend*, a Hollywood classic about a writer's struggle with alcoholism. Ironic, because both of my mother's brothers and later her only son—me—would become alcoholic writers.

I think my mother, in typical alcoholic fashion, always blamed my father, and later all the other men in her life—including me—for all her bad breaks, bad behavior, fuckups, and failures. That's pretty much par for the course for alcoholics: that singular ability to destroy their own lives, then point the finger at everybody *but* themselves. Being a potential alcoholic waiting to happen myself, I grew up believing I was the Big Jinx; that that's why my father and Bob had both run off and abandoned me. With typical unconscious alcoholic self-loathing, it was all *my* fault. Me me me! The eternal Curse of the selfish, self-centered alcoholic mind—a worthless piece of shit the whole universe revolves around. I may not think much of myself, but I'm all I ever think about.

To add to my emerging dark pathology, when I was six, Doris found a husband who really suited her needs—or rather, the needs of the Curse. Husband number three, the Nowhere Man, was a classic co-alcoholic. No good drunk should ever be without a partner in crime, and this guy would be hers for the next forty-odd years as she slowly drank herself into a long, troubled state of boozy stupefaction in well-appointed style and comfort.

Cigano stops and closes his eyes, conjuring up an image of his stepfather, Len, the ineffectual gray Nowhere Man. "Hold on," he mumbles, leafing through the pages, searching for the story he wrote about this creepy old ghost, the stepfather he had despised all his life. "Ha. Here it is. Ya might like this thing. It's a little short piece about when they first met. I was thinking of trying to fit it into this book somewhere. Wrote it right after I got sober. It's called *Boy Meets Girl in Hollywood*." He lets out a bitter little snort as the words run across his mind like a poison-pen letter.

○   ○   ○

The glamorous A-list party is in full swing as the up-and-coming PR man struts in the door like he owns the joint. An ambitious newcomer to the sun-splashed West Coast network of movers, shakers, and high-rolling star-makers, Leonard B. Kaufman moves across the livingroom floor with an affected jaunty-jolly stride, surveying the sumptuous Bel Air home of his employer, Hal Bernstein. And yes, that is "the" Hal Bernstein, king of the sanctified realm of public relations—indispensable friend to the rich and famous, the Beautiful People of 1960s Hollywood, a glittery dream factory of gimmicks and cleverly devised madcap "publicity stunts."

Strains of Brubeck's *Take Five* waft through the chattering night air as Len takes in his new boss's sprawling mansion. What a spread! He's never seen anything like it. But he's determined not to let it show. He looks down, sneaking a glance at the mirror-sharp shine on his new Florsheims. Hal Bernstein has advised his new employee to "dress for success," and that's just what he's done. Cary Grant is in the crowd. Big Game. No point looking like some schmuck who just stepped off the Greyhound from Newark.

Len smiles as a white-jacketed waiter hands him a Martini from a silver tray. Not much of a drinker, Kaufman is more of the lampshade-on-the-head-at-the-office-Christmas-party type. He looks around for a spot to set down the delicate glass. Then it occurs to him that it might make a nice little prop. After all, when in Rome and all that. Taking a frugal sip of the bitter elixir, Len begins to circulate. He moves through the crowd, mixing, mingling, stopping for a bit of small talk with some of the big shots, before politely moving on. Len doesn't want to wear out his welcome. This is networking, California style, and the sky is the limit for him if he plays his cards right.

Then he sees her. His stomach freezes. An angel, standing right before him, bathed in the indefinable air of stardom. Hollywood Royalty. A Queen! A Star! Artie Shaw's ex-wife is the most beautiful gal Len has ever laid eyes on! He stops, frozen in awe. He stares. He ogles. He gawks like a *meshugenah*. For the life of him, he can't take his eyes off her. Doris Dowling is sitting at a lively coffee table in the center of the room, surrounded by other glamorous Hollywood types. Bohemians, actors, writers, directors, intellectuals, beatniks. Len knows the type. Communists. Fags. But he feels confident. After all, he's dressed for success, and the world is his oyster.

He moves forward, slowly, without taking his eyes off his radiant prey. Doris is laughing, sparks flying around her in wild, crackling kinetic electricity. Her eyes are all fire, glitter, and shimmering, glimmering light. Leonard B. Kaufman is in love at first sight. Just like in a movie. He inches closer until he's standing right over her, slightly to her left. He lingers there, listening, intent on every word spilling from her ruby-red lips as she debates method acting with another striking young woman. An actress! An honest-to-God Hollywood starlet! A living doll! Stealthy as a big-game hunter, he hangs on to Doris's every gesture and inflection, watching, waiting for a chance to say something witty, to get her attention just long enough to shove his shiny new Florsheim in the door.

She never stops talking. Doris is the center of attention. She seems to sense Len's presence lurking beside her, but she studiously ignores him. Nonplussed, he remains at her side. He is her servant, her faithful lapdog. He hovers around, waiting for his chance, laughing whenever she laughs, paying rapt attention. As she expounds on French existentialism and God knows what the heck else, he nods—as if he gets a word of what the dickens she's talking about. Doris might as well be explaining algebra to a billy goat, and she knows it. Len doesn't give a hoot. He'll stand there all darn night if he has to. To heck with Hal Bernstein. To heck with Cary Grant.

Then the clouds part and the sun shines through. With a sidelong glance, she addresses him. "Don't you agree, dah-ling?" Len nods his head up and down like Howdy Doody, grinning to split his handsome but rather dull face. He would agree to paint his ass cheeks blue and jump into the big kidney-shaped swimming pool with Bernstein and Cary Grant under each arm. He is her slave. Doris hands him her empty glass, deftly relieving him of his untouched Martini. "Do be a dear and fetch me another drink, dah-ling," she coos. Len's heart sings like Sinatra with strings.

It's been said that the beginning of every relationship contains the seed of its inevitable destruction. What if Moses himself had come down from the mountain at that very moment with tears in his eyes and the Ten Commandments under his arm? Could he possibly have warned the ambitious young dreamer that forty-five years hence, he would be feeding his Living Doll watered-down supermarket vodka from a plastic tumbler to wash down her Valium and Vicodin pills? Would Len have been able to see himself in the future, changing her geriatric diapers in a dark airless room, while a once-glamorous starlet quietly drank herself to death behind the carefully manicured façade of a spotless American Dream home?

Probably not. Most likely, Len would've stood up gallantly and socked that no-good party-pooping gray-bearded schmuck right in the kisser.

23. INTO THE WOUND

"THE PAST IS OUR VERY BEING."

—DAVID BEN-GURION

With a bitter grunt, Cigano closes his notebook. He looks up at Jaco and shrugs. "Anyway, this stuff gives ya some idea what I'm doing here."

"It's devastating! And I feel as if I'm right there in the story. It's quite a strange feeling, really."

Cigano feels another wave of gratitude. "Thank you, man. Means a lot to me, you saying that. It's been like pulling teeth, dredging up some of this shit, y'know. Sometimes it feels like a fucking exorcism or something."

"Would you read some more?"

"Why not?" Cigano grins, opening the notebook again. "Long as I'm goin' to hell here, I may as well shake hands with the devil."

The first time she brought Len home, I was six, standing in the hallway.

"*Dah-ling!*" I could hear her cheery "stage" voice calling out from the stuffy den. "Do come in! I want you to meet someone!" Her tone sounded too nice to be about anything good. I shuffled inside, looking down.

"Hi, John-o." Len gave me this big fake smile. I had that feeling of being a trained monkey, like when she paraded me around her parties in my pajamas. Only I wasn't in my pajamas. It was afternoon, after school. Cocktail Hour.

"Say hello to Lennie, dear!" She was slurring her words in that phony voice that always meant trouble. Len smiled as I managed an evasive grunt.

"So, your mom tells me you like ponies." He seemed kind of nervous.

Bob used to take me to the amusement park down on Beverly to ride the ponies. We'd stop by the Farmer's Market and he'd buy me root-beer floats and these little marzipan candies that looked like oranges in miniature wooden California orange crates. But that was a long time ago, when I was a little kid. Now I was six and what I really liked was watching Godzilla wreck stuff on the TV. I still liked staring at the dancing ghosts in the tree outside my window, but now I liked all kinds of new stuff, like listening to The Coasters singing *Yackety Yack* on the radio. Mostly, I liked sitting alone up in my room with my picture books. Why was this guy talking about the ponies? He didn't get it. He looked like everything I didn't like: creepy old guys in suits smelling of whiskey and tobacco who made me stand around at her dumb cocktail parties. And that stinky old "den." I never liked to go in there. Who was this stupid old dork? And why was she making me stand there like a trained chimp and act all polite to him?

"Is he one of them head doctors?" I crinkled up my nose, pointing to Len like a giant dog turd in the middle of the room.

"Heavens no, dear!" She sort of frowned with a goofy smile at the same time. "He's just Lennie. He's my boyfriend."

"Just Lennie" shifted in the big leather chair. I looked at him like my cat Swifty looked at a bug he wasn't interested in killing.

"Oh," I said. Sensing it was about to be over, I took a couple of steps toward the door, flinging a casual "Okay, see ya," over my shoulder as I grabbed the big golden doorknob.

After that, he started coming around a lot. I tried to avoid them when he was there, but sometimes it was impossible. One night as I snuck toward the kitchen, where I knew Grandma would be muttering in the black-and-white glow of her little portable TV set, my mother caught up to me in the hall.

"Dah-ling! There you are! Come into the den! Lennie and I have something mah-velous to share with you!"

Head hung low, I followed her in there. What now?

There he was again, standing at the bar in his stupid suit and bow tie and horn-rim glasses. "Hi there, John-o!" He was smiling that same phony smile. I didn't like the way he said my name. I wished he didn't know my name.

My mother went over beside him and started telling me how they were going to be married. ". . . And so Lennie's going to be your father now!" She kept talking, as if she could fill the awkward white space of the den with words, sounding all cheery and fake like she did on one of those TV commercials she got to be in sometimes. "Isn't that just *wonderful?*"

I was confused. But I knew better than to say what I was thinking. *What's so wonderful about it? How's this creepy old guy gonna be my father when I already got a father? And my real dad could twist this corny little geek's neck like a chicken!* They stood there with their stupid drinks, looking at me like they were frozen, like those people on *The Twilight Zone.* Nobody said anything. I guessed they were waiting for me to say something back.

"That's nice." I shrugged.

Cold white silence.

Finally, my mother spoke again. "Yes, it *is* nice, dear!" She laughed. They both laughed, even though I hadn't said anything funny. They seemed kind of nervous, like they felt guilty about something as they stood drinking from those stupid cocktail glasses. "Well, then," she prodded, "why don't you come and give your new father a great big hug?"

She might as well have been saying: "Why don't you kiss a great big bug?" I felt like my dog Princess, who could hear things beyond the range of human ears. But I knew my mother's cheery suggestion wasn't optional. Me and Len hugged coolly, and then it was over. I think he was just as creeped out with that hugging thing as I was. We all knew it was a big phony act. But that's just the way things were. My mother was an actress, and that acting thing was like a secret code we would all have to learn to live by.

Len was a Jew, she told me. Just like my father, whose real name was Arshawski before he changed it to Shaw. She'd married him 'cause he was Jewish, that's what she always said. *The bastard!* Even though she didn't like my father anymore, my mother always liked the Jews. Maybe 'cause she'd been raised by Grandma, who was Irish Catholic, and by those mean old "knuckle-smacking penguins" she always cussed about. My mother hated the nuns and the Church. When she was drunk, she would rail on and on about all the poverty she came from. "We lived right off the Negro district in Harlem," she would tell me. "There was nothing but filth and cockroaches." She would pronounce them cock-a-roaches. "There were mice and bedbugs. Ugh! I remember coming home one day and Grandma had the icebox pulled back and there were hundreds of those filthy cock-a-roaches creeping all over. Ugh! Cracked linoleum in the living room, windows that looked into alleys of dirty brick walls. Just horrible! How I used to dream about changing all that when I'd walk past those beautiful tall buildings along Park Avenue on my way to school! I think that was the most important thing in my life, to get out of there and get what the others had . . ." The Jews were rich and smart and they always stuck together. That's what my mother said. They had to be real clever to get away from Hitler. All I really knew about the Jews were those creepy black-and-white pictures of burned-out skinny naked Jew bodies in the Nazi camps I had to look at when she called me into the den. She'd make me sit there with her while she drank and listened to scary classical music like in the monster movies, showing me those pictures of piles of dead Jews. Those pictures were a lot scarier than the monster movies on the TV. And now this Len was a Jew. He sort of looked like that goofy guy on the cover of *Mad* magazine. Was the *Mad* magazine guy a Jew, too? My mother always told me the worst thing was to be an "anti-Semite" and hate the Jews. So after she brought Len home I even had to feel sort of guilty about hating him too much, 'cause of him being a Jew and all.

A conservative, dull-looking man in his early forties, Len stayed lurking in the background, a distant gray presence. A Nowhere Man; the 'breadwinner,' my mother called him when she was drunk—which seemed to be all the time after she married him. Right from the start, it seemed this dour little fellow's only real purpose for existing in our home was as a support system for her drinking, her alcoholism, the Curse; a lackluster little fact of life. And if my mother tolerated him, I instinctively hated Leonard Kaufman from the moment I set eyes on him, as if as a child I could see through that haggard bumbling *Mad* magazine Guy mask and perceive the true malevolent reason for him coming into our lives. Still, we all tried playing our parts in a carefree family sitcom, sitting down together at the big empty dining-room table where nobody had ever sat before. It always felt weird being in there: cold and clammy and wrong. My mother would play this happy lady, always trying to direct our conversations to suit whatever show we were supposed to be in. Len and I tried to go along with it to please her, but I don't think either of us knew our lines too good. There was a lot of silence at that big dining-room table. White silence: like the long white living-room carpet with the brown bloodstain in the corner hidden by an end table with an ugly statue of Medusa the Snake Lady. "Wall-to-wall." That's what Doris called that big white carpet; and that's what those "family dinners" were like: wall-to-wall. Three walls sitting at a big empty table, trying to act polite and not look at each other too much. I dreaded those dinners. I would always cringe when her phony stage voice sang out in the big empty white house. "Jono, dah-ling. Dinner's on the table!" Mercifully, that dinner thing wouldn't last long.

One night, her chipper "dinner conversation" started. She rambled on about the movies and all the books she'd read, about Sartre and Shakespeare and the Italian cinema, where she'd had such a glorious career and a carefree bohemian life before "his father," *that bastard*, came along and ruined everything. The more she drank, the darker the sitcom got.

"But that's enough about *my* life!" She let out a sarcastic snort, a hellish glare blazing in her dark booze-maddened eyes. "Not that it would interest you *men* anyway!"

Silence.

She'd been drinking a lot, and the Jabberwock cast its shadow across the long white void as she croaked out in that fake-cheerful TV voice. "So . . . why don't my two men tell me about *their* lives?" My mother was play-acting, reciting her lines from a carefully scripted carefree show: *The Men in My Life.* But I could hear the angry voices in the background. *Men! You're all the same! Bastards!*

"So how were *your* days today?"

Silence.

"Jono, dah-ling?" She kept smiling that big phony smile till it looked like her face was about to crack in half.

Shoot! That's my cue! What's my line? "Uh, it was okay." I shrugged with my mouth full of meatloaf. I hated that stinky meatloaf. I looked down as my voice trailed off into a void of pounding white silence.

She glared at me and let out a loud melodramatic sigh. *Shoot! I fumbled my line!* I chewed and chewed. I swallowed the meatloaf like a mouthful of dried-up cardboard.

She kept looking at me, a little too long. Finally, she turned to Len. "And how about you, sweetheart? How are things going down at the office?" That cheery voice was trembling on the edge of trouble. Like my dog Princess, only I could hear it. I pushed my meat loaf around with my fork.

"Oh, just fine . . ." Len shrugged. I guess he was caught off guard too. Didn't know his lines, either.

Silence.

The spotlight was back on me again. "And *you*, my beamish boy?" she chirped like a dying vulture. "How'd it go at school today?"

School! Shoot! What's my line? I could hear the steady grandfather clock ticking in the hall. *Tok tok tok.* I pictured the classroom where we all said the Pledge of Allegiance under the big ugly flag by a blackboard and a sour-faced man in a suit saying words . . . *Words . . . I pledge allegiance to the flag . . . Beware the Jabberwock! The jaws that bite, the claws that catch!* Angry voices and menacing words were shooting and buzzing around like wasps in my head. *Words. What are the words? What's my line?* I pushed the meatloaf around with my fork, trying to remember what I was supposed to say as the silence shouted: *White! White! Danger! Danger! Red! Tick . . . tock . . . tick . . . tock . . . Red! Blood! Blood! Tick . . . tock . . . Red! Red alert! Earthquake drill! Fire drill! Bomb alert! Duck and cover!! Duck and cover!!* I could hear the emergency school bells clanging and see the kids dropping from their seats like birds shot off a wire. *My line! Quick! The line!*

I heard myself mumbling. "Uh, you know, it was okay . . ."

Crash! Splaft! Her plate went over face-down on the table, squishy meatloaf juices seeping onto the long white tablecloth. "Well, that's just fine!" she snarled, draining her Martini in one gulp as she stood, toppling the chair over behind her. "Just bloody fine! I'm so goddamned delighted to be having such a grand, stimulating dinner conversation with my two charming men! Ha!" Her flashing eyes scanned back and forth from me to Len like Nazi searchlights. ***"Men!"*** she spat, storming out and slamming the door so hard, the plates and silverware clattered on the table. I could hear her curses and shouts echoing down the long white hallway. ***"Bastards!"***

The obscene meatloaf stain spread out over the frilly white tablecloth like a bloodstain. Len just sat there, looking down at his plate. I could hear her voice raging from the den, then the sound of breaking glass crashing from the walls and floors. I got up and shuffled through the dark empty kitchen and out the back door into the cool night air, feeling relieved I didn't have to sit and finish that crummy cardboard meatloaf.

24. GODZILLA

" . . . SOME SAY IT WAS THE WIND AND RAIN . . . THE
VILLAGERS OF OTTO ISLAND, THEY SAY IT WAS . . .
GODZILLA!"

-RAYMOND BURR

The tattoo man stubs out his cigarette, then reaches across the table and lights another. He eyes Jaco, who smiles and nods back. Feeling as if he's being forced to watch some old movie he hates, Cigano sighs out a long plume of smoke as he turns the page. Reading on, he marvels at the odd childlike tone emerging from his mouth, as if he wasn't just reading the words, but channeling the voice of a long-forgotten little boy.

○ ○ ○

I went back to taking my meals in the kitchen, watching Godzilla on the little black-and-white TV set while I ate. I bet Godzilla wouldn't take any crap from her stupid booze demons! Grandma always kept me company in the big empty white house. After school we'd sit in the kitchen together and I'd listen to her complain about her life. Since I was still too little to complain about my own life, I liked having Grandma there to do it for me. It was almost as good as the TV shows. She'd stand at the kitchen counter, puttering around and chewing on her words like some worn-out old cartoon character.

"Back in th' Great Depression, things wuzzn't all cozy and cushy like this, boy! She don't know how lucky she got it. None of 'em do.

Hurrh! I had ta go ta woik cleanin' houses at five a'clock inna mornin', gettin' up before sunrise, and I wouldn't get back till after dark. Walkin' past all them long soup lines. *Tsk.* What else was I s'posed ta do? I had four kids ta support all by myself. Tsk! Five, if ya count that no-good drunken bum, Harry. That's ya mother's fathah, ya grandfathah. *Tsk!* By th' time I'd get home, dog tired from woikin' all day an' walkin' up five flights a tenement stairs, he was already inna bag, throwin' all th' foinacha around, bustin' up th' place. *Tsssk.* Th' kids would be hidin' out on th' fai-ah'scape. *Tsssk.* He used ta come in drunk an' wreck everything. *Tsk!* And me woikin' my fingas to th' bone. *Tsk!* Agh, what a life! Only time I ever got any peace was when th' bum was in jail or off on a spree. *Tsk!* He'd be gone fa months at a time, runnin' around wit' all dem no good doity crooks an' Gypsies. An' me all alone wit' four kids ta raise. *Tsk!* What a life, I tell ya. She thinks everybody's got it so easy? Hah! I sure didn't have no colored maids or fancy rich Jew husbands ta leech offa, I tell ya, boy . . ."

Grandma would go on like that for hours. Sometimes I'd go up to my room to get a comic book, and when I got back, she'd still be talking. I guess Grandma was a little shell-shocked. The Great Depression and all. I was only eight so didn't know what a Great Depression was, but it didn't sound too good. We spent a lot of time together in the kitchen, me and Grandma. The best part about having Grandma around was she would let me watch the grownup shows on the TV. My favorites were the old black-and-white horror movies. Scary stuff like *The Mummy* with Boris Karloff and the Christopher Lee *Dracula* shows. Grandma said I watched too much "morbid" stuff and that I'd get nightmares, but she didn't make me stop. I didn't care if I got nightmares anymore. I was a big kid now and I wanted all the scary movies I could get. They were never scary enough to suit me anyway. Sometimes you'd have to sit and watch half the movie before you even saw a monster, and then it was just for a second. And when they did finally show you the monsters, it was always a big letdown. As I got older I craved bigger, better monsters.

Then one day Godzilla came along. Now there was a *real* monster! Big, ugly, destructive, and just plain mean. That one I could really sink my little teeth into, sucking up all the drama and disaster like Dracula sucking on a neck. The part I liked best was when Godzilla would get loose and run around all pissed off stampeding through the crowded downtown cityscapes, like my old postcard memory of "a long time ago."

And then he'd just start *wrecking* stuff. I loved it! A part of me was kind of scared of Godzilla, like I was scared of my mother when she was drunk. But another part of me sort of wanted to *be* Godzilla; 'cause nobody ever messed with Godzilla! I guess you could say Godzilla became like my "male role-model." I'd sit at the kitchen table watching Godzilla wrecking stuff on the TV while Grandma puttered in the background, muttering her long gray monologues to the dishes.

My grandmother's parents had come over from Ireland to escape the Potato Famine, she said. I didn't know what a Potato Famine was, but whatever it was I figured Godzilla could kick its butt. She would tell me how she'd grown up rich, then had to raise her kids like "dirt-poor shanty Irish" after marrying a "no-account Gypsy." Grandma was a widow from two husbands. Her first one was my mother's father Harry, a Lithuanian Gypsy who'd died in some place called Skid Row right after I was born. I didn't know where Skid Row was, but it sounded pretty creepy. I never knew my real grandfather, but Grandma used to tell me and my cousins not to drink or we'd end up on that Skid Row place like "that no-good Gypsy bum."

Her next husband was the Grandpa I knew. Grandpa Wilson was nice. He used to take me on long drives in the country in his big De Soto. I called that car the Bathyscaphe 'cause it looked like the submarine from that movie *20,000 Leagues Under the Sea* where there was a sea monster like the Jabberwock. I always felt safe in the Bathyscaphe with Grandma and Grandpa Wilson. Wilson was a tall big-boned Okie with a long angular face like an oak tree. I always thought that's why my mother called him an Okie, but one day she told me it was 'cause he came from someplace called Oklahoma and he was stupid. I didn't care, 'cause he had a big friendly smile and he was nice. We used to ride along the dry dusty back roads outside Los Angeles, through all the orange groves and farms with eucalyptus trees and big date palms that looked like space monsters from *The War of the Worlds*. I'd jump up and down on the blue felt seat in the back. When I got tired, I'd sit staring out at the yellow rolling farmland, making up elaborate stories about the tall palms dotting the hillsides being space invaders from Mars. Grandpa Wilson was the captain of the Bathyscaphe and I was his head sailor.

"Look, look, Grampa! There's a whole bunch of 'em out there!"

Grandpa Wilson grinned back at me. "Ya better keep an eye on 'em for me while I drive, sailor. Lemme know if they start comin' this way."

"Geeze, Wilson," Grandma Mabel nagged. "Why ya wanna go and egg th' boy on like that? Ya gonna put all kinda ideas in his head!"

"Guess yer grandma can't see 'em. Her eyesight ain't what it useta be."

"Aww, g'wan witcha, Wilson," Grandma whined.

Then, Grampa Wilson died. A "heart attack," Grandma said. I didn't know what a Heart Attack was, but I guessed it was something bad like a Potato Famine or a Great Depression. She said he'd "gone away." I asked her if Grandpa Wilson had gone to Skid Row, where my other Grandpa went. She guffawed and told me Grandpa Wilson had gone to some other place way up in the sky. After a while, I forgot about him. After Grampa Wilson died, Grandma moved in with us. She was sad a lot after that. But she'd always been kind of sad. That was just Grandma. I was glad to have her around all the time, even though her and Doris didn't get along too good. I guess my mother mostly wanted her there to have a free babysitter for me.

Grandma used to stand at the kitchen counter while I sat watching the little TV on the table. She'd slice up meat and carrots, celery and potatoes, and throw them all together in a pot of boiling water till the meat turned gray. A dash of salt and she called it a stew. One time my mother came in while Grandma was chopping away at the counter and started yelling at her. "Jesus, Mother, that's filet mignon! Do you have any idea what that costs?"

"Well, ya don't gotta getcha liver in a twist just cuz I used some of yer precious filly whachamacallit for my stew. *Tssk!* Maybe I oughta just eat th' dawg's food. *Tsk!* Excuse me fa livin'!"

"Oh, never mind! Jesus, I need a drink!" She stormed out cursing as Grandma muttered into the boiling gray stew.

I sat glued to the TV, waiting for Godzilla to come and start wrecking stuff.

With a sigh, Cigano throws his notebook down on the table. He looks up and shrugs. "Anyway, I still got a long way to go with this thing."

"I'm telling you, Jonathan Shaw, it's really good."

"Thanks." He stubs out his cigarette. "No accounting for bad taste."

"I've been wanting to ask you, Jonathan Shaw. Is it all true?"

The tattoo man rubs his chin. "Most of it is, yeah. I take a few little dramatic liberties with things here and there. Someone told me once that veracity is no excuse for lousy storytelling, so ya always gotta emphasize the truth with the capital T. But yeah, it's all basically rooted in fact . . .''

"So that part about your father, he really just abandoned you completely after they divorced?"

Cigano nods. "Oh yeah. And the part about her shooting at him, it really happened too, not exactly the way I described it there, but she really tried to shoot the guy, and after that he was gone with the wind. But fuck, with shit like that going on, wouldn't anybody split?"

Jaco ponders the question. "Leave the wife, yes, but not abandon an innocent baby like that. I don't think people should ever desert their children. Your father did you a great wrong."

Cigano takes this in and sighs. "Look, kid, I get what you're saying, and on some level you're right. But me writing about it isn't like 'Boo hoo! Poor me! My daddy didn't love me and my momma was a lush so I became a junkie.' Shit, man, I know lots of people had it worse than I did, and they didn't go and fuck up their lives. I'm just trying to tell things as I remember 'em, y'know? God pity me if I ever start feeling like any of it's an excuse to feel sorry for myself. Like they say: 'Poor me, poor me, pour me a drink.'"

Jaco nods. "You wrote that you never really knew your father, but you seem to know a lot about his life. How? Because he was so famous?"

"Yeah, well, that's part of it. But I also did a lot of my own research."

"So that time you wrote about at the beginning, that was the only time you ever saw him, when you were a baby?"

"Not exactly." The tattoo man stifles a yawn. "I saw him a few times when I was a kid. Not very often, though. My mother and him couldn't put their own grudges aside for the sake of the fuggin' kid they had together. Poor bastards." He shrugs. "Argh, they were both a mess. Ignorant misguided intellectuals. A matching pair of emotional basket cases. Anyway, it's only recently since I got sober that I spent any real time with Artie."

"So he's still alive . . ."

"Oh yeah, man. Mean as a fucking rattlesnake. Alive and kicking and ruling Hell. Ninety-two years of boiling piss and poison." Cigano laughs, shaking his head. "And still sharp as a fuggin' buzz saw, too."

He reaches over and flips through another notebook, then starts to read out loud again.

25. THE TROUBLE WITH ARTIE SHAW

"IT DOESN'T MATTER WHO MY FATHER WAS; IT MATTERS WHO I REMEMBER HE WAS."

—ANNE SEXTON

I would always get lost looking for the old man's place, riding along those sterile prefab avenues beside the Ventura Freeway, a gantlet of shopping malls, American flags, basketball hoops over garage doors, and spotless rosy-faced children playing in plastic manicured yards to the hissing of sprinklers on summer lawns. Real *Leave It to Beaver* shit. After spending most of my life in third-world countries, I always felt so out of place in that squeaky-clean alien netherworld. A solitary leather-clad tattooed biker rolling through the bland suburban scenery, I must have looked like the fucking Horseman of the Apocalypse to the old man's neighbors.

Artie's house sat hidden away at the end of a little cul-de-sac on a street that looked like all the others. His living room overflowed with memorabilia from another time and place: walls crowded with artwork by legendary painters; books, magazines, sculptures and tchotchkes; mementos of the old man's life were everywhere, barely a surface free from the clutter of time and Artie Shaw's unhappy, self-obsessed solitary genius.

On one of my first visits, I sat across from him at a big Chinese teakwood table piled high with all kinds of books. It was as if he could read enough books to somehow master all the truth in the universe. I glanced at my watch, shifting in the chair, as Artie sat across from me on a big leather sofa, playing with his hearing aid. Before he spoke, I could already hear his voice. *"What a world you came into, kiddo . . . Jesus, Doris. Jesus, Doris! What th' fuck!?"* My father's voice: soft, but with an odd undertone of irony; egocentric, neurotic, self-assured—yet tainted with a distinctive, high-pitched, narcissistic angst; a vague tone of arrogance, the sort of deeply entrenched bumptious verbal swagger that only the hand of Death might ever dispute.

He looked up without seeing me, growling through an expertly trimmed silver mustache. "I don't like pork!"

I raised an eyebrow. "What . . . ?"

"I don't like it."

I tried for a smile. The best I could manage was an awkward grimace, wondering how I'd wound up sitting across from this cantankerous, mean-spirited old lunatic.

"It's the *idea* of a fucking pig. I just don't like it! They're *pigs*, fer Chrissake! Filthy creatures! They eat all kinda shit. No. I don't like it . . ."

As he expounded on his dislike for the expensive gourmet prosciutto sandwich I'd brought him, my eyes scanned the airless room like a camera. Restless and jittery in my skin, I was dying for a smoke but I knew the old man would pitch a fit and start lecturing me if I dared to go out on the patio. *"Jesus, Jono! When are you gonna quit smoking those filthy things?"* My eyes wandered to a dusty bar in a corner with a table lamp made from an old clarinet. A bottle of Cutty Sark. I longed for a drink. But, just for today, I was still sober. *Almost a year now! Eleven months. One fucking day at a time.*

The old man droned on. "Nope, I just don't like pork. Now if ya give it to me as chicken or something, I'd eat it. Sure. The taste is all right. I just don't like the image of a goddamn pig."

Artie stopped talking and the room filled with an interminable roaring silence. I could hear my watch ticking, my nose hairs growing, my balls sweating. *Drip. Drip. Drip.* I ran my hand through my hair, eyeing a Picasso in a dusty wooden frame on the wall. I was about to say something when his voice burst into the silence.

"So, anyway, it's time to eat!" He got up, strode into the kitchen, and sat down at an old wooden table cluttered with books, magazines, newsletters, journals, and piles of yellowing unopened mail. There were two generic frozen dinners. Artie sat down and started eating right from the container. "Try some of this macaroni, Jono. It's a bitch, man!" He pointed to the chair.

I sat and picked up a fork to eat the strange plastic-looking food. I tried a small bite. Not too horrible. After a few more bites of munching, crunching, excruciating silence, Artie spoke up again. "This is the real reason I moved back from Spain."

I cast him a confused look. "What?"

"Ralph's, man! I missed being able to go to Ralph's Supermarket!"

A glaring image flashed into focus in my mind: a five-year-old boy, lost in an endless white American supermarket aisle: a sprawling fluorescent forest of towering boxes and cans and packages, bottles, rolls and products, plastic labels, wrapping and packaging stretching away forever. The kid in my mind looked frightened, an anguished look of confusion creeping across a familiar little face. Then, in a tiny voice, timid as a cartoon mouse, I could hear his words leaving my mouth. "Oh, yeah. Ralph's."

"Hell, yeah! Check out this beef stew, man!" The old goat grunted and shoved another plastic container across the table. I felt a sudden urge to get up and run out the door. I glanced at my watch. I'd only been there an hour. *Fuck! God, grant me the serenity to accept the things I cannot change!* The old man rambled on, as old men do, reminiscing as he chewed with his mouth open. "This table here, it came from the farmhouse where you were born, Jono. Well, you were born in a hospital in New York City. But you were conceived on the farm, way upstate in Pine Plains. Boy, that was the best place I ever lived . . ."

I sat staring at him in mute bafflement. *What the fuck? What's he saying? Did he screw my mom right here on this fucking table? Who **is** this old freak? How can any human being be so completely self-obsessed?*

Artie went on, rapping with a withered, ghostly white fist on the tabletop. "Yep, it's my favorite souvenir of that place. And I have by my bed a little rug with a train for a little kid's bedroom. I look at that thing when I get up at night to piss and I think of Glenn Miller's stupid record, *Chattanooga Choo Choo.* Hah! How do ya like that for a title? A big hit. Ya know why? Cause people are *stupid! 'Pardon me, boy, is that the Chattanooga choo choo?'* Jesus. I think about that every morning. And at night, I think of my father."

As he rambled on, I pictured myself again as a little boy called Jono, sitting by the record player in my mother's den, holding an album. *Artie*

Shaw and His Big Band. An introverted, lonely, haunted little kid sitting all alone, staring at a photograph of the father he never knew. As the image faded to gray, I fixed my eyes on the old man. "Yeah? So whaddya think about your father, Artie? What was he like?"

"He was an asshole!!" he spat. "I remember him, *hungh*, makin' fun of me as a kid when I played the saxophone. When I won five bucks in a talent show for playing that horn, he said, 'They gave ya five dollars for blowin' on that bloozer?' That's what he called it. A bloozer, a blower! A contemptuous word in Yiddish. *He* gave me the contempt I had that eventually made me leave the music business! It wasn't a manly thing to do, ya see, to go up there and blow on a horn in front of all those people. That's what his heritage was. I mighta stayed in the business if I had any respect for it. I had no respect for it, 'cause *he* gave me that contempt! And I think, 'If you were around now, ya prick, and could see all the letters and honors I get and the amount of people that have been influenced by what I did,' ya know, I would tell him, 'Up yer ass!' But I was just a kid. *Argh*, he was a selfish bastard . . . I left . . ." Artie paused for a beat, editing himself. "*He* left when I was fourteen."

"That's a formative age," I heard myself say in an attempt to steer the old man's monologue into something like a conversation.

Artie looked across the table and an ocean of distance, as if seeing the odd tattooed stranger across from him for the first time. Our eyes met. Before I could speak again, he averted his glance and slipped back into his discourse. "It sure *was* a formative age, man! He and my mother would fight to the point that I useta cringe under the thing. He was gonna come and kill her. And me! I would say to her, 'Why don't ya shut up?' I used to think to her, 'Stop naggin' him, the guy's gonna, he'll murder ya,' ya know?"

Artie paused and sighed like a tired old wind-up toy winding down, looking off into an invisible realm of haunted spirits beyond the dull suburban kitchen where we sat like strangers. In that moment I felt something stirring within me for the first time; a feeling of something like kinship with this sad babbling old ghost, my father, slouching off to Forest Lawn in an AstroTurf bubble of resentment and self-pity.

Finally, he started up again. "*Arghh*. What a fuckin' way to live! It's a wonder I didn't become an alcoholic, too. I think to myself, I'm ninety-two fucking years old, man! My father died at fifty. The prick!"

I shifted in the chair. *I'll be fifty in a coupla years. Does this guy even know my fucking birthday?* I heard myself speaking again. "So it was never any good with you and him? Your father?"

The old man sighed, winding up again. "I remember when I was a kid, he was great. Saved my life! My earliest memory, earliest, I don't know how old I was but I was in a crib, and I looked up and I saw a head floating on the ceiling, shadows, lights from the outside, and it was like a devil. But I didn't know what a devil was, all I knew was this frightening thing, and I screamed, and he came in and picked me up and held me. And, you know . . . comfort."

I nodded, studying the old man's hands; ghostly white shapes dancing in the air between us; a pair of translucent albino crabs scuttling across the shifting sands of time.

"So he did some good things when I was young. But when he got older, he got very nasty. He got very disappointed in life. Sick man . . ."

"How so? How was he sick, Artie?"

I watched those hands, now resting on the table.

"Argh, he was a failure, an ignorant peasant. Illiterate uneducated man. His name was Arshawski, ya know. In those days, a name like that wouldn't fly in show business, so I became Artie Shaw. Anyway, that's your background, Jonathan, your grandfather. On my side. On your mother's side, ya had your grandmother, what was her name? Mabel. Hah! The bleeding Irish martyr. And you got that drunken Gypsy for a grandfather! Hah! Forget it! Boy, you really had some setup!" The old man let out a cold guffaw.

I forced a laugh like the croak of a dying bullfrog as I shifted in the creaky wooden chair.

The old man fixed me with a wry look. "How the hell did we ever survive, Jonathan? How the hell do people make it?"

I shrugged.

"You!" He leveled an accusing finger at me. "You did everything ya could to kill yourself, man! You did this, you did that." The hands were up off the table again, gesturing to mimic taking a drink, a shot of heroin in the arm. "You were really *trying* to die, y'know?"

I nodded. "Yeah, man, I know."

Artie shook his head. "But nature just wouldn't let you."

26. A LONG TIME AGO

"NOT ONLY DOES THE PSYCHE EXIST, BUT IT IS
EXISTENCE ITSELF."

—CARL JUNG

Cigano is standing in the cool tiled bathroom, pissing. He can hear Jaco's voice from behind the door.

He calls out over his shoulder. "Whassat, kid?"

"Your father. I had no idea he was such a famous musician."

Cigano yells back. "Yeah, man, Artie Shaw, big name in jazz."

"I've heard of him, in Brazil." Jaco speaks over the flushing toilet. "Maybe from my mother. But I never imagined . . ."

"Yeah." Cigano emerges from the bathroom, wiping his hands on his jeans. "The old man was a big deal back in the swing era. Big band stuff. Way before your time. Shit, way before *my* time." He chuckles and sits at the table, massaging his eyes. "It's funny. All my life, I never told anyone who my father was. It's like I was ashamed of it or something. I always hated it when people made a fuss about me being the son of this great man I didn't even know, like it was some big honor. I dunno, maybe it was just hard for me to acknowledge I even had a father, y'know, one who couldn't give two shits about me. It's only recently that I started to come to terms with that heritage. But, yeah, Artie was big-time back in the day . . ."

"And what about the Gypsy you wrote about?" Jaco asks him. "Your grandfather? He was a Gypsy, yes?"

"Yeah, well, I haven't written too much about him yet, I guess 'cuz I never knew him. I still gotta learn more. I got a feeling there's something real important there. But it's been hard to find much information. I been reading through all these old stories my Uncle Robert wrote about him."

"Your uncle was a writer?"

"Yeah, man. My mother's older brother. I'm trying to put all these obscure family stories into some sorta linear time frame, but it's kinda confusing." He scratches his head. "It's weird, going over all this history. There's so many blind turns and detours, it gets kinda daunting." He pauses. "Memory is such a subjective thing. It can get pretty surreal when you got all this emotional baggage attached to people and happenings; it all gets a little distorted. Like I remember certain things happening when I was maybe five, six, whatever, but when I start going over the times and places where they actually occurred, it turns out I was really like ten at the time, and I think to myself, where did all those years in between go? What happened? Where the fuck *was* I all that time?"

"Where do you think you were?"

"I dunno, I guess I just blocked out a lot of stuff." Cigano sighs. "This shrink I saw after I got sober told me I was a textbook case of post-traumatic stress. Then you pour hundreds of acid trips and hard drugs and booze into the mix, and it's a miracle I'm even sitting here today, much less able to remember anything, y'know?" He pauses again, rubbing his face. "But for me, it's the feelings attached to things that's important." He smiles. "The good part is that it gives you a certain distance from all the emotion, all those traumatic memories that used to drive me to drink myself into a puddle of piss. It's become like this cathartic process now, where I feel like I really *am* writing about some fictional character I'm not all tied up with, y'know? I guess it's what they call detachment, creative license, whatever. It's a real blessing, 'cuz it's hard to take yourself too serious when you become like a cartoon character. I guess what I'm really trying to convey here is the subjective essence of my experiences. If I've learned one thing doing this work, it's that human experience is all the same shit, it's universal, y'know?"

He turns and opens another notebook. "Here. Check out this part."

After watching my mother use my father for target practice, my next memory is from around three or four: a blurry green Mexican road sign seen through a car windshield as I sat with my mother in border traffic. Her long red fingernails tapped on the big black steering wheel, *tapita tapita tapita,* and a song played on the radio. *"Lo-ove, love is strange. A lot of people, take it for a game."* There were dusty figures of dark-skinned men in straw hats, kids in tattered clothes, burros trudging by in the heat, as my mother pulled an alligator-skin flask from her purse. *"Once you get it, never wanna quit, once you've had it, you're in an awful fix, many people don't understand, they think loving is money in the hand."*

The rest of the memory is cloudy and dark, parched with a sepia hue like an old postcard. I was delirious with typhoid fever, my disease-stricken entrails dry as a hot desert wind blowing through a weak little body I couldn't identify as my own. There was a shabby hotel room; a Mexican divorce certificate sitting on a table anchored by a bottle of rum. I was lying on a bed drenched in sweat. My mother's face hovered above me as she clawed at the shirtsleeve of a Mexican doctor who was poking at my chest.

My mother was my best friend when I was little, very protective and loving in her own odd way. As the booze-fueled Curse drove an iron wedge between us over the years, she would always remind me that she'd never left my side as I'd lain there sick and dying. The more poor Doris screwed up, the more she felt a need to affirm that it was her will that caused me to survive after the doctors had told her I was a goner, as if the very force of her love had manifested my recovery—thereby absolving her of the crime of having borne me.

That was when I first imagined that black-and-white city skyline and those weird words. Over the years, I would recall other little details: a hotel room. My mother's angelic face looking down on me. A five-gallon water bottle. A long shiny corridor. A Bible. But the one clear image I carry like a tattoo through this life is that shadowy skyline, like an old-time vision of New York City, and that haunting, familiar phrase, *A LONG TIME AGO.* I have no idea where it comes from. It's one of those weird little puzzles that maybe you'll only know the answer to after you die. But I cherish it like a sacred icon, because it's mine and it connects me like an anchor to some deeper reality, like a past life, a throbbing crystal- blue vein linking this mad earthly incarnation to some higher order of mystery and magic; a surreal, abstract perception I can't explain or define, but comforting somehow. It also seems to hold a clue to the deepest roots of my own madness, having first appeared in the delirious hallucinations of a moribund fever-struck child, my first conscious knowledge of Self emerging from pounding visions of impending death—as if my whole life began as a hallucination. Maybe that's why I could never take any of it too seriously, this world with all its trials, tribulations, hurries, and worries; its rules, regulations and social rituals, hustles, hassles, and stress; because it was all a big border-town mosquito-ass backwater delirium fever-stew to me. Like that old nursery rhyme. "Row, row, row your boat." But a lullaby takes on another tone when you know something like that as your first experience of life. Life is but a dream; a dream about waking up to yourself in a faded yellowed postcard vision of a Tijuana hotel room with a murky diseased water bottle humming from a throbbing corner, and knowing something vague and faded about *a long time ago*, and then hallucinating a life; a long delirious fever-dream; a pounding crashing nightmare symphony of raging infernal machinery.

Maybe that's how it all began for me, my lifelong existential dis-ease; with the fundamental idea that the world around me was nothing but an angry hallucination. Maybe that's where I first came to regard life as an unfriendly condition—a malevolent Curse that could snatch you from loving arms of peace and comfort and throw you into a boiling churning world of darkness.

〇   〇   〇

Cigano sighs as he sets the notebook down and shuts his eyes. Listening to the sounds of the hot Mexican afternoon outside, his inner vision expands under a wave of golden light as he sits breathing himself down, down, deep underwater, into a realm of fuzzy slow-motion pictures.

A smiling young Artie Shaw appears, covering a baby's neck with kisses. Cigano can feel the warm sandpapery tickle of the man's face on tender skin. The baby squeals with laughter as Artie's voice echoes, *"You know, comfort . . . comfort . . . comfort."* Past and present merge. Oily shadows spread into dark moving shapes as a pair of ghostly white hands appears. Long red fingernails reach out of the darkness, snatching the baby away from its father. There's a sound of breaking glass, a bottle crashing, a confusion of hazy yelling, angry shouts and curses, as the baby's cries of delight begin to fade, shifting, morphing into primal screams of animal terror. A pounding heartbeat emerges, joining the baby's wails, growing in intensity as darkness expands, engulfing all. The cries and angry shouts grow dim, giving way to the monotone of a heartbeat rising in volume, taking on a primitive drumbeat rhythm, then becoming a loud, steady clanging, banging mechanical din. A naked infant emerges from the darkness, screaming; an agonized wailing newborn engulfed in a confusion of grinding gears. Its howls disappear as the pink naked body is swallowed up in a raging whirlpool of hacking blades, clanging chains, slamming hydraulic presses, and screaming drills.

With a start, Cigano opens his eyes and looks around. The room seems changed somehow. As he reaches for a cigarette, he realizes he's covered in sweat. He wipes his face with a towel from the table and takes a long, deep breath.

27. JABBERWOCKY

"IF IT AIN'T ONE THING, IT'S THE MOTHER."

— ANONYMOUS

As the tattoo man sits fanning himself with his notebook, his listener sits across from him, as if lost in his own quiet thoughts. Cigano gets up and stands before the little fan on the dresser, stretching his arms over his head like a big bird flexing its wings. "It's funny," he muses, "the things ya remember once you start digging. Soon as you take that first step, fuck, man, it's like some crazy portal just opens up and the universe starts downloading all sorts of clues into your brain, and then the right people just start coming outta the woodwork."

Jaco looks up. "What do you mean?"

"I dunno. All kinda weird stuff. Like when I was first getting sober and starting to write, I ran into this guy at one of those alcoholic meetings. I didn't recognize him, but he knew who I was. Said he'd seen me on some television talk show. Turns out he was someone I'd grown up with, used to hang out with my crowd when I was a teenager. Jacob. He was a half Jew with Gypsy blood, like me. Good guy. Anyway, I was just starting to write about my past, and suddenly here he comes, boom, like magic. So we get to talking about our fucked-up families and stuff."

As he talks on, his old friend's face floats across the waves of his memory.

"The first time I visited your home, Jono, I don't know if you remember."

"It's all kinda fuzzy, man. A lot of the past is like a black hole for me."

"I know how it is, Jono. Don't worry about it. It takes a while to get our brains back. Anyway, we were around thirteen. You took me up to your room and played In-A-Gadda-Da-Vida *on the record player while your mom sat in the living room, drinking all by herself. I remember how the living room was full of all these strange, disturbing art objects. Your house and your mother really scared me and made me feel real uncomfortable and alienated."*

"Ha! And you were just visiting! I hadda live there." Cigano guffaws.

"Well, I'm glad you overcame the odds. You're doing good. Keep going, Jono. It gets easier, believe me. A day at a time . . ."

Cigano grins. "Well, I did keep going, and here I am now, trying to piece together the Great American Novel or some shit. The funny thing is how as soon as I started writing, bang, here comes this guy. And that was just the beginning. After that, all kinds of things started falling in place. Like right when I was starting to think about my Gypsy grandfather, wondering how he was related to my family's alcoholism, within days, bingo! I came across all these old stories my uncle wrote about him!"

"You didn't know about the stories?"

"No. Nothing. That's the wild thing, bro. They just came to me right when I needed 'em. Like magic, I found a whole box of writing with all these old photographs sitting in my mother's garage. It was like stumbling onto a treasure chest. It blows my mind, man. Synchronicity. And it's been like that ever since I started, all kinds of people popping up with information, and always right when I was starting to think about those exact things. Here, check this out." Cigano picks up his notes and starts reading again.

○   ○   ○

Other kids got Dick and Jane, Hardy Boys. Growing up with Doris Dowling, I got Hieronymus Bosch and *The Tibetan Book of the Dead*. It was a bizarre introduction to life for an American kid in the 1950s. My mother's unconventional bedtime stories were pretty surreal, too. I guess she meant well, but if she was trying to raise a drug-crazed paranoid psychopath, she couldn't have done a better job. She used to read me this one spooky poem, a jumble of rhyming nonsense words called *Jabberwocky*.

One night when I was around five, I was lying in bed clutching my stuffed koala bear to my chest as she sat reading to me. I watched her as she spoke with a studied dramatic cadence, her blood-red lips intoning a grim warning. "Beware the Jabberwock, my son! The jaws that bite, the claws that catch!" As she rolled her R's and exaggerated each word with studied theatrical precision, the sounds began to take shape in the room's air, changing into smoky letters drawn by her breath. "Beware the Jubjub bird. And shun the frumious Bandersnatch!" As my vision followed the eerie little forms, the letters began morphing into blades, bat wings, and spindly claw-like tendrils, rising up and swirling around in menacing shadows, like a flock of dark birds, merging into a big word hovering before my eyes: *BEWARE.*

"—*Dah-ris!*" A voice, a flashing nether-memory of clotheslines strung between Manhattan tenements, and the spell was broken. The dark floating shapes faded into the air and disappeared as Grandma stood in the door, a gray wisp of a guardian angel, hands on hips, scolding. "Whaddya wanna read that kinda morbid junk to th' boy for? Ya gonna give'm nightmayahs!"

"Oh, hush up, Mother!" my mother snapped. Grandma faded into the hall and she turned back to me. With a wink, she read on, her shiny eyes beaming with love. "And hast thou slain the Jabberwock?"

I nodded and clapped as she set the book on the quilt, crying out the next part we both knew by heart. "Come to my arms, my beamish boy!" She chortled with joy as I jumped into her embrace, snuggling in warm maternal comfort. "Oh frabjous day! Callooh! Callay!!"

She planted a cold red kiss on my cheek, and I snuggled in her hair. It was ticklish and cool and smelled of tobacco smoke and musk and mink fur and Martinis, and the crisp, cool California winter night.

28. NIGHTMARES

"I ALSO HAD NIGHTMARES. SOMEHOW ALL THE FEELINGS
I DIDN'T FEEL WHEN EACH THING HAD ACTUALLY HAPPENED
TO ME, I DID FEEL WHEN I SLEPT."

—ANDREA DWORKIN

By the time the nightmares began, my mother's world had become a hellish battleground of warped instincts, festering resentments and fears, brooding complexes, and violent traumas; all the fun-filled ins and outs of that singular spiritual emotional maladjustment known as alcoholism; a deadly multi-generational plague I would come to know as The Curse.

As I learned the rules of the game, one cold October night I was jolted awake by a loud noise outside. I crawled out of bed and stood, shivering, in my pajamas, looking out the window. Mommy was down in the driveway, dressed in a glittering gold lamé evening gown, sitting in the passenger seat of a white convertible. She took a pull of Scotch as a bald guy in a suit tried to grab the bottle away. She twisted like a snake and took another sloppy swig, spilling booze down the front of her sparkly dress. Then the bottle broke and she jumped out of the car, hollering her lungs out. When I called out from the window, she looked up and cussed me out something fierce, telling me to shut the hell up and get back to bed. I jumped under the covers with my teddy bear and cried myself to sleep.

The first rule I learned that night was to keep my mouth shut, always, no matter what. The next rule was that there were no rules; because just when you thought you knew what they were, they changed. And it wasn't just a spectator sport. As soon as the Nowhere Man came along to join in the fun, I learned it was a game the whole family gets to play.

I guess my grandmother was right about that stuff on the TV giving me nightmares. Or maybe they came from somewhere else. Since I was a little boy, I used to have this one recurring dream. It was always the same. I would lie frozen in my bed, paralyzed, my mouth clamped shut, unable to move or cry for help. I tried to fight, but I couldn't budge. The Jabberwock had me! As I tossed and moaned in my sleep, the dark shadow would engulf me, pinning me to the bed. I struggled to cry out. Gasping for air, I tried to fight back as it bored down on me, sucking away my voice, my breath, smothering me and pulling me deeper. I fought hard, pushing up with all my might. Finally, with a mighty burst of strength, I would break free and bolt from the bed. My koala bear soared through the air as I scrambled down the long empty hallway and across an endless stretch of plush white carpet, screaming, crying.

"Mommy! Mommy!" Trembling, I flung the door open. Her room was empty. "Mom-my . . . ?" My voice sounded far away, like it was coming from a tiny animal's mouth in another place.

Her bed was unslept in. Tears ran down my face as I turned and rushed downstairs, then came to a halt before the big empty living room. I turned and ran back up the stairs. Maybe that's when I first became so good at running from the things I was afraid of—the first dark seed of an escapist character trait I would refine over the years, eventually coming to define the entire pattern of my life.

At the sound of breaking glass, I ran to the window in her room. Breathing hard, I could see her down below, raging, spitting, hissing like a wildcat, cussing. I kept quiet this time. As I looked on, their shouts merged in my head with a sound of pounding machinery, blending together into a booming din. I stood by the window looking out, covering my ears with both hands to make it stop. But the noise would never stop; those angry voices would echo and buzz in my head for a long, long time.

29. GUNSMOKE AND BALLOONS

Cigano sets the notebook down as if it suddenly weighs a hundred pounds. He closes his eyes and listens to his breath blending with the steady pounding of machinery from the port. After a while, he sits up like an archeologist finding an important clue to some musty old mystery.

"Shit! Hold on, I just remembered something." He grins, picking his pen up off the table and scribbling into the margin of the page. "My father's theme song for his band! Gotta write this shit down before I forget." He finishes and looks up with a triumphant smile. "The title of the thing was *Nightmare*. Hah! What a fuggin' life, kid."

He turns to another page and reads on.

O   O   O

My favorite picture book was called *The Red Balloon*. It was about a boy who had this big red balloon that was his best friend. One day he lost his balloon, and he was sad and lonely. The book was from France and the pages had all these different photographs like from a movie. In the end he got a bunch of new balloons, all different colors. He was standing on a rooftop holding them by their strings, and then he floated off with this big bouquet of balloons. I used to have these dreams where I'd be floating away with balloons. That's where it must have started, my desire to escape; a powerful lifelong compulsion to travel.

But I was always a restless kid. Confused. Alienated. And curious. I heard somewhere that cats always landed on their feet when they fell. I wanted to find out if it was true. It was. One day, I held my cat Swifty out my bedroom window. Looking up into a concrete winter sky, I took a deep breath and let him go. Poor old Swifty. I never meant to hurt him, but it was a long way down. One of the maids saw me and told my mother, and she made a big fuss over it. Swifty was okay. He just ran off and never came back. I don't think I even got a spanking. My mother always said she didn't believe in "discipline" like that. But there was a big squabble between her and Len over it. More angry voices. That's when they took me to see a head doctor.

The guy's office was littered with toys I didn't want to play with. He said something to my mother about me "acting out," and she wrote him a check and took me home. Walking to school the next morning, wandering those wide empty streets lined with big shiny parked cars, I wondered where Swifty had run off to. The streets of the neighborhood always seemed so cold and barren. There were never any people around, just a lot of empty cars sitting at the curb, big metal bubbles of isolation and solitude. I hated those stupid cars. I used to scratch their paint with my house key and spit on the windshields. As I got older, I'd puncture the tires with a switchblade and pry off their hood ornaments. The shiny colorful enamel Cadillac emblems were my favorites. I kept a collection of them in a cigar box under my bed.

At school, there was this ugly old nurse in a starched white uniform. She had a big hairy wart on her chin, like a witch. She stabbed me with a long silver needle and I cried. After that I didn't have much use for school. I can't remember it too well. I wasn't really there, I guess. I was just floating away, riding the winds with my colorful fantasy balloons, over Paris or Istanbul or Mexico; anywhere I could get away to, all alone in my head.

Besides my two cousins, I never had any friends or playmates. Shelley Winters had a little daughter about my age who would come over sometimes. But then my mother started a big fight with Shelley, like she did with everybody, and they stopped coming around. I spent a lot of time alone watching the TV. The only company I really had besides Grandma and Bozo the Clown and Captain Kangaroo were the maids. Since my mother wasn't home much, they would change the channel and I got to watch the grownup shows.

One day, I was sitting at the kitchen table with Louise, my favorite maid. She was a big fat colored mammy and she was real nice. Louise was my best friend in the whole world. We were watching one of those old TV Westerns called *Gunsmoke*. The show was about this little Indian girl the settlers had taken in after some mean cowboys killed her mommy and daddy. She was real pretty and she had a long black braid. Suddenly my mommy was there on the show. I rubbed my eyes. Mommy was dressed like a cowboy lady and she was being real mean to the little girl. I didn't understand what my mommy was doing in the television box. I guessed that since she wasn't home much, *that* must be where she went. But she didn't act like herself. Mommy was nice when she wasn't drinking. But this one in the TV set was just plain mean. She grabbed the little girl by her braid and dragged her over to one of the big tubs the horses drank out of. She shoved her down and held her under the water, drowning her! As tears rolled down my cheeks, Louise ran up and told me my mama was just "play-acting," but I was still pretty upset. I think that was when I first began not to trust my mother.

Grandma would come and sit in the kitchen with Louise, saying how it was a shame the way her daughter carried on, going out at night with all those dirty no-good Communists and sodomites. She was a godless floozy and a drunk and she'd end up in that Skid Row place, just like her no-good father. Later I asked my mother about why she was on the television doing mean things to little kids. She told Louise to put up the TV and that was the end of it. I thought it was 'cause she didn't want me to see her doing more bad stuff to kids. It was like she had some mean secret life. From then on, nothing she said or did could ever change that.

30. NAZI NURSEMAID

"THE TERM RAPE IS ORDINARILY USED IN REFERENCE TO THE
PHYSICAL, SEXUAL VIOLATION OF ANOTHER HUMAN BEING.
THERE ARE OTHER FORMS OF RAPE WHICH VIOLATE THE MIND
AND SPIRIT OF A HUMAN BEING IN WAYS WHICH MAY OR MAY
NOT LEAVE PHYSICAL MARKS. JAILS AND MENTAL HOSPITALS
ARE FULL OF PEOPLE WHO BEAR NO PHYSICAL MARKS TO
SHOW THE RAPE WHICH HAS TAKEN PLACE."

—DR. PAT ALLEN

After the television ban, Louise started listening to the radio. She
loved the rock 'n' roll station with Wolfman Jack. I would sit in the
kitchen while she cooked and cleaned, listening to Smokey Robinson
and the Miracles, Little Richard, Jackie Wilson, and Chubby Checker.
My favorite group was The Coasters. They had this song I loved about
a bad kid, a troublemaker named Charlie Brown. That became like
my theme song. "Walks in the classroom, cool and slow, who calls the
English teacher Daddy-O? He's gonna get caught, just you wait and see.
Why's everybody always picking on me?" That was my favorite, and
another one called *Yackety Yack*. Louise taught me how to do the Twist. I'd
sing and dance around the kitchen, and Louise would whoop and holler
with her big toothy smile when I shouted out the words I knew by heart.
"Yackety yack! Don't talk back!" Louise's favorite was Sam Cooke. One
day I came home from school and she was all excited. She'd heard on
the radio that Sam Cooke was appearing at the Shrine Auditorium
downtown, along with The Impressions, Sam and Dave, and all the best

colored radio stars. I begged her to let me go with her and she said she'd ask my mama. After that, it's all we talked about.

The night of the big show, she held my hand real tight as we moved through a sea of sweaty dark faces, right down to the front. It was a big deal. There were no white people there. Everyone was finger popping and jiving and singing along with the music. A curtain came up and Sam Cooke was standing in front of us in a shiny gold suit, like a god. He started singing, "Darlin' youuuuu send me," and the colored ladies all started screaming and crying. Louise was jumping up and down. I jumped and shouted too. I felt like I was in a big happy family. I loved that night more than anything.

I remember coming into the kitchen the next morning, feeling happy. I pulled the oven door open and sat on it, warming my butt while Louise sang with the radio. I would dream about going away to live with her and all the nice colored people who sang and danced and loved Sam Cooke. I wished I could be a little colored boy. Louise could be my mama, and Sam Cooke could be my daddy.

One day I came bouncing in after school and the kitchen was empty. Louise's radio was silent. I stood there listening to the refrigerator breathing, wondering what was going on. "Louise . . . ?" I called out. No answer. I ran through the house calling her name. I found her in her room, lying on her little bed, sobbing into the pillow. She told me Sam Cooke had been shot dead. I hated seeing Louise like that. Her big toothy smile was my sunshine and the whole world had just turned gray. A few days later my mother got drunk and started a big fight with Louise. I don't know what it was about, but I think Doris was jealous of her. Louise packed her stuff and left. She cried and held me close as she gave me a going-away present. She'd saved up and got me a pair of pretty wooden elephants to hold my picture books together. She was going to keep them for my birthday, she said, but now that she was going away she had to give them to me early. After that, I was alone again. Those two strong ebony African icons always reminded me of Louise and Sam Cooke when I sat in the empty kitchen on cloudy winter afternoons, warming my butt on the oven door, the sink cold and the refrigerator breathing, the rock 'n' roll radio silenced forever.

Growing up in Hollywood royalty wasn't all glamour. I was up in my mother's room one night, watching her get made up in the mirror for a party. This was before the Nowhere Man, before her drinking got real bad; before they stopped inviting her to parties. She'd just hired a new maid, a no-nonsense German nanny named Wolfie, to watch the beamish boy with echoes of angry yelling and pounding machinery banging around in his head. I didn't like Wolfie. She was ugly and she wore a starched white uniform like the mean nurse at school who stabbed me with the big long needle. I kept thinking about the creepy pictures of naked Jews, those dried-out ribcages and bony death grimaces all piled up in German concentration-camp death heaps. That's why the Nazis were bad, my mother always said. I looked up at her as she was putting on her makeup. "Is Wolfie a real Nazi, Mommy?"

"I don't know, dah-ling . . ." She gave me a funny smile in the mirror. "But you better be a good boy and mind Wolfie, just in case . . ."

It happened a few days later while my mother was out drinking with her friends. Wolfie was bathing me in the big white bathtub. I wanted my mommy to give me my bath. Wolfie told me "madam" wouldn't be home till late and to keep still. She scrubbed my ear so hard with the washcloth, it drew blood. I yelled out and splashed water on her starched white dress. Suddenly her big beefy knockwurst fingers were grabbing the back of my neck in an iron Nazi death grip as her big manly hand stuffed the clammy white washrag into my mouth and down my throat. "Ya! Now you von't scream, brat!" I struggled and my rubber ducky flew up into her chiseled face. That's when Wolfie pushed me underwater and held me there, squeezing my throat like I squeezed my ducky to fill it with water to squirt at the wall. She kept me down almost long enough for me to fill up with water like my ducky. A bar of Ivory soap floated overhead. The last thing I thought of was my mother dunking the little Indian girl on the TV. There was a warm golden light as my hands clutched at Wolfie's apron strings, and then I was holding on to a cluster of balloons, lifting me up out of the water till I was gone, floating far away.

I don't remember much else. But I never splashed water on Wolfie again.

The tattoo man takes a deep breath, mumbling to himself. "Stupid fucking clueless bastards . . ." Hearing his voice catch with a stifled sob, he looks up from the blurry page, feeling restless and uneasy.

31. THE CURSE OF A HUNDRED GENERATIONS

"VERY DEEP, SOMETIMES QUITE FORGOTTEN, DAMAGING
EMOTIONAL CONFLICTS PERSIST BELOW THE LEVEL OF
CONSCIOUSNESS. AT THE TIME OF THESE OCCURRENCES,
THEY MAY ACTUALLY HAVE GIVEN OUR EMOTIONS
VIOLENT TWISTS, WHICH HAVE SINCE DISCOLORED OUR
PERSONALITIES AND ALTERED OUR LIVES FOR THE WORSE."
—TWELVE STEPS AND TWELVE TRADITIONS

As the tattoo man reads on, a scene unfolds behind his eyes in a glowing amber fog: little Jono is tucked tight into bed. He's tossing around like a madman in a straitjacket. Out of the darkness of a dream, a handsome dark-haired man in a suit stands under a spotlight playing a clarinet. Multicolored balloons dance on the dark stage, undulating in swaying shadows like underwater vegetation. The boy runs up, grabs a big cluster, and floats away, high above rooftops, trees, and green rolling hills. Happy, joyous, free, he sees a fuzzy gray city skyline and the familiar words *a long time ago*. Rising up into pink cotton-candy clouds in a dark blue sky, a fresh wind blows in his hair as the sun's golden light warms his skin. But his hands grow tired and weak. He holds on with all his might. His fingers burn as the strings slip from his grasp. The sleeping boy clutches at his bedsheet as dream turns to nightmare. His hands let go and he falls into a cold, dark ocean. Sinking, deeper, deeper, water fills his mouth and lungs and he begins changing, morphing into a squidlike creature propelling itself through the murky depths. An ominous reptilian shadow appears and engulfs him, pulling him down, down. He struggles to escape, but he's paralyzed!

○   ○   ○

I was awakened by a piercing scream. *My* scream. Eyes open wide and gasping for air, crying and blubbering in terror, I bolted from the bed and ran down a long white-carpeted corridor that never seemed to end. The harder I ran, the farther I seemed to get from my mother's door. The Jabberwock was closing in from behind! I could feel its cold breath at the back of my neck as the sounds of pounding machinery filled my head, blending with the sinister music reverberating in the cold white empty hallway.

"Mommy, Daddy, Mommy, Daddy!" I burst through her door. The room trembled with the thunder of dark angry Jabberwock music from mad-eyed Russians. She was sitting all alone, wailing, spitting, drunk. Dancing with the demons. The Curse of a hundred generations. She turned and faced me with a heart-stopping scowl, her dark eyes glazed and possessed.

As I ran up, she put out a rigid hand, holding me back, regarding her beamish boy with a devastating glare. "*Daddy?!*" She growled with a merciless smirk. "*Da-ddy? Hah!* That's a laugh, boy! That bastard! I coulda had some career till that goddamn son of a bitch came along! Hah! And *you!* You even *look* like him! *Bastards!* And now you want your precious da-day?" Her tortured eyes glistened with poisonous hatred, two dark portals opening up into a hellish realm of cold, empty white silence. Tears welled up in my eyes as she raised a dramatic hand and railed on. "How sharper than a serpent's tooth it is to have a thankless child! Away, away!"

I was sobbing when Grandma Mabel rushed in, her voice raised over the music. "Sweet Jesus! What's all th' commotion here? My Gawd, Dah-ris, are ya deaf? Turn dat racket down already! Ya gonna give ya-self a heart attack!"

My mother pushed me away, screeching. "Go! Get the hell out of my sight! Both of you! Get out! *Out! Away, away!*"

Grandma led me off by my hand, out of the room and down the hall, muttering under her breath. "Just like her father, God pity his soul. Aghh, ya can't never talk to 'em when they're on a drunk!"

Grandma was never fazed by my mother's drunken scenes. She'd had a lifetime of it with a Gypsy husband who'd died in the gutter, leaving her with nothing but bad memories, four "temperamental" children, and an alcoholic Curse that would rage down through the generations like a caravan fire.

○   ○   ○

The tattoo man stops reading and lights a cigarette.

Jaco gives him a quizzical look. "Whatever happened to that babysitter who tried to drown you? Did you tell your mother?"

"I can't remember if I ever told her about that." Cigano looks up at the ceiling, rubbing his chin. "I don't think so. I didn't really trust the old lady, because of her drinking, y'know. She was so crazy and unpredictable; it was like growing up on a fucking minefield. And I was just a little kid. I didn't know *what* the fuck was going on, so I just kept things to myself . . ." He closes his eyes, struggling with the words. "But the old lady wasn't really evil or anything. She was just really sick, a hopeless alcoholic, poor thing. Messed up as she was, I always knew she loved me more than anything. Poor soul." He shakes his head. "She really did do the best she could. Her best just wasn't very good. Like most alkies, she couldn't get over her own childhood traumas, so she started drinking more and more, till . . ." He shrugs. "Hang on a minute." He picks up a pen and starts scribbling into the notebook. "Just remembered something. Gotta write it down here before I forget."

He stops and looks up. "I just added a little addendum to that part.

"'Sometime later,'" he reads, "'my mother and Wolfie locked horns over something, I don't remember what. Maybe I told her about the bathtub. All I remember is more angry voices, more blood, another ambulance. Even if you were a Nazi, you didn't want to fuck with my mother.'"

Cigano laughs out loud. "Sometimes ya just gotta laugh to keep from cryin'."

32. THE GYPSY

"WHEN THOU TILLEST THE GROUND, IT SHALL NOT
HENCEFORTH YIELD UNTO THEE HER STRENGTH; A FUGITIVE
AND A VAGABOND SHALT THOU BE IN THE EARTH."

—GENESIS 4:12

Jaco sighs. "I'm still curious to know more about your grandfather,
the Gypsy? I used to see Gypsy camps in Brazil, out in the country. The
men rode on horses, wearing hats and vests. Some of them had silver
buttons going down their pant legs like Spanish matadors. I remember
the women's colorful dresses and shawls, exotic-looking people, but so
secretive. I was always curious about their culture. That's why they call
you *'Cigano'* in Brazil, no? Because your grandfather was a Gypsy?"

"Yeah, well, I wrote some stuff about him, but nothing exotic like
that." The tattoo man laughs as he stands up and stretches. "Like I said,
I never knew him, but my mother totally worshiped him. She was his
favorite, that's what she always said. But she also feared him, I think,
because of his drinking. She never really said as much, but that's the
impression I got from things my grandmother said. By all accounts he was
a real nasty drunk. I always sensed he was real significant to my mother's
alcoholism." He stands staring out the window. "It's funny. I remember
talking to this psychic one time, an *Umbanda* medium in Brazil, this old
African *Mãe de Santo*. She went into a trance and told me she could see
a Gypsy standing behind me. When she told me what he looked like, I
realized it had to be my grandfather. She described him to a T from the

pictures I'd seen. She's the one who first told me I was a *filho de Ogum,* a son of *São Jorge.*" The tattoo man takes hold of the Saint George medallion hanging from his neck and kisses it. "She called me '*Cigano,*' but I never told her about having Gypsy blood. She just knew. She gave me this *guia* for protection, told me to always wear it." He looks down and fingers the long necklace of shiny red crystal beads hanging across his chest. "Then she told me some really fucked-up stuff about my grandfather's childhood back in Lithuania . . ."

"What sort of stuff?"

He frowns. "She said his mother, my great-grandmother, died in childbirth, and he'd been brought up by the men in his Gypsy clan, his father and uncles. They were like a gang of hit men, robbers, highwaymen. She told me he'd seen people being tortured and murdered when he was a kid. She got dizzy and nauseous. She felt so much pain and anguish around his spirit, she almost passed out. It all made sense to me from what I knew about him. My grandmother would talk about how he'd been in the Marines back in World War I. Maybe he did so good in the war 'cuz he already knew about killing. I remember asking different family members about his childhood, but they just told me he never talked about where he came from or anything before he came to America as a teenager. I always thought that was weird, y'know?"

"Nobody knew anything at all?"

"Not much. All they could tell me was that he was this charming con man, a scam artist. All I knew about him growing up was that he could charm the birds out of the trees. That's what my mother always said. Maybe that's where I got my larcenous streak. That's what my mother used to say, that I had 'larceny in my heart,' just like her pop. It's funny, 'cuz once I started digging a little deeper, it's like I was saying, how as soon as you start working with an intent, all this stuff just pops outta the woodwork? Well, that's what happened, it just fell into my hands. I stumbled across all this information about him and started piecing it together like a jigsaw puzzle."

Cigano leafs through another notebook. "Here's something I wrote that I put together from things my grandmother and Doris let slip out."

He begins reading again, conjuring up a shadowy vision of a ratty shotgun flat in a New York tenement slum, once upon a time, a long time ago. *A long time ago.* The words echo in the hazy golden air of his mind as he focuses on the page, which describes rows of clotheslines crisscrossing skeletal fire escapes and soot-blackened brick walls. A dingy yellow light shines from the window of a cramped cold-water apartment. Inside, a haggard young woman sits in a threadbare easy chair, reading a worn black Bible, as Harry and a pair of Gypsies stumble through the door, drunk, talking loud.

Young Mabel looks up, holding a finger to her mouth. "Harry, be quiet! Please, the children are sleeping. *Ssshhh."*

"Don't you shoosh me, woman! Go fix us some goddamn food. Go!"

Mabel knows better than to argue. She disappears into the kitchen.

Harry stumbles into the children's room, fumbling for the light switch. With a cocky expression on his booze-reddened face, he staggers over to where his ten-year-old daughter Doris is sleeping. He shakes her shoulder. "Hey! Wake up, my little princess!" Little Doris stirs, groggy, alarmed at the looming shadow. She can smell the liquor on him, the evil spirits of the Curse. Half asleep, she lies rooted to her bed taking short breaths, saying nothing. Harry shakes her again, twisting her arm. "Get up, Doris! I mean it! C'mon! Get 'em all up, and bring 'em in the front. Go! Now!!"

"Papa! Leggo!" She cowers. "You're hurting me. Cut it out!"

Muttering, the Gypsy fumbles in his coat pocket and pulls out a weathered snub-nosed revolver. Doris's eyes widen as he brandishes the gun in her face. "I said *now*, ya little whore, goddammit!"

Barely breathing, she gets up and shakes her older brother Robert, whispering, "Pssst! Get up! He's cockeyed again! And he's got that gun outta hock. C'mon! We gotta get out there . . ."

Under Harry's watchful eye, Doris and Robert herd their two siblings into the living room. The four groggy children stand in the doorway, shaking like cartoon mice in thin cotton nightgowns. They range from six to twelve. Harry staggers over and lines them up by height like dolls. Any hesitation results in his pointing the gun at them. "I been telling my friends about what fine good voices my kids got. They wanna hear ya singin' now. Go!" He waves the pistol around. "G'wan! Sing, goddammit! Now!"

Little Doris begins, poking her older brother in the ribs. He joins in and the four start singing in squeaky unison; it's a song they've learned at school. "My coun-try 'tis of thee, sweeeet land of libertyyyy."

Harry smirks with lopsided pride, taking another swig from a tarnished silver flask as Mabel cowers in a corner, quietly reciting the Ninety-first Psalm.

Cigano closes his notebook, feeling more compelled than ever to unravel the mystery of his maternal grandfather. He knows that somewhere in the life and death of this shadowy figure lie the roots of the Curse, the alcoholic plague that has followed him all his life. He riffles through his leather bag, flipping through a big manila envelope filled with old papers. He pulls out a folded page of delicate stationery covered in spidery handwriting. "Here's something my mother wrote." He squints at the paper. "Found it in that old box in her garage. It's dated 1976. Looks like the beginning of a letter to someone, talking about her family. Probably some fleeting attempt to get honest during one of her half-assed ventures into psychoanalysis." He sucks his teeth and reads.

> *I was born in Detroit, where my Pop was a car salesman for the Ford people or some such thing, probably a front for a somewhat less respectable vocation. The family moved to New York when I was a year or so old, so I was raised in New York City, the middle child of four. I had a three-year-older brother and sister, Robert and Connie, twins, and another brother, Richard, my junior by five years. What I was told in later years about the family goes something like this: Mother came from an Irish Catholic family, and my father was a Gypsy who came over on a boat from Lithuania. He was a Marine in World War One, and swept her off her feet at an Armory dance. She's regretted it ever since, but as she mellows with age, sometimes there's a sweet pleasure in her regret. One night, as the story goes, she went to a USO dance, and met this compelling young Marine, and although knowing nothing about him, married him shortly thereafter. Mother was lace-curtain Irish—soon to become "shanty" Irish, as she was summarily disowned from her genteel family for marrying a Greenhorn. She had two sisters and an older brother (shell-shocked, institutionalized victim of the war, seldom mentioned as I grew up). My mother and her siblings were raised by their grandmother. Their own mother was a refined lady who spoke French, played the piano, and couldn't stand the noise of children. She had a "delicate constitution," suffered what was politely referred to as a "nervous condition," and retired to a sanitarium when her children were still small. I never did get a clear picture of her father, my grandfather, beyond that he was hardworking, a gentleman, and died when Mother was in her teens. I think my grandmother's subsequent*

commitment depleted the family's resources and they were on the verge of genteel poverty by the time Mother met Pop.

Pop? What about my Pop? Liar, hustler, charmer, cheater, promoter, pipe dreamer, card-shark, criminal, and drunk. A full-blood Romany Gypsy, he originated in Lithuania, hitting the shores of New York in his early teens. One night when he was drunk, he told us his original name was Zilionis—too much trouble for the immigration authorities, so they renamed him Smith—or so he told our mother when, years into their marriage, she discovered, to her everlasting shame, that she had been tricked into marrying a "dirty no-good Gypsy." I doubt the Immigration people had anything to do with Pop's name change, though, since, ashamed of his Romany roots, he never presented himself to anyone as anything but a born-and-bred American. When he met Mother, he was a Chief Petty Officer.

Pop never spoke of his origin or his people, or anything having to do with his life before coming to America. It was as if it simply didn't exist. Well, along came the twins, Robert and Connie, and Mother was happy with her new babies. Pop, by all accounts, was a super hustler, and even though the true source of his income was always mysterious—and undoubtedly shady—the living was good. Then, along came me, and things were still okay. Pop was successfully selling stocks, supposedly. If he was really selling stocks at all, I imagine they were in phony gold mines or some-such larcenous activity. Then along came a baby brother, Richard, then the market crash and the Great Depression. Pop started coming home drunk, then stopped coming home at all. Finally, he was sent off to Sing Sing. He was never the same after that. By the time he got out of prison, I was working in Hollywood and Italy. He disappeared on the Bowery. My older brother Robert tried to track him down, without success. Nobody knows how or when or where he died, but he'd been destitute for a long time by then. Poor Pop.

33. X MARKS THE SPOT

"THE FACTS ARE TO BLAME, MY FRIEND. WE ARE ALL
IMPRISONED BY FACTS: I WAS BORN, I EXIST."

—LUIGI PIRANDELLO

Cigano talks at Jaco over his shoulder as he pulls out a stack of
yellowed typewritten pages. "I've started to piece together a portrait of
him from these stories I told you about." Cigano grins. "Thankfully, my
uncle Robert wrote about him a lot. Seems Robert was pretty close to his
father, in a weird kinda love-hate way. Anyway, there's all these old short
stories." He unfolds a stack of papers. "Check it out."

X MARKS THE SPOT— BY ROBERT SMITH

*I didn't know what my father did. I guess most children don't really
know what their fathers do; some sort of funny notion about going to
work. When he was around, my father went to a mysterious "office"
every morning, and that was it. In the evening, he'd come home,
usually bringing the paper with him.*

*At the time, a sensational murder case was all over the front page:
"The 3X Killer Strikes Again." My parents would sit in the living
room and talk about the news, while we kids grabbed the comics in the
back section and read them lying on the living-room floor. And since
they were talking about the 3X killer, of course we became fascinated
and read about it too. There were photographs of how the murders*

*took place, around Times Square, I think. The victims would get a
letter with an X on a sheet of paper. The newspaper pictures showed
how the victim would emerge from a building in the evening and begin
walking. He would start to cross the street between intervals of traffic
and then be gunned down in the middle of the street. Little white
dotted lines illustrated the victim's progress from his emergence from
the building to his body lying in the gutter. Next to the body, at the end
of the white dashes was a large X enclosed in a circle. The caption
read: "X MARKS THE SPOT." The killer was sending letters to
the newspaper, announcing when he would strike again, and always
signing each message: 3X.*

*I came home from school one day, opened the mailbox, and brought
up the mail. A letter had arrived for my father. When he returned in
the evening, my mother showed it to him, her face drawn and pale. On
a single sheet of paper was written: "X MARKS THE SPOT." My
mother was worried. My father dismissed the whole thing as a joke*

*She persisted in her fears, my father telling her to forget the whole
thing. Nothing happened, but I think it was about then that I began to
have vague suspicions that my father had some kind of connection with
the underworld. Names were continually mentioned in hushed tones. I
had the impression they were both mysterious and dangerous.*

"Wow!" Jaco hands the story back. "That's a strange story."

"Oh, that's just the tip of the iceberg, brother!" Cigano guffaws,
folding the page and opening another. "Listen to this one."

HARRY GETS 'BLIND DRUNK' – BY ROBERT SMITH

*Robert opened his eyes to darkness and the sound of a man's hoarse
shout. Groggy, he reached out for his father. The short, strange yell
was repeated. He felt over the mattress where his father slept. There
was only space. He was alone. Now, it came as a rapid succession of
quick, guttural grunts. Wide awake, he listened, straining to apprehend
some element of the familiar, some reassurance in the dark.*

*That baritone resonance sounded again, made clear as song by its
note of terror. "Don't! Don't let it get me! Hunh, hunh. Stay away!
Hunh, hunh, hunh, stay away!" There was the crash of a chair, a
series of wild, incomprehensible thuddings against the floor.*

Robert lay still, rigid. Then, catching his breath, he eased out of bed. In the dining room, he saw him—not clearly at first—crouched behind a chair in undershirt and shorts. Breathing with an abnormal noisy sibilance, his father clutched the chair, rattling it on the floor. Robert's scalp crinkled, a shiver going up his spine. But it had nothing to do with his mother. She wasn't there. The boy began to feel easier. He's insane, he thought. There was a curious kind of consolation in the thought.

"Keep away!" Harry swung the chair around, using it as a shield against some unseen tormentor. "Keep away," he shouted. "Mabel! Tell her to keep away! Mabel!"

The light was snapped on. Robert saw him clearly then. His mad gray eyes opened wide, staring. His hair seemed wet, plastered down. Long strands, very black, fell over his brow and curved about the side of his face. His jaw was slack, a trace of saliva at the corner of his partly opened mouth. He looked around, dazed, in the sudden clarity of light. Then he began to whimper, a low-pitched, grunting, anthropoid sound.

"What are you doing on the floor?" Mabel barked. "For God's sake, man, what's the matter?" She stood in the opposite entrance to the dining room, a slender, very pale apparition in a long white flannel nightgown. "Whaddya making all that racket about?"

Harry saw her and jumped comically back. "Stay away!" he shouted, then scrambled behind another chair, crashing against the table.

"Stop it!" Robert's mother barked. "For God's sake, what's the matter with you?"

"Mabel? Is that you, Mabel?" He craned his neck forward and peered ludicrously like a sick turtle. His head swung around and pointed far off into the corner, quaking. "Your crazy mother's come back from the grave, Mabel. Don't let her get me! Oh God! She's after me! Mabel, she's after me!" He scrambled around again, making those strange grunting sounds, then went darting into the other room. Robert could hear him, shouting. "No, don't let her get me! There she is, over there! Don't you see her? Oh God, Mabel! Don't let her get me!"

"There's nobody there." Her voice was flattened, overawed, stunned.

When Robert entered, Harry was crouched behind the sofa. He approached and touched his father's bare arm. Harry sprang up and grabbed the boy's wrist. "Who'zat?" he gasped, staring him in the face.

"It's me. Robert." The boy struggled to pull his hand free. "Pop," *he pleaded, trying to loosen his father's steely grip. "Pop, cut it out."*

"Izz'at you, son?"

"Yes," he said, almost whining. He felt foolish and afraid.

His father pressed forward, a stupid wide-eyed question on his face. "Is that you, Robert?"

"Yes," said the boy, prying at the hand. "You're hurting my wrist, Pop." He glanced at his mother and two sisters, who were crowded in the doorway, watching with frightened faces. He made a grimace of annoyance and waved them away.

"What's the matter with him?" his mother asked.

"Nothing!" Robert snapped. "Go on to bed."

"You shut up! Don't talk to me like that!"

Harry jumped, startled. "Who'zat?" he said, clutching Robert. He jerked himself around in their direction. The girls shrank back. But apparently he hadn't seen them.

"Nobody," Robert said. "C'mon, Pop, let's go back to bed."

Robert was upset by their standing there—what did they want? Why didn't they beat it? But he was deeply embarrassed, aware of the fact that his father, dressed only in shorts, was exposing himself. There was something humiliating about their standing there, watching.

"Is that you, Robert?" his father asked again.

"Yes, Pop." He groaned. "Come on."

"Take care of me, son. Take care of me."

"Okay, Pop, I'll take care of you."

Harry began to grope for his face. Robert pulled back.

"Where are you? I can't see anything," Harry cried. "Put the light on, Robert."

"The light is on."

"No." He shook his head. "It's dark. I can't see." He frowned and glanced vacantly toward Robert. His voice was choked, grotesquely pathetic. "Is . . . is . . . the light on?"

"Yes," said Robert, shutting his eyes. "The light's on."

Twisting his face into an exaggerated question, his father repeated his words. "The light's on?" Then nodding in a stutter of facing the incomprehensible, he said it again. "The . . . the light's . . . on?"

"Yes." Robert sighed. "The light's on."

"But Robert." Harry shook his head. He swallowed with emotion, and spoke again. "Robert, I, I can't see. Robert, I, I can't."

He covered his face with his hands.

The boy gazed at him, feeling helpless and cold. How long was this going to go on? He slid an arm around his father's shoulder and tried to lift him. "C'mon, let's go to bed." It was like trying to move a wall.

Harry pulled back. "Ya don't understand!" he shouted. "Can't you understand? Can't ya see what's the matter? Robert, I'm blind! Can't ya see I'm blind?" He began to cry.

"It's just temporary, Pop."

Still sobbing, Harry rose to his feet. "Help me into the kitchen, son." He threw an arm over the boy's shoulder and Robert staggered along under his father's erratic lurches. They made their way into the kitchen. Robert guided him down into a chair next to the table.

"Pssssst!" His mother in the hall signaled to him. "Pssssst."

Robert looked at her and shook his head.

"Is the light on?" Harry demanded.

"Yes, the light's on."

He shook his head hopelessly. "Robert, I can't see anything."

"Pssst!" His mother called again. Again, Robert shook his head.

Breathing hard, Harry seemed to be trying to get a grip on himself. He let out a deep sigh and straightened, his voice suddenly firm. "Hold your hand in front of my face, son."

Robert passed his hand before the staring eyes. "Do you see it, Pop?"

Harry shook his head, his mouth a sag of despair. "No-oo!"

Robert was about to turn and see what his mother wanted, when Harry spoke again. "Try it again. Hold up four fingers."

Robert held his hand up. "Do you see it?"

"No." Harry's voice broke and he buried his face in both hands, moaning. "No, no, no, God! I'm blind! What's to become of everybody? What's to become of everybody? God has punished me, Robert! I'm blind!" He began to cry uncontrollably.

Robert slipped away and went over to his mother, as she pestered and whined. "What's the matter with him?"

The boy shrugged. "I don't know. He says he can't see."

"You better get an ambulance."

Robert spoke back in an intense whisper. "He's faking!"

"Get your clothes on," she told him, "and go out and call

an ambulance."

"Okay." He didn't feel like arguing. And the possibility of his father spending the rest of the night in a hospital, the possibility of his not being there, seemed wonderful. He hurried into his clothes. His mother handed him a nickel.

"What do I say?"

"Say your father's gone blind! G'wan!" She shoved him to the door.

He could hear his father moaning, lamenting the fate of the family as he left. Going down the stairs, Robert felt there was no chance of his father being taken to the hospital. He suddenly hated the idea of making the call. People would see an ambulance in front of the building. And what would the doctor and everyone say? Going to all that trouble just for a drunk! But it was nice to be out in the cold night air. The quietness was soothing. He wished he could just keep walking all night. But his mother was up there with his father, and Robert was suddenly worried. He went into the drug store, entered a phone booth and made the call.

Returning to the apartment, Robert found his mother and two sisters hovering around Harry. His father seemed subdued now, sad, gripped in the somber awareness of the whole tragic scene. Blind. He spoke in gentle, appreciative tones, clutching the two little girls to him. "That's all right. Don't worry about me. That's all right, dollings."

Connie turned and saw Robert. "Did you call the ambulance?"

He nodded.

"Who'zat?" Harry moved his head like a blind man. "Who'zat?"

"Me, Pop."

"Is that you, Robert?"

"Yes, Pop."

"C'mere, son."

"Okay, Pop. Wait'll I take my jacket off."

As he started back for the closet, his mother intercepted him. "Did you call them?" she asked.

"Yes, they ought to be here soon." Robert was suddenly tired, sick of everything. "He's faking," he said dully.

"What do you mean, faking?" his mother snapped. "He's blind! He can't see anything."

"Arrgghhh!" Robert pulled back, waving her off.

"Well, I'm sorry, mister, but you don't know everything."

"I know he's keeping everybody awake again," he sneered as he started to take off his jacket.

She stopped him. "You'd better go down and wait for them. I don't want them ringing every bell in the building again."

"Okay." He turned and headed for the door. As he stepped into the hall, he heard his father calling him. He closed the door and ran.

Outside again, Robert sat on the stoop, his hands thrust into the side pockets of his jacket, shivering in the cold night air, wishing he were in bed. But he was glad to be out of the apartment. He wished he never had to go back. And he was already suffering the embarrassment of facing the men who would arrive with the ambulance. He wanted to hide. He felt a rise of excitement as they entered the block, the red light flashing importantly as they pulled over in front of the building. Attracting attention again! he thought, with a quick glance over the deserted street.

As they started up the steps, he said, "Are you looking for Smith?"

"You call an ambulance?"

"It's upstairs."

They made no attempt to lower their voices, and it seemed to Robert that the noise they were making could be heard throughout the entire street. He tried to explain that his father couldn't see.

One of the men said, "Is he drunk?"

Robert hesitated, then nodded. "Yes."

And then they were all crowding into the apartment, important and officious, taking over. His mother and sisters faded back in a hush. His little sister, Doris, peered at them and giggled.

They confronted Harry in the kitchen. "What seems to be the trouble?" went the booming voice.

A different tone to his father's voice; still subdued, but there was a challenging ring. He was talking to strangers, and that peculiar maudlin thickness vanished. He sounded almost reasonable; a trifle pompous.

Robert eased himself out of the kitchen and listened from the living room, hoping they'd just take him away. The voices were indistinct, confused. A silence. And then Robert caught a final note. "Well, it's up to you, but the smartest thing to do is to go to the hospital."

"No, no!" He heard his father cut in. "That's all right, boys." He heard the scrape of the chair, a shuffling of feet, sounds that he recognized as their getting ready to leave. With a sinking sensation, Robert moved closer to the hall, his eyes tremulously blurred. That dirty lying son-of-a-bitch, he felt with a rush. That dirty liar. Liar!

"You're the boss," one of the men said. "We can't make you go if you don't want to."

Accompanying them to the door, Harry was the expansive man of the world. "Thanks for all the trouble, fellas. Appreciate it. I really do appreciate. But I'm perfectly all right."

They're leaving! Goddammit. They're leaving. And now we'll have to spend the rest of the night, the whole night, with his talking and raving. Robert felt as though he couldn't put up with it anymore. And he knew that the moment they left, the whole idiot routine would start again. He followed morosely into the hall.

The door buzzer suddenly sounded, and there were the brass buttons and blue coats of two cops, shoving the half-open door wider. The police, he remembered with a sinking dread, always answered all the ambulance calls. They greeted the driver and attendant, asking what was up. The narrow hall was suddenly crowded. The men seemed gigantic. Talking loudly, the cops were filled in on the story.

"You're sure you don't want to go to the hospital?" one of the cops asked Harry.

Harry's jaw was tight. He spoke in a low, menacing tone. "I don't see where that's any of your goddamn business."

"Now wait a minute!" The other cop cut in. "All we asked is a civil question."

"A civil question . . ." Harry spoke softly, nodding. His voice was still low and he talked through clenched teeth. "Who gave you dirty bastards permission to come into this house?" He moved close to them.

"Hey! Watch your language! Watch your language, fella!"

Robert, to the rear of the men, farther back in the hall, shrank against the wall, amazed. What was he saying? Who did he think he was? The impulse surged up in him. Go on then, go on! Get yourself arrested again. Get yourself arrested!

"Get out!" His father was growling. "Get out!" His voice got louder and nastier each time he repeated it. "Get the hell outta my fucking house, ya dirty no-good sons-a-bitches!"

"Now listen, we're going to take you in if you don't behave . . ."

Robert noticed them shift position, moving apart. He saw how *they let their clubs slide down into their hands, the thongs catching their wrists, their grips tightening over the handles.*

"So, you're going to take me in?" His father grumbled sarcastically, looking from one to the other. "Big men. Going to take me in, huh? Got a badge and carry a gun. Take off that fucking uniform and I could beat the shit out of both of you bums. Now get out, before I throw yez out."

"Okay," one cop said, "that's it. Get your clothes on." He grabbed Harry by the arm.

Harry stood stock still. "Get your hands off me," he said, tightly. "Just get your clothes on . . ." The cop jerked Harry's arm.

There was hardly room in the narrow enclosure to move around. Robert held his breath as he watched. Harry twisted away like a snake, swayed back, and brought around a hard fast punch at the cop's head, slamming him against the wall.

For Robert, barely a few feet away, the nightmarish fight had begun. The three of them were wrestling around, crashing against the wall. Harry, getting an arm free, tried to throw another punch. The cops' hats were knocked to the floor, and for the space of a few seconds, they backed off slightly. Then, a club came whirling around and cracked Harry across the face, covering it with blood. Harry closed and grappled with the cop. The other cop swung his club against the back of Harry's head. The loud, hollow clunk seemed to reverberate in Robert's ears. The cop hit him again. And then the two of them were beating him down. Harry, on one knee, was struggling to push himself up against them. This time both cops had an arm free. Before Harry could make it to his feet, they were bringing the heavy clubs down in long, savage swings, cracking him solidly across the head, each time with an ugly, incredibly loud, resounding clunk. Harry kneeled motionless. One after the other, whack, whack, whack, everything they had behind each swing, the clubs kept coming down. He didn't fall. He just stayed in the same position. His head was covered with blood. With each crack of the club, blood would spatter all over. Patches of hair flew from his scalp. It had to kill him! How could anyone stand it? He didn't go down, and they just kept it up.

For Robert, it seemed to go on, and on, and on. The cops were breathing heavily. The walls were splattered red. Harry suddenly lunged up after them again. He swung and missed. He was knocked over and one cop went down on top of him. Robert saw Harry's face squeezed tightly against the floor, being ground down under the cop's knee, all twisted out of shape. The other cop slipped a handcuff over his wrist. Agony came over Harry's face as the cop tightened the cuffs. And his mouth, barely able to get a sound out, his face unrecognizable. "All righ', aw righh', 'at's enough," he slurred, finally defeated.

They lifted him. He stood swaying on his feet; Robert couldn't understand how he was still able to stand at all.

One of the cops turned to him. "Go get his overcoat, son."

Robert went to bed alone that night, as he had so fervently wanted to. He lay there in misery, unable to sleep. Unable to cry.

34. A TRIP DOWNTOWN

"IT IS A SIN TO BELIEVE EVIL OF OTHERS, BUT IT IS
SELDOM A MISTAKE."

–H.L. MENCKEN

"Jesus!" Cigano shakes his head. "Growing up with that kinda shit
going on, no wonder my mother was so messed up! And I thought I had
it bad as a kid." He unfolds another page. "Listen to this next one . . ."

A TRIP DOWNTOWN – BY ROBERT SMITH

*His mother was standing in the kitchen in a ragged-looking cotton
housedress, doing something to the sweater she held in her hands.*

*"Hi." Robert greeted her, walking in. She peered up at him as he
leaned against the sink. She turned her attention back to the sweater.*

"Did you eat?" She spoke out of the side of her mouth.

"Nah. I'm not hungry."

*She looked up at him again, wearily exasperated. "I can fix ya
something."*

"I don't want anything, Ma. I'm not hungry."

*She breathed deeply and placed the sweater on the shelf beneath
the cupboard. She filled a pan with water, placed it on the stove, and lit
the gas, then occupied herself with cutting up a head of cabbage.*

"What about Pop?" he asked.

"I don't know." She spoke listlessly. "I'm sure I don't know

anything about it."

"Well, what did he do?"

"He's in jail again. In the Tombs." She began fixing tea. "That's all I know about it."

Robert crossed his arms. His lips were compressed.

"Your father's in a lot of trouble this time, I can tell you that. A man was around here asking questions. I don't know. Why come to me?" She made a brushing movement with her hand. "I don't know anything about what that man does. He doesn't bring in any money. He doesn't support his four children."

"Who? Who was around?"

She enunciated carefully, giving the appearance of a stiff smile to her mouth. "A po-lice de-tect-ive was around."

"What did you say? What did he want?"

"I told him about your father. I told him about what I've had to put up with here, the abuse I've taken." A self-dramatizing note of wonder came into her voice and she shook her head. "'Madam,' he said, 'I don't know how you ever stood it. I don't know how you ever put up with that no-good bum. Well, he won't bother you again'." She nodded, a question wrinkling her brow. "You know, he's known."

Robert was irritated. "What do you mean, 'known'?"

"Well, f'cryin' out loud, he's got a police record!"

The boy began to breathe fast. He didn't know what to say. Something had happened, something remote and unreal, something his father did in his mysterious life beyond the house. It was hard to grasp the idea of what went on beyond the door of the apartment, as his father had no tangible existence at home anymore. He knew the door wouldn't open again. Something mysterious had occurred out there, and the return back from that emptiness into which his father daily disappeared was barred forever now. He stood there, unable to feel sympathy or concern. Whatever had taken place had happened away from his own experience.

His mother was drinking tea. There was a fear in him—a sense of the irrevocable. An erratic shift of breeze from his father's world had passed unnoticed into the house, erasing a family. They were talking in the same tones, but something had changed forever. He was vaguely conscious of the door; and conscious of his mother's presence—her puttering about.

Finally she peered up at him and asked, in a curiously reticent prying tone, "Do you want to go down to see him?"

He shrugged. "Well, sure."

"I think someone ought to go down there."

"Did you visit him?" he asked her.

She pursed her lips. "I haven't got the time."

"Well, didn't anyone go see him, for chrissakes?"

His mother glared at him. "Just watch your language, mister. You're not out on the streets."

"Didn't anyone go see him?"

"I don't think it's a very nice place for your sisters to go. It's not the most respectable place in ihe world, ya know."

He looked at her. "You mean no one's even paid him a visit?"

"Doris isn't old enough. She's not permitted. Constance goes to see him. Tssk!" She shook her head. "I'm sorry, but I don't approve of a young girl going to a place like that."

He nodded, his lips set, no longer listening. Without Harry, what would his mother become? A persistent accusation, monotonous and dim—someone alone.

As Robert approached the Tombs, he remembered the familiar neighborhood; the same part of town where his father once had an office, where he set up shop for his mysterious comings and goings. One-Twenty Wall Street. It was strange that he was still able to remember. He must have been only four or five at the time—not much more. There was a blond lady. He remembered playing with the typewriter. When he left with his father, Robert had carried a writing pad and a whole box of yellow pencils. The streets had been deserted; it was close to evening. And now that he thought of it, it could only have happened late on a Sunday afternoon. The memory of those big, intimidating streets was strong. It had taken the massive reassuring grip of his father's hand to keep him from terror. They had walked along, the two of them. There was no one else; nothing stirred. There were sides of buildings and no sky; no people, not a city—a strange, empty world of walls and imposing gray angles. Fragments of that short excursion returned to him now, and with it a vague shadow of dread.

In the formidable hollowness of the area, the Tombs was an anachronism; its high walls of heavy stone blocks seemed curiously warm. He rounded the corner and saw a gathering of people near the big green metal door at the base of the wall. A sign in gold lettering said: "Visitor's Entrance." It was too early. He walked a short distance beyond the group and, lighting a cigarette, leaned against the railing. Most of the visitors were women. After a while, a movement began. He walked back and joined the line, which had started to form.

Just within the entrance, a guard sat on a high stool, a ledger opened on the stand before him. Robert told him his name and assured him he was over sixteen. It was his father he was visiting.

"Sign here."

Robert signed. The guard extended an arm. "Follow the arrow around to the right."

Bars ran from ceiling to floor, cramping space, forming a maze. It was like being caught in an overcrowded zoo, where it had become difficult to tell which were the cages. One had the uncomfortable feeling that the bars included you. And the noise was incredible, out of all proportion to the number of people. The voices were excited, shrieking; a weird amplification of some violence and confusion that seemed to be taking place nearby. He looked around. The placid faces of the guards—the lack of concern on their faces. A riot must be taking place just around the corner, he thought, hidden from view, and they didn't care. Or this was a scene from a dream, which would soon become frightening.

A guard glanced at his pass and led him down a long aisle of booths to an unoccupied cubicle. The din was deafening. He was told to wait. Peering through a heavy grilled screen, he saw another row of stalls, similarly screened and sectioned off. A guard strolled along the space between the two rows of booths. Beneath him, a sign: "Do not push anything through screen." The prisoners were on one side of the aisle, visitors on the other. In order to talk it was necessary to shout, and since the room was filled with people, everyone was in competition with everyone else. Sixty people in a long, narrow enclosure, shouting through screens across a six-foot aisle at someone behind the screen. The intensity and violence of the noise seemed an insane, frenzied struggle for speech; a primitive battle to be heard. Robert wasn't certain whether or not there was anyone in the opposite cubicle. Then, some figures appeared. A gate in the background swung open and his father, little more than a silhouette, materialized against the screen.

"Hello, Pop," Robert shouted and, because of the need for

shouting, was unable to even smile a greeting.

"Hello, son," his father yelled back.

"How are you?"

The question seemed to irritate Harry. He nodded quickly, perfunctorily. "I'm all right. I'm all right. Listen." He glanced around in annoyance. "Listen, will you tell your mother to come down here?" He pressed forward and spoke louder. "It's very important I see her, got it?"

"I'll tell her," Robert yelled. "Do you need anything?"

"I need some money. I got no cigarettes."

"I've got two dollars. That's all I have."

"Take it around . . ." He stopped and looked around in annoyance, then began again. "Take it around the corner and give it to the man at the desk. That's a good boy."

"Okay, Pop." He took a breath. "What happened? What's this about?"

His father shook his head, his mouth open, an anguished squint on his face. "I'm being framed," he shouted. "I'm the fall guy, the sucker. I didn't get a cent of that goddamn money. Those lousy sons-a-bitches cleared out and left me holding the goddamn bag. Your mother has to do something. She's gotta get me out of here. I want her to go see some people. She can raise the money for bail. I've got to talk to her." He was agitated. "I've got to get out of here. Court'll be adjourned for the summer and I'll have to spend three months in this goddamn hole before I'm even tried. Tell your mother to get the hell down here, will ya?"

"I'll tell her, Pop. I'll tell her." But even as he said it, he knew it was useless. His mother would piously proclaim her own innocence: "It has nothing to do with me. What can I do?" And she'd probably be right. The chilling thought, even then, was that she wouldn't even try. He didn't know what to say. "Do you get any exercise?" he asked.

"No. No. This is a terrible place. Terrible."

They were both silent. The yelling and shouting all around them was beginning to upset them both. His father shook his head and, pointing around, indicated that it was useless to try to talk.

"Okay, son, take care of yourself."

"I will. I hope everything turns out all right."

His father nodded, waved, then turned and beckoned to the guard.

"Good-bye, Pop."

"Good-bye, son. Be a good boy."

The guard opened the door. As Robert saw Harry pass next to the guard, he was struck by the difference in size between the two men. The guard seemed to tower above Harry. His father had somehow become smaller than he could ever remember him being. For the first time in his life, his father seemed frail. Robert turned to leave, a sinking sensation clawing at the pit of his stomach.

35. THE LAST TIME

"DON'T TALK, DON'T TRUST, DON'T FEEL."

—CLAUDIA BLACK

Cigano stops reading and sighs. He looks up at his young listener. The kid appears to be in a trance. The tattoo man shuffles through more pages, grimacing as he looks into the weird typewritten communications from another world, another time, a long time ago. He lights a cigarette, then pulls out another stack of papers. "This one's pretty tragic."

THE LAST TIME I SAW POP – BY ROBERT SMITH

His face was beginning to seem wizened, Robert thought. A Tartar's face. Bronzed. Strongly defined cheekbones with the smooth shine of a red apple. Yes, and the eyes were slanted. Near the corners, the radiation of fine lines were a tiny fan; long, thin pencil marks drawn straight across his brow, permanent now, even without the habitual frown. As the years were added, the skin had been drawn tighter, until his face, more and more now, approximated a skull. None of the sags and folds that were the ugliness of the old were there. Still, the violence was in his gestures; an anger without direction.

Baring his teeth, Harry broke the roll and buttered it. "Here." He thrust half across the table at Robert.

"I'm not hungry."

"Eat it!"

"No." Robert let out a nervous laugh. *"I'm not hungry."*

"Eat it," his father snarled.

Robert shook his head. Harry shrugged and stuffed his mouth. As Robert sat opposite him in the Automat, he watched his father with solemn eyes, not trying to formulate anything. But his eyes were hollowed and dark. The mask of Robert was watching, an observing that has nothing to do with any of the reasons of seeing, but is statement and question and fact itself. I see. I see. A silence is in me. There is nothing I can say. My feeling means nothing. Words are gone. Everything is through, and now all I can do is see.

As he listened to Harry's positive, contrite, domineering tone, the necessity began, the ritual process of his father building himself up again. He will never hear me, no matter what I say. He's never heard me. He's never heard a fucking word I've said. He knew he could never ask for his father's understanding. He knew he could never talk to the man. He wanted to reach across the table and beat his face in. He wanted to shake him by the throat. He wanted to shout. Listen to me, you son-of-a-bitch! Listen to me! Just shut the hell up and listen, goddam you!

He looked at Harry with tight lips. He heard his father's voice, paying no attention to the words. Robert watched the face. Harry was talking, eyebrows slightly lifted, the expression composed, slightly harassed but also somewhat tranquil; eyes shaded, cast downward, reflective, unseeing; without luster. The attentive tilt of his head; attention paid only to what he himself said. Words, their soft lulling resonance of reason and logic. Robert listened coldly, hostile, not giving a damn what he said. Harry wasn't speaking to Robert anyway. The words were cast up in front of him, were made to resound as a force against silence; an inner voice spoken. Robert was there only to add substance to Harry's latest fantasy. How could the man hear anyone? The realization infuriated Robert as nothing else he could have done. And it carried with it the years of lies, broken promises, the lifetime of self-deception, which had brought ruin to anyone who ever trusted the man, and misery for those who depended upon him. Robert could've reached over and hit him. Instead, he leaned back in his chair and lit a cigarette. His breathing was shallow, but he watched Harry steadily as he talked.

"All I need is a stake! Now this!" Harry slapped the envelope,

twisting down the corners of his lips in speculative approval. "There's a good thing. Good for three—four—hundred a week! I stay up there in the Catskills a couple months, and I got a stake! That's all I need. With a couple thousand dollars in my pocket, I'm back in business, business! Up there, ya get everything for nothing. Ya got the country." He looked angry and shook his head. "An' no drinking! Listen, I'm through. Ho ho!" He looked squarely at Robert. "I'm through with . . ." He waved his hand, his face showing disgust. "Oh, I've had enough. More than enough. In the fall I got me a stake. I'll come back to the city and start a corporation, and there'll be plenty for all. Plenty! Listen!" His voice grew belligerent. "I made it before an' I'll make it again. Couple thousand dollars!" He wrinkled up his face. "I get myself a front. I can start operating again." He looked toward Robert and waved his distaste in the air of the Automat. "No more of this cheap fucking shit . . ."

"Yeah, Harry. Look, what time you gotta leave?"

"I get a bus at four thirty."

O   O   O

"Hey, Bob!"

Walking north along the Bowery, I stopped, caught like a guilty child stealing away. I swung around and saw my father hurrying toward me, momentarily stalled by two colored hobos who stopped on the sidewalk.

"Hey, Bob!" He called again, louder and sharper as he emerged from between the coloreds, edging his way past—a little roughly, frantic. His eyes lit on me as I stood there reluctantly, waiting for him to catch up. The look on his face was haunted. He seemed jaundiced, the eyes underscoring a shallow hollowness. He came up, breathing heavy. His face was dirty and the cheeks were sunken. The gray unshaven jaw put years on him. He looked at me, caught his breath. His head tilted up. The tip of his tongue touched his dry lips, and he said nothing.

"Hello, Pop." My voice was slow, matter-of-fact. I was staring at him.

The shift of emotion that took over his face seemed an expression as simple as relief. That slight movement of his raising up as he drew *in a deep breath was much more than the fading of anxiety from his expression. That instant of something disappearing from his face was something I couldn't permit myself to feel. I turned away and began to walk slowly, he at my side. I was stalling—I didn't want to recognize yet that I felt empty and helpless. I felt an enormous distance. He wore a soiled shirt. Unshaven, hollow-cheeked, a red welt on one side of a sallow face, the lips colorless and thin. How strange! Harry's biggest concern, all his life, no matter what the circumstances were, was to always appear neat and clean. He put faith in the necessity for a respectable front. "Appearance, appearance, look at your appearance," he would always tell me. Now, that unfamiliar spectacle of total inadequacy and defeat stirred irrational extremes in me. It wasn't grief that I experienced. It was a horror that I hadn't quite succeeded in blotting out. The moment he saw me there on the Bowery, I realized, wasn't just relief. I saw Death leave his face at the very sight of me.*

Suddenly, I was looking full at his face, a helpless face, a poor, unhappy wretch, made even more pitiable in the rage his voice raised in me; made even more conspicuously broken. And with a rush of feeling, I recognized in his baffled bluster of anger an asking for help. He had never known how to ask. Then, as quickly as it had been called up, that dark rage was gone, and I was overwhelmed with a sense of love. I reached in my pocket and pulled out a five-dollar bill. I handed it to him. The victim I had always carried with me was gone forever. No retribution was possible. I could only attack him by attacking the image of my father that dwelt within myself.

"Man!" Cigano takes a deep drag and sighs out a cloud of smoke, stubbing out the cigarette. "Reading this stuff is like, I dunno, man, it's like seeing ghosts . . . "

He pulls another thick stack of loose pages from the bag.

36. THE BAD SIDE

"THERE ARE SOME SOLITARY WRETCHES WHO SEEM TO
HAVE LEFT THE REST OF MANKIND, ONLY, AS EVE LEFT
ADAM, TO MEET THE DEVIL IN PRIVATE."

—ALEXANDER POPE

HARRY'S BAD SIDE – by Robert Smith

*Doris and Connie would not be quieted. I can't recall his ever having
succeeded in driving them off. Courage lay in my sisters' crying. Almost
berserk, he'd go after them, and they would pull back. But a moment
later, they'd be as before, close to his side, crying, "Daddy, Daddy,
please go to bed." Their voices would rise sharply at every threat to
their mother. They'd scream in unison each time he lunged at her.*

*Standing there in his shorts beside the bed, a drunken distortion on
his face, Harry cursed her steadily, not in sporadic outbursts, but with
an increasing, pounding brutality that continued for hours; his language
an incredible idiot repetition, while beneath it ran the incessant, timid,
birdlike refrain of Connie and Doris. He might suddenly become
maudlin, "all right, dollings," allowing himself to be led off by the
arm. "I won't hurt . . . that dirty, stinking bitch, your mother!" And
then, just as suddenly, he'd begin cursing her again. At other times, his
rage would focus on the girls. "If you little whores don't stop, if you
don't get away and stop," his jaw working, trembling, his voice rising,
"I'll break every goddam bone in your fucking bodies! I'm warning ya
now!" But they'd be back as soon as he turned. Usually, it was only*

the foul language and the shouting. There were other occasions, though, when the night would become a delirium of violence.

Harry was in their mother's room, calling her names, every few minutes sounding a final note, then turning again to resume the verbal savagery. Robert first heard the chattering then, the only sound against those horrible words. It rose louder and louder. He couldn't imagine what it was or how it was done. He had the impression that his father, standing beside the bed, was making some mocking, ridiculous noise. The realization that it came from his mother sent a chill through him.

His father finally went to bed. He slept with Robert. The apartment was quiet, the lights were out, still the chattering continued—the same eerie sound from his mother. And Robert would hear her on other nights, her teeth chattering; nights when there'd been no fight; nights when his father was out of the house. He'd listen, wide awake, perfectly still; a faint, muffled clicking in the darkness, slowly increasing—a strange sound, like dull castanets, ebbing and rising. Mute, frail, unflinching, there was always a deep silence in his mother, inviolate and remote, more frightening than anything Harry's behavior revealed. The boy couldn't understand. What was she doing? He had no idea what it meant. If she'd been crying . . . but this! He couldn't respond. It seemed like grief, yet somehow not quite human. He could never grasp what she felt. None of them ever tried to comfort her. He was sure the others felt as he did then: desolate . . . afraid.

◗   ◗   ◗

In the sharp speculative glance, the slight narrowing of lids— as though seeking the distant perception out there instead of within— Phil the psychiatrist was watching me. I don't recall our discussion. Whatever it was about, the subject had become irritating, and I had lapsed into a stubborn, somewhat hostile silence.

"What's going on?" he asked.

I shrugged.

Phil persisted. "What's that expression on your face?"

"Expression?" There was no feel of any expression. Why did he ask? I considered for a moment. He's reaching, I thought. "Sadness?" I said at last, more as a guess than anything else,

Phil moved his head. "No . . ." He dragged the word out,

uncertain, unable to release it quickly. "I think . . . it's more like . . . desperation."

My face, its expression, suddenly became part of me. I recognized the look I wore. It was desperation, all right. Utter desperation. I could hear myself speaking again, tonelessly. "It's my father's face."

I'd seen that expression on my father's face one day when I was little. I'd noticed the way he sat there, the way he looked, sitting at the kitchen table. It was early one morning. He was wearing a business suit, ready to go. I was quiet. Everyone was silent. I may have felt sorry for him. I don't know. I probably just wanted to get out of the house. I think that moment told me who my father was, and erased the possibility of my hating him. I saw a human life as a tragedy, a disaster. I didn't dwell on it. I was little. I wanted to get out of the house; just walk past and forget.

○   ○   ○

Harry was wearing an undershirt and a pair of shorts. Robert finally got him to bed. Breathing heavily, a fluttery, noisy exhalation, wet and stinking, his breath smelling like a fart, his father threw an arm over the boy's shoulder and hugged him close. Robert shivered and tried to edge away, but there wasn't any space.

"I love your mother. I do." Harry's eyes were closed; dozing. "I do, son." A soft, cloying tremolo that was somehow obscene. "I love your mother. She's the sweetest, most wonderful person in the world." Still talking to himself, explaining very carefully, in the weird accentuations of a girl addressing her dolly, "I love all of you. And you, you're my first-born. I love you. Always respect your mother, son. Always respect her. Remember, your mother's a lady . . ."

It went on and on . . . and on. Robert lay there, dazed, scarcely hearing him. Interludes of silence, a muttering incoherence, and then the voice would begin again. He heard his father's jaws working, a grinding of molars. Robert could almost feel the rage, the clumped, accumulating words building pressure, backed up to his throat. Then, as though violently forcing the clenched mouth open, he would spit. "Your mother! That rotten whore!" A mist of fetid saliva dampened the boy's cheek and neck. "Your mother!" His father thrust himself up on an elbow, twisted toward her room, and let out a stream of filth. It became steadily more violent. There was no response, and this goaded him. His inadequacy against the dark and silence soon became too much. With a promise to "beat the shit out of her," he was up again. Reeling against the furniture, crashing through the apartment. And there were the girls' screams again. "Don't, don't, don't, Papa! Go back to bed! Please go back to bed!"

I remember my mother standing in the kitchen, drained of color, delicate features, sniffing—the unlikely sight of long black hair down her back, lips tight, staring at him—a butcher knife gripped in her hand.

Eventually, the boy got him started back to bed. "C'mon, Pop, let's get to bed." It seemed as though he'd been sounding that theme for hours.

"Okay, son. Okay." He threw his heavy, naked arm around Robert's neck. "Help me, son." He swayed, deliberately lurched, stumbling against the boy so that he almost knocked him over. His muttering started again, grew louder. He stopped. He brought his hand to his face. His features worked in a ludicrous display of emotion, as though he were struggling to get control of himself.

"C'mon, Pop. C'mon, go to bed."

The eyes glazed, out of focus, he looked at Robert uncomprehending. His jaw dropped. "Uh?"

"Let's go to bed. It's late. I've gotta go to school tomorrow."

That same steady, stupid stare. "Wha'?"

"I've gotta go to school tomorrow," Robert pleaded.

Breaking into an insane grin, his father reached out and tousled his hair. "He-eyyy, you're gettin' to be a big boy there! Hey!" A whisper, an intimate, ridiculing condescension. "Tell me something." His face filled with amusement. "Are you the tough guy on the block?"

"No." Robert looked at him dully. "Dad, I've gotta go to school!"

Nodding vigorously, he understood. "Oh, yes. Sure, sure." He walked a few steps and then stopped. "Hey, tell me something . . ."

Robert waited, but his father said nothing. "What?" Robert asked.

His father frowned, then went on. "How you doing in school?"

"All right."

Now grave and fatherly. "I want ya to study. Yer gonna be somebody. Know why?"

The boy listlessly shook his head.

"Because you're my son, that's why! And just remember . . ."
Tapping his forehead. "It's what's up here that counts. Be somebody,"
he growled. "Get wise to yourself. Don't ever work with your hands."
The thought seemed to bring a sudden silence.
Robert nodded. He waited.
"You can do anything ya want, anything, if ya like it. And just
remember, your pop is here to back you up. And don't let nobody tell
you nothing. You do what ya wanna do! And never mind these punks."
Then suddenly curious. "What do you want to be when you grow up?"
"I don't know."
"You wanna go to West Point?"
"If I could get in."
"If you could get in! Whattaya talkin'?" he snarled. "If you
could get in? Congressman Murphy's a personal friend of mine." His
fist thudded against his chest. "My son? 'Why, sure, Harry. West
Point? Only too happy to oblige.' Whattaya talking about? I tell
them! I don't ask. Yea-ah, that's right. Your old man. All he has to
do is say squat and they all shit. That's right. Yeah, your old man!"
Again hitting his chest. "I tell them. Understand? I tell them. And
believe me," he pointed a finger, "they listen. When Major Harry
Smith says something . . ." He turned and started shouting. "That's
right! Aristocratic Dowlings!" Sneering. "Aristocratic Dowlings!
Scum. Filthy scum! Ya know where her mother is? Huh? In a lunatic
asylum!" Looking back toward her room. "There's yer aristocratic
Dowlings for ya! Your Uncle Willie's nuts! And that's where your
mother's gonna wind up! In the bug farm!"
"Pop . . ." he whined. "C'mon, I gotta go to school!"
He suddenly gave the boy his attention, a hard, speculative stare.
His voice was cold. "Don't you interrupt me. Don't you ever interrupt me!"
"I'm not interrupting. I was just . . ."
His eyes were narrow. Nodding, he held up a big white-knuckled
fist. "You just watch yourself. Remember that. Just remember that!"
There was nothing stupid about his expression then. He sounded sober.
Robert stared ahead in silence.

Cigano looks at Jaco. "This next one's pretty depressing. When I first
read it, I was like, 'Fuck! Bingo! There it is, the dirty little roots of the
Curse!' I totally got the chills, like somebody was walking over my grave."

DOWN BY THE RIVER – by Robert Smith

On the deserted streets by the docks, where the markets were unheaped for the coming day, a few bars open, shipping warehouses, huge trailer trucks, crated fruits, produce—in that neighborhood, I lost him. Ugly streets where nothing stirred at night. Cobblestone gutters and shadowed recesses, where a red neon sign illuminates the strange movie-set atmosphere of the waterfront, where dramatic darkness gathers around the pale, theatrical light of a solitary lamppost, where nobody passes, where one imagines the habitation of rats. A lone drunk, a bum, asleep on a loading platform. Wet lips, snoring, choking, churkeling, yum yum, and a haraaaah, yum yum; smacking of lips, and mumbling mumble, to ease into snorking hisssss of heavy breathing.

That's how I remember him. Not in the doorway or on the sidewalk—not without a flop—but Harry, my father, beside me, drunk and snoring. The stench of him, of his breath, and me trying to avoid it with my face turned. The coldness of the plaster wall on my cheek, and the place I burrowed my nose between the mattress and the wall. Wide awake, I lay there, making myself small, imagining myself so small, as small as possible, so that his arm, his knee, or any part of him shouldn't touch me, huddling the covers up as a barrier between us. Nothing would provide against the stink, and, trying not to, but compelled to hold my breath, or not breathe as much, so I wouldn't take in the smell. Then finding myself half-smothered, suddenly inhaling deep lungfuls of stinking him; holding myself rigid, while writhing in agony within.

I would lie there, night after night, with him in the same condition. Somehow, the nights ended. Somewhere, I faded and woke on a bright morning, told to get ready for school. I felt deeply embarrassed for my mother and my sisters, shamed by the way he would lie there, flat on his back, naked, exposed. I would crawl from between Harry and the wall, desperately concerned to keep him from coming awake.

On different occasions I'd try to get away and sleep somewhere by myself, the floor, anywhere. His rage would be almost out of control. "You try to do that to me!" He grabbed me by the throat. "Ya dirty little son of a bitch, I'll break every fucking bone in your body, goddammit. I tell ya where to sleep! Ya see this fist? Oh, oh, oh . . ." Shaking his head, the huge red knuckles passed back and forth under

*my nose. "You're getting too big to spank. One a' these days . . ." A
drunken wave of maudlin endearments might follow that were a great
deal more horrible.*

*But I grew up. Perhaps it was the need, or some deep human
warmth I knew in him—distant memories and separation, the rolling
emptiness of years when our family disappeared, each of us children
alone, moving our individual course. I don't know how it was for the
others, but for me, I was everywhere alien to my surroundings. There
was always an aura of coldness, of something gone, the absence of
a family, forever gone. Each became a stranger. Solitary, wandering
Gypsies, without a homeland or a clan. Like him. That legacy, that
past I so deeply hated, hung on. And I think I felt I was always far
away from home. And in those years, somehow, I acquired a father.
Not the kind of man that should care for children. I don't know
what he was. I'll never know. A strange and ugly picture. Yet, in that
period, I acquired a father. And I knew that we had always had one,
although we didn't know him at all, really.*

*In those streets and alleys of the port, the streets around South
Street, down by the river, the sleeping ships, the small melancholy light
of neon from a bar in the distance, rats and warehouses and an empty
street where a solitary bum rolls along. That's what my mother always
called him, "a dirty drunken bum." And in the end he was. That was
his neighborhood, and whatever friends he had, that's where he could be
found. I tried to locate him there not long ago. I asked around in places
where he was known. From the way he was living, and from the things
said, or not said, I know my father is dead. I'll never know how it
happened or where. The district around the docks, I guess, is as close as
I'll ever get.*

Cigano sighs and folds the yellowed pages, then puts them back into
the envelope. He drops it on the table, its weight suddenly too much for
him to bear.

37. DISCIPLINE

"YET MAN IS BORN UNTO TROUBLE, AS THE SPARKS
FLY UPWARD."

—JOB 5:7

Late the next afternoon, after hours working on Jaco's growing tattoo, Cigano is alone again, sitting on the bed scribbling furiously into his notebook.

O   O   O

Following my mother and Aunt Connie out of the police station, my heart sank as I spied the gray specter of my stepfather sitting behind the wheel of my aunt's wood-paneled white station wagon.

"Get in, you monsters!" My mother pointed to the back door.

Aunt Connie stayed silent. Len pulled away and drove. Everybody was quiet. As we neared home, the old lady started in again. "And to think I've wasted the best years of my life. I wouldn't hear of it when they spoke to me about discipline. Noo-oo, not for *my* boy. Ha! And here's the thanks I get!"

"Well, there'll be a few changes made now," Len piped up.

My stomach went cold. I wanted to murder them both. Who did they think they were, that red-lipped mouthy old whore and her pet hamster showing his teeth at me? I wanted to bash their heads in with a hammer as the car pulled up in front of our house. I took a deep breath and got out. Aunt Connie drove off with my cousins still sitting in the back. Nobody said good-bye.

I was "grounded," Len informed me in the living room. I winced at the coward's triumph in his voice as he ordered me up to my room. Closing the door behind me, I could hear my mother banging around downstairs, raging, hurling incoherent insults and threats around the sterile white walls. I was trapped. Who the fuck was that little gray nothing, telling me what to do? The eucalyptus outside my window was quiet and still in the windless night. Boiling with rage, my skin burned. I spat on the floor. I punched the wall till my hand hurt. The urge to climb out the window and run off into the night was almost overwhelming. I looked around my room, seeking relief in the steady blink of the little Christmas lights I'd pinned to the walls. That shadowy blue cave was the only place I ever felt secure: my own private fantasy world where they couldn't reach in and bug me. But it felt unsafe now, invaded. I could hear her muffled raging down there, and him talking in his low, droning "reasoning" tone. I pressed my ear to the shiny blue door.

"Well, Mr. Know-It-All, I *know* the boy needs discipline, but are *you* going to give it to him? Ha! That's a good bloody laugh! You can hardly bring yourself to be alone with him for an hour."

"That's not really fair, Doris."

"Fair? What's fair got to do with this? I've tried to step aside and let you do your job, but Jono's strong-headed, and he's used to getting what he needs from his mother. Then you come along wanting to play daddy, but he's never trusted you. He doesn't trust anybody!"

"Well, if you'd just give me a chance, Doris."

"Oh, so now you want a chance with the boy? Well, fine! Here's your chance, Mr. Big Shot! Here's your big bloody chance! You just go upstairs now and you tell him how things are going to be around here from now on. I'm through dealing with it. Jesus, I need a drink! You want to go play father? Fine! You go up and have a talk with him. You two. Man to man!"

"Fine, Doris, that's just what I'll do!"

I couldn't listen anymore. The whole thing made me want to puke. Why couldn't they leave me alone? I just wanted to be old enough to get the hell out of that place. Neither one of those stupid old creeps was gonna tell me shit! I dug through the pile of LPs I'd swiped at the big new department store across from the railroad tracks by the liquor store. I picked one by the Rolling Stones and put it on the turntable. I lowered the metal arm, and the speaker crackled as the music began to play. "I can't get no satisfaction . . ."

That was better. I liked the Rolling Stones, the way they looked on the album cover, dark and tough, like a gang. Their hair was long and covered their eyes and seemed to shout *FUCK YOU!* to all the stupid parents and stark white walls and neighbors and police stations and schools. The music played and the Christmas lights blinked, taking me away to a calm place in my mind. I pulled out a comic book, *The Amazing Spider Man*, and got lost in the life of Peter Parker, who lived in New York. He had a motorcycle and a girlfriend. He was a straitlaced normal guy who worked and went to school and loved his grandma. Peter Parker had it pretty good.

Suddenly, Len opened the door without knocking. He stood in the doorway, milking his big entrance with his best Alfred E. Neuman Man in Charge look. Pathetic. Without a word, he strode across the room and yanked the needle from my record with a stifled screech, like the yelp Princess made when she got hit by the car. Poor Princess! Run over and killed, all because that stupid old creep left the gate open. Everything was wrong, and it was all their fault! I wanted to murder them both. Maybe I'd even get to be on one of those Wanted posters someday.

The shadows grow long in the late afternoon light as Cigano stops writing. He gets up and lights a cigarette. His hands are shaking. He needs to eat something. He looks at his watch. 7:15. He can make it in time for that little Alcoholics meeting by the *mercado* if he leaves now.

He grabs his jacket off the chair and shoves his cigarettes into his pocket.

38. HALLUCINATIONS

"WE ARE SO CAPTIVATED BY AND ENTANGLED IN OUR
SUBJECTIVE CONSCIOUSNESS THAT WE HAVE FORGOTTEN
THE AGE-OLD FACT THAT GOD SPEAKS CHIEFLY THROUGH
DREAMS AND VISIONS."

—CARL JUNG

The next day, the tattoo machine buzzes as Cigano works. He is sweating as late afternoon sunlight streams through the window. Holding Jaco steady in the creaking blue wooden chair, he concentrates on an elaborate outline covering the young man's arms and working its way across his torso. The tattoo man's mind wanders as he works, conjuring up details of the meeting he went to last night, composing, writing in the silence of his thoughts.

JOURNAL ENTRY – Veracruz, April 2002:

A blue-and-white sign hanging on the wall. UN DIA A LA VEZ. ONE DAY AT A TIME. Look down. Cold dirty scuffed-up linoleum floor. Feet. Pants legs. Shorts, skirts, shoes, socks, sandals. Human beings. Shit. Look up again, a deep-sea diver coming up for air. There is no air. Shirts, arms, skin, faces, mustaches, colors, textures, dirty plastic and metal chairs. Made in China. A cheap plastic orange clock hanging on a peeling powder-blue wall. Telling time. Time. A minute at a time . . . tic tic tic . . . Shit. Voices. Addicts. Alkies. Losers. Lost souls. Alcoholism. Recovery. Little signs hanging on the wall. Easy Does It. Keep Coming Back. One

Day at a Time, blah blah blah, and this is it: the long fucking road back. Long and hard and tough. Tough Love. Tough lives. Tough luck. Tough shit. Fans spinning. Hard to hear the voices. Voices, voices, talking, talking, blah blah blah. My mind is spinning around and around like the creaky overhead fan in this stifling airless hole. My mind is making too much fucking noise, talking too loud for me to hear what the fuck they're saying in here. God, I wanna get up and run! My brain is a restless cesspool of irritation and discontent. My feet are on fire. I don't wanna be here! Don't wanna be anywhere. Don't wanna be. And that's exactly why I ended up here in this pathetic little circle of recovering fuckups, with rancid taco acid coming up in my throat from the big empty hole in my gut where a heart should be. Where else am I gonna go? This is the last wagon on the last train, last fucking stop. Hell is waiting. I feel like dogshit. Too many cigarettes, too many drugs, too many doses of cheap liver-rot rum. Remember. Too many hangovers and too many whores. Too many mental emotional physical beatings. Too many memories. Too many sleepless restless lonely nights and bad nasty selfish self-destructive self-hating habits. Too many thoughts and ghosts and scars. Too many thrills and spills and self-inflicted harms, hurts and dramas, traumas, terrors, tortures and chills. Too many nightmares and too many fears. Too much pain. And now I'm here. Shit. Clean and fucking sober, looking down at this ugly scuffed dirty linoleum floor. Feet. Legs. Shorts, skirts, shoes, socks, sandals. Look up. Look around another drab windowless room full of angry frightened lonely lost souls. Like me. Fighting the void. Voices. Like mine. Talking, telling, sharing, screaming, barking like motherless homeless loveless stray dogs howling into the godless winds of nowhere, clamoring for any little scrap of salvation . . .

Jaco is talking.

Cigano looks up. "Hunh?"

"I couldn't stop thinking about those stories you read."

"Which ones, kid?"

"The stories about your grandfather, the Gypsy. Is that all true?"

"Yeah, pretty much, I guess. Far as I can tell, he really brought the wrath of God down on my mother and her siblings when they were kids. That's how alcoholism works, bro. It's like an inherited curse, some kinda fucked-up karmic burden. Anyway, he seems to have been the real architect of adversity for my immediate family of origin. It all ties back to him."

"I see what you mean." Jaco winces, then goes on, milking the conversation to keep his mind off the constant irritation of the needles burning into his flesh. "So you think he was the root . . ."

"My uncle's stories were pretty explicit." Cigano nods, not looking up from his work. "My grandmother told me some pretty hair-raising tales about him, too. But, like I said, he died right after I was born, so I never got to see any of it firsthand. But maybe I sorta did anyway . . ." His voice trails off.

"How do you mean?"

"Well, like I was saying, that kinda alcoholic imprint always seems to echo through the generations, y'know. It all bubbles up to the surface eventually in all kinda weird behavior. My mother was really messed up, poor thing. She'd get super violent when she drank. But sometimes she was even worse when she wasn't drinking. That's how it is, y'know, alcoholism, that's why they call it ism, not was-m, 'cuz even after people quit drinking for years, there's still all these nasty alcoholic character traits that live on. I guess that's where she got her mean streak from, that dark side. From her father. It's a family affair." With a wry grin, he stops talking and works on in silence.

After a while, he sets the machine down, pulls his gloves off, and reaches for a smoke. "Anyway, that's my family, my ancestors, whatever. The Gypsy's a ghost, but I swear he feels so fucking present in my life. Always did, in a weird way. Other times, my whole family history seems kind of unreal, even my own life. Sometimes it all feels like a big long hallucination." He stops working and wipes ink and blood off Jaco's skin with a wet paper towel. He nods, and the kid gets up to look in the wall mirror.

As Jaco stands regarding the intricate abstract tattoo designs taking shape across his body, he seems to be searching for words. "Hallucinations." He sighs. "I've never taken any drugs, Jonathan Shaw, but I think I know that feeling." He falls silent again, staring in the mirror, then looks up. "I came up here on a ship from Brazil, you know? It was my first time at sea. At first when the ocean got rough I became very sick. One time, late in the night, the shadows from the moonlight started to look really strange, like the hallucinations you describe. Frightening, really. That and the rocking motion from the big ocean waves, you know . . ."

Cigano studies the young man's hands as he talks. Not like a sailor's hands. Too smooth. For the first time, he notices the kid is wearing a silver ring with a five-pointed star. It looks a lot like one he used to have.

"Yeah, kid, I know."

39. SINS OF THE FATHER

"ESPECIALLY AS ARTISTS, WE HAVE TO CELEBRATE OUR MEMORIES."

—MEINRAD CRAIGHEAD

The next day, Cigano is at work again, filling in a wide section of black shading across the kid's shoulder. As his hand repeats the familiar motions of his craft, he pictures his father's hands, fingering at the air of his living room as he talked late into the night; as if the old man were still playing an invisible instrument after half a lifetime away from making music. Cigano wonders if it will be the same for him after he quits making tattoos. As he works on, he reminisces, falling deeper into the hypnotic rhythm and cadence of his work, remembering another conversation with his father; so many long evenings spent with the old man. Artie would talk on for hours, and always the old jazzman's fingers absently playing at the air, talking about himself, his life; downloading his memories into Cigano, as if trying in some fumbling way to make up for all the time he'd never spent with the strange tattooed son he'd long ago abandoned.

As the buzzing lulls him into a familiar trancelike state, Cigano thinks back to another dinner with Artie, and then he's there again, composing the words, writing down his recollections and impressions in the journals of his mind.

○　　○　　○

"Ya want me to drive, Artie?" I ask my father as we walk over to his car, parked in the dimly lit driveway.

"What?" He shouts into the darkness, gripping his cane with one hand, adjusting his hearing aid with the other. "Can't hear a fucking thing with this goddamn thing. I've hadda take it back three times already, goddamn it!"

I repeat my offer to drive his car over to the restaurant.

"Nah, I can make it. You can park it for me when we get there," he concedes, an afterthought, as if speaking to an underling, a servant. "I don't see too well in the dark . . ."

"Great." I mumble as we get into the car. Artie doesn't hear.

Speeding along the dark Ventura Freeway in his fully loaded new Lexus, the old man's hand seems to take on a weird life of its own, playing with the radio dial in a most extraordinary way, and suddenly my ears are assaulted with a loud, surreal cacophony of gangsta rap, evangelical radio preachers, Mexican news broadcasts, fast-food chicken ads, folk songs, and frenetic techno music. It's as if he's in a trance of some sort. If that ghostly white hand weren't continually fiddling with the radio dial, I'd think he'd fallen asleep at the fucking wheel. The car careens across the blurry white lines at ninety miles an hour, and suddenly I feel like a helpless little kid again, sitting on Mr. Magoo's Wild Ride at Disneyland. I look around and realize there's nothing to do but pray. I start to pray. *Yea, though I walk through the shadow of the Valley of Death, I shall fear no evil, for Thou art with me.*

He tunes into a screaming rap music station, "Word up, yo, word to ya motha' yo yo yo, niggas," with his head cocked to one side like a distracted parrot. I sit there beside him, feeling my asshole pucker like a sea anemone caught in a swirling whirlpool of hip-hop and horn-blaring mariachi music, static, easy listening, opera, more static, heavy metal, classic rock, opera again. *Fuck!* I'm watching the highway, frozen silent in escalating waves of terror as he sideswipes thundering eighteen-wheelers, narrowly avoiding instant annihilation for us both. Morbid thoughts race through my brain like wasps. *Fuckin' bastard's ninety-two years old. Every hour above ground's a fucking bonus for his wore-out, wrinkled old ass! What about me? I'm just getting started again now, ya selfish old prick!! God, please don't lemme die here with this demented old crow! Not now, please! Not today!*

Finally, the old man looks up from the radio like a sleepy basset hound and explains that he's looking for the news station. *Riders on the Storm* is playing, "Into this life we're born, into this world we're thrown," and then we're hurtling down an off-ramp and I can feel myself breathing again. *Yes! We're gonna make it one more time. Another day. Thank you, Jesus, for another dinner with this narcissistic old mummy, my father. And now I get to pick up a hundred-dollar tab at some fancy suburban eatery again 'cuz Artie only gets the bill when he drives us to that cheap greasy Chinese heartburn factory next to the taco stand in the strip mall. Fucking tightwad old bastard really thinks he can take it with him. Shit!*

We pull to a lurching halt in front of La Dolce Vita Trattoria. Artie snatches his heavy silver-tipped hardwood cane from the floor, almost bopping me on the chin with it as he unfolds himself from the car, cussing and complaining, one pissed-off, irritable old bone at a time.

○   ○   ○

Cigano stops to wipe the tattoo clean, still thinking, remembering. It must have been awkward for the old man. Yeah, it had to have felt pretty fucking weird to suddenly find himself sitting with a middle-aged son he'd spent a lifetime neither acknowledging nor caring to know. But as intimate as Artie's long rambling monologues ever were, he always maintained a certain clinical distance: that subtle defensive barrier, as if the old man unconsciously feared that this imposing stranger with grinning gold teeth and a face like the devil himself had come back from the dead to avenge the helpless child he'd abandoned to an alcoholic mother; as if some guilt-ridden primal core of his father shuddered at the notion that now in his old age, facing the specter of death and teetering over the grave, this scarred, brutal-looking tattooed thug had crawled back from the depths of Hell just in time to give him a final shove.

As he works on, squinting into the void of memory, Cigano thinks of how maybe that's where Artie got his mean streak: an unconscious resentment against Death itself—as if somewhere deep in his core, his indomitable ego simply couldn't accept the idea of his own mortality. He can hear the old man's voice again, humming in his inner ear, as if arguing with the Grim Reaper, saying: *"I'm Artie Shaw, fer Crissake! Ya can't take me! Don't you know who I am?"* That fucking voice! Calm and assertive, yet always kept in check somehow with that odd underlying egocentric edge; a subtle, urgent *something*, bordering on a shrill manic hysteria.

○   ○   ○

" . . . I used to have this dream about a crazy woman, coming at me with a knife." The old man rambles on in Cigano's memory, eating from a twenty-nine-dollar plate of linguini. "Found out when I was in Freudian analysis that it was about my mother. Later, it was Doris, *your* mother, coming at me with a fucking gun. Same thing. It's a strange world. It's amazing people ever survive . . ."

"But if ya knew she was so messed up, Artie, why'd ya wanna marry her?" I look at him, remembering the pile of corny, almost childlike love letters I'd come across in my mother's garage.

SAVOY HOTEL, LONDON, 1951 –

Sweetheart: I just finished reading the most beautiful piece of prose I've ever read in my life—that last letter of yours, the one you so idiotically told me to tear up without looking at it. You, my little furry-eyed beloved, stink. I'm not sure I love you at all if you're going to go on making cracks like that about letters written by my girl. However, if you can go on writing such letters I'll allow you to go on telling me to tear them up—so the whole thing winds up a kind of dead heat. Oh baby, darling little one, you'll never know how that helped. I've been going around under my own private dark cloud. Then your letter—and presto! The sun comes out. But only for a few seconds, because after that I'm back to missing you again worse than before. Oh, dear sweet Jesus Christ! How I do love you, to say practically nothing at all of how I already begin to miss you with a deep, deep, sad, painful ache way down somewhere in the buried center of me. And now, darling, it starts getting bad—very very bad. Missing you, I mean. I wouldn't have believed it possible for anyone to feel a need for anyone else to the extent I do for you. It's actually quite difficult for me to believe it—except, of course, that I must, since I feel so strongly about it. You know what's really the wildest part of this whole letter-writing business, don't you? The first thing after my first phone call to you—I sit down to write you and start by apologizing for whatever gaucherie I'm about to commit re love letters, etc. Then I get a letter from you (written under the same circumstances on your end) and it starts the same way. I think we ought to compare these particular two

letters when I get back, just to see how similar both beginnings are. As I remember my own, it's almost identical to yours, in content— all of which seems to prove something or other about us in regards to each other, although I can't quite make up my mind as to just what. Anyway, I adore you, I adore your letters, and I feel lousy that you're so bloody far away from me. I'll have to fix that real quick. I will, as soon as I can get my goddamn job of work finished here. So, my lovely little one, that's my story, in essence. I want you here with me, and not only here, but also anywhere else I have to be. For keeps, as far as I'm concerned, but that only if it works out to make you happy. I think it could easily work out that way, but how can I know for sure with such a brief history to look back on? So what it all boils down to in the end, is that I want us to start working on a longer history, and I want it to begin immediately if not sooner. As to how you feel about that, and how it may or might affect or cause whatever complications regarding your own plans (aside from me)—well, you know my story and I hope yours is the same kind of story, but please let me know if it is and I'll take it from there. In short, whichever way you want it I'll understand—until we can thrash out the one big sixty-four-dollar question of whether we're going to go along with separate plans or work out one overall master plan that will tell us we have no plans apart from one another. Which latter is something I most fervently and ardently hope for and want. For, as I say, I do love you. Moreover, although it's been a relatively short time since I started loving you, curiously enough I can't remember at this point the time when I didn't love you. That's it. Not period, but exclamation point. Right now there's just room left on this page to tell you you're the most amazingly wonderful thing that's ever happened to me. Period! I love you, I adore you, I may as well go all out and say I need you. Oh God! So much I can't begin to say. So long, my little shrill and strident one, and God bless the little furry corners of your eyes. I adore you – Your everlovin' globe trotting fella,
Art

The old man grunts as he shoves a massive shrimp into his mouth. "Yeah, well, ya never really know how fucked up they are till the mask comes off. Your mother and I got along for a while. Till we got married. Hah! The great institution of marriage! That's the great destroyer! After that, we did nothing but fight. But she convinced me that having a kid would make things all right. Well, what did I know? We really planned it, you know . . ."

As Artie chews his food and talks, I set my fork down and push the plate away. I picture a young Doris and Artie sitting in a plush living room in the country, smoking cigarettes, drinking cocktails, and fighting. My mother has a significant bun in the oven under a fancy designer maternity dress. She's drunk, yelling, spitting, raging at her famous husband. I can almost hear her angry shouts bombarding me in the womb. "*I shoulda gotten the abortion, you bastard! If it's a boy, I swear to Christ I'll put its goddamned eyes out and drown it at birth, so help me God!*"

"Yeah, we planned it, all right." The old man drones on. "And then you were born. Oh, boy, you were the goddamn baby Jesus! And she was Mary, Mother of God! *Argh*, what a business! She was fucking nuts! When we split up and she moved away to California with you, I told her, 'Jesus, you're not hurting me, Doris, you're hurting him. You're taking the kid's father away from him!' But she wouldn't hear it. She was gonna show me! Hell hath no fury. So, what are ya gonna do? She just wasn't very good mother material. You at least found the mental muscle to get out. How old were you when you left home? Fourteen, fifteen?"

I nod, absently picking at my eighteen-dollar plate of eggplant Parmesan again, relishing the tiny spark of validation my father has finally tossed me.

The old man snuffs it out. "Yeah, well, there's still a lot of her bullshit in you, kid. I can see it." He snorts into his plate.

"Yeah, so whaddya expect, man? She did raise me, y'know. At least she gave it her best shot . . ." I can hear my voice turning shrill as I bite my tongue to hold back the words fighting to get out: *That's more than **you** ever did, ya selfish old prick!*

"Well, her best wasn't very good!" the old man spits back.

I can feel a black pit of anger swelling in my gut. I push the food aside and throw my napkin on the plate. Longing for a cigarette, a drink, anything to take the edge off, I take a deep breath and the smoldering rage begins to subside. I can hear myself speaking again. "Well, I survived, didn't I?" *No thanks to you, ya self-centered old bastard.* "I guess that's all that matters now." I hear myself going on calmly. "And now is all I got."

A long surly silence.

I break it. "So what about *your* mother, Artie? What was she like?"

Artie devours another greedy mouthful and looks up as if noticing me sitting there for the first time. "*Arrgh*. My mother was pretty tough. I mean I loved her, sure, she was my mother and all that. I had a hell of a time getting rid of her. As I got older, she was like a fucking Jewish albatross hanging around my goddamn neck. And me traveling around the country with a band." He guffaws. "Just picture it, man, this old lady following her grown son around like some lovesick cunt, like a fucking groupie or something, for Chrissake. I was a rock star in those days, ya know, like fucking Elvis, Mick Jagger, and here I've got my mother along with me on tour, on the bus, backstage, coming to parties with the band, can ya picture that? *Arrrgghhh*. Very weird scene, man. Mothers just don't know how to get outta the way. They keep wanting to be 'mother.' They keep wanting the authority of that: 'I'm your mother!' What the fuck is that supposed to mean? You were my mother when I needed a fucking mother! At eight, I didn't need ya anymore! Get the fuck outta my bag, man!" The old man pauses and looks away, staring off into a realm of phantoms, memories, ghosts.

"I couldn't go to her deathbed." He begins again in that shrill, defensive, self-assured tone. "I was feeling hate. And love. Mostly hate, yeah. For what she did to me, trying to make me into a surrogate husband after she ran my goddamned father away . . ." Artie trails off.

I break into the rare pause in the old man's endless monologue, prompting him for information, feeling like a junkie whining for a fix. "So, your childhood?"

Artie snorts. "*What* fuckin' childhood? *Arrgghh*, I musta been like most kids, a real pain in the ass. Boy, I really did some stupid things!"

I hear myself reply, as if from very far away. "Yeah, me too."

40. TATTOOS

"SHOW ME A MAN WITH A TATTOO AND I'LL SHOW YOU A
MAN WITH AN INTERESTING PAST."

—JACK LONDON

Coming up for air from a sea of memory, Cigano sets his tattoo machine down on the table and throws the rubber gloves in the trash. He pulls a cigarette from the pack, lights up, and looks over at the kid.

"Have you written about how you first got into tattooing?" Jaco asks.

"Funny you should ask that, man." He grins, lighting up. "Must be all this tattooing's giving me ink on the brain or something. I was just gonna read you this thing I wrote about my first real impression of it, back in the sixties."

As he stares into the page like a deep-sea diver, reading through a cloud of smoke, the words stir up a new flurry of memories: the first time he ever saw those mysterious little symbols that would someday make up the roadmap of his destiny.

○   ○   ○

Nineteen sixty-five was the year of the big Watts riots. I must've been about thirteen when the ghetto exploded in the August heat. After charges of police brutality came to a boil in the hyper-segregated Los Angeles Basin, fierce rioting broke out in the all-black inner-city neighborhood. As the urban battlefields burned, panic swept the whole city. The news media fanned the smoldering embers of a longstanding racial mistrust into a full-scale black/white Armageddon. Television anchormen warned that the burning and looting could soon spread to white neighborhoods—an absurd notion, since the violence was contained to a distant inner-city slum, far from the affluent suburbs. To make a perfect shitstorm worse, the racist police chief denounced Watts residents as "monkeys in the zoo," adding new insult to decades of racially targeted cop abuse. Frank Zappa summed up my take on the whole racial tone of my country when he said: "I'm not black, but there's a whole lot of times I wish I could say I'm not white."

In a media-generated tizzy, Len—a bleeding-heart armchair liberal who'd never had a black person at the house, except to clean it—packed up the Caddie and insisted we leave home. We drove to a quiet beach-front community in Malibu, where he said we could "wait things out safely" in a small rented vacation house. This was right down the road from Doris's old theater mentor John Houseman's luxurious beachfront mansion. The following weeks were a typical "family" disaster. Every night, Doris would get plastered with her theater friends, then come staggering back down the beach to carry on drinking alone and raising hell for the rest of the night. The "beach house" Len had rented was just a shack compared to home, where it was easy to avoid each other. Now we were forced into close contact, my worst nightmare. Seething with boredom and indignation at Len for sticking us in a "pauper's shanty," one night my mother got drunk as a fiddler's bitch. In typical scandalous meltdown, wailing like an angry ghost, she tried to drown herself in the ocean. A couple of burly surfers jumped into the dark, raging waves to fish her out, buck naked, kicking and screaming like a drenched wildcat. As I stood on the sand cringing in embarrassment, Len looked on in silence, useless as a wristwatch on a sweet potato.

I soon made friends with some kids from down the way and did everything I could to stay away from the house. We started hanging out with a hard-drinking, out-of-work movie director named Sam Peckinpah, who was spending the summer at the beach. Peckinpah—who would go on to direct classics like *The Wild Bunch* and *Straw Dogs*—was the kind of rugged role model my friends and I could relate to. We spent our evenings with him sitting around a bonfire, getting buzzed on his beer while he delighted us with ribald tales of adventures in Mexico and the Orient.

Sam was the kind of real man's man I'd always pictured my father to be—a polar opposite of my gutless stepfather. When Len got wind that "his son" was spending more time with "this Peckinpah character" than at home, he started a smear campaign to turn the other kids' parents against him, making up all sorts of evil rumors about the poor guy. It was like the Doormat's Revenge. After convincing my mother that Sam was a "bad influence" on her beamish boy, they slapped a chickenshit dusk-to-dawn curfew on me.

Bored and discontented, a few kids would meet up on the sly in the morning and take the big blue city bus down to this sprawling old amusement park, The Pike, by the port in Long Beach. That's where the cool kids hung out. The tough kids. The troublemakers. The juvies. Disneyland was over in Orange County, a world of plastic white-trash suburbs. Disneyland was for momma's boys and fairies. The Pike was more like it: a rundown time warp of blue-collar factory workers, bikers, sailors, and drifters loitering on the hot summer boardwalk, smoking cigarettes and drinking beer from cans.

One day, I went down with another kid. After spending all our money on games and rides, we were standing in front of this dingy tattoo parlor, peering in the window. A dusty ship in a bottle sat next to a stuffed weasel wrestling with a snake and a blue-and-white statue of a sailor. The haunting little objects seemed frozen in time under rows of faded old carnival photos of sideshow freaks: tattooed men and women staring out from rusty cages of long ago. Hundreds of colorful little pictures like comic-book panels covered the nicotine-stained walls: from floor to ceiling, an endless loop of pinup girls, skulls, daggers, dragons, shooting stars, crosses, saints, anchors, panthers, and goofy cartoon ducks. I was hearing jungle drums. It was like a religious experience; a portal to another world; a familiar place I'd always known, deep in some lost forgotten region of my soul's memory.

I rose up on my tiptoes, focusing on a picture of a high-masted ship sailing through a colorful sea of naked ladies, tigers, anchors, horseshoes, mermaids, devils, and old-time cartoon characters. Every inch of space was covered with mystery and magic. I wanted access to that smoky other world. I needed to see all those tattoos right up close. My guts raged and my mind raced as I inched toward the door. My hand hesitated. Just as I worked up the courage to go in, I saw the little sign: *YOU MUST BE 18*. I stood there frozen, the ominous words holding me at bay like a cross before a thirsty vampire. I moved back to the window and peered inside again, longing to know the secrets within. I could smell the soot on the ledge, and my ears pounded with excitement. People were moving around in the back, sailors crowding around in a corner where a skinny old guy with bare arms covered in fuzzy blue-green hieroglyphics sat hunched over another guy. I could hear a muffled buzzing sound, and I knew exactly what was going on.

Nobody had ever told me about tattoos, but staring in that dusty window I knew I needed one. The tattooed sailors were drinking, passing a little bottle around. One guy had this great big eagle with a ship covering his whole chest. I wanted to grow up real fast and be eighteen, to disappear into that smoky haven and never go back; to go wherever sailors sailed to, sailing off on a billowing ship of dreams across a painted watercolor horizon, far as a young boy's spirit could fly on a pair of fuzzy blue tattooed wings.

As my breath fogged the window glass, suddenly a big hairy hand grabbed my arm in a vise-like grip. My heart froze as a booming voice bored into my ear. A stocky red-faced man with a crew cut stood towering over me, yelling "Gotcha, ya little turd!"

A group of bikers watched with amusement as my friend darted off into the crowd. A tall, lanky guy with a long, blond, nicotine-stained beard stomped over, facing my stocky captor. "Hey, man, give th' kid a break!"

The angry shopkeeper ignored him, bending my arm back, growling. "I saw you, ya little bastard!"

As I struggled to break loose from his beefy grip, a stack of comic books slid from under my shirt and fluttered to the ground. As the man bent to pick them up, I broke loose and bolted. The biker who'd defended me extended a casual motorcycle boot, and I tripped and fell to the pavement. He turned away laughing as that huge, hairy hand of guilt plucked me from the ground like a cat snatching a baby rat.

41. PRISONER OF WAR

"UNDER TYRANNY, IT IS RIGHT TO BE A REBEL!"

—ROBERT FANNEY

The old lady was really dressed to kill this time, all pimped out in black patent-leather heels, mink stole, pearl necklace, even her best movie-star sunglasses. The great Doris Dowling working without pay or critical acclaim again, playing the role of Distraught Parent for some idiot police sergeant. Satisfied with her latest command performance, she escorted her wayward son down the steps of the Long Beach station house, huffing and puffing all the way.

I couldn't tell if it was just another well-rehearsed act, or if she was really pissed off. She sure looked pissed. Grim-faced and muttering under her boozy breath, she shoved me into Len's hearse-like Cadillac. She slammed the door behind me like a coffin lid and got in front with her husband. Adjusting his glasses, the old Nowhere Man navigated his big white Jew Canoe away from the curb, easing defensively into the late-afternoon traffic.

Doris was milking it hard as she turned sideways, railing at her juvenile delinquent son. "You're grounded for good now, boy! I've had it with your crap! I'm calling the boarding school first thing in the morning!"

Boarding school?!? I stared at her in mute shock.

Her eyes blazed like a rabid bulldog. "That's right! You're going off to boarding school now, damn you! And you can consider yourself lucky! I should've left you to rot in Juvenile Hall with the rest of the goddamn delinquents! And to think! To think I threw away a brilliant caree-ah, at the height of my fame, to play some, some . . . suburban PTA matron! And for what? To raise a troublesome, ungrateful, sullen little sociopath? A comic-book–reading idiot!"

"Well, boys will be boys, Doris." Len interrupted her grand Oscar Acceptance Speech in a weak pretense of coming to his errant stepson's defense. "My goodness! When I was a young man . . ."

"Shut the hell up, you fool! Jesus! 'Boys will be bo-oys.'" She mimicked him, rolling her mad eyes. "I am surrounded by imbeciles!"

"I was just saying, dear . . ." He tried again, not getting it. Poor old chump. He never got it. I might have been amused by his bumbling attempt to assert his manhood if I hadn't been burning with hate.

"'I was just sa-aying, de-ear,'" she spat back. "Just shut the goddamn hell up and keep your bloody eyes on the road, you dimwit! What the hell do you know about it, anyway? Nothing! That's what you know!"

Len fell into another brooding silence. I was almost embarrassed for the guy. I wished the spineless little drone would just pull the car over and give her the back of his hand for once, like Sam Peckinpah or Artie would have done. But there was no Artie. No man. No father; only this stupid gray little worm with his habitual brooding silences. I hated him, even more than I hated her for marrying such a big fat nothing.

Doris turned around in her seat like a snake, aiming her deadly venom at my face again, eyes blazing in a hellish mixture of boozy rage, pep pills, and puffy-eyed, vodka-logged hangover; the unbearable weight of her anguished lot in life. "I wouldn't listen when they told me the boy needed discipline! No! Not my Jono! Not my beamish boy! And this is the thanks I get! Hah! How sharper than a serpent's tooth is the sting of a thankless child! Just like his bloody father, that puffed-up egotistical windbag!"

Disgusted, I turned away. *Blah blah blah.* I'd heard it all before. *Fucking old bitch! Where does she come off acting all haughty and self-righteous?* Sulking in the back seat, I flashed back on coming home from school when I was a little kid to find her passed out naked on the kitchen floor, drunk and covered in blood from self-inflicted knife wounds. I remembered running over to the neighbor's house, crying. I thought of the ambulance and the shame and confusion raging in my heart as she was carted off to the hospital. Where was the All-American Mom waiting for her beamish boy with a steaming apple pie on the kitchen counter? No such luck. Her and her husband were a shame and a fucking disgrace, a pair of stupid old martini-slurping hypocrites!

As we rode on through Venice Beach, the sidewalks were alive with denizens of a sixties counter-culture dream: runaway kids, longhairs, bikers, willowy hippie chicks with flowing hair and tie-dyed Gypsy skirts. They were all sitting around out on the sidewalk, free as alley cats, panhandling, smoking pot, playing guitars, grinning and laughing; happy, carefree, stoned. As the car rolled to a stop at a light, I sank down in the back, trying to hide my face, cringing in shame. I was a hostage, a prisoner in that shiny Cadillac; a glaring status symbol of their phony superficial American Dream reeking of poisonous suburban angst. And there they all were, right outside the window, passing me by on the sidewalk like fantastic fish in some exotic aquarium. Those kids had everything I longed for. I slunk down, horrified that someone might see me with those bickering old squares. Waiting for the light to change was an excruciating eternity of seething humiliation.

"Look at those scum!" Doris glared. "Filthy little degenerates! Juvenile delinquents! Is *that* what I've raised? Over my dead body! God! And to think those are somebody's children! Argh! Outlaws! Scum! Lock the doors, Len! Jesus! They're all on drugs!!"

I was in Hell. As the light changed, I saw a beautiful doe-eyed hippie chick. My heart jumped into my throat as she looked at me. She smiled and gave me the peace sign as my face flushed red, white, and blue with embarrassment.

"Look at that little tramp! If I ever catch you running around with something like that, I'll disown you, you hear me, boy?"

As my mother raged on, I glared at the sorry old spooks. My guts overflowed with the bitter poison of my miserable life. I felt like puking as the Cadillac waddled off like a crippled funeral wagon, taking me back to my sterile white teenage mausoleum.

42. LOVE IT OR SHOVE IT

"THE WORLD IS FULL OF PEOPLE THAT HAVE STOPPED
LISTENING TO THEMSELVES OR HAVE LISTENED ONLY TO
THEIR NEIGHBORS TO LEARN WHAT THEY OUGHT TO DO,
HOW THEY OUGHT TO BEHAVE, AND WHAT THE VALUES ARE
THAT THEY SHOULD BE LIVING FOR."

– JOSEPH CAMPBELL

Sure enough, they sent me to the dreaded boarding school she'd
been threatening me with for months. The place was called Chadwick
Academy, and I hated everything about it, especially its pretentious
pseudo-British name. Chadwick. It sounded like one of those stick-up-
the-ass butlers in boring movies about tightwad ruling-class creeps. The
kids there were all spoiled trust-fund brats, a bunch of goody-two-shoes
scholastic overachievers who went in for sports and wholesome extra-
curricular activities. It was like being sentenced to live somewhere south
of Hell. I was a pissed-off stranger in a very fucked-up land.

The boys' "dorm-mother" was a hatchet-faced old crab named Mrs.
Maxam, a scowling, overweight Orange County Republican with a stiff
upper lip and an All-American chip on her shoulder. The pro-Vietnam
flag-waving redneck took an instant dislike to me, and the feeling was
mutual. Like the sadistic Nurse Ratched in *One Flew Over the Cuckoo's Nest*,
that gray-haired authoritarian closet lesbian had me pegged as a troublemaker from the get-go; and in a futile effort to break my rebellious spirit,
she singled me out for all sorts of random punishments.

○   ○   ○

Cigano stops reading and pulls out some old letters. "Here's one I wrote home from that place. Found it with all that old stuff in Doris's garage." He squints at his awkward adolescent scrawl. "Fuck! Look at this shit!" He laughs, handing the page to Jaco. "God, I'd totally forgotten how miserable I was there. Check it out, man! No wonder I was so fucking disturbed!"

12/2/66 – DEAR MOM,

I just finished my homework and decided to write. I'm real happy about coming home this weekend. I'm fed up with Mrs. Maxam. Yesterday I left the pistachio nuts you brought me outside my box and she took them away and passed them out to everybody in the dorm. Then she walked right past me with a handful of nuts and said, "Mmm, these sure are tasty, too bad you can't have any." This place bites. I want to come home. I promise I'll be good. I can't wait for the weekend. Write soon. Love, Jono

"That's so sad." Jaco shakes his head as he hands the letter back.

"I was only like twelve, thirteen years old, man, just a dumb kid." Cigano sighs as he puts the letter away. "Clueless fuggin' bastards . . ." He grumbles under his breath as he turns back to his story.

○   ○   ○

I was at war. My frantic pleas to come home fell on drunk ears. But my stay at Chadwick wouldn't last. It was the mid-'60s, and the Vietnam War was raging on the nightly news. Unlike most of my upper-middle-class schoolmates at the ultra-conservative prep school, I was against Vietnam. I would cringe every time I had to walk past old Maxam's room and see that ugly pro-war sticker on her door: *AMERICA—LOVE IT OR LEAVE IT!*

One evening, thoroughly fed up with Chadwick, the war, Mrs. Maxam, and the American Dream, I swiped the big American flag from the utility room where she stored it at night. I smuggled it out of the dorm and went out into the woods. I sat down under a big oak tree with a flash-light and, with a ballpoint pen, sketched a perfect little swastika into the middle of each of the flag's fifty stars. I figured I was making some kind of anti-war statement when I snuck it back on the shelf; or maybe I was just bored and wanted to stir up the shit. When Mrs. Maxam unfurled it at the flagpole the next morning and saw what I'd done, she freaked out and immediately accused me of vandalizing her beloved Old Glory. This time I'd clearly gone too far. Knowing I'd been caught red-white-and-blue-handed, I tried to stifle a nervous snicker. The grim-faced old dragon punched me right in the face. Unable to beat a confession out of me, she marched me down to the principal's office. This time, even Doris's mink stole and rhinestone-studded sunglasses wouldn't cut it. I was expelled from Chadwick Academy, and that was that. I was just relieved to be out of there, whatever it took.

43. CAPTAIN CRINGE

"THERE ARE NO HEROES. IN LIFE, THE MONSTERS WIN."

—GEORGE R.R. MARTIN

Within weeks of being home, I was back in trouble with the law. After a string of new shoplifting busts, my mother was at her wits' end. There was talk of sending me to military school. But after the usual round of threats, yelling, chest-pounding, and gnashing of teeth, I was just "grounded" again. I was an angry, frustrated thirteen-year-old. Still, I was glad to be back in the sanctuary of my cluttered cave where my record collection of albums by The Fugs, Mothers of Invention, Jimi Hendrix, Cream, Coltrane, Miles Davis, Willie Bobo, Paul Butterfield Blues Band, Django Reinhardt, and Artie Shaw lay comfortably strewn across the floor. Stacks of EC and Marvel comic books littered every horizontal surface. My mother had always hated my interest in comics. She was forever telling me I'd outgrow all that "low-class trash." But I didn't outgrow it. I dreamed of becoming a comic-book artist.

I was sitting in my room one evening, drawing. My prized collection of shoplifted Rapidograph pens and colored pencils sat on the desk alongside an open copy of Zap Comix. The big eucalyptus tree outside the window was still, and I could feel the Jabberwock wiffling through the cold night wind. An indistinct stench of burning rubber filled my soul with futility and doom. My skin burned red with a desperate longing to escape that hated white prison and never go back.

My eyes darted around my little space, taking in the glossy shine of the dark blue walls as I thought of Grandma standing in the hallway, looking in as I painted the whole room blue. *"Why ya makin' it such a dark cullah, Jono? You'll go blind in there. Ya can't see nothin'."* I had no way to verbalize it then, but that was the whole point. The less I saw of my reality, the better. I remembered breathing in the paint fumes that day, getting a buzz as I watched the white walls turning a deep dark blue. Blue, yeah, because the rest of that shit place was white: stark, sterile, soulless white; the color of ambulances and hospital corridors and the absence of all color and life. Fuck that! Blue was the only color for me. The color of escape; a dark shiny hue of deep ocean dreams and fantasy and the darkening sky at dusk stretching far away from that soulless creep-fuck limbo of repulsive freak-show terrors, a lifeless white void of starched white uniforms and clammy white washcloths stuffed down a child's screaming throat. Yeah, blue was the color, alive and shiny like a hard protecting armor; because no matter how bad things ever were, I could always disappear into that dark blue grotto, the one refuge where I always felt safe and inviolate, a pirate captain sailing the Seven Seas to a faraway cobalt world where they couldn't hassle me with their angry jabbering static.

Sitting at my desk, I could hear their idiot chatter downstairs. I cringed at the familiar sound of Doris raging into the night and the dull muffled murmurs of their secretive conversation; the hysterical rise and fall of her voice and the low, steady, serious hum of Len's pathetic whine. The whole thing took on the steady cadence of a foul, septic tide washing up on the shores of Hell. Disgusted, I got up and switched on the old stereo I'd smuggled up to my room after she replaced it with a bigger one for her solitary drunken self-pity parties in the den. I dropped Coltrane's *Giant Steps* onto the turntable and turned the volume way up to drown out their bickering. Was I turning into her, I wondered, locked in a dark little room with my own solitary music? If they would just shut the fuck up! I sat back down at the desk, got out the Zig Zags and rolled a fat joint. I lit some incense, cracked the window open, and sat there smoking. As the weed burned deep in my lungs, I got out my sketchpad and started working on my latest comic strip.

My tongue played at the corner of my mouth as I inspected my progress.

THE AMAZING SAGA OF CAPTAIN CRINGE. The title blasted

across the top of the page in bold graphic lettering, calling up fuzzy childhood visions of sinister, spindly shapes. The opening panel showed a scruffy wisp of a downtrodden little bum sitting all alone on a barstool in a sleazy skid row bar. I'd named my comic's hero Wilfred Wormus. I sucked in another hit of weed. The smoke filled my lungs like a pair of fleshy balloons expanding. My fantasy exploded onto the page as my pen scratched over a panel, working the story into life, when suddenly the pictures began to spill off the paper, onto the desk and across the room, filling my senses with animated sound and motion. My mind fully blown, I sat back in my chair drooling like a science-fiction movie zombie as the drama consumed my awareness.

I was Wilfred Wormus.

From across the dingy barroom, three bullies emerged from the shadows. A massive muscle-bound brute named Killer grabbed me by my throat, hauling me off the barstool. I strained in my chair as the big thug held me in the smoky air, spitting into my face. "Woimus, ya creepy little punk!"

A second sidekick chimed in. "Dat's right! You tell 'im, Boss!" My eyes bugged in terror. I was caught like a fly in Killer's terrible bully grip as the next panel sprang to life.

Killer was yelling, spitting, raging, pointing his big stubby finger at me. "Get th' hell outta here, ya doity bum, and don't come back!"

I turned to another page as Coltrane's saxophone riffs danced in the air. Grinning, I sat back reviewing my artwork, touching up a detail here and there. The next part showed my protagonist a few hours later, brooding and weeping in a shabby roach-infested skid row flophouse room. Standing under a bare light bulb, Wilfred Wormus vowed revenge on his tormenters. I scanned the page, muttering to myself, rehearsing my hero's words. "Someday them bastards will *cringe* when they see me coming!" I lit another joint and inhaled, closing my eyes, sinking deep into the movie playing in my head. I could hear a narrator's tinny voice droning all around me, telling the unfolding story in a bombastic Walter Winchell-style radio announcer's tone. "And so-oo, the next evening, pulled by the invisible hand of fa-ate, Wilfred returns to the bar for a rendezvous with destinyyy."

In my stoned-out vision, I watched Wilfred Wormus enter the barroom. The shabby little man looked apprehensive but determined. I swallowed. No turning back. Wilfred knew he would die if he didn't get a drink. Suddenly, my heart froze with Wilfred's as he saw the bully approaching.

Killer fixed us with the cold brutal eyes of a rabid Saint Bernard as he came stomping across the sagging floorboards, barking "Hey! I thought I told ya to stay th' hell outta here!"

I could feel my own lips moving as Wilfred groveled and pled. "Aww, please, Killer! I just gotta have a drink. Just one dr—"

Killer dashed a mug of beer in my face! I could hear the other two bullies chattering as I felt the icy liquid seeping into Wilfred's ragged shirt, running down his shivering, emaciated carcass as his towering aggressor's sadistic laughter filled the dark blue space of my room. "Drink up, sucker! Hahaa!"

The pungent smoke lit up my senses, filling the air with angry words and visions. The narrating voice droned on, louder and clearer now, drowning out the sound of Coltrane's sax as I drifted into the next animated scene. "Suddenly-yyy, an incredible chemical change occurs in Wilfred Wormus! His filthy unwashed clothes and rancid toxic sweat mix with the stale beer, resulting in a strange and powerful supernatural reaction-nnn! He begins to change into the ferocious, invincible . . . CAP-TAIN CRII-IINGE!!"

I could feel Wilfred's scrawny body expanding, growing and ripping through my clothes like the Incredible Hulk! I looked down and saw a pair of huge muscular arms. My bare torso was covered in exotic, abstract, primal designs tattooed all over; dark, spindly, blade-like claws and tendrils crisscrossing my body, reminding me of the word *BEWARE* from a long time ago. Wilfred held his bulging tattooed arms above his head as I heard my own voice reverberating in a deep triumphant booming bellow. "I HAVE BECOME MASSIVE!"

Wilfred and I were transformed! Through the smoky vision, I saw our imposing shadow towering over the three bullies as they cowered in a corner, cringing under the menacing superhero bulk of Captain Cringe. The radio announcer's voice rattled on in the background. "Captain Cringe! Yes-ss! Something in the booze has indeed changed Wilfred! It has suddenly made him powerfu-ull! And something else! Something more! They all CRINGE when they see him! Besides his rippling muscles and hairy legs, what is it that makes them all CRINGE before him? Could it be the strange, mysterious markings that cover his powerrrful-ull new body-yy . . . ???" I watched in stoned-out glee as my comic-book alter ego ran amok, tearing up the barroom, destroying everything in his unstoppable path, slaughtering our foes in a brutal, bloodthirsty, homicidal rampage!

Suddenly, the gory heart-pounding action sequence froze. Long red fingernails reached like squirming spiders into the periphery of my vision, grabbing, gripping, ripping the frozen cartoon panel in half, exposing my grim unwelcome reality again. My mother was in a rage, towering over me like Godzilla, tearing up all my drawings and comic books! Before I knew what was happening, it was too late! Snapping out of it, I looked around in horror. Len was standing behind her in the doorway, a silent gray phantom holding my bag of weed between his fingers like a dead rat, a dour look on his dull face.

"I've had it with you and your crap, boy!!" Doris screeched, rampaging through the shelves and ripping my cherished comic collection to shreds. "These damn cartoon books are the reason you sit in a dark room all day! Brooding, filling your head with this trash! My only child has become a thief and a vandal! A common delinquent!" She faked a melodramatic sob and railed on. "A goddamned drug addict!"

Paralyzed, in shock, I cursed her under my breath. I looked up at Len, my eyes pleading. *Make her stop, man!* He just stood there with his usual pathetic hangdog "fatherly" look of stern, empty, brooding nothingness. He crinkled up his forehead and cleared his throat. "Why were you shoplifting again when you have everything you need here, Jono?" His vapid eyes poked at me like a stern Alfred E. Neuman. "Just tell us the truth, son. Was it to pay for these drugs? Are you hooked on this stuff?"

Son? Drugs? Hooked?! My cringeometer jumped into the red as I glared back at him in disgust. *Stupid pussy-whipped dickless old creep!* I jumped up and bolted out the door, brushing past them and screaming till my lungs hurt.

"I hate you fuckin' people!" I could hear myself shouting, my unstoppable rage bouncing off the cold white walls as I ran down the stairs and slammed the back door behind me.

44. BORN TO RAISE HELL

"I HEARD PAPA SAY TO MAMA, TO LET DAT BOY BOOGIE-
WOOGIE, 'CUZ IT'S IN HIM, AND IT'S GOTTA COME OUT."
                                        –JOHN LEE HOOKER

"And that, my friend, was the bitter end of my budding teenage art career." Cigano laughs as he closes his composition book with a lively snap and picks up another one. "This next part," he mumbles, leafing through the pages, "I dunno about getting into it just now, man." He shrugs. "I never thought I'd even live to write about this stuff, much less read it to someone."

Jaco shifts in his chair, saying nothing. Loud mariachi music blasts from the cantina below as the roar of a mufflerless bus rattles the windows.

Cigano looks up and sighs. "I dunno, man. I guess this is where the whole 'confession' part comes into this thing, some real painful memories I'd totally blocked out. So many feelings came up while I was writing this stuff: rage, sadness, repulsion. Kinda like lancing a big horrible diseased goiter. I never thought I'd be able to remember so many details of the past when I started writing this stuff. It hasn't come easy, believe me . . ." He begins scratching his head fiercely, as if trying to jump-start his brain. He stops. "How can I explain? Didja ever feel like you left something behind and you should maybe go back and look for it, like before it's gone forever?"

Jaco nods.

"Yeah, well, dredging some of this old shit up has been like pulling teeth without painkillers, bro."

"I see what you mean. I'd like to hear more. But if you prefer not t—"

"Naw." Cigano takes a deep breath. "It's cool. I guess it's about time to take another look at this mess. Just gotta keep goin' . . ." he mutters, opening the notebook like a tomb.

"By the time I turned fourteen," he reads, "I was itching to get out of there for good. Leaving home was all I could think about as I quietly planned my escape. The comic-book incident was the last straw for me. I'd always been a dark, introverted kid, but after they destroyed my comics and confiscated my stash, threatening to turn me over to the cops, it was all-out war." As he reads, the tattoo man pictures a worn pair of dusty black-and-white high-top sneakers standing in the dirt. "I became a brooding teenaged stoner," he reads, "with murder in my heart . . ."

As he turns a page, the fuzzy yellow picture expands in his awareness, growing sharper, more focused in his mind, till he can clearly see himself as a shaggy-haired teenager standing behind a hedge at the side of the neat white house. Throwing furtive glances around, young Jonathan stares down at the shiny edge of a big hunting knife. He grins at his scruffy reflection in the blade, baring his teeth like a feral cat. Looking around again, he tucks the knife into his belt and creeps like a pirate around the side of the house, ducking below the windows. He finds a new spot and crouches down behind a big eucalyptus. He starts carving into the virgin tree trunk. Sweat runs down his face. Wood chips fall at his feet as he works with all the desperation of his pissed-off young soul, till the sappy green flesh is covered in bold primitive designs like the ones on Captain Cringe. The young vandal stands back staring at his handiwork with a grim, rebellious pride.

Cigano shakes his head and returns to the page. "As I fell into a whirlpool of brooding isolation, I would spend whole days alone in my room smoking weed, fantasizing scenes of bloody retribution and playing with my knives. A petty criminal and merchant marine named Richard Speck had just made headlines for slaughtering eight nurses in a mad booze-fueled blackout. The news reports showed a crude tattoo on his arm: *BORN TO RAISE HELL*. I thought the hard-drinking whore-chasing sailor looked cool with his slicked-back hair and badass tattoo. With no other channel for my teenage alienation, I found in Speck a new role model to rival even Godzilla. Utterly powerless over my own life, I imagined how it would feel to be a serial killer like Speck. I daydreamed of breaking into the whitewashed suburban homes in my neighborhood, tiptoeing around in those houses behind their neat manicured façades. I pictured myself butchering people like Speck did, thinking to myself how easy it would be to literally get away with murder since nobody would ever suspect an innocent-looking neighbor boy.

"As the sixties progressed, my mother's alcoholic rampages worsened as she started mixing an assortment of pep pills, downers, and other weird prescription drugs with her steady booze diet. Her freaky mood swings got more unpredictable and violent. A climate of fear and distrust reigned at home as the bombs rained down on Vietnam. The ominous shadow of the family Curse was closing in on us like a dark clammy net. Paranoia clouded the air we breathed. That's when the restless demons of the Curse began to really bare their teeth.

"To mark the series of tragic events which would seal my family's unhappy fate, once and for all, my mother's younger brother Richard died from cirrhosis of the liver at the ripe old age of thirty-seven."

Cigano winces and looks up from his reading. "As a lifelong hope-to-die alcoholic myself, I can tell ya, man, it takes a whole lotta real dedicated drinking to stew your guts into mush so young. And believe me, brother, I didn't keep from drinking myself to death for lack of trying."

Shaking his head, he turns to the next page.

45. NEW YORK, NEW YORK

"IN A ROOM WHERE PEOPLE UNANIMOUSLY MAINTAIN A
CONSPIRACY OF SILENCE, ONE WORD OF TRUTH SOUNDS
LIKE A PISTOL SHOT."

—CZESLAW MILOSZ

My uncle Richard—who, until his sudden death, I'd never known
existed—was a writer in New York City. Even though he couldn't
write as well as his older brother Robert, he'd managed to publish
an uninspired little novel, in which he savagely took the piss out of a
star-struck, narcissistic young woman for her shameless ambition. The
character was a thinly disguised takeup of his sister Doris. Poorly written
as his book was, he managed a wonderfully bitter hatchet job on my
mother. The character's haughty, narcissistic dialogue captured her to
a T, depicting her as an unfaithful, shallow, ill-mannered, loathsome
creature who cared for nobody and nothing other than her fancy house
in Hollywood—which she describes in boastful detail to a pair of young
New Yorkers who poke fun at her snooty airs. After the book came
out, my mother, mortified by her brother's hateful portrayal of her, cut
Richard off like a diseased limb.

I was fourteen when she got the news that her estranged sibling had
bought the farm. I remember her getting real upset when the call came
from Robert. She flew to New York with Grandma and Aunt Connie to
bury her baby brother. I think she felt kind of guilty for having turned
her back on her New York brothers in her pursuit of fame and fortune.

Back home from the funeral, she went on a violent weeklong bender that ended her up at a posh Beverly Hills drying-out clinic. While she was away "resting up from her trip," Len and I slunk around the big empty white house, a pair of guilty shadows avoiding each other like witnesses to some dirty little crime.

Those were bad times. After she got out of detox my mother was irritable, restless, and cranky; a ticking time bomb. We all tiptoed around the sleeping rhinoceros in the living room till it was unbearable. I stayed away, cutting classes and spending long, aimless afternoons shoplifting, smoking weed, sniffing glue, and skulking around the neighborhood plotting my escape. As the months dragged on, I kept getting brought home by truant officers and cops. More trouble. That's when a new game of Musical Homes began. In a last-ditch attempt to be free of my rebellious antics, they decided to send me away again, this time to spend the summer with my uncle Robert and his family in New York.

Uncle Robert was an unpublished, ne'er-do-well bourbon-soaked bard who lived with his wife Peggy and their three kids in a ratty beatnik basement apartment on the Upper West Side, near Harlem. For years, Robert Smith had lingered on the fringes of New York's bohemian intellectual art crowd like a drunken fruit fly hovering around the likes of Kerouac and de Kooning. His most prolific literary efforts were dedicated to an endless stream of impassioned letters bombarding his well-heeled sisters and Grandma Mabel, begging for "loans" to finance the Great American Novel he was always on the verge of selling. The years went by in a boozy blur of rejection slips and tragicomic drunken misadventures while the money they sent him went to the Blarney Stone Tavern at the corner of Broadway and West Ninety-sixth. One day, a drinking buddy took one of Robert's manuscripts to a prestigious publishing house where he had a friend who was a top editor. After reading it, the editor raved about turning it into a bestseller. Excited, the friend ran back to surprise Robert with the happy news. Robert asked for his manuscript back, ostensibly to make a few minor revisions. That evening, following in his father Harry's footsteps, he got drunk. Crazed as a rabid squirrel, Robert Smith ran outside and threw his Great American Novel onto a garbage fire.

My first day in New York found Uncle Robert in a fit of restless writer's block. He came home with this big stump of wood he'd found in Central Park. He sat in the living room drinking, building a slow wobbly pyramid of empty beer cans and carving at the stump with a nasty-looking hunting knife. He'd grunt to himself from time to time, but never spoke to anyone. Nobody said a word. He made this big unruly mess, then finally stood up and growled, "*Agghh,* fuck it!" He walked out the door and disappeared for the next couple of days. His wife Peggy wouldn't dare touch his "modern art sculpture" or clean up the pile of wood shavings he'd left there. Everyone just tiptoed around this big old tree trunk in the middle of the living room with a knife sticking out of it like it was some kind of sacred totem.

Aunt Peggy was a shell-shocked, goofy short-order waitress who slung sweaty hash to surly Negroes at a Harlem greasy spoon to support her husband's beatnik lifestyle and keep their three kids, my cousins Hillary, Justin, and Malcolm, clothed and fed. As soon as I arrived, Malcolm— my elder by a year—took me under his wing. We became an inseparable pair, stalking the streets around Riverside Park with his gang of big-city junior hoodlums. He became the big brother I'd never had, quickly replacing Richard Speck and Godzilla as my new role model. Malcolm looked like a young version of his father. A slouching sixteen-year-old boxer and all-around tough guy, Malcolm Smith's brooding James Dean figure was legend on the streets and handball courts of the Upper West Side. To me he was a larger-than-life heroic character right out of *West Side Story.* He kept his Golden Gloves trophies lined up on the window-sill by his bed where you could look up and see feet scurrying by out on Columbus Avenue. I remember him grinning at me on my first day there: "See this fist he-ah, Jon? I knocked a goddamn subway cop flat on his fat ass d'utha day when da dumb basti'd come ovah and tole me to put my smoke out on da friggin' train, heh-hh! Woo, boy, and all dem people just sat there mindin' their own damn business too, hee-hh!"

My hero's well-behaved siblings both seemed to want little to do with Malcolm's sullen hellfire antics, so I became his full-time sidekick. His best friend was this weasely smartass kid named Louie. Louie was half Italian and half Puerto Rican. His dad was some kind of big-shot hitman for the Mob or something. He was always talking about his old man "whackin'" guys who got "outta line." Louie always had the best pot, too. We'd spend the long humid summer afternoons hanging out in the neighborhood, smoking the nickel and dime bags he sold. The three of us would sit for hours with our feet dangling from a cliff over the river, bullshitting and throwing cigarette butts down into the Hudson's dirty waters. Whenever we had a few bucks we'd go sit in the balconies of the musty, cavernous old movie theaters in Times Square, watching Charles Bronson movies, sniffing glue and drinking cheap Muscatel. Sometimes we'd take the train down to the Village. Macdougal Street was our hangout. There was always a lot going on down there. Louie and Malcolm would get into pickup games with the colored kids from Brooklyn at the basketball courts on Sixth Avenue while I hung around smoking cigarettes and watching the world go by. I was quite impressed. Summer in New York was a dream come true. I was fifteen years old and feeling right at home somewhere for the first time in my life.

Malcolm was a tough guy on the street, forever teaching me boxing moves and sucker-punches. But at home my big cousin was a dedicated artist; a painter with a wild van Gogh-ish flair and a poet who loved Poe, Kafka, and Shakespeare. He was also a gifted stand-up bass player—bow and all—with a scholarship to Juilliard. Malcolm was clearly Uncle Robert's favorite kid, despite the occasional beating he took from his father to "straighten him out." In the beginning my uncle eyed me with suspicion, scowling in silence from his easy chair where he sat holding court surrounded by piles of empty beer cans. He never "threw me a beatin'" like he did his son, but I think he was worried I was some sort of stuck-up Beverly Hills movie brat. Luckily, Uncle Robert soon realized I despised Doris's stuck-up airs as much as he did. That's when we sort of bonded. My uncle and I would take turns imitating her fake British accent, making fun of her and her husband. Uncle Robert would share his Rheingolds with us and show me his brawling scars, bragging about all the "jive niggers" he'd knocked off barstools on upper Broadway. "Dis one big spade pimp gave me this one heah when my back wuz toined, see . . ." He lifted his shirt to show a twelve-inch straight-razor scar. "Never toin ya back on a goddamn nigger, Jon! Dis ain't no fuggin' hippie-dippy California love-in he-ah, got it?" Malcolm and I would drink our beers and nod sullenly under the low basement ceiling with people shuffling around overhead.

46. SUMMER IN THE CITY

"I GUESS I WAS JUST DIFFERENT AND, LIKE DOGS, THEY COULD SMELL IT. SO I NEVER HAD MANY FRIENDS."

—SOL LUCKMAN

One humid Saturday in July, Grandma Mabel, who was visiting for the summer, took Malcolm, me, and his little sister Hillary to Coney Island. Their introverted older brother Justin—who was some kind of math genius and never spoke to any of us—was off at his special egghead school.

Under my direction, the three of us promptly ditched the old lady on the boardwalk after she stopped to chat with some other old crows. Once again I was the Ringleader, the Troublemaker. After spending all our money on hot dogs, salt-water taffy, and rides, I coached the other two on the fine art of shoplifting, and off we went on an hour-long stealing spree. We grabbed all kinds of cheap trinkets from the concession stands and gift shops in the busy arcades till our pockets were bulging. Hillary, who was only nine, ended up getting us busted. When some security cops saw her snatching a kewpie doll and shoving it into her pocket, they followed her till she led them to us. They snagged the three of us and took us into a little room behind the roller coaster. We sat looking at the floor while a skinny guy in a white shirt and black tie went on the loudspeaker and paged our grand-mother to come get us. We weren't charged, because Hillary was so little. The cops even acted like it was kind of funny. But Grandma

Mabel was mortified. On the subway ride back, we begged her not to tell Robert, but she said it was for our own good.

Hillary got sent to her room after a half-hearted spanking from Peggy. Then Robert, who was already plastered, lashed into Malcolm with the fierce, wild-eyed savagery of a barroom brawler. I watched in horror as my tough-guy hero stood there silently playing punching bag for his father, taking a man-sized thrashing like a man. All these "souvenir of Coney Island" keychains and seashell bracelets flew out of his pockets every time Uncle Robert punched him. I just stood frozen in place, waiting my turn. But when he was done beating on Malcolm, he just glowered and told me to "Shape up or ship out" and that was the end of it. I felt guilty for being the Ringleader and egging the others on—especially when I saw my cousin's two black eyes, split lip, and bloody nose. But Malcolm never ratted me out to my quick-fisted uncle. He just grinned and said: *"Don' worry 'bout it, Jon, it ain't nut'n'."* Malcolm was a stand-up guy.

There was this girl who lived across the street. She used to come up and flirt with me as I sat out on the stoop with Malcolm and Louie and their gang. Linda something-or-other, some long Italian surname, was a pretty thirteen-year-old colt with high hips and endless legs. She wore her long brown hair in loose, friendly braids. She had these big piercing black eyes that made my stomach churn like a cement mixer. Louie told me she had a "hardon" for me and that I should take her down to the boiler room and "ball" her. But Linda was a virgin and so was I. The closest we ever got to "balling" was fumbling around on a bench in Riverside Park one day where she let me kiss her and feel up her peachy little breasts. Her timid pink tongue was cool and tasted like the salt-water taffy from Coney Island. That was the first time I'd ever been with a girl. I thought I was in love; but after our frantic little make-out session, she always avoided me and kept her haunting dark eyes lowered when she passed us on the street. I was crushed.

Zeroing in on my awkwardness like a big brown sewer rat, Louie quizzed me about our walk in the park. When I just shrugged, he started breaking my balls for not "poppin' her cherry" in the bushes. Miserable and consumed with regret, I wanted to die. Malcolm stepped up and saved the day. "Hey, ma-aan, give da guy a break!" He scowled at his friend. "My cousin Jon here ain't no ignorant animal like you fuggin' spic-wop monkeys around hee-ah, see? He's from California, see, and he's a gentleman! Got it?" Louie got it. That was the end of his bullying. Even with his hit-man dad, he didn't want to be on Malcolm's shit list. That's the way it was around the neighborhood. There was a pecking order out on the stoop and down on the corner, and my big cousin the Golden Gloves champ was top dog. Nobody fucked with Malcolm.

Despite his streetwise tough-guy swagger, though, Malcolm was a sensitive soul. A hopeless romantic, his favorite movie was *Romeo and Juliet*. He must've seen it twenty times. You never saw a guy so hung up on a film! It was all he'd talk about. We'd lie on the grass in the park smoking reefers and staring into the hazy summer sky, and he'd tell me how he was going to meet his "soul mate," just like in *Romeo and Juliet*, and how they'd move upstate to the country and make abstract art and progressive jazz together. I loved listening to Malcolm's high-flying dreams about music and writing and art. Then he'd jump up and start waving his arms around. "C'mon, Jon, let's get da fuck outta here! I gotta show ya sump'n'." We'd march down to the musty old subway station on Broadway. Jumping into a grafitti-covered train screaming out of the dark tunnel like a metallic dragon, we'd clatter downtown and clomp around the Museum of Modern Art for hours while Malcolm gestured at paintings by Klee, de Kooning, Kandinsky, and Dalí, all these great artists I'd never heard of, saying, "Woo, boy, now dis is da way a guy's supposed ta paint, maa-an! hehh-ehh!" I'd stand beside him, nodding like a young boxer listening to ringside instructions.

But Malcolm also had this weird dark side. The Curse. Sometimes he'd get real gloomy. He'd sit on the stoop brooding and not talking to anyone. His pals always left him alone when he got like that; they just talked around him like he wasn't there. I could relate to my big cousin's moodiness. Sometimes we'd both sit out there staring into space together. It was cool to finally have someone to brood with. Uncle Robert was all hung up on Sigmund Freud. He would take Malcolm aside for an hour or two every few days and they'd go sit in his room and talk. Nobody was allowed to disturb them when they were in a "session." Aunt Peggy proudly informed me in her thick Bronx drawl that Robert was "psycho-analyzin'" his son. Malcolm would never talk about those amateur head-shrinking sessions with his father, but I think it kind of messed up his head, and he'd always be in a dark, creepy mood afterwards.

As August descended over the ghostly half-deserted metropolis like a moldy blanket, my return to LA crept and darted around our muggy subway days like a nervous shadow. I didn't want to go. There was talk about me transferring to a local school and staying on in New York. Malcolm talked to his father. Robert seemed to be all for it—scheming to hit up his rich sister and her fancy Jew husband for more cash to foot the bill for my room and board. Long distance calls were made. Len was ready to cut Robert a fat Hollywood check, but the old lady wasn't having it. Furious, she accused her big brother of trying to "seduce" her son away and "turning me against her," and that was the end of our big plan. With a heavy heart, I packed my suitcase and boarded a big Pan Am jet plane back to California.

47. MARRIED TO THE MOB

"THE REAL LONELINESS IS LIVING AMONG ALL THESE KIND
PEOPLE WHO ONLY ASK ONE TO PRETEND!"

—EDITH WHARTON

Back in my unhappy home, I rebelled. Truancy. Shoplifting. Vandalism. Burglary. Trespassing. Drug busts. All the trademarks of a pissed-off juvenile delinquent. My mother got her money's worth out of her mink stoles, pearl necklaces, and rhinestone-studded sunglasses. She seemed to almost revel in all the drama, as she became a frequent, well-rehearsed visitor at principals' offices, police stations, and Juvenile Court.

Finally, they sent me to see a Beverly Hills headshrinker. A Dr. Finkelstein or some shit. I used to call the faceless old Freudian analyst Dr. Frankenstein. I'd sit in a stuffy leather armchair, a prisoner in his dark book-lined office. My dirty Converse sneakers fidgeted like two trapped birds as the old shadow just sat there stroking his close-cropped gray beard and staring at me, saying nothing. I said nothing. We both sat there the whole fucking session, saying nothing. Then the time would be up. My eye was already on the door as the gray-headed doctor glanced at his watch and gave me a dull look. I'd get up and split without saying good-bye.

I knew my mental health wasn't Doris's real motive for sending me there anyway. The old lady just wanted someone with a diploma on the wall and some kind of "authority" to wave a magic wand over her troublesome kid, then send him back all patched up and ready to play his part as a walking, talking prop in her big production of "The Happy Family," a cheery Hollywood blockbuster she craved a starring role in.

I was "acting out" again. That's what the head doctors called it. Acting out. It had an official ring to it; like a diagnosis of the clap, measles, diarrhea, the flu. Something curable. The old lady latched on to all the fancy pseudo-therapeutic double-talk like a pit bull with a hambone. It gave her something to sink her perfect whiter-than-white teeth into. Something to blame. After that, it was "the boy is acting out" this and "acting out" that, ad nauseam. But there seemed to be no tangible cause or standard course of treatment for that mysterious, exotic malady. From my mother's twisted, boozy perspective, her beamish boy was fucking up her big movie, as if some defiant anarchist method actor had thrown away his lines in a lighthearted sitcom, hurtling the cast and crew into a churning maelstrom of confusion and chaos. And Doris didn't like that sort of dilemma. How would she? Alcoholics are basically directors, control freaks, dictators. They always need to know exactly what's going to happen next. Insecure and paranoid by nature, they want all their ducks lined up in neat little rows; and my unpredictable anti-social antics didn't fit the script. But what seemed to really piss her off the most was that by "acting out," I was a threat to the status quo, a menacing chink in the clean white fortress wall of practiced respectability so important to the survival of her Grand Production.

Growing up in an alcoholic home is like being in the Mob. There's always an unwritten Code of Silence. *Omerta.* You never discuss "Family Business" with "Outsiders." Even as the family members brutalize and butcher each other to death in a hundred subtle and not-so-subtle ways, there's always this ironclad Us Against The World mentality that must be preserved at all costs—like a hardy protein shell protecting a deadly virus. By getting into trouble all the time, I'd committed the Great Cardinal Sin, threatening to bring the dreaded Outsiders in on Family Business: cops, truant officers, Juvenile Courts, school authorities, psychiatrists. God forbid those big bad Outside Intruders might discover that behind their carefully maintained whitewashed façade maybe there was something unwholesome, something strange and unhappy going on in The Happy Family's happy home: some dirty little secret pounding away in a dark corner like a reappearing bloodstain on their spotless white wall-to-wall carpet. And so I became a Threat. A Fly in the Ointment. An Informer. A Snitch. A Rat. A Fink. A Liability; dispensable, for the good of the Organization.

○   ○   ○

The tattoo man pauses and looks at Jaco, grinning. "It's funny, man. Right after I wrote that last part, I ran into this guy I knew, at a recovery meeting. Richard O'Connell. I hadn't seen the guy in like thirty years. I was sure he musta ended up dead, like most of my old friends. I was really glad to see him alive and sober, after God knows how long. Anyway, we went out for coffee and started talking about our families. I gave him copies of some of my writing about my mother's drinking, stuff like that."

He chuckles. "Having grown up in a similar alcoholic shitstorm, I figured he could dig it. Anyway, he comes to see me a couple of days later and sure enough he starts telling me how much he could relate. It was a good feeling."

Cigano smiles, seeing his old friend's grinning face in his mind's eye.

○   ○   ○

"I really dug where you wrote about families, Jono, the way they always band together like gangsters, even when they're bashing each other's brains out. That part really cracked me up. After I finished laughing out loud, I started remembering all kinda stuff about my folks. You remember how nuts my mother was, right?"

"Well, I remember how she was always screaming and breaking shit; yeah, man."

"Fuck, that ain't the half of it, Jono. My old lady made your mom look like Mary Poppins! So when I was reading your thing, I suddenly flashed back on this time my mom and dad were totally beating the crap out of each other in the living room. I ran down and started trying to break 'em up, and then all of a sudden my brother walks in and puts a fuckin' shotgun up to my head!"

"Whoa! That's a nice family get-together! What happened?"

"Well, the neighbors were out walking the dog and they heard all this screaming and commotion and then they saw him holding this big gun on me through the window, right? So they ran home and called the cops . . ."

"How dare those dirty busybodies interfere with family business?"

"Yeah, man! Exactly! Why can't people just mind their own damn business, right? So get this. There's my folks beating each other to a bloody pulp, and my brother's holding this big old shotgun to my head so I won't 'butt in,' when all of a sudden the cops are banging on the door . . ."

"It ain't real fun till they call nine-one-one."

"Yeah, right? So dig this, Jono. It was just like that thing you wrote, like as soon as somebody was trying to put a stop to it, all four of us were right up there in a flash, standing at the front door like a united front, all grinning and nodding at the cops while my dad's standing there telling 'em, "Er, there must be some mistake, officers. Everything's just *fine* here." The minute the cops split, of course, my brother pulls the shotgun on me again, and my parents go right back to punching each other's lights out. Business as usual. My old man was a fucking expert at that shit! Old school Irish. 'No problem here.' My mother would be so fucking pazooed she'd be out on the front lawn at three in the morning, down on all fours barking like a fucking Rottweiler and my dad would be like, 'Oh, your mother's just a little . . . tired. You boys go back to bed. Everything's fine.'"

Cigano chuckles at the memory. "Running into Richard that day was really cool for me. A couple of shell-shocked survivors, sitting around cracking up about all these horrible traumas like it's a big fucking joke! It's not all doom and gloom, y'know. No matter how fucked-up things were, by sharing this kinda shit there's a kind of identification that's pure magic." He grins. "That's where the word 'compassion' comes from, y'know. Its Latin root means something like 'shared suffering.'" He shrugs. "I can honestly say I don't regret any of it. After a lifetime beating myself over the head and hating the world, finally being able to see some humor in the whole fucked-up deal is like finding buried treasure."

Jaco nods as the tattoo man turns to another page.

48. OUR GANG

". . . WE WALKED THREE ABREAST IN THE COBBLESTONE
STREET, DRUNK AND LAUGHING AND TALKING LIKE MEN WHO
KNEW THEY WOULD SEPARATE AT DAWN AND TRAVEL TO THE
FAR CORNERS OF THE EARTH."

—HUNTER S. THOMPSON

Back from New York, I started running with a bunch of neighborhood kids. They would become the family I'd never had. Loyal. Available. Stable. Fun. My gang was a group of shaggy visionaries, artists, musicians, poets, and likeminded teenage fuckups. It all started with a guy named Jerome Ali who came bopping down the street one afternoon. We got to shooting the shit, then went out and stole a Triumph Bonneville together. We stashed the bike in his garage, where he lived upstairs in the attic.

My new friend was from a big Arab/Italian family. He had the dark, engaging looks of a young Omar Sharif. We shared a passion for comic-book art, and he knew all about avant-garde literature, foreign art films, and jazz. Jerome was a poet, a painter, and a real good guitar player. Like many young guys, I wanted to learn to play. That was the big thing back then. Hendrix was God, and rock 'n' roll was a one-way ticket to the Promised Land. Jerome taught me a few licks, and we started a band. Ironically, my own father was one of an elite few to make it as a musician. More than just a visionary player, Artie Shaw had been a superstar celebrity, a predecessor to the rock icons of my generation. When Jerome found out who my father was, and that my mother had been in *Bitter Rice*—one of his favorite foreign art films—he flipped. He always seemed confused by my taciturn distaste for my parental legacy, since Jerome pictured my mother and father as heroic Muses of the Arts.

I smoked my first opium-laced hashish up in Jerome's little attic cubbyhole, while practicing guitar riffs to the haunting sound of Gabor Szabo's *Gypsy 66* on his record player. I set the guitar down and shut my eyes, nodding, drifting off with that dreamlike music to exotic faraway lands. It was great; the first time I ever felt completely at ease in my skin. Getting high and sneaking into rock concerts and movies became a regular thing for us.

One day we went to see a new Brazilian art flick called *Orfeu Negro*, hunkered down in an empty theater balcony smoking a joint. It was an exotic stew of color and sound; a magical world of godlike dancing Negroes. As a Bossa Nova soundtrack filled the dark musty air, I watched, hypnotized by the visions weaving a spell of longing across my soul. Right then I knew I was seeing my destiny. Rio de Janeiro, Brazil. I became obsessed with going there. I watched *Orpheu Negro* so many times that the story and its breathtaking tropical setting became essential elements of my being.

By the time I was sixteen, I practically lived at Jerome's place. I was at the Alis' dinner table every night, a new family member—no questions asked. Jerome's mother was everything I'd always wanted in a mom. She cooked spaghetti with meatballs, and Jerome's father and older brothers and sisters sat around the round kitchen table fighting like convicts. There was always loud talk and laughter there, especially when Jerome's father, a big-spirited Italian tradesman, sat down after work. Jerome's home and family were everything I'd always longed to belong to.

Through Jerome I met a whole bunch of other new friends. There was Chris Anderson, another artist, and his bright-eyed fifteen-year-old sister Melissa, who would become my first girlfriend. There was Steve Hartman, a tall, gangly Jewish orphan with a sick sense of humor who lived with a speed-freak older sister. We would hang out at her place and use her binoculars to form a stoned-out Peeping Tom club. Patrick and Billy Butcher were a pair of outgoing young Irish brothers with a fluttering assortment of fresh-faced blond sisters. There were lots of others, like Kim Gordon, Danny Elfman, and Lou Beach, who would go on to become world-class artists and musicians.

Richard O'Connell was Jerome's best friend since childhood and our gang's unofficial guru. A handsome, charismatic seventeen-year-old drummer with intense blue eyes, O'Connell loved jazz, chicks, and cars—which he was a specialist at stealing. He was forever pushing the limits of our adventures into sleepless drug-fueled days and nights of mayhem. His enthusiasm and energy were contagious. We'd drop mind-bending handfuls of LSD and pile into some big, shiny luxury sedan O'Connell had hot-wired. Next, we'd be standing around nodding and grinning as he hustled us into a shadowy Negro jazz club downtown. We'd stand in a dark corner popping our fingers to the John Coltrane Quartet's mad telepathic musical epiphanies; the next afternoon, still tripping our eyes out, we'd ride up the coast to a hidden cove Richard knew. We'd listen to the jazz station on his ever-present transistor radio and eat fishy raw mussels right off the rocks as we marveled at Charie Parker's high-flying be-bop riffs. Our gang was generally feared and admired by our neighborhood peers, and there was always something new and exciting going on.

49. DRAGON LADY

"A HALLUCINATION IS A SPECIES OF REALITY."

—TERENCE MCKENNA

"My first acid trips with my friends were all it took for me to see the advantage of 'turning on, tuning in, and dropping out' of the uptight world of consensus reality once and for all," Cigano reads. "Having found a way to change my world without having to leave home, things quickly turned weird; and the weirder it got, the more I avoided my house like a snake pit. Sometimes, though, going back was unavoidable, like one cold night, tripping balls at three in the morning, I went home to get a jacket."

Nostalgic strains of psychedelic music weave through the tapestry of Cigano's mind. "*The killer awoke before dawn. He put his boots on. He took a face from the ancient gallery, and he walked on down the hall.*" Like a shaky dime-store magician, the tattoo man's hands gesture madly. The sound of traffic from the street below blends with his words as he takes up his story again.

Approaching the big silent mausoleum, I had a disturbing vision of Doris and Len sleeping inside like a pair of mummies in an Egyptian tomb. I tiptoed up to the back door in the dark, trying to be as silent as the ants on the outside wall. But those ants weren't silent at all! I could hear their tiny footsteps pounding in my brain like angry troops marching off to war. Trying not to breathe too loud, I fit my key into the lock ever so carefully.

I tiptoed across the darkened kitchen, stealthy as a cat. I cracked the hallway door and looked around. The coast was clear. As I started slinking up the stairs, I heard a noise in the living room. *Shit!* I froze, the blood rushing in my veins like Niagara Falls. My heart was pounding like a giant drum. I shut my eyes tight. Swirling patterns of the most incredible colors raced across my vision. I felt I'd be sucked off into outer space if I kept my eyes closed a second longer. Prying them open, my eyelashes screeched like a pair of rusty old beach umbrellas unfolding. It was excruciatingly loud. *Fuck!*

"Jono . . . ?" My mother's voice called out. "Dah-ling? Is that you?"

I couldn't move. I didn't speak, fearing my voice would crack a hole in the universe, that I'd fall in and never get back.

"Jono, dah-ling . . . ?"

I took a deep breath. Struggling to maintain, I crept to the big white living-room doorway and stopped. Through the swirling patterns, I could see an image of my mother forming. She was sitting on the plush white sofa all alone, wearing a long, flowing white nightgown. Reading a book, she looked like a queen sitting on a throne. Regal. Unflappable. She seemed to be sober.

"Hi . . ." I mumbled, inching forward, keeping my eyes to the floor. My voice sounded amplified, like it was coming from a giant megaphone. I clamped my mouth shut again and kept my eyes averted. I knew if the Queen saw them she'd be able to read my mind. She'd look right into the depths of my soul and see all the colors swirling around and the jig would be up.

"Hello, dah-ling." She was smiling. "How was your evening?"

"Uh, fine." My voice was a booming, rasping, metallic croak.

"That's nice, dear . . ."

She began making conversation, talking about the book she was reading. She seemed to be making a special effort to sound all casual and calm. Something was wrong. Her voice was too normal. But I couldn't focus on her voice. I could barely distinguish the strange language she was speaking; and even if I could, the words were drowned out by the rushing flames spitting from her mouth as she shape-shifted into a hissing reptilian dragon!

"You seem a bit pale, dah-ling," the creature hissed at me. "Come and let me feel your forehead. You look like you're burning up."

Burning! Flames! Oh God! I stood still as a pillar, frozen in terror as the giant lizard thing lifted a long spindly claw and beckoned. *Oh God, no!* My brain shouted *RUN!* in a thousand tiny voices of terror. *I'm gonna die if that fucking thing comes near me! This isn't real! It's the acid! Maintain!* I kept urging myself to stay cool. But I knew that horrible creature could read my thoughts. *Maintain, man! Just make it up to your room and everything will be all right! Don't let it see your eyes! Go! Go!*

"Uh, I'm just a little tired, Doris," I croaked as the dragon flicked its long black tongue out like a snake, then settled back on the sofa with the book my mother had been reading. "I'll see ya in the morning," I mumbled as I bolted up to my room, pouring sweat and taking the stairs two at a time.

50. THE BIG VISIT

"GRIEF CAN TAKE CARE OF ITSELF, BUT TO GET THE FULL
VALUE OF JOY YOU MUST HAVE SOMEBODY TO DIVIDE
IT WITH."

—MARK TWAIN

All in all, I think it was a relief for Doris and her husband not having me around much. Out of sight, out of mind. Definitely out of *my* mind. As I grew increasingly absent, they sure didn't send out any search parties; and that casual new attitude became a quiet truce. By the time spring rolled around, my mother and Uncle Robert were back on speaking terms. The old lady must have figured Malcolm had been some sort of stabilizing influence on her troublesome son, since I hadn't been in trouble with the cops in New York—at least as far as she knew; and so it was decided that my big cousin should come spend the summer with us.

By the time Malcolm arrived in June, I was almost sixteen. I only went home to change clothes or to hit up the old lady for cash. My mother's sporadic handouts were called an "allowance." That had a nice respectable ring to it. In truth, it was more like hush money: an unspoken bribe to stay away as she pursued the all-important task of drinking herself stupid. I had no problem with the arrangement. I'd had enough of their shit to last me a lifetime, so I just took the cash and ran the streets with my gang. I couldn't wait to turn my New York hero on to the scene.

The day of Malcolm's arrival, after some polite formalities at home, the two of us ran right out to see my friends. Malcolm was an instant hit with Richard O'Connell. An accomplished jazz drummer with the energy of ten African percussionists, Richard was thrilled to have a bona fide Juilliard musician in the ever-evolving musical mix. And like O'Connell, Malcolm loved handball. They went right down to the alley behind the liquor store where there was a brick wall. The two of them hit the same note that day, a sweet note. They became fast friends.

In the weeks to come, there were all-night jam sessions in garages around the neighborhood. There was lots of pot smoking and wine guzzling and foxy chicks. It was the perfect scene to roll out a proud welcome mat for my big-city hero. One warm summer evening there was a big acid-fueled band practice in the Butcher brothers' garage. Malcolm labored away at the old upright bass Richard and Patrick—the Bat—had "liberated" from the high school band room. Sweating like a bricklayer, he labored over the big instrument till blood ran down the bass's neck. Richard leaned over his drum kit, gawking. "Jesus, Malcolm, yer hands are fuckin' hamburger meat, man!" Malcolm just nodded and shot him a maniac grin. "Keep playin', ma-aan!" Finally he set the bass down and stomped out into the yard with the Bat. After rummaging around in a tool shed, Malcolm came back wearing these big leather gardener's gloves. He played on till after sunrise. Richard was most impressed.

The next day, as if to do his new friend one better, O'Connell boosted a big, roomy Lincoln Continental. We all piled in and tore rubber up the coast highway, tripping on acid. The radio blasted us through Big Sur and Monterey. By the time we rolled into San Francisco, reeling under the beatnik spell of North Beach, we'd talked ourselves into the notion that there were all these underground tunnels in Chinatown where they kept the secret opium dens. Wild-eyed and sleepless, we set out on a mission to find one, trudging up and down and banging on all these "Chinese Businessman's Association" places' doors, winking and grinning like idiots. We ended up being chased by a gang of angry Chinamen brandishing meat cleavers and bats. Cackling like mad crows, we stumbled off through the narrow Chinatown alleys that smelled of fish guts, temple incense, and Jasmine tea.

There was this pair of cute sisters who always hung around; the "Boobsy Twins," Jerome dubbed them. They had the hots for my cousin and me. Betty, the one who liked Malcolm, would sit in front of him during our late-night jam sessions, wearing a miniskirt with no panties. As we played, sweating to keep up with Richard's frenzied drumbeats, Betty would uncross her long, elegant legs and flash Malcolm a sneak-peek at her sleek, shaved hardwood clam. I had a massive boner straining at the back of my thrift-shop Stratocaster, but Malcolm just kept thumping away at his big stand-up bass. My romantic cousin wasn't at all impressed by Betty's vulgar demonstrations. He was, however, quite taken with her younger sister, Silvia—the one who Richard said had a crush on me.

One afternoon, after a call from O'Connell to come hang out at the two sisters' place, Malcolm and I were up in their bedroom smoking weed with some other kids. Richard was out in the backyard screwing one of their girlfriends in the bushes. Malcolm was sitting in a corner with Silvia. From the corner of my eye, I saw he was starting to hit it off with her, looking in her eyes and putting his hand on her knee as they talked in intense, hushed tones. I was happy for him and a little relieved too, since I'd always liked her sluttier older sister Betty better. Betty had given up on Malcolm by then and was busy flashing her business at Howie, our other guitar player. That didn't bother me, since Howie was kind of a dork. Some of us even suspected him of being a secret queer. We were all smoking weed and drinking their parent's booze as Hendrix blasted *Purple Haze* on the stereo, when I saw Malcolm and Silvia making out on the sofa. Perfect! I was glad. Malcolm had seemed a little down since coming to town. Suddenly someone killed the music and kids started scrambling around. Betty and Silvia's folks were home from dinner, and Betty was lighting up a bunch of incense, opening the windows to let the pot smoke out. The party was over. As the car pulled into the driveway, we all beat it out the back door.

On the way home, Malcolm didn't talk about Silvia. He was in one of his quiet moods, so I let it go. For all his street-wise big-city ways, my cousin didn't have any more experience with chicks than me. I even suspected he was still a virgin. The weeks went by and nothing happened with him and Silvia. The one time I mentioned her to him, he just got this funny faraway look and didn't say anything. I didn't think any more about it.

A few weeks later, a bunch of us were hanging out at Patrick's. The Bat's parents were away for the weekend and it was a full house. Malcolm wasn't around. He'd been going out in the afternoons looking for a summer job. But Silvia was there, flittering around like Twiggy in a shapeless black-and-white summer dress. I was alone in the Bat's room, sitting on his little single bed smoking a joint and reading one of his comic books, when Silvia walked in and shut the door behind her. I looked up as she glided over to the foot of the bed. Eyeing me with a shy grin, she reached down and pulled the dress over her head. She stood before me all shaggy-haired and naked, staring at me with big Bambi eyes; and then she was in my arms, a hard-bodied woman-child, and we were kissing, feasting on each other like a pair of lust-struck wolverines. I struggled out of my jeans and she moaned into my mouth as she guided me into her hot wet hole, writhing around on top of me, a delirious blond ferret in heat. It was a religious experience as we fucked like sweaty animals and passed out in a humid heap. When we woke up, we did it again.

I'd already been de-virginized by one of my gang's horny fifteen-year-old chicks. Melissa wasn't really my type, but she was kind of cute: slutty, bubbly, and fun. She had these massive snow-white tits with perky pink nipples, and she wanted to fuck all the time. She'd jumped on me one afternoon in the back of a stolen car, initiating me into the wonders of teenage sex. I liked it so much, I promptly fell in love. We went around like boyfriend and girlfriend for months, holding hands, even making plans to run away together. Puppy love. It was all good till I got her knocked up and she had to get an abortion. I thought Doris would hit the roof when Melissa's mother called and told her that her daughter was pregnant by me. But that was one time the old lady came to my rescue. She sat down and had a nice "girl-to-girl talk" with Melissa—who she'd always called a "little white-trash tramp." Doris put on her sweetest Understanding Parent act that day and talked her into the abortion—which Melissa didn't really want. Doris arranged the whole thing, and that was that. I think my mother had actually had her own experience with abortions after marrying Len—though she never told anyone that was the reason she'd mysteriously "lost" his baby. Before I knew what was happening, it was done. Poor Melissa! I'll never forget the day we broke up; her big, teary blue eyes boring into my soul as she stood by my door, screaming "You killed my baby!"

With Melissa, sex had always been sort of clumsy and fast. With Silvia, it was intense. Powerful, raw, and compelling. The more I got, the more I wanted. The only problem was that, unlike Melissa, I didn't really like Silvia—except for the sex. There was something creepy about her, the way she talked and dressed and generally carried herself, that I couldn't stomach. Out of bed, she irritated the shit out of me. I wanted nothing to do with Silvia as a girlfriend or even as a friend. But in the sack she was a wild-eyed, screaming fifteen-year-old fuck goddess, an insatiable nymphomaniac, a force of nature. I could never seem to say no whenever she called to invite me over. It ended up becoming a regular thing; something obsessive and addictive—and absolutely disgusting to me. Still, I couldn't stop. Whenever the urge overtook me, I'd stagger over to her place, a sex-crazed, glassy-eyed fuckpuppet. We'd get right down to it, humping away like it was our last day on earth. Soon as it was done, I'd make some excuse to split, swearing to never go back . . . until the next time, and the next; and so it went, all summer long.

I never told anybody about my sordid little fling with Silvia. I think it got around anyway, though, since Silvia had to have bragged to her slutty older sister about having seduced me; and everybody knew Betty had the biggest mouth in town. I didn't know if it ever got back to Malcolm, since neither of us ever mentioned Silvia again. Meanwhile, at his father's urging, my cousin had started working as a stock-boy at this fancy Beverly Hills department store. Since then, he'd been pretty busy. O'Connell asked me about him all the time, and I promised to bring Malcolm around soon.

51. FREAKOUT

One Friday afternoon, Richard took me aside and slipped me a couple of hits of really strong acid: one for me, the other for Malcolm. I gave Malcolm his after he got off work. I suggested we drop them later that night and go trip out on the golf course together. Bored and restless after being cooped up in a stockroom all week, he swallowed the bright orange tab right on the spot. I followed suit and off we went.

The acid kicked in just after dark. By the time we made it across the neighborhood and hopped the fence, we were both tripping hard. The trees were pulsing with shimmering blood-red veins. Everything was alive and throbbing with frantic electric energy as we crept through the bushes toward the edge of the wide green fairway.

A weird paranoid shadow was creeping into my trip as I led the way through the underbrush. We hunched down and lurked in the murmuring bushes, looking out at the expanse of lawn sparkling like a surging ocean of van Gogh patterns in swirling moonlight. I'd brought along a flashlight and some candles. The idea was to get to Rabbit's Roost, where we could hide out during our psychedelic adventure. I'd done plenty of acid before with O'Connell, and we'd had lots of good times sitting up all night in pulsing fluorescent coffee shops, drumming alien percussion beats onto the Formica tabletops, making funny faces and giggling as we shared cosmic secrets via stoner telepathy. But there was a dark edge coming over Malcolm's trip. I could feel it like an unseen sinister presence.

As we started toward the distant bushes, suddenly my cousin veered off and marched out into the middle of the dreaded fairway, right out in the open. *Danger!* I sprinted behind him, struggling to keep up as he stomped into a sand trap in the middle of a felt-like circle of pristine lawn. "Hey! Whaddya doin', Malc?" I whispered, out of breath.

"I'm gonna sit in this sand he-ah, maa-aan." Malcolm was drawling in an eerie voice. He plopped down and started rolling around like a dog, howling. "Yeah! This is da beach, maa-an! He-eehhh! Th' beach of life, and the ocean's comin' down in great big death waves from outta th' sky. But I'm stayin' right here on th' beach, maa-aan, th' beach of life!!"

Confused and worried, I stepped into the pit with him as he lay down on his back in the sand, repeating the same crazy words. "Malcolm, get up!" I leaned over and held my hand out. "C'mon, man. Ya gotta maintain. We don't wanna get caught in here. Let's get over to the Roost! We can hang out there and nobody'll see us! C'mon, Malc, ya gotta get out of the sand trap!"

He wailed into the darkness. "Death is da trap, Jon, but I'm stayin' here on da sand, maa-aan, right here on th' beach of life! Heehh!"

I looked around. He was yelling really loud. *Shit!* Somebody was going to hear him and call the cops! I begged him to get up. We had to get out of the middle of the fairway! It wasn't safe. We were going to get busted! But the more I urged him to be cool, the more Malcolm freaked out, raving and shouting. I felt like crying. "Malcolm, buddy, ya gotta *maintain*, man!" I pled. "Just come with me, *please*, get up, let's go before the Man shows up!"

"The Man!! Get down, Jon!" He yanked me down into the damp, gritty sand with him. It was as if my mounting paranoia had infected his trip and now it was all raging out of control, sweeping back and forth between us in horrible waves of escalating fear. "They're comin'! Just lay here on th' beach with me! Don't worry, Jon! I got ya back!"

"Who's coming, man?" I felt a quick stab of panic, like when the "up" elevator you're in suddenly starts going down—only worse. Much worse. This elevator was going all the way down to Hell.

He held me down with his thick, muscular boxer's arm. Dark spasms of paranoia flashed through my vision as he sprang to his feet like a soldier on a raging battlefield. *"Hunnghhh!* Take dat, ya fuckin' sonsabitches!" He was yelling, throwing a flurry of punches at the chilly night air. "C'mon, ya fuckin' cowi'ds, come'n get me, haaa-aahh, haaa-aahh, I ain't scared of ya mothafuckas! Haaahh!!"

"Sssshhh! Malcolm, quit yellin', man. Somebody's gonna hear ya!"

My cousin was gone, ranting and screaming in the dark, duking it out with phantom shadows only he could see. "Father! **Faa--aatha!"**

"Malcolm, stop!" I tried to pull him away as headlights appeared at the far end of the fairway. "Malcolm! Be cool! Maintain! Cool it! C'mon, man, it's th' cops! We gotta split! Malcolm! Malcolm!" But there was no Malcolm. Only a crazed solitary warrior doing frantic battle with the invisible demons of the Curse. "Father! **Faa-thaaa!"** His agonized screeches rang out in the dark as the headlights drew near.

That was it. I ran and ducked into the underbrush. From my hiding place, I watched in horrified waves of revulsion as the car skidded to a stop on the path by the fairway, its red lights flashing into the night. I could hear an alien metallic voice booming through a loudspeaker.

"YOU THERE! DON'T MOVE! FREEZE!"

The last thing I saw was Malcolm's tall, muscular silhouette standing in the lights of the police cruiser, gripping the big metal rake the Mexican gardeners used to clean the sand traps, attacking the pristine lawn, screaming his lungs out. Big clumps of grass exploded like shrapnel in the headlights as the car doors flew open. I huffed back through the clearing and scrambled over the fence onto the street. I tore ass all the way home, only stopping to duck into the bushes of sleeping yards whenever I heard a car approach.

Breathing hard, I let myself in the kitchen door and crept through the dark house like a trembling fugitive. I hid in my room, tripping away the gloomiest, guiltiest, most hellish hours of my life. The image of my cousin back on the golf course wailing in the dark played in an endless loop of agonized shame. *"Fa-thaaa! Fa-thaa!"* I kept seeing Uncle Robert's vengeful red face as he pounded away at Malcolm with angry drunken fists: that brutal beating Malcolm had taken in New York for my transgressions while I'd just stood there watching. I could hear that Doors song playing in my head, the creepy words *"Father? Yes, son. I want to kill you,"* as I envisioned those weird "psychoanalysis sessions" and Malcolm standing there howling as the cops closed in on him like a pack of bloodthirsty sharks. I sat in the dark, tripping my guts out in recurring waves of self-hate and shame; feeling like a punk, a coward, a traitor, for running off and leaving Malcolm to take the heat from his father, from the cops, for stealing the girl he liked and treating her like a whore. I could feel every ounce of the terrible weight of betraying my hero as I heard the words of a Beatles song creeping into my head. *"Boy, you're gonna carry that weight."*

After an eternity, dawn came, and with it a slight sense of relief—tainted with the knowledge that Malcolm was sitting in a cell somewhere, bum-tripping. And it was all my fucking fault! That harsh inner voice kept screaming at me, telling me it was never going to be all right, never again. *"Boy, you're gonna carry that weight, carry that weight a long time."*

As the sun rose in the sky, its warm summer rays reflecting against the familiar eucalyptus leaves outside my window, the creepy stabs of horror began to subside. The acid was wearing off. I summoned the guts to pick up the phone. I dialed Operator and asked for the number. *"I'll connect you now, sir."* A robotic, nasal female tone. After a couple of rings, a man's serious voice came on the line. "Los Angeles Police Department. Sergeant Williams."

"Uh, I was, I'm, uh, looking for my cousin . . . ?" I stammered, holding my finger over the button, ready to hang up if he asked for my name. "I think he mighta got in some trouble last night, uh, with the police . . . ?"

"What's your relative's full name, sir?"

"Malcolm. Uh, Malcolm Smith . . . ?"

"Okay, hold on." Silence. Then the voice again. "Malcolm Smith. White male. Yup. He's here. Juvenile division. Let's see what we got . . . Unlawful trespass. Disorderly conduct. Under the influence. Vandalism. Destroying private property. Assault with a deadly weapon. Assaulting a law officer. Resisting arrest. Musta been some night! Bail's set at fifty thousand . . ."

"Oh, okay, thank you." I hung up the receiver with a fateful *thunk*.

I waited till I heard Len's car pull out of the driveway. I waited another hour till I heard my mother going down to make her coffee. I waited till she'd had time to drink it. She'd be in a better mood after she'd had her coffee.

I held my breath as I slunk down the stairs.

52. THE WEIGHT

"WRITERS, LIKE ELEPHANTS, HAVE LONG, VICIOUS
MEMORIES. THERE ARE THINGS I WISH I COULD FORGET."
—WILLIAM S. BURROUGHS

"My God, Len! I'm at my wits' end!"

I winced, pressing my ear to my door, as I got ready to slip out the back and meet Malcolm at Richard's, where he was lying low. Doris had already read him the riot act when she went to bail him out, pearl necklace, mink stole, rhinestone-studded sunglasses and all. Luckily for Malcolm, she'd acceded to his sullen plea not to call his father—probably more out of pride than anything else. I knew the old lady wouldn't want to lose face with her older brother for letting things get out of hand on "her watch."

"You should have *seen* him in that horrible cell, Len. Simply disgraceful. The boy was filthy, all covered in dirt and bruises. He looked like something the bloody cat dragged in! My God! His clothes were torn, and he was shoeless, like a derelict! God knows what the hell he'd been doing all night. Taking drugs, probably LSD. That's what the police said. They told me he was absolutely out of his mind. On drugs! Oh, God! I simply can't tell Robert. It would kill him! Especially now, right after poor Richard . . . Oh, Jesus! Why is this happening to me?" She started sobbing.

I shuddered and backed off from the door. The old lady was really turning on the waterworks down there. I couldn't tell if it was one of her regular acts or if she was really distressed. Probably a healthy dose of both; but I wasn't sticking around to find out. I beat it out the back door.

My cousin was sullen and uncommunicative when I found him at O'Connell's place. He and Richard were in a deep powwow, sitting at the kitchen table with their heads bowed together, nodding and drumming on the tabletop with frantic fingers and mumbling. They seemed to be tripping on some heavy shit. I stayed a while waiting to talk to Malcolm but they kept ignoring me. Feeling worse than ever, I wandered out the door. Did Malcolm know about Silvia and me? Was that why he'd flipped out on the golf course? Nowhere else to go, I trudged over to her place, seeking relief again where there could be no relief.

○   ○   ○

I saw little of Malcolm over the next week. Between his job at the department store and my mother and Len deciding it would be better if he moved out of their spotless white home, we grew kind of distant. He'd taken a room at a local boarding house, where he was supposed to stay out of trouble until his hearing at Juvenile Court.

One day I overheard them arguing downstairs. The Country Club was demanding an obscene sum of money in damages to drop the charges. Otherwise Malcolm would be prosecuted to the full extent of the law and probably end up in Juvenile Hall. When they tried to quiz me about the night of his arrest, I just shrugged and said I hadn't seen him that day, that I'd heard from some friends he'd been busted but I didn't know why. Malcolm kept tight-lipped too, and in the time-honored See No Evil tradition of my people the subject was swept under their spotless white rug—even as his upcoming court date loomed like a silent predator's shadow.

The weeks went by in a blur as I hung out with my gang. Richard O'Connell asked after my cousin, who had taken on extra shifts at work and pretty much disappeared. I shrugged and said I hadn't seen him lately. I guess I'd kind of blocked Malcolm out of my thoughts—partly from a guilty conscience, and partly out of some lingering fear that his creepy mental twist might be somehow contagious.

Then, on a cool October day, I came home and saw a cop car in front of the house. I ducked into the bushes and waited till they came out and drove off. Thinking they'd found my stash again and finally called the heat, I was about to sneak in the back to check my hiding place. My heart was beating fast as I watched my mother and Len emerge from the front. Len hurried to the driveway and started his car, looking especially stern and gray. Doris seemed to be crying behind her dark glasses as she got in beside him. I hesitated on the sidewalk, bracing myself to face the music, whatever it might be. As the car backed out, my mother lowered the window and called out. I shoved my hands deep into my pockets and shuffled over. Something was wrong.

"Jono, listen to me, dear." Her voice was trembling with a serious tone. "Your cousin Malcolm is in the hospital." Her dark eyes were darting around. "He swallowed rat poison. The woman at the rooming house found the poor boy moaning in agony on the floor and called for an ambulance."

Was this for real? I stared at her in shock. I had a strange sinking feeling that this had all happened before, like some creepy old movie I'd seen somewhere a long time ago.

Doris tried to stifle a terrible burbling little sob that gave me the shivers. Then she spoke again, in a dark whispering croak. "They, they say he's in very serious condition, honey. He might not make it."

○   ○   ○

The next morning, she asked me to come to the hospital with her. I couldn't bring myself to go. She told me it was all right, that she knew how painful it must be for me. That night, though, Richard O'Connell and I snuck into the Intensive Care ward. Malcolm was half-conscious as we stood at his bedside. His eyes were glazed, staring with an other-worldly look of chilling dementia. "Rats! Rats on bikes!" He moaned and ranted as I strained to hear the bone-chilling words bubbling from his mouth. "Rats runnin' around everywhere! *Oh! Ohhh!!*"

Richard and I looked at each other in horror as he raved on. "The screams! *Aghhggh,* horrible screams!" Malcolm stared right into my eyes. "Tell 'em all, ma-aan. Tell 'em about th' screams, Jon! *Arghhgghhh!*"

As I looked into those mad eyes, my blood froze. We just stood there looking down on him, shifting back and forth as he raved on. He seemed to be staring right through me with that red-eyed maniac grin, like Renfield from the old *Dracula* movie. Richard and I were both incapable of comprehending that one of us might actually be dying right before our eyes.

The next day, I went back to the hospital with my mother. They'd done a tracheotomy on Malcolm and he was getting oxygen pumped from a tube into a hole in his throat. It was really gruesome. My mother stood at his bedside, weeping. I felt so bad for her. For the first time in years, Doris seemed human to me; sad, fragile, vulnerable. I wanted to hug her and tell her how much I really loved her; but something stopped me. The Curse. It stood in the shadows like a smirking assassin, laughing at us all.

Malcolm lay strapped into his hospital bed, convulsing and babbling for another week before slipping into a coma. Then late one night my mother got the call. Malcolm's suffering had ended. Malcolm had been seventeen.

The long mournful boom of a ship's horn fills the air. As the tattoo man reads the last few words, he can hear his voice start to crack, buckling under a heavy weight of guilt and shame. A slow mariachi lament drifts up from the street, forming a melancholy soundtrack to his confession. Tears begin welling up in his eyes, catching him by surprise. He sets the notebook down and lowers his head. He takes some deep breaths and reaches for a cigarette, his hands quivering slightly as he lights up.

53. AN INTERCOURSE WITH GHOSTS

"THERE IS NO SEPARATION BETWEEN THE LIVING AND THE DEAD."

–JAMES JOYCE

"Robert and Peggy flew in from New York," Cigano reads, "to stand by, helplessly, watching their son die. They went home with his ashes in a box. After poisoning himself like his love-struck hero Romeo, Malcolm's remains would be scattered across a beach in Atlantic City, where they'd gone on vacation once when he was a kid."

He stops and riffles through a pile of yellowed typewritten papers. He looks up at Jaco and shrugs. "I couldn't feel anything, man. I never saw anyone on that side of my family again." He falls silent, leafing through the pages. "It was a real tragedy," he sighs, "the bomb that blew whatever was left of my family to bits. I dunno if Robert ever spoke to my mother again. I don't think so. Nobody ever talked about it. But when I was going through all that old stuff, I found this thing Robert wrote about Malcolm's summer vacation . . ." Slowly, reverently, Cigano unfolds the paper.

MALCOLM'S PET CHUCKWALLA by Robert Smith

The thing looks like an iguana, almost three feet long and ugly as sin. Wearing a pair of trunks, chuckwalla clamped to his back, little Malcolm walks onto the beach. It's really a sight, this three-foot-long lizard clinging to a kid's back like a leech, its lidded eyes half-closed in dreamy reptilian reverie, jogging slightly with the boy's jaunty stride. People approach and then turn around swiftly, to confirm what they thought they saw hanging down his naked back. It's a huge gray scaly reptile of some kind.

Malcolm carries a length of clothesline coiled in his hand. Selecting a clear space, he drops down in the sand and extricates Chuck from his back. He gazes fondly into its eyes for a moment, crooning softly to it, as though it were a kitten instead of this repulsive miniature replica of a beast that crawled out of the primordial ooze. Setting it on the sand, he ties the clothesline lovingly around its neck, plays out the rope and tugs the leash, encouraging it to walk around and enjoy the beach.

The thing inhabits the desert and ought to feel right at home. Stretched out on the sand everywhere, topless sunbathers lounge on their backs, eyes shut, enduring the heat. Chuck is motionless for a few moments, then he begins to sense the ocean. He's never heard so much goddamn water. He slips the leash and starts running straight for the moisture. And Chuck can really run; through, over, and around the sunbathers. Malcolm runs after him, yelling. Pandemonium. Shrieks, yelps, a great scrambling to the feet as the sun worshipers catch sight of the thing the boy is chasing. They don't know what it is, but it looks poisonous and dangerous as hell. Chuck cuts a swath through a cluster of half-naked ladies, leaving a cacophony of screeches in his wake. It dives into the water and is never seen again. Little Malcolm is very upset.

I didn't see Robert and Peggy while they were there. I didn't want to see anybody ever again. There were a lot of somber comings and goings at the house. Aunt Connie's station wagon stayed parked in the driveway every day. I didn't even want to see my cheery-faced "other mother." I couldn't face any of them. A dreadful sense of guilt haunting me, I would leave early in the morning, sneaking out the back like a burglar, and I wouldn't come home till late at night. I spent my days hiding out at friends' places or sitting alone in the alley behind the liquor store smoking weed, sniffing glue, and staring into space, trying to forget I existed.

Of all my shell-shocked, saddened friends who had known and liked Malcolm, Richard O'Connell, the devil-may-care Pied Piper, was the most affected. Poor Richard was grief-stricken. I think he felt responsible for Malcolm's death too, somehow. I was too numb to feel anything. I wandered around in a long waking nightmare, playing it over and over in my head, waiting for it to be over so I could wake up. But this was a nightmare there was no waking up from. There was a dark feeling of mourning everywhere I went. I couldn't even look at Silvia. A few days after Malcolm's death, my mother went to the rooming house to collect his things and found a pile of haunting missives to Silvia; tragic love letters he'd never sent. As I read through them, I was consumed with a powerful and persistent wave of shame. Poor Malcolm had died a virgin.

O   O   O

The tattoo man stops and picks up a page torn from a book and reads it.

> *Letter writing is an intercourse with ghosts, not only with the ghost of the receiver, but with one's own, which emerges between the lines of the letter being written . . . Written kisses never reach their destination, but are drunk en route by these ghosts.*
> *—Franz Kafka*

"Malcolm was real big on Kafka." He shrugs as he hands some more papers to Jaco. "Here's one of his letters. Turns out my mother saved 'em all these years, as if some part of her knew I'd find them someday . . ."

> **DEAR SILVIA** – *Here is a person who has kept inside him all his emotions, and then they come out in a flood. All the hate and love, the misery, loneliness and passion, causing my limbs to twitch in eagerness to escape this body, this jail, they have sat buried inside me, twisting and tearing at my guts to get out. But I know better, for I have lost my trust in people. Even with you, I am afraid to show myself. I thought I could trust you, that you were different. I saw in you a hurt, a loneliness, and I wished to draw your picture. I saw in you so many beautiful emotions, just under the surface, waiting to be unlocked onto a piece of cardboard, to glow over the world through your radiant*

*features and teach it shame for its hates, and show it the joy of living.
I see in you a dream come to life. I feel like a little boy watching a
hummingbird in all its beauty, breathless, watching its wings move so
fast they are just a delicate pattern in the air, and its scarlet body still
and alive below them. A still moment caught for all time in my heart
and my memory. Most people would say I sound too poetic, to get so
excited about a hummingbird. But I can't restrict myself to normal
conversation with you. Most people, when I tell them I place no value
on money and would rather buy paints than food, shake their heads
in pity and say, "That's the unfortunate way of the artist." But I
have something better than them. As they hide behind masks, denying
their emotions, trying to change the natural way of things, they become
old and wrinkled and cold. Not just on the outside, but on the inside.
They're afraid to show their real faces, afraid it will tear them apart.
Maybe it will, but it's a world they made, built upon their fears and
inhibitions. I deny it the right to judge me, deny it the right to affect me.
But even as I despise it, I have to feel sorry for it. It's thrown away
everything that's good. It wants to feel love, but it doesn't know how.
It's afraid it will be hurt, so it says love doesn't exist. But it does exist,
I know. There is something in this world more important than yourself,
someone you would die for, someone you feel only love for, someone you
want to protect, to show tenderness, generosity. Art, music and nature
are all forms of it. Love has so many facets. Like delicate patterns of
glass, it can take your breath away in its splendor. The love of a boy to
a girl, a mother to her child, an artist to the colors in which he paints
his soul, or a composer to those wonderful patterns of tones that make
up life. Love is universal, it involves all of yourself, body and soul, in a
life-or-death struggle for beauty. It's brutal and tender, and overwhelms
all other emotions, and is perhaps the only reason we exist. Without it,
what reason is there to live? I think even the smallest insect must feel
it. Why else should he do things that nature has dictated him to do,
even before he was born? Perhaps he is better than us with our great
reasoning powers that try to reason away our emotions and replace
them with something better. But we wind up replacing them with
something worse, like money, or any number of perversions that run
the world. Only with love have we any hope of being who we really
are, what we can be. Love is what I feel for music, for art, and for you,
Silvia—like some magnificent Beethoven symphony, a blazing fire of*

glory that makes my breath catch, involving all of life and death, an act of nature, and I feel it's time to tell you. I do not expect anything to come of it, and I will never again mention it, but I ask you not to be bothered by it. This is no sudden thing. I have felt this way toward you for weeks. When I first talked to you and we kissed that day, I was in a shocked state afterwards for weeks. Before that, I'd hardly noticed you. But I warmed up to you long before I knew your name, or had even spoken to you. As I grew to know you that day, I fell in love for the first time. If I seemed a little abrupt in leaving afterwards, it's because I really hated to go. The only way I could handle it was to not look back. All my life, I've only known one side of life, the bad side. Now I've finally tasted the joy of life. As an excuse for my misery, I once told myself that I had to feel pain to paint a dream, for dreams are for the miserable. I was right in a way, and wrong in another, for I am inspired now by my feelings, by my newfound freedom to paint my joys, not my nightmares or my misery. For I can now take a breath and know I'm alive for the first time, and paint life, not death. To paint beauty, not terror, and take more joy in every touch of color and every moving line than I ever could before. That experience in the golf course was so horrible, I felt like a little boy having a nightmare, then waking up to find it was real. Things so horrible that they defy every nightmare or horror I'd ever known before, fear times fear. It just wouldn't end, and it left me in a long, terrible state of shock. For a week afterwards, I had to go to sleep with a knife under my pillow, only to wake up screaming from a terror that nothing could help. I was sweating and thrashing around, and I wouldn't dare close my eyes for the rest of the night. It was only my feelings for you, Silvia, that brought me out of it. If it wasn't for your presence in my thoughts, I might still be running around in that maze of horrors. You lit a fire in my heart once more and let me breathe the joy of life. For that I am grateful. It's funny, the way you had the power to change my whole outlook on life, just by your unseen presence. You seem to glow all over with a freshness, an honesty and a rare beauty I've never seen in a person before. You have a quality like sparkling water running in a stream with trees hanging over it. All the world is quiet to watch this dream that nature has created. You always change, yet you're always the same, and always more beautiful than before. Therefore, I'll fill this silence around me with music that I'll write and dedicate to you, and call it The Joy of Life. I'll write

it for guitar and bass so I can play it for you. Goodnight, goodnight, parting is such sweet sorrow, that I shall say goodnight till it be the morrow.
  Love, Malcolm

"Poor Malcolm was just too pure and innocent," Cigano reads, "too sensitive to live in this miserable, greedy shithole of a world. I racked my corrupt heart and brain, wondering if he'd known about Silvia and me all along. Had I been responsible for my hero's death? Guilt rode me like a merciless horseman. I could never bring myself to speak to Silvia again. The dirty little spell had been broken at last; broken by the Curse."

54. SOMETHING DARK

"ALL SINS HAVE THEIR ORIGIN IN A SENSE OF INFERIORITY, OTHERWISE CALLED AMBITION."

—CESARE PAVESE

The following Tuesday night, just after midnight, only a week after Malcolm's death, my Aunt Connie's cat appeared outside my window, howling in the dark like a ghost. It was strange because my aunt lived several miles away. I hurried down and opened the door. My blood froze as the familiar creature looked at me. In that moment, I could swear I saw my dead cousin's spirit in those haunting feline eyes. The cat turned and darted off into the night. I stood reeling in the dark doorway, covered in goose bumps, thinking of one of Malcolm's poems, an eerie tribute to Poe called *The Cat People*. It felt like an ugly omen; something occult and dark. Something cursed.

Suddenly the phone rang in the house. I jumped as if grabbed from behind. I had a bad, sick feeling in my gut. Len was out of town on business. As I slunk back upstairs I could hear my mother's muffled voice talking in urgent tones from her room. I picked up the extension in my room and cupped my hand over the mouthpiece, listening.

"Just tell me what the hell you took, Con!" There was a weird desperation in her tone. "For God's sake, stay awake! I'll be right there! I'm on my w—"

I strained to make out Connie's faint slurry words. It sounded like she was murmuring from the bottom of a well. "Nev'min', Doris, I'm sleepy, can't take it anymore, can'takeit, th' basti'd's been holed up all night wit' that nutty psychiatrist. Pair a bastards, *arrgghh*, he told me he hates me an' went'n' locked 'imself in 'is office, said 'e's gonna get rid of me an' take th' kids . . . *arrggh*, well he can have 'em, he can have it all. I'm so tired, I jus' wanna go t' sleep forever now, Doris. Look after th' boys for me, sis, okay? Promise?"

"Nonsense, Connie!" My mother's voice broke in. "Listen to me! You're not going anywhere! You'll raise your kids, we'll get a lawyer and you'll get custody, don't worry. Please, Con! Just tell me what the hell you've taken!!"

"No-oo, Doris, no more! I'm gonna go t'sleep now, no more! Jus' promise y'll take care of 'em f'me, promise me 'fore I go . . ."

"Constance! Stop! You're talking madness, girl, stop it!"

"Promise me, Doris, y'gotta promise . . ."

"Jesus, Con! All right, I promise, nothing will happen to your boys, okay? Jesus! God! Now just tell me what th—"

The line went dead. I set the receiver down. A cold numb sensation was creeping into my gut. I could hear my mother's shouts in her room. "Connie, Connie!! No! Don't go! I'll be right there, Con, wait! Oh Jesus!" Then she was at my door, an overcoat thrown over her nightgown, hair all haywire, eyes puffy. She looked panicked and groggy at the same time. She seemed very old as she spoke in a grave rush of words. "Jono! Thank God you're home! Listen to me, dear, there's something wrong at Aunt Connie's house. We have to get over there right now. I need you to come with me."

She was as sober as I'd ever seen her. There was a desperate pleading look in her eyes I'd never seen before. I grabbed my jacket, putting it on as I followed her downstairs. Her frantic voice urged me on as we got to her car. "Please, honey, get in, hurry, we have to get over there right away!"

"What's going on?"

"I don't know yet, darling." There was a deadly serious tone in her voice as she backed out of the driveway. "We just need to get to her quickly . . ."

We sped in silence through the dark suburban streets. When we pulled into Aunt Connie's driveway, the lights were out, all the windows dark. As we stood at the big imposing front door, I thought of her cat howling outside my window. It was the day before Halloween and I had this creepy feeling of impending doom. I stood with my mother in the chilly autumn air as she rang the doorbell again and again. Silence. Something was very wrong inside that house. I could feel it in my center with a cold, relentless dread.

"C'mon, Ma." I grabbed her arm. I hadn't called my mother anything but Doris for years. It felt like somebody else was speaking as I pulled her behind me. Gravel snarled beneath my feet as we hurried toward the side of the house. I tried the kitchen door. Locked.

My mother stepped back and shouted up at the dark upstairs windows. "Connie! Con! Open the door. *Co-nnnn!* Ivan! *Iv-annn!* Peter, Steven! Kids! Wake up! It's Auntie Doris! *Con-neee!*"

"Wait!" I pulled my switchblade from my jacket pocket and started prying at the dark kitchen window. "I can get in here, Ma, just hang on. I'll go in the window and open up for you."

"Oh, yes, that's my good boy! Hurry, honey, hurry!"

I dug the blade in with steady pressure till I heard the latch pop. I raised the window and climbed up. Scrambling in over the big kitchen sink, I hit the faucet with my knee, spraying cold water all over my jeans. Shivering, I fumbled for the light switch by the door and let my mother in.

"Good boy!" She grabbed my arm and we hurried across the kitchen. "Stay right beside me, Jono, come . . ." She hurried us through the dining room, past the living room, turning lights on, then onto the stairs, calling out. "Connie, Connie, Con-nn!" At the top, my mother was breathing hard, still shouting. "Connie, Con-nnn!" She rushed to the door of her sister's room, wailing and pounding as she twisted the doorknob. It was locked. "Connie, for God's sake, Con, open this goddamn door! Connie! *Conn-nneee!!*"

There was a sound. I turned to see my cousins Peter and Steven and their little brother David, who was only seven. They were standing by the door to their room in their pajamas. "Jono!" Steve was staring at us. "Auntie Doris, what's goin' on? What are you guys doin' here?"

"Stevie! Peter! Where's your father? I need him to come and open this door right now . . . *bastard!*" She hissed under her breath.

"Lemme try it, Ma! Move!" I nudged her aside and put my shoulder to the door. It didn't budge. I leaned into it harder and the lock cracked.

My mother ran in as I hit the light switch. Aunt Connie was passed out on the big king-size bed, sprawled across a shiny blue satin bedspread in her underwear, her long blond hair sloshing over her face like a shroud. The phone was lying off its hook, on the floor, like a dead animal. My mother straddled her, shaking her, screaming in her pale, expressionless face. "Connie! Connie! *Wake up!*" An empty pill bottle sat on the bedside table beside a bottle of Scotch and an empty glass with a red lipstick smear on the rim. I walked over and picked up a little brown plastic bottle. Seconal. Red Devils. I'd taken one of those things from my mother's medicine cabinet once and got really fucked up. I knew what a whole bottle would do mixed with whiskey. I pictured Malcolm lying in his hospital bed, strapped in and dying; that ghastly white tube going into the hole in his throat.

I looked up and my uncle Ivan was standing in the room in pajamas with little blue airplanes on them. "Doris, what the hell's going on here?" he huffed.

My mother turned, shouting. "*Jesus! Ivan!* Call for a bloody ambulance, man, for Christ's sake!"

"Whatever for, Doris?" The Hungarian grunted as he stepped over, looking down at his wife. "Don't be silly." Smiling, he stroked Connie's arm. "She's just had a couple of her sleeping pills. Don't worry. She passes out like this all the time. Why, you couldn't wake her with a brass band! There's certainly no need to call anyone at this hour . . ."

"*Are you insane?!* She's taken an overdose, you ass! *Jesus!*" My mother's urgent fingers motioned me over. "Hand me the phone, Jono!"

Ivan grabbed the telephone out of my hand. I cursed him under my breath as my mother pleaded with him to let her make the call.

"That is out of the question, Doris! Absolutely not! I told you, she's only had a couple of pills. You're being hysterical now!"

I looked over at my cousins standing in the doorway, white-faced. My mother told Ivan to call his own goddamned doctor then, for God's sake. Again, he told her she was hysterical, that she was "overreacting." She kept after him, badgering, pleading, threatening. Finally he allowed that she could phone her own doctor and ask him to come, just to ease her mind.

While he was still talking, my mother looked up in anguish, wailing. "*Jesus Christ!* She's not breathing! *Oh God!*"

"Nonsense, woman." Ivan put a calm, steady hand up to Connie's mouth. Then he turned and strode into the bathroom. He came back holding a huge hypodermic syringe.

Doris stared at him. "What the hell are you doing with that thing?"

The Hungarian rolled his wife over on her side and slapped her butt like a barnyard animal. "This will pull her around and then you can relax, Doris. But you must promise me you will never tell anyone about this . . ." He looked up at my mother, waiting.

She gave him a desperate little nod. He shoved the long needle into Connie's backside and pushed the plunger down. Aunt Connie's face was gray as wet cement. My mother started shaking her again as Ivan disappeared into the bathroom. "Jono!" She whispered to me. "Get me my phonebook, quickly, honey, it's there in my purse."

I opened her handbag and handed her the red leather book. She found her doctor's home number, then grabbed the phone and dialed. "Stan!" She was whispering, talking fast. "It's Doris! Listen to me, it's an emergency . . . My sister Constance, yes, Connie, she's unconscious from barbiturate poisoning . . . Yes . . . I don't know, Seconal, I think . . . Yes . . . That's right . . . No, we haven't, not yet . . . Yes . . . Then you'll make the call? Oh, thank you, Stan . . . You'll meet us at Cedars?" There was a long silence as she listened into the receiver. Then she spoke again, her voice rising. "Well, that's what I *said* when I got here, to call a bloody ambulance, but her idiot husband was worried about a scandal or something, and he told me not to call anybo—"

The Hungarian strode up and took the phone from her hand. "This is Ivan Tors, Constance's husband." He spoke in a low, even tone. "My wife has merely taken a few sleeping pills. She's done this sort of thing before and she's always fine in the morning . . . Yes . . . I understand . . . Yes, but, the hospital? Don't you think you could come to the house, perhaps pump her stomach, just to reassure Doris. She's very upset and . . . Yes, but . . . "

There was an ominous silence as Ivan listened to the doctor insisting it would be best if we met him at the hospital, that he'd send an ambulance. After a moment's hesitation, Ivan whispered the address into the phone. He hung up and glared at his sister-in-law. "I'm going to go get dressed now, Doris." With a long huffy sigh, he stomped out of the room.

Struggling to pull her sister's inert body off the bed, my mother turned to me with panicked eyes. "Help me, Jono! Help me get her up!" I went over and held Aunt Connie upright. Her flesh was cold and clammy. She felt real heavy. She kept falling over onto the bed as my mother struggled a shiny pink bathrobe onto her body. Then she stopped breathing again. Doris started slapping her on the face. "Connie! *Connie!* Wake up, for God's sake, Con! Just hold on, Con! *Oh, Jesus God!*" No amount of slapping would arouse her. My mother stopped. I let go and she slumped over on the bed like a dropped puppet.

"Ivan! *She's not breathing!*" Doris screeched like an air-raid siren. "*I-vann*, get in here, we need help, *you son of a bitch!*"

"Relax, Doris." The Hungarian's voice called out from the other room. "I'm trying to get dressed in here . . ."

I crept over to the door. I could hear Ivan whispering. He had called the hospital and was telling them not to use a siren when the ambulance came, that it wasn't a real emergency, no reason to alarm the neighbors at this hour. "Asshole!" I cursed him out loud and walked back into the room. My cousins were standing behind my mother, watching in silence. They looked scared.

Doris looked around like a frightened animal. When she saw the kids standing by the bed, staring at their mother's motionless form, she motioned me over. "Jono! Take the boys out of here, please, darling. They shouldn't be seeing this."

As I turned toward them, my mother cried out again. "Look! She just took a breath! *Yes! Thank God!* Good, that's real good, Con, you just hang on and keep breathing. I'll be right back."

She stood up to comfort her shell-shocked nephews while their father reluctantly dressed to meet a slow-moving, siren-less ambulance. "It's going to be fine now, boys. Your mother will be fine real soon, don't you worry."

She rushed back. Poor Connie didn't look so fine to me. My mother sat down on the bed, holding her sister's head in her lap like a statue of the Madonna, as if trying by sheer willpower to sustain her intermittent shallow breaths. Connie just lay there in her arms like a broken doll.

I heard a car pulling into the driveway. The flashing red lights bounced around the white walls like silent fireworks. I could hear the Hungarian's beefy voice down at the front door, greeting the attendants gruffly, almost apologetically, like he was embarrassed to have inconvenienced them for such a trifle. Finally he walked them up the stairs and into the bedroom. The younger one, a handsome blond guy who looked like he could be Richard O'Connell's older brother in a white suit, took one look at Connie and yanked her from my mother's arms.

"Get the stretcher, Jim, quick!" He began barking out orders to his partner. I could hear him cursing under his breath as the other one came back with a gurney. They strapped Connie in and rushed her from the room and down the stairs, my mother following like a harried shadow. As I hurried behind them, I could hear the blond one mumbling "Why the hell did some goddamn sonofabitch tell 'em this wasn't a friggin' emergency?"

"I'll take my own car," Ivan called over his shoulder, disappearing across the dark driveway.

"We'll never make it to Cedars in time," the other attendant warned.

"Screw it!" The blond driver shouted out the window. "We're takin' her to UCLA; it's closer!" He slammed his door and hit the siren.

The sound pierced the cold night air like a scream.

55. SHUTTING DOWN

"I BELIEVE THAT TO PURSUE THE AMERICAN DREAM IS NOT
ONLY FUTILE BUT SELF-DESTRUCTIVE BECAUSE ULTIMATELY
IT DESTROYS EVERYTHING AND EVERYONE INVOLVED WITH IT."
—HUBERT SELBY JR.

Malcolm had opened the gates to Hell with his suicide, unleashing
the soul-shattering Curse of a hundred generations. My aunt was taken
to the same hospital where he had just died. She didn't last the night.

Connie had followed at last in the tragic footsteps of her star-crossed
lover, Pavese. But her first enthusiastic aficionado, Elia Kazan, had seen
it coming long before, when he'd written in his diary: "I had a terrible
fear that in Hollywood, this place where only the tough survive, this nice
girl was about to be eaten alive and left in a little pile of feathers."

I was numb to it all. I didn't want to go to my beloved other mother's
funeral, and nobody insisted I go. Unable to feel any more pain, I blanked
out, a primitive survival mechanism kicking in. As that foul contagious
wave of suicide raged through my family like a blazing fireball, my life
became a textbook case of post-traumatic stress. My heart was closed for
business; and it would stay that way for a long, long time.

My mother went stark raving mad. Consumed with guilt, remorse,
self-pity, and hatred, she drank more than ever. That just made it worse.
The Curse was closing in like a silent predator. Classical music boomed
in the den day and night as she raged and wailed, pounding the walls,
smashing the furniture and ranting about Malcolm, Connie, and Pavese,

as if there was some horrible occult connection between their deaths. Maybe there was. I will always remember her yelling at Len as she slapped him in the face the day Connie was buried. "How *dare* you invoke *God* in that corny speech of yours at my sister's funeral? How *dare* you? You stupid *ass!*" As her days staggered by in a drunken melancholy blur, she would pass out in a tragic heap on the floor, lying in a puddle of urine. Len, clueless as always, was as ineffectual as a dead possum. Me, I kept away from them both. I wanted nothing more to do with anyone— even my unfortunate orphaned cousins. The Ringleader was on permanent vacation.

Ivan Tors sold the house and moved with his sons to Miami, the happy home of Flipper, King of the Sea. I didn't see any of them again for many, many years..

○   ○   ○

Jaco watches as the tattoo man digs through his bag, pulling out more worn manila envelopes. He dumps a pile of loose papers and yellowed newspaper clippings out onto the table.

"What's all that, Jonathan Shaw?"

"More research, bro. I'm looking for this little side-note I wrote about Ivan. I've been doing a lot of digging here, coming up with all kinda weird shit. It's like peeling the layers off an onion, man."

"How do you mean?"

"Like I said, man, the more I go back over my family's history, the more I keep coming up with all these fucked-up coincidences. Like this part here." He pulls a page out of the pile. "Check this out.

"The success of Ivan Tors's popular *Flipper* series," he reads, "led to a huge proliferation of dolphin-based entertainment all over the world. A lucrative trade for the friendly creatures emerged. Culls in the wild were slaughtered by the tens of thousands. Their meat contains high levels of mercury, but it ends up being sold as fish for sushi, mostly in Japan. Years after Ivan's television empire collapsed, a veteran dolphin trainer named Rick O'Barry blew the lid off the whole dirty deal. O'Barry first captured and trained the original *Flipper* dolphins. The veteran fish-wrangler had a sudden change of heart when his favorite dolphin committed suicide in his arms, apparently despondent over its captivity. Racked by guilt for helping Ivan Tors open the gates to Hell for the intelligent peaceful human-loving species, he became a crusader against the worldwide dolphin massacre—all of which started with Ivan's disgustingly cute television series."

"Suicide?" Jaco says. "How does a dolphin commit suicide?"

Cigano looks up with a quizzical grin. "That's a good question, man. When I started doing all this research, I came across all kinda weird stuff like this. So I started looking into it, and it turns out dolphins can just quit breathing whenever they want." He guffaws. "Even fish were killing themselves to get away from my family!" He throws his notebook onto the table and snorts. "Talk about a motherfuckin' Curse . . ."

56. THE MAGGOT

"IT IS GOOD TO MAKE FRIENDS . . . EVEN IN HELL."

—SPANISH PROVERB

Soon after the final disintegration of my shell-shocked family home, I met a wild looking longhaired kid who lived in the neighborhood. A pockmarked teenage fuckup, Paul Magad had grown up being teased for his scrawny stature, a bad case of acne, and—last but not least—his surname. Kids at his fancy private schools nicknamed him Maggot. Paul never gave a shit. He was a loner, an outsider. Wherever he went, people took one look at him and bolted. Paul's father had been a successful Beverly Hills lawyer who went on to become a Superior Court judge. Like everyone else, His Honor had no taste for his son's delinquent antics; but Paul knew his old man would always bail him out of trouble, if only to protect his own standing, rather than out of any real concern for the son he saw as a living reminder of his own youthful transgressions. Paul's mom had been a beatnik junkie stripper in New York—an eclectic heritage, producing strange and bitter fruit.

In the wake of Malcolm and Connie's deaths, Paul Magad became my evil twin. An intelligent and sensitive kid, Paul's antisocial escapades were even more hardcore and destructive than my own. My new friend had been kicked out of more than one exclusive Beverly Hills prep school, narrowly escaping being sent to Juvie the last time—despite his father's influence—for making a bomb and blowing the principal's office to smithereens.

"It's simple, Jon. I've discovered a perfect method to get away with antisocial behavior and still maintain a good image." Passing me a crooked joint, he winked with a deadpan eye. "All one must do after committing an atrocity, my friend, is to tell them it was a practical joke. Yasssir! Everyone loves a practical joker, right?" Paul went on, grinning like a deranged midget. "If you get caught punching someone in a wheelchair or something, all you gotta do is tell 'em you were only kidding around, see? People will just smile and go, 'Hey, that guy's got a real good sense of humor, ha, ha!' They might even give you yer own teevee show! That Richard Speck guy shoulda just told 'em he was only joking, hehehe. He prolly woulda got off . . .'"

I was most impressed by Paul's perverse sense of humor. Nobody else was impressed. Not at all. Even the most jaded fuckups in my crowd were put off by my new pal. But I loved him. Where I had always been overly shy, brooding, and introspective, Paul was fearless, funny, and outspoken. He was into real hard drugs, too. Paul's only socially redeeming qualities were that he could read Baudelaire, Genet, Céline, Artaud, and Rimbaud in French; and he wrote amazing poetry when he was high—which was most of the time. He also played the classical violin like a virtuoso—a talent totally out of character with his ratty delinquent appearance. Despite a baffling blend of genius and mental instability, though, Paul had a heart of pure gold. Pirate gold. He was a good and loyal friend as he became my tour guide along the road to Hell. We started out hanging around with my gang; but as friends backed off, we fell in with more sinister kids. Druggies. Criminals. With Paul, I became a "head." That's also when I started writing a lot, usually high on cocaine, speed, pills, uppers, downers, and PCP, and still tripping almost daily on acid. A deep and effective transformation was taking place as I disengaged once and for all from the unhappy world of consensus reality.

Cigano opens another old notebook filled with jumbled handwriting, and an avalanche of imagery fills his senses. He can almost smell the scent of dirt-brown Acapulco Gold and Krylon spray paint in the alley behind the old liquor store as marijuana smoke expands in a kid's lungs.

On a transistor radio, Jimi Hendrix's guitar fills the air as a bottle of wine makes the rounds of friends sitting on the cracked asphalt.

"What's the word?" Paul shouts out in Cigano's memory.

The others yell back. "*Thunderbird!*"

"What's the price?"

"*Fifty twice.*" They chant like stoned aboriginal tribesmen.

"What's the reaction?"

"*SATISFACTION!!*"

Cackling and darting around like cartoon bats, they spray crooked psychedelic graffiti patterns onto the walls of Cigano's mind, flying through his head on colorful, swirling clouds of sickly-sweet smoke. *RREEEERR.* A high-pitched wail of panic stings the tattoo man's gut as a cop car flashes into his vision like a shark and the kids all scatter like pigeons. As he reads on, he can hear their sneakers slapping the hot summer asphalt as they dodge around corners, hopping fences, past pools and clotheslines; dogs barking, kids laughing and ducking into bushes, then fading away into the shadows of his memory.

◯   ◯   ◯

The first time I ever did cocaine, Paul and I were sitting in an abandoned house in the neighborhood. Drunk on wine, we rummaged through a pile of shoplifted booty. Paul looked up, grinning like the devil as he pulled a little bag of white powder from his pocket and cut out four lines on a scrap of broken mirror.

"What's that shit, man?" I asked.

"Seven more years of bad luck, brother!"

He rolled up a dollar bill and sniffed a line, then handed me the mirror. I stuck the banknote in my nose, as if I knew what the fuck I was doing, and snorted. My nostril burned like someone had stuck a hot match in it. I felt my face going numb as the coke ate into my brain, a million microscopic piranhas thrashing around in my blood. My hands began to shake as I tasted an alkaline drip at the back of my throat. Right away I wanted a drink! I thought of Wilfred Wormus as I fumbled in my backpack for the wine. *What's the word? Thunderbird!* I took a swig, then sat back and lit a cigarette, feeling a flush of euphoria, followed by an urgent need to take a dump.

I got up and ran for the bathroom, but Paul was locked inside. "Hold on!" he called out as I stood in the dark hallway shifting from foot to foot. I couldn't hold on! The cocaine was tugging at my bowels like an angry midget! About to shit my pants, I rushed into the dark kitchen and grabbed a stack of old yellowed newspapers. I laid them down, squatted, and wiped with scraps of mildewed news. Vietnam War, World Affairs, Real Estate, Economy, Politics and Sports, Entertainment, all raging in my throbbing bunghole as I inhaled the distinctive odor of my shit. I pulled up my pants and wrapped up the whole nasty business. Creeping over to the window like a burglar, I flung my guilty little bundle into the weeds like an abortion fetus. Feeling a new sense of lightness, I took another big swig of wine, lit another smoke, and sat watching the lively patterns swirling in the dusty air. Rays of sunlight cut through the shuttered windows like knife blades.

I felt good. Alert. Alive. Fearless. As I took another deep pull from the bottle, I could hear a familiar voice: *"Yess-ss! Something in the booze has CHANGED Wilfred! It has suddenly made him POWERFUL-LL . . ."* I started to laugh, harder and harder, till I thought I'd cry. With trembling hands I picked up the mirror and snorted the last line. Feeling that crazy burn numbing out my other nostril, I stood up and paced the empty room like a tiger in a cage, thinking, planning a world of new adventures for me and Paul . . . *Paul . . . where the fuck is Paul?*

My friend came back into the room grinning like a bandit. We sat up snorting the rest of the bag of sparkling flake and talking long into the night, grinding our teeth like a pair of chattering monkeys, rattling our frantic little monkey jaws and babbling on and on about all sorts of earth-changing, crucial, cataclysmic topics, ideas, and events; lost in a brave new world of grand plans—which we wouldn't even remember the next day.

All in all, cocaine seemed like a big waste of time. On some other level, though, that evening would mark an unholy bond between me and the Maggot, and a whole new direction in my life's crooked path.

57. GETTING OUT

"WE BECOME THE CHILDREN OF A DREAM THAT RECURS
OVER TIME."

–JIM CARROLL

"Paul and I were inseparable," Cigano reads. "My new best friend had graduated from cutting classes to being kicked out of school for good. I followed suit and stopped going too, embracing the proud title of High School Dropout. As we followed each other around the neighborhood like alley cats, Paul Magad came to replace Godzilla, Richard Speck, and Malcolm as a role model. The restless virus of adolescence had infected my numbed-out, shut-down soul, lighting up my brain like a mad flashing pinball arcade.

School was out forever, but we worked like honor students to bend the limits of our reality with drugs. What really sealed our unbreakable psychic bond, though, was the force of our one common need: a compulsion to get out. Out of our messed-up broken homes. Out of our boring suburban neighborhood, our stupid white-bread schools, our upper-middle-class straitjacket upbringings. Out of our unbearable situations, our families, our angry childhood memories. To that end," the tattoo man reads, "we wanted to get straight out of our fucking heads; and we did it by any means we could find."

Cigano reads from the next page, conjuring the image of two young friends sitting on a dusty sidewalk crowded with hippies, bikers, panhandlers, ranting acid casualties, speed freaks, winos, and wild-eyed idiot savants: a burned-out, faded snapshot in a musty basement of the American Dream. As his eyes scan the page, an old song begins playing in his head. *Ninety-six Tears*, by Question Mark and the Mysterians. He remembers how Louise had taken him to the Shrine to see them before his mother ran her off—like she always ran everyone off. Now they're just another mysterious question mark of memory as his voice wanders the smoggy, garbage-strewn alleys of the past.

$$\circ \quad \circ \quad \circ$$

The closest local escape hatch for us was the nearby counterculture mecca of Hollywood Boulevard. We fit right in with the legions of stoned-out, longhaired runaways there, refugees from stifling suburban wastelands like ours. We loved those dirty city streets where we could run amok on a holy mission of excitement, adventure, and fun. Our early excursions echoed the sacred childhood memory of that magical night when Louise took me to see Sam Cooke. But these outings were different. I was a teenager now, on my own at last, without restrictions or rules. Now I wasn't ever going back.

Hollywood was just a few miles from home, but that first bus ride with Paul felt like blasting off into outer space. Marching down the dark empty streets on our way to the bus stop, flashing our eyes out on Orange Sunshine, the night was a maze of melting Salvador Dalí landscapes, like the paintings at the Museum of Modern Art that Malcolm used to love. But Malcolm was dead now, gone forever, and I was in a hurry to leave all those sad, guilty old memories behind.

As we reached the corner, the acid kicked in harder. We fell to our knees, convulsing in snot-shuddering peals of laughter as the buses rolled by like thundering rocket ships. Tripping so hard we couldn't make it the last twenty feet to the bus stop, we lingered there for minutes. Or hours. Who knew? Time was nonexistent. Finally a big blue bus pulled to a stop and we made a mad dash for the door as it hissed open, a dragon's mouth swallowing us up like a pair of cackling Pygmies.

Our laughter mounted in hysterical waves as we sat in the back, smoking with a gang of Mexican kids. A transistor radio was playing. "Ya gonna cry, cry, cry, cry now . . . Ya gonna cry, cry, cry, cry . . . Ninety-six tears . . ." The thrill of the Run pounded in my blood like a sharp new drug. Everything was new and intoxicating: the feel of the cold, round aluminum rail in my grip as I sat in an ass-worn vinyl seat, staring out into the rolling stillness of night; taking off, blasting into space, stoned beyond all worldly measurement, grounded to Earth only by a lingering odor of old tobacco smoke, musty cookies, face-grease, and shoe rubber; a stale-breath residue of unseen hordes of bus riders haunting the dry dusty wind like spirits of the dead; restless souls of eternal night stirring up memories beyond memory. In that silent rolling moment, the ancient Gypsy blood of my restless ancestors seemed to awaken in me. Motion. Travel. The Run. Rolling along, leaving the past behind, traveling the long, lonesome road to nowhere, my soul came to life with a sense of peace I'd never known. I couldn't describe that abstract language of night coursing in my veins, any more than a cat on the prowl can define its own shadow roaming atop a fence under a full moon as the world sleeps, with a lone dog barking in the distance. More than anything, it was an absence of stillness that gave substance to that magical moment; a singular sensation of adrenaline pumping in hot-wired young veins like a shot of pure excitement; a big empty conveyance thundering down a foggy night road, tires bouncing over earthquake-cracked pavements in a sprawling lost civilization on the desert's edge; dusty patterns of dreams hanging in the dark asphalt air conjuring impressions and memories of far-off times and places; all this as the world flashed by in a fantastic ghostly slideshow. I was a ghost, invisible now, freed at last from the greasy straitjacket of myself; no more feelings, no more fears, no memories, no name; just there, anonymous and unfettered, lumbering along on an aimless night-train down crooked avenues of tall alien palms. And I wanted to howl like a coyote. I wanted to laugh at the absurdity of that stark, unearthly city at world's end. I wanted to cry and jump and shout and wreck shit like Godzilla.

As we approached Hollywood I looked over at Paul sitting across the aisle, grinning out the window like a hungry dog. The streets began taking on the look of a real metropolis, far from our stunted suburban backwater of roving cop cruisers and prying, uptight neighborhood eyes. Like a pair of stoned Martian explorers, we sat there gawking at twinkling corners crowded with dreamers, wanderers, crazies, and longhaired freaks like ourselves; and then the rumbling, groaning monster spit us out into the humid exhaust-fumed city heat, its doors opening, *wssssshhh,* a magical portal ejecting us onto the sidewalk with the force of a revelation.

My nostrils flared, skin and all senses alert. Frantic young legs propelled me along those gum-spotted, glittering sidewalks, littered with stars and famous television names, in an exhilarating new amusement park of life. Electricity crackled in the air, murmuring an enticing soul-language that was large, mysterious, compelling, and new as I merged with a crowded, crooked, winking, blinking mayhem of life; people, crowds, movement all bustling around, an overpowering high I'd been craving forever. I didn't know where I was, and I didn't care as it hit me like a spotlight.

We wandered the shadowy aisles of the old Hollywood Weird Museum, ogling the Cyclops Baby, rows of shrunken heads in dusty glass cases and mysterious two-headed mutant beings peering out of murky jars; and then we were on the move again, cackling and backslapping each other down the feverish sidewalk. "Oh, shit, look!" we pointed and giggled, gawking like gin-soaked yokels visiting the Big City for the first time, poking, prodding, sticking our grinning acid-tripping heads into all the city of night's little corners, a blinking neon forest of mad holy visions. Comic-book stores, tattoo parlors, a throbbing neon corner with a pizza joint where bikers lounged on the sidewalk: greasy Vikings in denim and leather jackets with sinister death's heads, *HELLS ANGELS* emblazoned across hulking backs, perched on fearsome machines purring at the curb like giant insects of doom. The world was all lit up like some mad fantastic Camelot, rock 'n' roll songs blending with a scent of tacos, chili dogs, and car exhaust in the humid electric air.

○   ○   ○

Cigano stops reading and closes his eyes, remembering another late-night talk with his father, sitting across from the old man in his living room.

"Those kids were all fucking nuts back in the sixties," Artie growls. "Neurotic and rebellious. Against, but never for anything constructive. Everything against. Well, they were right for being against all the political bullshit and the war, but what the hell did they wanna put in its place?"

Staring at his father, Cigano sighs. "Our apathy was just a product of our time and culture, Artie. Vietnam. Shit. I think wars like that are all about man's basic inability to live at peace with himself . . ."

Artie grunts. "I dunno what the hell that's supposed to mean."

"The so-called human condition, man." Cigano shrugs. "The

Buddhists say the source of all suffering is want. Other philosophies call it hell, or the bondage of self, whatever. For me, what you call apathy was just a symptom of that kind of deep inner conflict. We were just really pissed off, man, disappointed with the whole cockeyed social structure. There was nothing to believe in, so people just said 'Fuck it.' I dunno. I think my generation's social apathy had its roots in a general frustration with the whole crappy order of things, and a basic desire to find something better . . ."

"No!" The old man cuts in. "It was more than just apathy, Jonathan. They were very hectic. Rebellious. They were out there giving out flowers, lighting candles, having sex with anybody that came along. They weren't living. They were doing things, but to what avail? Nothing came out of that whole sixties movement. Nothing. It all just faded away. They grew a little older and they realized how stupid it was. It was a very strange phenomenon."

"It was a strange time. There's a chapter in this book I'm writing . . ."

"I remember it all vividly." Artie cuts him off. "Nobody knew what the hell that shit was all about. They only knew there was a great comment on the stupid society we had."

Cigano flinches. "Well, I was around fifteen, sixteen back then, and it was an important time, like a rite of passage for me and a lot of other kids . . ."

"Yeah," the old man interrupts again, "well, you were the right age to be in the middle of all that stupid shit. You all ran away from home and wound up sleeping on floors, didn't matter. Crashing anywhere. Woodstock. Lying around in the mud. What the hell were you people doing? It was a strange affair. And they still talk about it. Woodstock. Haight-Ashbury. What the hell was all that shit? A crazy thing. Millions of people gathering in the streets to protest. Protest against what, for Chrissake?"

"It's like Marlon Brando in *The Wild One*, Artie." Cigano tries again. "Ya remember when the girl asked him, 'What are you guys rebelling against?' and he just looked at her and said, 'Whaddya got?'"

Artie grunts and changes the subject.

Cigano shakes his head, wondering why the fuck he even bothers.

58. STRANGE DAYS

"ANY WORLD THAT I'M WELCOME TO IS BETTER THAN THE
ONE I COME FROM."

—STEELY DAN

Cigano looks up, still thinking about his father, wondering how
any amount of description could ever convey another time and place to
someone like this kid sitting across from him.

He shakes his head. "Yeah, Jaco," he sighs, addressing his confessor
for the first time by name, "ya kinda had to be there, I guess. When I
sobered up and started to write about that era, I felt like Rip Van Winkle
or something . . ."

Jaco gives him a confused look. "Rip van what?"

"Arrgh." He shrugs. "It's this old story, man, about a guy who falls
asleep under a tree and doesn't wake up for like a hundred years, and
everything's all different." He grins as he flips to the next page.

"Up in Hollywood," he reads, "we made friends and crashed
wherever we could. Hanging out on the dirty old streets, we lived day
by day and night by night, drinking cheap wine, smoking pot, dropping
acid, and running amok. Growing bored, we took off on the road, crisscrossing the land like a pair of punch-drunk missionaries from Hell; back
and forth, we hitchhiked to New York, then down to Texas and New
Orleans; through deserts, bayous, wheatfields, and the gray industrial
wastelands of America . . ."

JOURNAL ENTRY – EL PASO, TEXAS: *Got a ride with some crazy Indians and drank their tequila all the way from Tucson. After wandering around town here for a while, we guzzled a jug of wino brew Paul swiped from a little market down by the railroad tracks, then fell asleep in a parking lot behind a taco joint. Last thing I saw before I closed my eyes were the humble shacks and shanties of sleepy old Mexico winking and blinking in the lazy Mexican darkness across from the big barbed-wire fences of America. I woke up half-drunk in the middle of the night for a piss. I looked around, wondering where the fuck I was. I saw Paul curled up in a fetal position in his ragged blanket, snoring beside me, and I remembered. It looked like a big concentration-camp ghetto over there, all those bright Yankee searchlights, like some weird Orwell No-Man's-Land separating funky old Mexico from this No-Loitering No-Trespassing plastic neon spiritual ghetto in The Land Of The Free To Obey. A bunch of raggedy Mexican kids were standing on the other side, getting ready to hop that big fence and make a run for the gluey promises of the American Dream. If they only knew. I wanted to jump up and shout. Forget it, go back, amigos! This place will eat your fucking soul like a cheap roadside taco! One day I'm gonna hop that fence going the other way and I'll never look back.*

"We never stayed anywhere for long," he reads. "A restless urge to keep going percolated in our blood like strong truck stop coffee."

JOURNAL ENTRY – NEW ORLEANS: *Been stumbling around the French Quarter with a bunch of grinning Cajun oil workers from down on the bayou, riding around in the back of their beat-up old pickup, listening to accordion music. Met up with some goofy blond chicks from the suburbs who took us down by the river. We smoked some really harsh weed under the docks by an abandoned warehouse, watching the sweaty old Mississippi riverboats chug by. One chick had some pills she'd swiped from her mother's medicine cabinet. Musta been downers, cuz we passed out like a bunch of tangled-up puppets. When me and Paul came to in the middle of the night, the chicks were still knocked out, so we went through their purses and fished out enough bread for a meal at this all-night greasy spoon called Hummingbird*

Cafe, right next to the YMCA. The place was full of ancient Negroes and skinny white-trash guys who looked like dust-bowl ghosts. Real Twilight Zone shit, everybody looking like they'd been sitting there forever. After filling up on bacon and eggs with grits, we decided to get back on the road. Hiking up Elysian Fields to the Interstate in the eerie New Orleans moonlight, we passed rows of foggy, beat-up old Victorian houses, kinda like the ones you see in San Francisco, but different. Run down. Spooky, all covered in vegetation and banana trees and stuff, like shabby hollow-eyed phantoms peeking through a creepy midnight swamp mist. New Orleans is full of ghosts and zombies lurking in muggy night shadows.

"Like an old whore, the streets of Hollywood beckoned from afar. Back home from our travels, we succumbed all over to the glittery, greasy lies of our beloved, hated, inevitable City of Angels. Paul and I crashed a lot of parties in Hollywood, stoned-out gatherings that went for days on end. We'd hang out up at Jim Morrison's place in Laurel Canyon, or at Frank Zappa's big Log Cabin across the road, meeting all sorts of soon-to-be-legendary artists, musicians, actors, writers, poets, and freaks. As we stumbled through that thriving underground maze, taking all kinds of drugs with all kinds of people, we became teenage mascots to some of our favorite bands . . ."

Reading on, Cigano's mind's eye scans a brick wall in a downtown alley; a colorful psychedelic dance poster. *STRANGE NIGHTS: IRON BUTTERFLY AND THE DOORS.* He sees himself and Paul loitering by a big metal backstage door of the Shrine Auditorium, smoking a joint under the watchful eyes of a group of beefy bouncers. A black limo pulls up. Its passengers pile out like a band of Gypsies, surrounded by groupies and roadies. Jonathan spots his new pal Jim. As he edges toward the group, the Lizard King's eyes light up. "Yeah! It's Jonny Shaw and Mr. Pablo, people!" The rocker puts a friendly arm around his scrawny shoulder, passing him a cold can of beer as they all march in the door past the bewildered guards.

"As the good times turned weird," he reads, "a familiar paranoia began to creep over me like a clammy shroud. The acid trips became dark and scary. I just kept taking more, though, hoping to recapture that magical sense of unity I'd felt with my friends, but the trips just kept getting worse. You can run all you like, but you can't get away from your traumas. They're an integral part of you. Some things you never get over. The nightmares that had haunted my childhood were coming back again, with the full force of the Curse."

As the tattoo man continues, the nightmare that's troubled his sleep all his life trembles across the screen of his vision. He's in a beautiful house, the most beautiful home he's ever seen. He's just moved in. As he wanders through a sprawling living room with an expansive view of the sea from a large picture window, he notices a door he hasn't seen before. He opens it and drifts down a long hallway past many doors to mysterious back rooms stretching on forever. He stops and opens one, then stops again, frozen, bombarded with a dark, angry, malevolent energy that pulses and vibrates from the floor, the walls, the ceiling, like a living presence. A pit of terror wells up in his soul as he realizes the house is a living organism. It wants to devour him! He turns and flees, but he cannot awaken as he runs and runs and runs, screaming forever, down a long white corridor that never ends.

Shaking off the memory, Cigano finds his next page. "Were my recurring nightmares of a haunted house a representation of my childhood home? Or was it the creepy landscape of the haunted back rooms of my mind, returning to infect my life now through my acid trips and dreams?"

59. BLOODTHIRSTY ANGELS

"MEMORY IS FICTION."

–KEITH RICHARDS

As the bummers got worse, I became convinced people were conspiring to murder me. The acid paranoia would outlast the trips themselves, coming back in random unpredictable horror-show flashbacks, terrible visions of death, and worse. I began to suffer bouts of suicidal depression. The Curse had me in a headlock. It got so bad that if I so much as sucked on a joint, it would trigger a full-scale cinematic acid flashback.

The mind-expanding drugs of my early teenage years had opened the doors of perception into a hellish nightmare realm where tortured spirits of the damned clamored for my flesh. Like an animal recoiling from fire, I shied away from substance-induced mind expansion. Opting for something closer to oblivion, I developed a taste for harder drugs offering temporary relief from symptoms of major existential agony. Booze, pills, and heroin took the place of LSD, peyote, and pot.

On a very real level, those drugs would save my life. If it hadn't been for alcohol and the comfort it provided, I might have ended up killing myself like Malcolm. Drinking seemed to smooth those rough edges and bolster my courage, bestowing on me an ability to live and act extemporaneously. As I became friends with the bottle, a lusty, life-loving, drunken daredevil replaced the shy, introverted, self-conscious kid cowering inside me.

JOURNAL ENTRY – HOLLYWOOD: Another week gone by, broke, wasted, bored, wallowing around stoned on pills, stumbling crooked streets of same old washed-up blues contemplating Man's inhumanity to Jazz. Stir-crazy in the belly of Babylon. No money. No hope. No fun. Hollywood bartender wardens, Lost Angels of perdition, no credit, they say; fuck 'em, sez I, so me and Paul and The Bat get drunk on a bottle of wine we stole from the Hollywood Ranch Market. When it was gone we wanted more. Bat had some money, so we got a big old half-gallon jug of some cheap foul-smelling shit and started in again, drinking like a gang of ignorant peasants in an old horror movie boosting their courage to go out and commit some awful bloody irrevocable atrocity. We get in a car and split out late at night into cold sagebrush Malibu Canyon after a quick midnight raid on sleeping hippie marijuana patches of Topanga. Sitting in the dirt looking up at the stars, the madman Bat as fucked-up as me, we both understood the futility of talk. We lay back, drunk as toads, till we passed out wrapped in blankets on a cold surface of hard dirt, three little bags of sleep in haunted woods of night. Woke up still high and fuzzybrained looking around for lonely resemblance-hologram-shadow-eternal form of time and place, but it was all gone and this horrible waking-up place was AMERICA. "Where da fuck am I?" I grumbled. The sun had lied to me in my sleep and it was only ten in the shit-fuck morning, fog rolling down the hills in little packs of cold gray mountain spirits. We coulda slept a few more hours, but dehydration parched my sleep and colored my dreams dark and thirsty. Wide awake, still lying in the dirt, three restless stale-wine mummy cadavers, it was time to get out. The hangover visions were disturbing as we pried ourselves from the ground and drove breakneck down to the Coast Highway looking for cure-all breakfast relief. The old Malice Cafe or whatever it used to be called with its warm wood paneling and red leather booths and faded pictures of old-time movie idols looking down from the walls like a troop of greasy cherubs and its motherly old waitresses. The place was but a memory as we stood in front of what used to be, cringing and cursing before the super high-glossy PANCHO's RANCHO MALARIO or some such modern fluorescent pseudo-Mexican abomination and shit-fuck it's bleeding eleven in the morning or later and we're standing out in front of this truly hideous horror-show nightmare place looking at the fancy streamlined door like a pack of angry Pygmies. To our horror, the fucking modern hell-pit is CLOSED, even at this late Sunday hour, and there's this big intimidating sign outside saying: DRESS CODE blah blah and furthermore NO JEANS. What can you say about a pretentious shit-hole like that? Somebody ought to burn it down or blow it up or just get the fuck outta there fast as Paul suggested, so off we go toot sweet to the old drugstore coffee shop by the Malibu Colony, and there we found life and an honest-to-goodness old-time Sunday breakfast crowd. "Gee-whiz, this is more like it," we say, and all that bright early Sunday morning welcomeness should be able to cure any old hangover, we figure; so we sat down feeling all regular again and ordered the works—as if we even had cash to pay for it. Boy howdy! The Real All-American Breakfast: eggs coffee bacon O.J. hash browns and the newspaper Sunday Breakfast Section or whatever, enough good old Sunday morning normal living to really make ya feel all right. The Bat, fucking subversive crazyman, he gets an order of garlic bread, glass of tomato juice and I got a cup acup acup acup acupacupa JAVA TIME, goooood Lord, and it's near noon now, time for the good old dine-n-dash and they both get up to "go to the bathroom" and climb out the window while I go out the front door and start the car and then we're screaming along the sparkling coastline sideswiping Sunday families in their low-down-payment shiny station wagons and so begins the next angel-dust lost weekend here at the beginning of the end of time.

JOURNAL ENTRY – HOLLYWOOD: *Met up with some crazies on the Boulevard and got a big jug of wine, then went over to somebody's pad where we got lit up like confused fireflies. Some guy with a big bushy black beard you could stash a dozen rats in is tripping his brains out on dust and the stuff goes around and we're all getting pretty good on it when O'Connell tumbles in out of the night and the whole scene turns into a big drunken freak-out rhythm orgy drumming for hours on tables and chairs and tin cans and each other's heads and anything in sight into the wee hours until the sun came up. Positively religious, a lot of good energy and unity, like being on acid back in the old days again, but without all the paranoia, like revisiting the scene where all the past years of ugly bum-tripping started out and seeing*

*it now for what it was: nothing to kill yourself over, even if it was
a close call there for a while. At the end we're all sitting around in
a circle on the floor singing this crazy acid-chant that spontaneously
erupted as Richard sang out "The bottomless pit . . ." in a deep
serious baritone, and then all the rest of us start raising our hands in
the air like a gospel choir of frantic Jesus-intoxicated colored ladies
in harmony singing, "Ain't got no bottom!" And it goes on like that
for hours, that endless crazy mantra, "The bottomless pit . . . ain't
got no bottom," over and over till we're doubled over on the floor like
cackling Pygmies. Paul and I split with Richard, chanting it together
down the street, bopping along, just as we first did years ago on first
trips up to Hollywood, tripping our melting brains out, digging on the
pristineness of the morning, the crystal-clear comedown after another
big insane high-energy freak-session. And walking among the rushing
morningworld people we felt it again like a gang of bloodthirsty angels
sitting in bright morning coffee shop buzzglow howling like coyotes and
making crazy R. Crumb faces at each other and the whole lopsided
world and everyone who saw us thought we were bug-farm batmen
and they were right as we went tripping through the creepy franticness
of go-go-go-to-work morning rat race rush hour, lecherously eyeballing
pink-faced schoolgirls in their slutty short plaid skirts and knee-socks,
dog-drooling at their tender young carcasses and sharing our lunatic
sex fantasies with each other. Boy howdy, yeah! It's nice to have a gang
of brother-souls as demented as you are who are well aware of this
ugly bastard-culture's decrepit influence on our undernourished crooked
brains, and it's even better when you're talking about it with your own
kind and digging the whole thing and then you can go somewhere safe
to sleep it off till more later come.*

I started hanging out with a chick from my old gang. Ellen Janov was
the daughter of the infamous Primal Scream therapist, Arthur Janov, John
Lennon's psychic guru. Ellen and I had gone to school together and had
been pals. Now we were fuck-buddies. With her extraterrestrial teenage
beauty, extraordinary appetite for sex, drugs, and rock 'n' roll, and her old
man's connections to the rock elite, we wound up in the middle of some
pretty surreal scenes—including the inner circle of the Rolling Stones.

Ellen had been the childhood sweetheart of a brooding young artist
named Chris Anderson, my old girlfriend Melissa's brother. The love of

Chris's life had recently become the mistress of one Marshall Chess—heir to the Chess Records Empire—who was now managing the Stones. I was fucking Ellen too, as were O'Connell, Chris, and just about everybody else. Our gang had always been an incestuous lot. Now, thanks to Ellen's new situation, we all had the run of Chess's big house up in the Hollywood Hills. When the Stones were staying there while cutting an album in Hollywood, Ellen and I would do the dope runs. Ellen had the kind of look that was popular with rock stars of the day. Lolita on drugs; arm-candy for the middle-aged Marshall.

"Oh, look, it's the scream doctor's dough-taa." Mick Jagger raised an ironic eyebrow when he saw her on Chess's arm one night. "So the Screamer has loaned her out to Chess now? How chaahh-ming!"

The first time I went up to Marshall's with Ellen, there was this older guy sprawled out on a sofa as we walked in. His eyes were rolled back in his head, his mouth cocked open like a coffin lid, a cigarette burning down to a stub between his fingers. The ash was incredibly long.

"Fuck! It's Keith Richards!" I whispered as Ellen took the butt from his hand like a concerned parent, patting him on the head like a shaggy dog.

"Wha'? Wussat?" He opened one eye with a crooked grin. "Oh, 'allo, luv . . ." Mumbling, he reached for another cigarette, nodding out again before he could light it.

Keith Richards was a kindly older brother junkie to us—when he was conscious. The one time I managed to talk with him for a minute, he reminded me of an old Negro bluesman trapped in a white man's body, the antithesis of a glamorous rock star. He had this charming smile like a mischievous old pirate. And like a good pirate, he shared his booty with Ellen. Sweet Ellen shared with me, Chris, O'Connell, and the rest of our crowd, who hung around the house like stray dogs. That's when we were all just flirting with heroin as a part-time buzz. Nobody was strung out yet. Life was still a big long lazy rock 'n' roll party. The dark times were yet to come.

60. THE WAY WE WERE

"I HAVE A HOT MEMORY, BUT I KNOW I'VE FORGOTTEN
MANY THINGS, TOO, JUST SQUASHED THINGS IN FAVOR OF
SURVIVAL."

—IGGY POP

JOURNAL ENTRY – HOLLYWOOD: *Ellen and I walked
into this shop on Hollywood Boulevard today. It was like something
from a childhood that must have existed somewhere. Rows and rows
of sparkling, colorful little bottles of perfumed oils—that's what I like
about the crazy hieroglyphic glittery aesthetics of life. We were like
two timid animals standing there with all the shiny clicketyclacky. The
evolution of our little species is another matter. A question of circles. I
like to play with pretty colors. I should be locked up in the loony bin.
I like jugglers and midnight seesaws and jigsaw puzzles you can't see
right away. I like spookhouse alleys and dark winding pathways and
hypodermic needles and dirty little girls like Ellen. I like the wind and
rain. I like music. I like dreams and I like to piss on ice in the men's
room at Musso's when there's some rich rock star paying the tab for
Ellen and her stray-dog pack. I don't like high school principals and
cops and I don't like the cholos out on the boulevard in their noisy hot
rods. I don't like spiders and I don't like snow and I certainly don't like
anchovies on my pizza. Some things totally disgust me, like fat people
and cheap diner food with too much grease. Sometimes I like to be
disgusted and sometimes I don't. Sometimes I disgust myself. Oh, yes,*

and I like my beautiful friend Ellen very much today. I don't like what I'm writing here, though. I'm gonna stop so we can get high again and fuck some more before she has to go back up to Marshall's and feed her pet junkies.

JOURNAL ENTRY – HOLLYWOOD: *Survived another week, somehow. I've even been straight for a whole day now, no liquor or drugs, as I sit trying to piece together this last long lost weekend. It ain't gonna be easy getting through a day without any drugs or booze, but neither are the hangovers and drunk-driving busts, and God knows I've had my share of both lately. It just ain't easy any way you do it, so I'm just sitting around trying to stay clean today. Yesterday was another story: I was at the Hollywood Swap Meet, looking for something to steal and trying to keep straight. That was Sunday. All of Saturday night I spent in the drunk tank. I slept a lot in jail, but I woke up intermittently, thinking I was somewhere else. I was pretty bummed out when I realized I was locked up in a big cement room with a bunch of sleazy sleepers, not even any windows or bars, no idea if or when I was getting out. I was fucked. Anyway, Sunday, so there I am fresh out of the pokey, walking around under blazing Hollywood sun nursing a murderous hangover, trying to kill some time and keep straight for the rest of the day. At least I had my beat-up old car. I found it still sitting at the curb like a crippled roach right where I'd left it when the cops carted me off the night before. So I'm walking around the Flea Market after blowing my last five bucks on a too-big shirt and a pair of too-tight cowboy boots, when I hear a chick's voice calling my name. I look around and it's Ellen, who I was with before the cops dragged me to jail. She runs up and starts kissing me and playing with my leg. "Hurry, Jonny, take us to the Renaissance Faire." It was too good to resist. Ellen. Warmth, affection, female companionship—no matter how bizarre. I could hang. My sweet little dreamer was with two of the most curious people I've ever seen, a pair of queer-looking transsexual types; interesting, though, kinda Keith Richards-David Bowie glam-rock alien life forms. Intense, like Ellen, like all of her mad beautiful loser acquaintances. I say sure, let's go, and they all pile into my car and crack open a big jug of wine, and off we go. By the time we get to the place out in Topanga, I've figured out that one of Ellen's companions (who called himself-herself Danielle) was a guy.*

*The other one, his/her playmate, Wednesday (or was it Wendy?) I
still wasn't too sure about. We hustled ourselves into the employee
parking lot and made our crooked way to the fairgrounds, me in these
ridiculous too-tight cowboy boots wishing I'd stopped at my rooming
house for some normal boots first. My dogs were really barking. I had
this big camera I'd ripped off somewhere and a nice woolen
man-woman's sweater I'd put on after we ransacked a car in the
parking lot. The closer we got to the gate, the more I wished I'd
brought better shoes. Pain! Ellen and Danielle skipped right through,
blowing kisses at the guards and leaving me behind with Wednesday
or Wendy or whatever. By the time I get to the gate I can hardly
walk, so I had to be supported by Wednesday. I still wasn't sure
about her/his sex but I couldn't care less, in such agony I couldn't
walk without her/his assistance. As I hobbled past the baffled-
looking guard, leaning on my weird transvestite crutch, I could see
Ellen and Danielle up at the top of the hill waving and shouting,
cheering us for our excellent ruse to get in without paying (little did
they know it was for real and I was hanging on to this bizarre
woman-man for dear life). After we're all together again, the three of
them jump into this insane dervish-dance, and I lay my broken
carcass down on the ground, feeling totally miserable. I pulled the
goddamn boots off my blistered inflamed feet, and from that painfully
prone position I took a few photos of them dancing. A big crowd
gathered and stood around watching as they danced around like
maniacs. There was a bagpipe player and all these weird medieval
music types with lutes and harps and shit, playing faster and faster
and the dancing got weirder and more frenetic. Then my companions
all skipped away like merry children, leaving me to put the accursed
boots on and hobble along behind. It was impossible. I was dying.
After a few limp strides, I gave up, sat down by a glass-blower's
booth, and took off those shitty boots, feeling hungover and abandoned
and sad. A couple of very straight, touristy-looking middle-aged
ladies approached. "Dear boy," they said in a weird old-world
accent. "What the matter be with ye?" "My back is broken," I
wailed. "I'm crippled forever, God is punishing me, I can't walk,
help!" They instructed me to lie down and turn over face down in the
dirt. I obeyed. When you're down and out, what else you gonna do?
"VE MAKE ALL BETTER," they declared. Before I knew what*

was happening, these old witches were gathering boulders from the surrounding terrain and placing them on my body, literally burying me under the weight of the goddamn things, giggling. "I vish ve have camera, he look so fun-ny, heheheee . . ." Goddammit, people were staring at me in that ridiculous position! I could barely move my head to see the dusty feet scuffling by. By now I knew they were just fucking around, this whole demented routine was of no use at all. Just as I was about to shrug the rocks off, a pretty hippie chick approached and bent down to my absurd snake-eye level. "Hurt yer back?" she asked. "Yeah," I gasped, "but these rocks ain't doing no good." She chased the old hags away, flinging the rocks off my back. Ahhhh. I could breathe. She straddled my back, feeling all the muscles and bones, and went to work on it. Shortly I was able to move. She told me "Good luck" and to move around and stretch it a lot. I thanked her (she was so beautiful) with boozy tears in my eyes. Then I hobbled over to this fantastic giant oak tree where I was supposed to meet my friends if we got separated. I sat in the shade, oblivious to the festivities, and fell asleep. An hour later, I woke up rejuvenated. Hangover gone, feeling good, I got up and walked around a bit, greeting people with a friendly/freaky eye and picking up scraps of food here and there. I ran into Wednesday. I still wasn't sure about the gender but felt more relaxed around her/him/whatever, just glad to see anybody. We walked as she told me about her past hours and I told her about mine. My sweet Ellen had consumed about a half gallon of vodka and passed out after pissing on Danny's feet, falling over, bruising herself, fucking up her face and her tattered Victorian dress. We found her flat on her back, laughing, playing and rolling in the dust with Danny and humping his leg. She looked like a wilted peacock after a thunderstorm. Fuck! They carted her off on a stretcher, five or six security guys, real anxious and uptight. They growled at me as I tried to take a picture, ordering us all to keep back. After we got to the infirmary, they mellowed out and even gave us a ride down to my car in one of their golf cart things. We proceeded down the great cosmic sparkling Pacific Coast Highway to the nearest market, where we quickly and efficiently ripped them off for everything in sight. The way Danny's hands moved through the produce, deli, and even liquor shelves was pure magic. Then we drove to Santa Monica, where Wednesday's mother was the building manager and she/he had her/his own apartment. It being Mother's Day, we stopped in to see the mom, a lot of people coming and going. Mom was cool, and we all laughed and exchanged pleasantries before making it down to #24 which Wednesday called home. By then I knew she was a girl (by birth, if not by choice). We drank and ate and Ellen and I got on the bed and started making out. We took our clothes off, getting ready to fuck, but all these weird people kept coming and going, including Wednesday's little brother, about eight, real cool little kid. I was struck with impotence for about an hour with all those people watching. How embarrassing! But I tried, God knows I tried, to get it up and get it in there. It really seemed important at the time, but people were shouting and talking and moving around. It was like trying to fuck in a train station. I picked up some interesting bits of conversation, lying on top of Ellen's heaving yearning body, including some great humorous comments about our fucked-up sex struggles, all in good fun, but I dunno, these group gropes just don't do it for me. Wednesday even got on the bed and gave me a blowjob, but nothing worked. My sword was blunted, bummed out by all the pressure, even if the only real pressure was in my mind. Finally they split and I got the dick in. Ellen and I worked it out for about fifteen minutes, but people started filtering in again and I gave up and pulled my jeans on. Fuck it. A whole hour of diddling and fiddling for fifteen minutes of so-so sex. Forget it. Ellen was all worked up by now and trying to get it on with everything in the room, including Wednesday's little brother who just went "eww, gross" when she flashed her pussy in his face, begging him to lick it. Wednesday passed out on the bed next to us with her little brother. Ellen and Danny and I took off to his place in Hollywood where we did this weird ritual to "consecrate" some Egyptian Sphinx statue and he gave us some crazy voodoo keepsakes and showed me his scrapbook (truly freaky). From there, Ellen and I made it over to my room in the back of a crumbling old wooden house where we finally managed to fuck like champs. Then we smoked some grass and crashed. I didn't sleep too good. Not used to crashing in my own bed anymore. Ellen looked like an angel passed out beside me. A fallen angel, but what other kind could I want? If I wasn't so crippled and fucked in the head, I would fall in love with her like everybody else does—but that would just fuck it all up. I'm just glad to have her for whatever stolen moments from Marshall and poor love-struck Chris. We fucked some more in the morning, then I had to do some "business" Paul had cooked up. We got ourselves together and I drove E. back to D's, and with a torn-up kiss, I split to meet P.

JOURNAL ENTRY – HOLLYWOOD: *Another Saturday night and I got that same old empty feeling of futility that comes over me. Bored to tears after days without booze or drugs, I got out and went to the Rainbow. Sat at the big table in the back with some of the Led Zeppelin crew, and even mooched a few free drinks off of Robert Plant himself. Nice cat, friendly and real down-to-earth. No stuck-up rock-star pretensions. After they split, I went to this party up in the hills that got busted by the cops and all the lost children of Hollywood had to split, me hot on their trail. Nothing happened at the next place and I wound up at Danielle's pad in the lower Hollywood slums, three in the morning, drunk and stoned and craving more of anything I could get. At Danielle's, I met these murderous-looking Vic Tanny biker angel-dust freaks. I got loaded on the stuff and went on this mad bummer freakout, a massive mental meltdown where I saw police snipers and CIA agents and spooky shadows crawling around in every bush, weird paramilitary goons armed to the tits on street corners, getting ready for Armageddon. I'd been transformed into an evil midget and shit-fuck could hardly drive my car. My stumpy little midget legs couldn't reach the gas pedal. Go ask Alice. Somehow I made it back home like a sweaty fugitive Pygmy and wrote two pages of really demented bloodthirsty shit before passing out. When I came to the next day and looked in my journal, I couldn't even remember writing any of it. The horror! It's come to this! The walls were closing in again. I made a few calls and tried to hustle myself a trip to San Francisco with these jive-ass filmmaker kids I met before the party got busted under the ruse of me being a photographer with this big-ass camera I ripped off the other day. Nice try, but it did not happen. I made more calls and managed to get Tony Fried to come with me to this coke hustler's place, under the premise of us copping and selling an ounce to some non-existent big shot if he'd put up the money. Tony showed up without money, of course, so the ounce didn't happen, of course. We did get a gram "to sample" and did all the coke ourselves. I* *feel responsible for so many bad things. I'm turning into a sleazy little hustler like the rest of them! I even ripped off this big long elephant-trunk telephoto lens I know nothing about from the hustlers who hustled me into hustling Tony—and God knows who they ripped off for that—one big ripoff hustle jungle. We wound up driving around, ending up at this party in Silver Lake with a bunch of crazy Mexicans. I went into the medicine cabinet and found a bunch of Valiums and got real stoned. Only thing I remember after that is waking up in a room in Hollywood to snores of sleeping zombie coke hustlers. It took me about a minute to get the fuck out of there back to my room and passed out again. I was awakened by frantic calls from Ellen and Danny. "Come to the Renaissance Faire," and off we go, another freakish horror show, worse than before, Ellen making out with some out-of-town boy she'd picked up. I almost fucked a slutty chick from Encino behind a trailer, but before I could get my pants off Danielle got busted ripping off a vase, a big fuss, we got kicked out and split back to Hollywood, then off to this big party up in the hills—posh house, private fashion show, drinks, good food, a few snorts of China White. I was feeling pretty good, stoned. I marched upstairs to where all the fashion clothes were, trying them on. Next, I'm down at my car, ripped out of my skull, sporting a five-hundred-dollar designer coat, Danielle and Ellen with their own pilfered goodies. We get in, but the car is stuck in a ditch. We tried pushing it, no dice. A Cadillac comes along. Guy wouldn't give us a push, fucker, I threatened him and made "menacing gestures" (probably just gave him the finger, I can't remember a thing, but that's what the police report said). The Fat-Cat-Caddy-Jockey roared off and we got the car going. But just as we got down the street, there's Fat Cat talking to the cops. Why me? Ellen and I got busted for under the influence. When we got to the station, the cops breath-tested me and said I wasn't drunk and decided to drop the drunk driving charge. They had to book me for something so they wouldn't look stupid since I was already there and all, so they wrote me up for an old warrant. Luckily, I had eighty bucks cash, and I was out in fifteen minutes. From there I hitched up to Rodney's on Sunset (bumping into the Vic Tanny dust-freak midget bikers at the Ranch Market, sweet Jesus, I'm associating by sight with all the zombie wolfs in town!). I hustled myself another ride to my car with some knucklehead from the Valley who thought I looked like a real authentic Hollywood hipster. Went to*

Rodney's, then home. Called Ellen. She was okay, still with her little tiger boy. I said I'd talk to her tomorrow, blah blah. Now I'm home with a lot of court dates, ass kissing, job hunting, and straightening out to do tomorrow. Another weekend all blown to hell. At least I got a new winter coat out of the deal, something to wear to court. Ho hum. P.S.—at the end of this weekend that was supposed to be booze and drug free, I've done coke, grass, heroin, booze, angel dust, Valium, and a brain-melting assortment of other weird downers, and driving all the while, yo ho ho and a bottle of cat piss rum.

After underlining a few passages, Cigano sets his old notebook down, mumbling "Man, what a little shit I was! I'm lucky to be alive."

He falls silent, staring off into space, then looks up at his listener, shaking his head. "Most of 'em weren't so fucking lucky, man."

With a long weary sigh, he picks up the book again.

61. SURF CITY

"YOU CAN'T STAY IN YOUR CORNER OF THE FOREST WAITING
FOR OTHERS TO COME TO YOU. YOU HAVE TO GO TO THEM
SOMETIMES."

—A.A. MILNE

Late one hot summer afternoon, I came to with a brutal hangover. I cracked my blurry eyes and blinked. Another strange bed. Another strange chick snoring beside me. Kind of chubby. Not much to look at. What the fuck? I reached over the inert body and found my smokes. Sitting on the edge of the bed with a clattering ball of dread bumping around my gut, I lit up with trembling hands, wondering where the fuck I was. A heater was blasting, all the windows closed. Breathing in a stifling stench of cat piss, garbage, and sickly-sweet incense, I wanted to puke. Piles of glittery silver clothing and gaudy colorful platform boots and shoes were strewn around, like a gorilla had arranged the dark little space. Waves of dry-mouthed panic swept my brain. My head was pounding. I couldn't breathe! Where the fuck was I? What happened last night? Where did I leave my fucking car?

In the last few months, Paul had been hanging out with this older chick we met at a party. This one was pretty straight. She kept a steady job and even had her own place down in Hermosa Beach. Never one to snub a free meal ticket attached to a pussy, my friend had wasted no time moving in on her. Whenever I needed a break from Hollywood, I'd go visit him in that factory-lined working-class suburb by the sea.

One time we hitched to Tijuana and holed up there for a week with a gang of junkie hookers; usually, though, we just hung around his place in Hermosa, drinking wine. As I struggled into my boots and stumbled out the door, I knew it was time to go see Paul. Fuck the car. I marched down to Sunset and stuck out my thumb.

Feeling better an hour later, a cool ocean breeze was blowing in my hair as I trudged along the coast highway, breathing in a nostalgic beach-town aroma of pizza and fish tacos. The bubbling human rhythm of used-car salesmen and bank tellers enjoying an early Saturday night out with their attractive top-sirloin dates filled the trembling air. An overhead sign loomed up ahead:

THE SOUTH BAY CHAMBER OF COMMERCE WELCOMES YOU TO SCENIC HERMOSA BEACH

I grinned, picturing a bevy of snappy businessmen with shiny white Pepsi-Cola smiles greeting me with a warm, open-armed welcome to that fine, tinsel-toned industrial wasteland of hamburger efficiency and oil-change readiness. Plodding along the sprawling commercial avenue, I looked down at the colorful twinkle of broken-bottle chips glittering in the gutter, trying to ignore the fleeting universes of suspicious eyes flooring it past in big easy-terms muscle cars; regular workaday inhabitants of a white-trash neon desert by the sea, probably wondering who the hell was this solitary hobo shadow in worn dirty jeans, and where the hell did I come from with my long tangled hair, and where the hell was I going with a three-day booze stubble, and what the hell did I do for a goddamn living.

I hung a right and walked up to the scruffy old Victorian house. I stared up at the window of Paul's little attic pad, picturing my friend up there, playing his violin at sunset like a crazed twentieth-century Nero. The three-story wooden relic reminded me of the kind you see in block-long rows, interrupted by the occasional corner grocery, in places like San Francisco. Next to this one, though, just a lonely used-car lot with hundreds of colorful, sun-bleached plastic banners blowing in the wind like celluloid gravestones; hard-dirt vacant lots and broken-down picket fences were the backdrop, dotted with the occasional rusty oil well. I stood taking in the barren scenery, feeling a melancholy tingle in my gut as I wondered to myself what that ghostly hybrid netherworld must have looked like in the old days, back before the oil industry and aerospace projects brought jobs and prosperity to the sleepy little coastal towns spewing north from the Mexican border. California dreaming, I racked my brain, wondering why I wondered so much about stuff. I really hoped Paul had some wine. Too much restless wondering about the nature of things was nothing a few drinks wouldn't fix. I walked around the back and started up the long flight of creaky wooden steps, then paused and lit a cigarette, watching the dark expanse of ocean from the second-floor landing.

At the end of the next flight, I found a note pinned to Paul's door: *BACK BY NINE. P.* I looked at my Timex. Almost eight. The door was open, so I let myself in. Shit. Paul was supposed to be home. Good old Paul, always happy to see me and hand me a beer and a joint when I showed up out of the night. I wandered around the empty pad and switched on the stereo: a new addition since my last visit; probably "liberated" from some unfortunate neighbor's home while they were off at work. Paul always had that special knack for "acquiring" things in a most mysterious fashion. I found a record and set it down on the turntable. To the scratchy sounds of Art Blakey's Jazz Messengers, I bopped into the kitchen. The shelves were pure art. Paul art: a bottle of Ovaltine that looked like a holdover from the Great Depression. A couple of rusty cans of tuna. Dark brown ketchup in an ancient bottle. A battered tin of sardines. A box of stale Cap'n Crunch. I opened a cabinet. A package of tampons, a half bottle of muscatel and half a bottle of apple juice with a white film floating on top. I chose the muscatel.

I went back in and flipped the disk. The other side was even scratchier. I didn't care. I sat on the lumpy sofa sipping the sweet syrupy wine. I picked up last week's paper and scanned the comic section for a while. I eyed my watch again. Twenty minutes after. I wished Paul would show. The music played and I sipped the wine. What did it matter? I'd only come there to get away from Hollywood; to get into cars and get out again; to get drunk all alone and feel the wind on my gas-station-restroom-Borax-washed face. That's all that mattered. I just needed to wander off like that sometimes and see something new, anything, anywhere. But that old restless itch wasn't done. I felt cheated. I wanted to get up and move again, to keep going; maybe stick my thumb out and ride all the way to Mexico City; just say fuck it all and never go back. Why not?

I poured another glass and sat listening to the stereo playing *A Night in*

Tunisia. I drained the bottle, daydreaming of Tunisian nights and feeling like an alley cat waiting for an old lady to come with a meal. I thought of going out for a walk, but I had everything I needed. Jazz, wine, cigarettes. All was good. I didn't even bother going through the drawers and cabinets like I might have done elsewhere. There was nothing to find. The Jazz Messengers played on and I leaned back on the sofa, staring out the cracked window at the sea stretching off into infinity. I put my feet up on the coffee table, trying to shove my restless travel thoughts to the side, but the more wine I drank, the stronger that nagging, rambling itch became. I was growing bored and restless again, my mind playing with old nostalgic memories of hitchhiking cross-country with Paul and all the places we'd been. Another powerful urge to get up and wander off into the night began to emerge from my muscatel high. Then, just as I rose to my feet to split, the door opened.

"Jon!"

"Paul. What's up, brother? How ya doin', man?"

That kind of question always brought my friend to life like a mad animated underworld marionette, bursting with anecdotes and lurid descriptions of life in the surreal back rooms of his twisted vision of America.

With a crooked grin, he started. "The bitch kicked me out, man. Took my keys, told me to hit th' road, Jack!"

"But yer still here, brother." I laughed. "What's the deal?"

"She went outta town for the weekend. Visit parents, whatever." He shrugged, gesturing at a broken window. "I let myself back in. *No problema.* I got till Monday before she's back."

"Whaddya gonna do then?"

"I dunno." He grinned like a hungry wolf. "Go back up to Hollywood with you, I guess. Just been hanging around here, doing a little writing . . ."

That was the signal. I knew what came next.

62. A WARM WELCOME

"WRITING IS A SOCIALLY ACCEPTABLE FORM OF
SCHIZOPHRENIA."

-E.L. DOCTOROW

We sat on the floor surrounded by pages of Paul's illegible scribbled manuscript. My friend squinted and shuffled, sometimes shouting, sometimes barely audible, through reams of his marathon novel-in-progress, *Babblings of a Madman*. While the title might have sounded a little pretentious to the uninformed, I could hardly call it misleading. Knowing Paul Magad as I did, it was just simple truth in advertising.

As much as I missed having him around up in Hollywood, it kind of sucked he wouldn't be down in Hermosa anymore. Those quiet literary interludes there with Paul were always inspiring. I found myself wishing I could express myself with words as well as him, despite the long pauses when he sat bent over his scattered pages like a confused ape, grunting in painful attempts to decipher his own haphazard speed-freak scrawl.

> *It's positively radioactive. It all started when I made fun of some asinine book she wanted me to read. Can I help it if I can't fit into these girls' normal lives? I just don't identify with our heroes of modern literature, upbeat characters like Jonathan Livingston Seagull. But all is not lost. At least there's one mainstay of our popular culture I can fully relate to. He happens to be a used-car salesman in Southern*

*California, who has captured late-night television audiences with
his dog, Spot. Yes! Cal Worthington is a real honest-to-God, unsung
Western hero. Speaking of dogs and spots, at this exact moment two
dogs are howling eerily outside my window, and I'm seeing spots from
shooting a huge load of crank. It's all making me extremely uneasy.
Try to picture this situation, if you will. I'm sitting in a room alone,
stoned and growing increasingly paranoid, with enough speed coursing
through my veins to give the whole building a heart-a-choke. The
sounds of the city are strangely amplified. These Pavlovian puppies
down the road hear a faroff siren in the night and respond with the
most blood-curdling wails, undoubtedly under the influence of a little
moonlight. I've got to get out of this place before I eat a bug. So, I go
sit in an all-night Laundromat. If you're reading this, you already
know I spend a lot of time in all-night Laundromats, and you're
probably wondering what sort of demented fascination I have with
these places. Please allow me to enlighten you: it's two in the morning
and all the housewives are fast asleep. No music is being piped in at
this late hour, but all the dryers are whining eerie high-pitched sound
frequencies. To replace the housewives, there is a man in his early
twenties, replete with mustache and sideburns, doing his laundry.
He is making quite an issue of ignoring me, standing up reading a
newspaper, with his back fastidiously turned to me. I bet if some
Cosmic Power suddenly forced us into some inevitable confrontation, he
would still avoid looking into my eyes. Why? How can I convey this
empty situation? Maybe I shouldn't call it empty, since the moment
is positively pregnant with all sorts of vibrant radioactive vibes. It's
not that the other guy doesn't like me, I suppose. I'm really not that
paranoid. Nor do I think I could be frightening him in some way, not
by just sitting in an empty late-night Laundromat. But he was here
FIRST, so I'm The Intruder. It's a territorial thing, I would imagine.
But you, dear reader, must know as well as I do that, in reality, he is
the intruder. Because I have ulterior motives for being here, you see.
Yes, Virginia, I didn't come here at two in the morning merely to wash
my clothes. I'm here, in truth, to absorb all the radioactivity emerging
from this particular situation. There is a sign on the wall that says
MAYTAG COMMERCIAL WASHERS. Maybe you take the
"radioactivity" reference as some sort of poetic metaphor. Forget it.
It is not! You may not know it, but this whole place is buzzing like*

*a spaceship right now! The lights are very bright. The linoleum is
scuffed-up and dirty, but never mind that. It almost has the sanctity of
a library or a church to me as I sit waiting for something momentous
to take place. Anything could happen here! I can imagine a marching
band descending out of thin air playing John Philip Sousa marches.
Perhaps if I concentrate I can actually make it happen! In the
meantime, I find myself slipping into a cross-eyed state of limbo. I'd
better stop right now, or I might not ever be able to come back to this
Laundromat, or even Planet Earth, for that matter. Would that be so
bad, I wonder? The human condition is ripping my eyeballs apart!
Everywhere I look, I see silent screams of wretchedness and despair.
I'm no exception, of course. And still, I can't help but wonder, sitting
in this stationary spaceship at two in the morning, why is this such a
futile existence? I actually have the nerve to ponder the validity of other
people's lives? To figure out what purpose they serve? Who the hell
am I to judge the purpose of anyone else? I am everybody else! I want
to cry for all of us, for our plight, our trivial position in the universe.
We're nothing but lobsters in a tank! And suddenly Inspiration comes
to me with a thick Irish brogue, urging me to make a field goal, do it
for the Clovers, do it for the Shamrocks! Don't you remember seeing
that film on a Sunday-afternoon television matinee? When the coach
urges O'Clancy to do it for the Clovers, for the Shamrocks? A real
tearjerker . . . And time marches on. So you think I'm crazy, eh?
Television! That's what did it to me! At the age of two, I could sing
all the cigarette commercials! TV has literally short-circuited my brain!
It sends out the radioactive spores that enter my bloodstream and alter
my chromosomes, or something to that effect. Yeah, well, maybe all
that speed might have had just a teeny weeny bit to do with it too. I
mean I shot a lot of CRANK before coming over here. But still, if it
wasn't for all that meth—ouch—I wouldn't have ever discovered the
radioactive properties of all-night Laundromats in the first place, I
kid you not. Still, I'm not ready to cut down on my daily allotment of
spores, not ready to kick such a heavy-duty habit just yet. I just had a
really disturbing thought. What if our popular television personalities
all suddenly put their hands through the screens and reached out and
turned all the televisions off? Imagine the anticlimactic silence that
would pervade the living rooms of America. When I was fifteen and
all strung out on heroin, I would really enjoy watching the daytime*

soap operas. I couldn't actually follow the convoluted plots, but the detergent commercials were incredible! What I liked most was when they would show the Brand X Detergent. I would be reminded of women in Laundromats, in bleak Middle American winter settings, and I would get a certain pleasurable pain from watching those off-brand detergent commercials. I imagine all that must have some masochistic overtones. You would have to be pretty deranged to understand it, I suppose, but hey, I'm just thrilled with my discovery of a whole thriving subculture of the American Housewife; a noble creature who has made her trips to the Laundromat a veritable way of life. It keeps me up all night, sitting in places like this, hoping for a mere glimpse of it in all its foamy Whiter-Than-White splendor. She sweeps all the dirt under the rug so she won't have to miss a minute of her favorite Soap Opera (did you know they call them Soap Operas because of all the detergent advertisements on the commercial breaks?). Her husband comes home a few hours later, only to find a skeleton sitting on the sofa, glowing with radiation. He sits down across from his wife and flashes her a sparkling Colgate Toothpaste smile. "Why, you're positively radioactive, dear!"

I was cackling like a deranged jackal as Paul looked up from the disheveled pile of papers, grinning. I beamed at my friend like a proud parent. I loved his depictions of the demented little world he inhabited; the way he described even the most mundane events in such mad apocalyptic language. And Paul was always writing; a huge inspiration to me. Since the day my mother destroyed my fledgling comic-book efforts, I'd given up on drawing. Now, all I wanted was to write. But, other than my random spaced-out journal entries, I was too busy staying high to do it with any regularity or focus.

"Fucking beautiful, Pablo!" I grinned as we rose up. "Hey, let's truck on down to the store, brother, get some more wine, some food, whatever."

"You're buyin', I'm flyin', man!" said Paul. Navigating around the pages scattered across the frayed Persian rug, we staggered out into the night.

Carloads of rolling eyeballs tracked us like snipers as we crossed the avenue, making our way to the little corner market. As we strode in, a ruddy middle-aged cashier shot us a cold look. This wasn't Hollywood, I remembered. They weren't used to seeing longhaired weirdos. I shrugged up the aisle, looking for something to eat. I picked out a container of lemon yogurt, brought it up to the register, and handed the grumpy old clerk a twenty. As I waited for my change, I noticed the button on his apron. An American flag. *AMERICA—LOVE IT OR LEAVE IT.* Great.

"Y'ain't got nothin' smaller?" Whitey shot me a sour glare. I was a Dirty Commie Peace-and-Love Hippie Bum. The Enemy.

"Sorry, man, that's it. Hey, could I get a plastic spoon?"

"Ain't got no silverware here. This ain't a restaurant, boy."

"Yeah, okay, man, whatever."

I got my change and wandered back down the aisle looking for Paul, who was still bathing in the sacred radioactivity of the bright fluorescent space. Halfway down, I spotted a box of plastic spoons on a shelf. I picked it up. Forty-eight plastic spoons for forty-nine cents. I pulled a spoon out and set the package back on the shelf. Now there were forty-seven. I was eating the yogurt as we walked out the door. The cool lemon flavor really hit the spot after that sweet wine.

As we got to the corner, I felt someone grab me from behind. "I got 'em, Tony!" Whitey was shouting to a beefy red-faced younger guy who rushed up, scowling at me like I'd just kicked his pet puppy.

"What th' fuck's goin' on, man?" Paul stepped over.

Whitey swung around and glared at my friend. "Shut th' hell up, ya little faggot, or yer goin' t' jail with yer pal fer shoplifting!"

Shoplifting? Jail!?! For taking a plastic spoon? What the fuck? I spat on the ground as the cop car pulled up. That big sign flashed across my mind. *THE SOUTH BAY CHAMBER OF COMMERCE WELCOMES YOU TO SCENIC HERMOSA BEACH.* I winked at Paul as they ratcheted the cuffs on my wrists and shoved me in the back.

On my way to the pokey, I wondered how they'd dig old Doris's mink stole and movie-star sunglasses down here in Scenic Hermosa Beach.

63. FORGOTTEN BOY

"THE FAMILY IS THE ASSOCIATION ESTABLISHED BY NATURE
FOR THE SUPPLY OF MAN'S EVERYDAY WANTS."

—ARISTOTLE

One warm Hollywood night, a guy called Iggy Pop was playing in this hole-in-the-wall called Rodney's on the Sunset Strip. I'd never heard of him, but Ellen said we *had* to go to this show, so off we went, me and her and Paul. The place was a cramped dark little hovel. People were crowding around a stage the size of a tampon waiting for the show to start when all of a sudden this wild-eyed bleached-blond scarecrow came lunging out of the darkness screaming into a microphone. Holding a big deadly-looking knife in his other hand, he started cutting himself up and rubbing blood all over everyone!

It was a wild performance, even from our jaded perspective. We were all into Hendrix, The Doors, The Mothers, Spirit, Buffalo Springfield, The Stones, and so on. There were always a lot of bands playing around Hollywood and we went to all the shows, sometimes as guests of the groups. But we'd never seen anything like that freak. On some level, I really related to this Iggy's raw, violent angst and brutal urgency; maybe because I felt just like him. Bored. Pissed off. Restless. Volatile. Self-destructive. Doomed. Kids like Paul, Ellen, and me were like Punk rockers, years before there was Punk rock. We were social outcasts, anarchists, outlaws; outsiders, like Iggy's Forgotten Boy. Whatever they wanted to

call us, we were never anything remotely resembling "Flower Children."
For us, that whole "Flower Power" thing was nothing but a load of
bullshit media hype. I always thought it was all government propaganda
contrived to discredit the growing social discontent and opposition to
Vietnam. What better way to deflate a nationwide wave of anti-war
protests than to portray it as the childish whining of pampered middle-
class brats with flowers in their hair—rather than what it really was: a
popular dissatisfaction with the established order? Meanwhile, my own
sense of personal dissatisfaction was taking its toll.

JOURNAL ENTRY - HOLLYWOOD: *Been shooting
smack every day for a week. Suffering from a severe case of the Bends,
holed up in this little room getting high on death, an intravenous
skeleton dinner. Check myself out on the bathroom scale down the hall
at least three times a day just to make sure I'm still here. I know, I
know, I baked this rotten old cockroach pie myself, but strange incidents
have been coinciding with my sad little soul-suicide; like I've been
reading this book,* City of Night, *and really starting to see things
that way as I wind through its morbid passages. Like when I went up
to San Francisco a couple of weeks ago, trying to run away or go back
to better times or something. After driving all the way there, I spent the
next four days skulking around the streets like a phantom; never spoke
to anyone or visited Coit Tower or City Lights or Chinatown. Besides
copping some beat junk off this jive Fillmore spade, the only other
living soul I interacted with the whole time was this lonely, white-
trash hitchhiker I smoked a joint with as I rolled into town wired on
bennies. I felt a kindred spirit in him, with his six-in-the-morning-no-
place-to-go-nobody-to-go-with existence. But at the same time it was
so pathetic, shades of* City of Night, *Jesus. His horrid hangdog-
homeless-hobo reality scared the shit out of me, like I could see my
future in the cracked mirror of his hollow bummed-out jaundiced eyes.
As the paranoia kicked in, I dropped him off on a street corner with
some lame mumbled excuse. That sordid little interaction would set the
pace for the rest of my time there. Back and forth from Berkeley to S.F.
like a bored old cabdriver. Finally I gave up and drove back to LA in
defeat, beating myself over the head all the way down the cold clammy
unforgiving Pacific coastline. Didn't even see Big Sur, just flew past
like the devil was after me with fire. That failed attempt to recapture*

*the old feeling of good times on the road was the first manifestation
of a terrible freakish restless loneliness and homesickness, living like
a crustacean at the bottom of a dark ugly well, crying, shooting up,
vomiting, and dying.*

Good times gone, flip-flopping between hangovers and a series of
low-grade heroin habits, I started looking for a job. I was usually too
broke to pay the ten-dollar-a-week rooming-house rent, and I didn't like
hitting the old lady up for money anymore; too many creepy strings of
emotional blackmail attached to my mother's occasional "loans." And
unlike my more resourceful sidekick, I couldn't hustle enough cash on
the street to save my life.

JOURNAL ENTRY – HOLLYWOOD: *Borrowed some
ID and got a job at this restaurant in Westwood. PJ Clark's. Fancy
pretentious overpriced grease pit. Burgers. Beer and wine. Plastic
Italian food. Wasn't too bad at first, all the free wine I could drink;
pretty cheap shit, but like Jessica, one of the waitresses, told me,
"It's always cheaper when it's free." I made fast friends with the
cook, Vinnie, this skinny junkie from Chicago. Jessica was Vinnie's
old lady, and we hit it off right away—mostly cuz Vinnie hated the
manager Mickey as much as I did. Mickey was a real asshole, bossy
little wannabe mobster momma's boy. Nobody could stand the prick.
One day I walk into the kitchen to pick up an order and there's Vinnie
standing with his dick out, pissing into this big bowl of stew. I was
shocked, didn't know whether to shit or go blind. I was about to beat
it out of there like I didn't see nothing when Vinnie flashes me this big
shit-eating grin and we both busted out laughing. After that I could
do no fucking wrong. I had a hard time keeping it together when I
saw that faggot Mickey sitting at his table in the back scarfing down
Vinnie's "special" stew! After work, I'd go on dope runs with Vinnie
and Jessie. We had some fun times, before I got canned. I remember
when I started I brought this real uptight lady her Caesar salad,
then like a minute later she's calling me over, real loud. "Oh, waiter!
Waiter!" She's standing by her table bellowing like a stranded water
buffalo, so I run over and she's pointing at her salad bowl, looking
like she's about to cry. I look down, and there's a fucking BAND-AID
wedged in between a bunch of croutons and lettuce and shit. There*

might as well have been a big FUCK YOU note from Vinnie tacked to the thing. I had to fight to keep a straight face. Then Mickey struts over, acting all official. "What seems to be the problem, ma'am?" I dunno what happened, cuz it was the end of my shift. Mickey looked real pissed the next day though, marching around with a big stick up his ass like he'd swallowed a fucking dog turd, but he never said anything more about it. I think he was just waiting to catch Vinnie red-handed fucking up the food so he could fire him and not give him his paycheck. I wound up getting the bum's rush first. It all started when I got this big table of obnoxious drunks. They were ordering everything on the menu, being real fussy, asking me all these stupid questions like what was "yummy" to eat and where were the tomatoes grown, like were they "hothouse" tomatoes and was the cheese local or imported, and if the beef was "cured" and "aged" and all kinds of stupid shit like that. How the fuck am I supposed to know? It's just fucking food, you dumb fucks. Gimme a fucking break. They were really putting me through the hoops, running me back and forth to the kitchen all night, sending shit back 'cuz it wasn't cooked right, complaining about the wine. What the fuck? I'd been drinking it all night, on top of a bag of dope me and Vinnie split earlier. I was about ready to go back into the kitchen and puke into their fucking soup when Mickey comes running back all huffy and starts ragging on me about how one of these asshats complained to him about the service, telling him I had a "bad attitude" and all this kinda shit. Fuckers! To top it off, when they got up to split, me and Juan the busboy go over to clear the table and there's like a fucking two-dollar tip sitting there! IN COINS! I couldn't believe my fucking eyes. That did it. I scooped up all those quarters and nickels and ran out to where they're strolling down the sidewalk, not a care in the world. "Hey man, ya forgot something," I shouted. The main guy turned and I threw the money in his smug cat-fucking face. The guy starts yelling like an old cunt and then Mickey comes running out before I can punch him in the face and tells me to go inside, that he'd "handle it." Whatever. When he comes in, he tells me I'm fired. Just like that. I tell him it's fine by me but I want my pay, so he says to follow him upstairs to his office. Then the dirty little shit-weasel tries to screw me out of a hundred bucks, telling me he had to refund those ass-monkeys' dinner tab and was taking it out of my pay. That was the last fucking drop. I told him

*if he didn't cough up my fucking cash he'd be sorry. "Whadda gonna
do, kid, sue me?" he smirked. That was it. I jumped on him like a
tiger and grabbed him by the lapels of his cheap suit. Before the fucker
knew what hit him, I dragged him to the door and threw him down the
stairs. Who's the fucking tough guy now, shit-for-brains? It was worth
the hundred bucks. Good thing I used somebody else's ID to get hired.
I'd seen enough cops lately to last me a fucking lifetime.*

After a brief career in the "service industry," I got a part-time
stockroom gig at this fancy Hollywood lingerie place. I discovered the
Mexican smack dealers had a soft spot for that stuff, so I traded loads of
stolen frilly silk panties for heroin. I still wasn't ready for a full-time life of
petty crime, though, so next came a dull procession of mindless manual
day-labor gigs.

JOURNAL ENTRY - HOLLYWOOD: *Got busted driving
without a license, stoned blackout drunk and all fucked up on pills.
Cops took my car. Now I'm on foot, crawling around like a crippled
toad. Had to take the fucking bus to work today. The horror! It was
like sitting in a cloudy aquarium surrounded by a bunch of sick,
dying fish to go labor like a convict on a chain gang all day long.
Another hot smoggy summer afternoon, beaches crowded with summer
sun-worshipers and their dogs, and me slaving away in Beverly
Hills, lugging heavy furniture around for a bunch of plastic-faced
millionaires. To add insult to injury, the fuckers treated me like garbage.
They seemed to see themselves as far superior to me, a common laborer
sweating and cursing in the burning heat. They sat back in their loose-
fitting pastel colored shirts on wicker lawn-chairs, drinking imported
beer, watching me unload their refrigerator off the hot oily truck bed,
humping their precious wooden heirlooms, struggling and grunting
like a fevered ape, up to their big extra-wide front door. They never
winced as my balls exploded under the weight of their obscene wealth.
It was sadistic. Roman. But I knew better than to fall down yelling,
"Arggggh, ya got me," like some tragic cowboy gunned down in an old
Spaghetti Western. Why give the heartless bastards the satisfaction?*

After getting the sack for backing a moving van over an old lady's prize
rose garden, there was a series of shitty mindless grunt jobs—enough

miserable slave-wage manual labor to keep me pissed off and drowning in a cesspool of self-pity for years, thinking of my millionaire father who wouldn't bother to piss on my head if my hair burst into flames. Still, I could never work up the nerve to become a straight-up burglar like Paul. Too paranoid. I would've been a disaster, he scoffed, rubbing it in that I couldn't even steal a fucking plastic spoon without getting popped.

64. INTO THE ABYSS

"HE WHO FIGHTS WITH MONSTERS SHOULD SEE TO IT THAT
HE HIMSELF DOES NOT BECOME A MONSTER. AND WHEN
YOU GAZE TOO LONG INTO AN ABYSS, THE ABYSS ALSO
GAZES INTO YOU."

—FRIEDRICH NIETZSCHE

"Paul had always been absolutely fearless. And he had a real knack for putting himself right in the middle of all sorts of weird, sinister worlds and netherworlds. I remember how, right after we'd first started hanging out, he would disappear for days on end sometimes on mysterious visits with a bunch of crazy hippies out in the wilds of Topanga Canyon. There were lots of wild chicks up there, he said, and he'd always come back from those sojourns telling enticing tales of sex orgies, plentiful drugs, and all-night jam sessions. I was curious. One day I went with him to check out the scene."

Closing his eyes, the tattoo man stares into the foggy mist of the past. He can see a pair of dusty boot-clad feet planted in the dirt alongside the Pacific Coast Highway. A young hitchhiker looks up at the Santa Monica Pier looming in the distance, covered in a dreamlike haze. Feeling the bite of a cool fishy ocean breeze blowing his long hair into his eyes, young Jonathan pulls his old buckskin coat up around his neck and looks down at the guitar case between his feet; that old Martin he and Paul stole from a party at Stephen Stills's house in Laurel Canyon. Whatever happened to that thing? Cigano wonders. He shrugs and turns the page. "I looked over at Paul as he slouched at my side, thumb out, collar turned up on his leather jacket, holding a suspicious-looking violin case in his ruddy grasp like a scruffy Baby Face Nelson." With a sigh, the tattoo man reads on.

Paul's hippie friends lived in their own little world out there: a weird Wild-West outlaw freak compound tucked away in the dusty scrub-brush hills. One star-splashed summer night we were sitting up there in a packed dirt clearing, surrounded by a gang of dirty-faced kids who looked like they hadn't bathed in weeks, passing joints and wine bottles around a blazing bonfire. The acid was kicking in strong as a pretty dirty-blond chick rubbed against me like a feral cat. She nibbled at my neck, sending goose bumps down my arms. An intense-looking older dude named Charlie winked at me and smiled like the sun.

Charlie reminded me of a wizened old Indian chief as he picked up the Martin we'd brought and started playing. Singing with an ancient leathery growl, stirring up vibrations from some weird other dimension, his hypnotic rhythms weaved through the sage-scented night air like a pounding Aborigine dirge. A bunch of the girls joined in with a haunting angelic harmony behind Charlie's raspy wail. As the singing rose, Charlie Manson's lyrics took over my brain, words hovering around the blazing fire like mad fireflies as Paul pulled out his violin and dove into the swirling wall of sound like a frantic bumblebee; chords and chorus growing in intensity, pulsing colors, flames jumping and dancing like wild Gypsy spirits into new tunnels of awareness, tattooing that night into my soul's memory forever.

Cigano can see details emerging in his vision like an old horror movie: a dilapidated wooden sign emerging in a fuzzy yellow glow, and those unforgettable words: *SPAHN'S MOVIE RANCH.* He pauses, clearing a catch in his voice, then continues his story.

That innocent hippie gathering would soon be shoved, squirming like the inhabitants of an overturned rock, down the world's collective

gullet as The Manson Family. Screaming headlines and freaked-out newscasters fanned the hysterical flames of terror sweeping a shell-shocked nation; and the die was cast. With a blaring *Life* magazine cover portrait of Manson looking like Satan's Little Helper, the mainstream media machine triumphantly announced its official nightcap to a naïve and childish dream: The Death of Peace and Love. That would be the definitive boost to a New World Order in America; another quantum leap into institutionalized mass murder, political corruption, journalistic deceit, and sheep-like popular apathy. The whole Manson affair was just the kind of brutal catalyst the powers-that-be needed to bull-whip rebellious masses of anti-war types back into their pens—while creating yet another much-desired public reaction: the inevitable demand for more Law and Order; one more baby step toward a totalitarian police state.

Those were weird times. Only God knows what really led up to the tragic bloodbath, but having shared some crucial moments with the people right in the thick of that dark ugly weirdness, I was shocked to learn of their supposed involvement. Having crossed paths with Charles Manson long before his name became the Registered Trademark for Evil, I was baffled. Charlie had seemed pretty cool. I couldn't believe the reports depicting him as some kind of murderous Satanic Pied Piper. Maybe he was kind of intense and weird, but it had seemed like a good kind of weird, like that Iggy Pop guy. Weird, but harmless. After all, in a world gone mad with Vietnam and the American Dream unraveling like a schizophrenic speed-freak nightmare, weird was the only way to be sane; and those were very weird times: apocalypse times; fertile times for all sorts of grim nasty weirdness.

I had no idea at the time of my stoned-out pre-teen snuff fantasies just how close I might someday actually come to crossing the line into a bloody shit-storm of homicidal madness. Luckily for us, our sporadic visits to the Spahn Ranch would be just another piss-stop on the road to Hell. By the time it all went Helter Skelter, Paul and I were long gone from the murderous freak-outs of the doomed and demented Manson Family.

65. SINISTER FORCES

"IF IT IS TRUE THAT THE GODS OF ONE RELIGION
BECOME THE DEMONS OF THE ONE THAT REPLACES IT,
THEN WE IN AMERICA MUST DEAL WITH GENERATIONS OF
DEMONS ONCE WORSHIPPED HERE, WHO NOW WANDER
THE COUNTRYSIDE, THE CITY STREETS, THE INTERSTATE
HIGHWAYS AND DEAD END ROADS, THE THEME PARKS AND
FAST FOOD RESTAURANTS, THE SHOPPING MALLS AND
PARKING LOTS, THE PEEPSHOW PARLORS AND CATHEDRAL
AISLES, LIKE HUNGRY GHOSTS ON A MISSION FROM HELL.
WE GAZE WITH HORROR ON THEIR CRIMES, AND DON'T
UNDERSTAND. WE STARE INTO THE EYES OF THEIR HIDEOUS
CREATURES, AND DON'T UNDERSTAND. WE CLEAN UP THE
CRIME SCENES AND MOP UP THE BLOOD, AND DON'T
UNDERSTAND. WE IMPRISON, INSTITUTIONALIZE, EXECUTE TO
MAKE IT ALL GO AWAY . . . AND DON'T UNDERSTAND."

–PETER LEVENDA

I'd been living in Hollywood at a cheap transient hotel around the time of the Tate-LaBianca murders. Between odd jobs, Paul and I survived by hustling stepped-on drugs to weekend hippies from the suburbs. Inspired by my friend's prolific literary output, I began to write in earnest. One night I swiped a copy of Kerouac's *On the Road* from the all-night newsstand and my mind was officially blown. My artistic-minded buddy Jerome Ali had told me all about the Beat writers, but aside from the excerpts he showed me, I'd never really read their stuff. After the book's title grabbed me, I sat up till dawn, reading it from cover to cover. Over the following months, Paul and I would read *On the Road* again and again. That book became our Holy Bible. Our plan was to follow in the footsteps of Jack Kerouac and our Beat Generation heroes. In the grand tradition of the failed pipe-dreamers and doomed drunken authors of my mother's unhappy bloodline, I, too, was determined to become a writer.

○   ○   ○

Cigano stops reading and digs through his travel bag. He pulls out another manila envelope and dumps a pile of yellowed photographs onto the table. He picks out an old picture of himself sitting by a dirty window, looking like a character in an old *film noir* movie. Hair slicked back, with a cigarette tucked behind one ear, he resembles Wilfred Wormus. Even the room seen in the photo is reminiscent of the skid-row flophouse in his old Captain Cringe saga. A flurry of memories flutters across his mind: his old rooming house, an oily black-and-white image of himself staring out the window into the flashing neon night.

Closing his eyes, the tattoo man can see a shadowy hand shuffling through typewritten poems and notebooks filled with a tiny speed-freak scrawl. The hand clears a space on the table and uncaps a short dog of whiskey. Laying out a line of sparkling yellow powder, the young writer snorts it, pulls the smoke from behind his ear and lights up. Cigarette dangling from his mouth, he begins pounding away, like a deranged marionette, at a beat-up Salvation Army typewriter.

JOURNAL ENTRY – HOLLYWOOD: *Another ugly day in the clutches of the Criminal Justice System with all the usual courtroom absurdities; a malevolent monkey zoo of repulsive subhuman empty-headed piss-eyed creatures from hell; screaming babies, bad clothes, body odors, bail-bondsmen, lawyers, cops, judges, juries. A hellscape of struggling brainless turds floating in a dirty fishbowl, nothing better to do than lurk around these drab soul-stifling purgatorial waiting rooms sucking shit from the asses of brain-dead public officials who wouldn't even be there if it weren't for the mass stupidity that reigns supreme in this world. After getting sprung on a 200-dollar bond, I came home, popped some downers, chugged some wine, and passed out waiting for this fancy Chinese chick I've been*

*fucking. Woke up around midnight and looked outside. It was like
another world. There was this crazy hot summer rain hissing down,
crickets chirping in the alley. Smell of damp earth and sage, car fumes,
wet asphalt, and gasoline. I didn't know what the hell was going on
up in the skies; thought it was a UFO attack or something till I saw
lightning and heard the thunder. The world had changed. Artificial
energy pumping through me from the wine and pills, I went out and
walked barefoot through the streets in the big* City of Night. *The
pavement was cracked with quiet sighs of disaster, like it might just
split open and swallow this phantom shadow who walks alone like
a mad Chinaman's ghost. Lost City of the Fallen Angels with your
glowing 3 a.m. streetlights that nobody sees, you lie too still. It's not
healthy. Where are your street-corner musicians, your sidewalk cafes,
your joyful dancing brown-skinned girls? A solitary truck rumbles
by and is gone down the dark empty street, intent on some important
midnight mission. A cake to deliver. Shit. Where is your past, my
burned-out young friend? When do you dream? Am I but a dream? A
figment of your unsure imagination? Who is this ragged catlike figure
who walks the lines of your urban deception? I stop to light another
pale cigarette before moving on to seek the eternal fix, the answer to
no particular question. Whispered conversations, crooked lines to
greater events zigzagging around your worn-out welcome mat like the
directions of a suspended whistle. Where am I to go? Please show me
some sign that you're alive, that you are the Holy Mother of Chaos.
You have gone disturbingly laconic tonight. It's not right. Give me some
rumble of disaster in the distance and I'll go my way and leave well
enough alone. Stop your Cadillac for this humble hitchhiker. Don't
you see, like old lovers, we need each other's company in this faceless
gray arena. I seek your foul axis again because you have already led
me half the way. This city speaks to me in tongues as I wander her
endless blind alleys like a giggling Zen monk, seeking the inscrutable
smile of her derelict wisdom. I'm turning all the wrong stones over,
getting too far from walking the Righteous Path as I walk these hungry
cold-nighted streets. My nocturnal visions haunt me. I want to know
of days gone by. Are they the same as this insane Here and Now as I
stop to inject more inspiration into my arm? No, I'm not happy in this
converted crabshell. I want to remember other times and places. Fuck!
Burned out at last. Your clouds hang low over the hot gray cities of*

my thoughts. This is my day of reckoning, I know, but clouds of you gather and rain falls upon placid waters, water pail, glass of beer in hand, looking so ridiculously unnerving to soothe the sounds I see and swallow, ingesting the whole bloody freak show without a prayer. I am a sneaky nocturnal hunter, obvious but unseen, a gaily colored savage sneaking about, confined by the walls of Forever. Oh, that their burden may break my trembling back, that their midnight mice may shout to me in my sleep—for even an escape artist must rest upon the pinnacles of his own undoing. That's how I spent my childhood, you know, hiking in the hills behind your houses. The cactus flower was always there but I never stung myself until now; the wound isn't much, though; could easily be taken for needle-marks on a random junkie arm. You see, I was stung by a poisonous spider once—and while that's pretty much in the order of things, the psychic swelling never did go away. Sunday afternoon, walks in the park, etc . . . But clouds of you gather as furtive gray figures emerge from dark crevices. I explore your nightlife bars 'n' grills all night long, but with the rising sun I feel like Rip Van Winkle sleeping too long and all that. Where is this goddamn bitch when I crave the old Chinese water torture of another stolen kiss?

○   ○   ○

My latest girlfriend was an elegant sixteen-year-old Asian beauty named Stefani Kong. O'Connell brought her around one day, hitting me up for a ten-spot to go cop, then tossing Stefani aside like a used snotrag as he ran out the door. Or maybe she planned it that way all along. Either way, that was the last I saw of that money, but not of Stefani. As she joined Ellen in the nightly parades though my bed and my life, I learned my new lover had grown up in the same elite Beverly Hills circles as Ellen. As life got weirder in Hollywood, random coincidences like that became the norm. Stefani was the daughter of Marlon Brando's longtime Chinese lover, Anita Loo (aka Anita Kong). Brando, coincidentally, had been tight with both of my parents. He'd also starred in *On the Waterfront*, directed by Elia Kazan, my aunt Connie's old flame. Like Ellen, Stefani was heir to a bizarre Hollywood subculture of Beautiful People. Her sister China would marry and collaborate with the eccentric British filmmaker Donald Cammel. Cammel directed *Performance* starring Mick Jagger, one of my favorite movies of the day. Cammel, whose dark visionary films were filled with all sorts of weird occult references, had been bounced on the knee of none other than Aleister Crowley as a child. Through his friendship with Stefani's mother, he would go on to collaborate with Brando, before shooting himself in the head while Stefani's unfortunate sister watched his final dark performance.

With Ellen, I'd been a regular visitor to Frank Zappa's home in Laurel Canyon where she babysat his kids. With Stefani, I found myself hanging around Brando's sprawling hillside mansion, in another stoned-out whirlwind with another young refugee from the Hollywood hamster wheel of fortune spinning dangerously out of control. As we fucked away the windy summer nights in Marlon's heated pool, the sparkling city lights spread out at our feet like a jittery jewel box, the irony of being with a stepdaughter of the same man who'd rested his hand on my mother's belly to feel me kicking in her accursed womb wasn't lost on me.

To add to a weird string of coincidences that would come to define my twisted reality in truly twisted ways, years after my aunt Connie's suicide, I learned that she and my mother had participated, along with Cary Grant and other celebrity friends, in a hush-hush "study program" at UCLA, where, under the guidance of early LSD researchers Drs. Sidney Cohen and Oscar Janiger, my mother and her sister became among the first unofficial guinea pigs to ever drop acid in a clinical environment. Could there have been more to my family's madness than met the eye? Among whispered rumors that both my hated stepfather Len and my uncle Ivan Tors had been OSS operatives during World War II, those same friendly family psychiatrists' research would later be co-opted by shadowy government agencies for top-secret mind-control experiments. All this, coincidentally, linked together many of the ensuing political assassinations and other bizarre events that would mark that truly bizarre time in history.

Cigano stops reading and pulls out a paper. "Check it out, man. I Xeroxed this thing from this crazy book I came across called *Sinister Forces*. It kinda sheds a whole new light on some of those fucked-up coincidences. I knew all kinds of weird shit was going on all around me back then, but I didn't have a clue at the time what the hell it all came down to. Listen to this part . . ."

During the Watergate era, an unsettling revelation was made: that for twenty-five years (or more) the CIA had conducted psychological experimentation upon both volunteers and unwitting subjects—both at home and abroad—to find the key to the unconscious mind, to memory, and to volition. Their goal was to create the perfect assassin and to protect America from the programmed assassins of other countries. This project was known by the name MK-ULTRA . . . We do not know who the test subjects were. We don't know what was done to them. We don't know how they have been programmed, if at all. We don't know what they might do. Or what they have already done. We do know, however, that some of our more colorful criminals have spent time at the same institutions receiving CIA MK-ULTRA funding for this "special testing." People like Charles Manson and Henry Lee Lucas, for instance, as well as "Cinque," the leader of the Symbionese Liberation Army that kidnapped heiress Patty Hearst.

The more acid I took, the more I started seeing all kinds of hidden meanings behind things. In 1953, the year of my birth, for instance, there had been a lot of UFO sightings; by the mid-'60s, the whole country was spooked. The CIA had pulled together a team of so-called "experts," hoping to downplay all the speculation about extraterrestrial weirdness. One of the chief players in the original UFO furor had been Orson Welles—who, coincidentally, had directed a film with my mother.

As the weird coincidences hovered around my head like flying saucers, my mother's close friend Thelma Moss, a well-funded researcher of "Paranormal Phenomena" at UCLA, began dating a guy named Sidney Gottlieb. I almost shit when I learned this Gottlieb was the same CIA chemist who had been in charge of the MK-ULTRA program. What did it all mean?

As my paranoia mounted, all the weird happenings felt as if they'd been planted in my brain by some malevolent Outside Force. Sensing sinister paranormal communications encrypted into all these baffling circumstances, I felt like a broken broadband radio picking up alien frequencies. Incapable of judging my place in the confusing psychedelic stew swirling around me, I thought I was going nuts. It was miserable.

Meanwhile, more weird coincidences kept coming, swarming around in my head like angry wasps. A musician I knew named Taylor was sharing a house with John and Prudence Farrow, Mia Farrow's siblings. John Lennon—who, coincidentally, was a regular visitor at Ellen's home in Benedict Canyon—had written the song *Dear Prudence* for Prudence Farrow. He had also co-written *Helter Skelter*, which would later become known as Charles Manson's apocalyptic snuff anthem. This all came crashing into my awareness when I was hanging out with Ellen one afternoon around the time of the Manson affair and hearing John Lennon's haunting primal wails wafting up from her father's study.

My world was getting smaller and freakier by the day. Deadly forces seemed to be closing in. Whenever I dropped acid, the presence of Death was unbearable. Ominous signs were everywhere I looked. Prudence Farrow's sister, Mia, had just starred in Roman Polanski's Satanic thriller, *Rosemary's Baby*, right before Polanski's pregnant wife and friends were butchered like pigs in their Benedict Canyon home—a pad where Ellen and Stefani's inner circles often partied—and just a stone's throw away from both girls' houses. Polanski was also a close friend of Stefani's mother. My friend Taylor also knew Polanski. He'd even been at a party at Polanski's only days before the slaughter. And Mia Farrow's brother had just been telling him about weird CIA mind-control projects involving major Hollywood players.

As this cryptic tapestry of morbid syncronicity enveloped my world, I took increasing doses of acid in a desperate attempt to crack its invisible codes. In a naïve quest for mind-expansion and freedom, I had turned on, tuned in, and dropped right out of the American Dream—inadvertently plunging myself into a living American Nightmare.

66. THE TRIAL

"THERE ARE NONE SO ENSLAVED AS THOSE WHO FALSELY BELIEVE THEY ARE FREE."

—GOETHE

By the end of the 1960s, the whole city was in a paranoid frenzy over the unsolved Tate-La Bianca murders. Fear was the air Los Angeles breathed. The ensuing three-ring Manson Trial capped this off with a bang. That wild, sensational public sideshow had something in it for everyone: celebrities, sex, drugs, rock 'n' roll, and high-profile Hollywood intrigue—along with creepy hushed rumors of all sorts of unholy behind-the-scenes perversity, the occult, and secret government conspiracies galore.

For me, the mysterious string of dark coincidences kept coming. A week after the massacres, homicide cops showed up at my friend Taylor's house, having found his fingerprints at the crime scene—where he'd been partying days earlier. Another uncanny fluke involved a girlfriend of Ellen's, who'd been driving home drunk along a deserted stretch of Mulholland Drive one night to avoid the cops, when she happened across the murderers' discarded bloody "Creepy Crawly" clothes after stopping to pee in some bushes.

O   O   O

The tattoo man digs through another envelope. "Here!" he breathes, handing a yellowed paper to Jaco. "This is another one of Malcolm's old letters. He wrote this to me just before he died. Check it out."

DEAR JONO – *Remember the other day when we all dropped acid at Richard's house and I was trying to tell you about this terrible scream I heard but I couldn't describe it with words? Well, I'm going to try to tell you what happened now. It was in a place called Tuna Canyon, an isolated spot up in the hills of Malibu, near Topanga, where you took me with O'Connell when I first came here, remember? I was with a guy named Grek, you remember him, he worked next to me at the Broadway. He was leaving for college, his last day at work, so we went out after our shift to celebrate. We had been to a place called the Village Inn and gotten pretty drunk, and we decided to get some beer and go to the canyon. We drove up a windy road that went way up into the hills, miles and miles, till we reached the top. We thought we could see all of Malibu. There was no light but the stars and the city below, no wind, and thousands of crickets. The hills all around were black, the air was silent, all those crickets like violins on a high tremolo, adding to themselves, like a nervous guilt waiting for something to fill it. Not a soul around. Just miles of black hills and winding roads and rock cliffs and trees. We sat on the dirt at the top, drinking beer, talking. Then we stopped in pure terror. The night was suddenly pierced by this long, blood-chilling scream. At first, we didn't know if we had really heard it or not, it was so far off, it came from the black hills. Everything stood still in shock, and then it came again, louder this time, a woman's scream, the most horrible sound I've ever heard. It had no note to it, it was not a tone, it was pure terror, a running scream, and it echoed and echoed like a thousand screams. We couldn't move. I couldn't speak. We were filled with terror for a girl who was running blindly in the mountains, screaming, facing certain death, murder in some horrible form, pain and death, and so alone, not another person out there in the miles of blackness. It came again, farther to the right now, a woman running and screaming with all her heart, body and soul. Not for help, there was no hope of that, just screaming, and so unnaturally. We jumped into the car and our drinks splattered on the ground. We drove toward the sound, tearing up the road. Not out of bravery; we were too scared to feel that or anything*

else except to get away, thinking we could be next. But we drove toward
the sound. It just snapped something in us. It was so primitive and
so urgent, so terrified and raw. Not a lovers' quarrel or something like
that. It just kicked your insides out and made your blood run cold. It
sent a shiver down your spine and into your bones, because it was for
real and had death in it. After driving up the road about half a mile,
we stopped. A cliff was on one side, but it didn't seem to matter. We
sat there and listened, not breathing, but it didn't come again. It was
all over. Somewhere in the back of my mind, I was thinking someone
was dead now, and I hated the blackness and the silence, that goddamn
silence. It was like a wall between us, like standing inside a cage and
watching some girl being beaten to death on the other side and smashing
yourself against the bars to get through. But it was hopeless from the
start. We drove toward the area where it came from, literally shaking,
expecting to see some insane murderer jump out on the road, or a body
lying in the bushes, something, anything. After we had gone about two
miles into the hills, we came upon a car parked on the side of the road,
which was very unusual because nobody ever went there. It was the
first car we had seen, and we had been there for several hours. There
were no lights on and no one was near it. It was parked on the edge of
the cliff that runs along one side of most of the road. We went past it
and we knew the killer or killers of that girl were still out there. Maybe
they were coming back for us. There was nothing we could do. It was
over. We drove away. It has haunted me ever since. I just had to tell
you now.
Love, Malcolm.

"Pretty fucking creepy, right?" He looks at Jaco. "The place he was
talking about was just over a hill from where the Manson Family lived.
We didn't know about any of that shit at the time, but looking back now,
I dunno . . ." He shakes his head, staring at the floor.

Jaco whistles and hands the letter back.

The tattoo man looks at it like a dead rat. "Yeah, right? Weird shit
like that just kept getting weirder, man. Death was literally in the air.
After Malcolm's suicide, when I read this thing again, I always wondered
if he might have been, I dunno, like tainted, y'know, touched somehow
by the same creepy occult weirdness that had spawned the whole Manson
thing. God only knows what the fuck was lurking in the ether back then.

It was a weird time, man, especially for a fucked-up kid tripping on acid every other day."

With a sad grunt, he picks up the notebook and returns to his narrative.

○   ○   ○

After Manson and three of the chicks we'd partied with at the ranch got busted for the Tate-LaBianca murders, Paul and I became obsessed with the case. We started going down to the Hall of Justice every day to sit in on what would go down in history as the most infamous and wildest murder trial of all time. That weird psychedelic sideshow was a metaphor for so many fucked-up themes in my life, I just needed to be there. We would sit in front of the courthouse with some of the Manson girls who, not being allowed in the building, littered the sidewalk like hollow-eyed war orphans. We made friends with the defense attorneys who would stop to banter with them after court. The lawyer I got to know best was this chubby longhaired guy named Ronald Hughes. Even though Paul and I had associated with the defendants, we were never officially connected with any of them, so getting in was pretty easy. After a while, Paul got tired of waking up at seven in the morning. I kept going to the trial alone, hanging out with the chicks every afternoon and giving them firsthand accounts of the day's events.

My lawyer pal, Ron, was the third of a string of inept public defenders who'd been appointed to represent one of the girls, Leslie Van Houten. Out of Charlie's three pretty young co-defendants, Leslie was the least loyal to him; but she'd copped to being at one of the murders, helping hold a victim down while another snuff-junkie stabbed them to death, so she was in for the long haul. She'd given her first lawyer the boot after he'd pissed Manson off by trying to separate her case from the others. Her second attorney had also argued that because she was nuts—supposedly having been brainwashed by Charlie while tripping on acid—she was unfit to stand trial with him and the other girls. Van Houten wouldn't go along with either lawyer's strategy, claiming she'd been influenced by television and Vietnam when she'd joined the bloody two-day kill-fest. Charlie, a seasoned ex-con, didn't want any of his bitches to be tried separately, probably because he was hoping to get off by throwing them to the lions. At his behest, Leslie fired both lawyers, and the next one was my new friend. A stoned-out law-school slacker with no trial experience, he had originally been Manson's lawyer before being replaced. The Manson trial was a surreal media circus right from the start, an ongoing game of Musical Lawyers: another diversionary tactic of Manson's, apparently, to match the rest of his theatrical courtroom hijinks. Ron Hughes, like his predecessors, hoped to get Leslie a separate trial by proving she wasn't right in the head when she got caught up in the mayhem, but had been drugged, mind-controlled, and turned into a bloodthirsty murder zombie by Manson. When, near the end of the trial, Ron unveiled his strategy—butting heads with Charlie in court by saying he refused to "throw a client out the window"—Ron Hughes became The Enemy. A few days later, he vanished.

Ron's disappearance was especially significant to me. Over the months, we'd become pretty tight. He lived in a friend's garage in West LA, where I used to hang out with him after court. We spent many an evening smoking weed as we pored over the piles of trial transcripts littering his floor. We used to go on weekend camping trips together, accompanied by Manson Family kids. We always went to a remote mountain hot springs in the rugged wilderness outside Los Angeles.

The first time I went up there with him, we were with three of Charlie's sidewalk groupies. After driving for hours crammed into his beat-up VW Beetle, we all dropped acid. Ron made a turnoff and parked at the end of a long dirt road in a big looming canyon in the middle of nowhere. We hiked a rugged trail by a winding creek up to the steaming hot pools. Set in the shade of scraggly oak trees, it was an idyllic spot with birds singing and lizards scampering in the underbrush, surrounded by soft little patches of fluffy green grass. The creek bed was shallow and dotted with big smooth river rocks, forming a natural hot tub. As the girls got naked and slipped into the pond, I lowered myself in, coming on to the acid. The ensuing swirling psychedelic hot-tub orgy was one of the coolest experiences of my young life: me, Ron, and three hippie chicks, tripping in the pool and fucking up on the grassy knolls. It wasn't hard to persuade me to go again the following weekend—and the weekend after that. We took those trips all summer.

Then, one cold windy Friday afternoon in late November, Ron called me on the pay phone at my rooming house to tell me that he was going the next day. I'd been laid up with a low-grade dope sickness, a bad case of strep throat and the flu, so I hadn't been to the trial for a few days.

Feeling weak as a dying hamster, I declined his invitation—a decision that may have saved my life. That would be the last time I ever spoke to Ron Hughes.

There were heavy rainstorms all weekend up in the mountains. When Ron failed to show up in court on Monday morning, the judge ordered a recess till he could be located. According to the people who'd been with him, the intense rains had gotten his old VW bogged down in the mud. They'd given up trying to move it and hitchhiked home, they told the cops, leaving the overweight lawyer behind. As the fierce Pacific monsoon raged on, the area was declared hazardous and evacuated by the park rangers due to flash flooding. Ron's car was found a few days later, covered in mud, with stacks of the ever-present trial transcripts in the back seat; but no sign of Ron. The judge appointed a new attorney and the trial staggered on without him. The search went on, despite growing doubts he'd ever be found alive. Four months later, the same day the jury returned with death verdicts for all four defendants, the news came that Ron's remains had been discovered in a shallow creek bed.

There was much speculation the Family had snuffed him for trying to go against Charlie, but there was never any proof of foul play. His decomposed carcass had been chewed up by wild animals, making it impossible to determine the cause of death. No one was ever charged, but the prosecutor later claimed a Manson associate had told him in private that Family members on the loose had gone on to murder another forty people, and that Ron had just been the first of a long string of unsolved "retaliation killings."

The Manson trial dragged on for nearly a year as I sat in the courtroom watching, listening, observing, scrutinizing; and wondering, always wondering, just how close I'd come to stepping over that bloody line myself. It was with Ron's death that I first began to sense the unseen presence of some angelic Something watching out for me, protecting me and keeping me alive. Not that I was ever willing or able to cooperate.

67. THE GARBAGE PEOPLE

"I HAVE ATE OUT OF YOUR GARBAGE CANS TO STAY OUT
OF JAIL. I HAVE WORE YOUR SECOND-HAND CLOTHES . . .
I HAVE DONE MY BEST TO GET ALONG IN YOUR WORLD . . .
AND NOW YOU WANT TO KILL ME? HA! I'M ALREADY DEAD,
HAVE BEEN ALL MY LIFE."

                                                    —CHARLES MANSON

My fascination with the case outweighing any sense of self-preservation, I kept going to the trial. Even before Ron's disappearance, I'd seen my share of weirdness there, like the day Manson leapt from his seat and lunged at the judge with a pencil. I was there again when they finally let him take the stand.

Charlie was a good talker; intelligent, coherent, sincere, and down to earth; nothing like the crazed, bloodthirsty serial killer portrayed by the media. He seemed to be enjoying himself as he hammed it up for the crowd, shifting between roles of jailhouse philosopher, idiot savant, and guru: an eloquent and poetic speech from a man facing the gas chamber.

The courtroom was packed that morning with spectators, reporters, lawyers, and cops. Watching from the back of the crowded wood-paneled space, I strained in my seat to see the main attraction. As Manson was called to testify, a kinetic, electrical buzz filled the air like the surge of impending power before a lightning storm. People were talking in hushed, buzzing tones. An eerie silence fell over the room as Charlie was sworn in and took a seat in the witness stand. Surrounded by the official trappings of the court, he looked like a bewildered child, diminutive and out of place, flanked by bulky meat-fed detectives in suits. Charlie had seemed so large sitting around the fire with his kids, his people, his Family. Now he was oddly diminished, a caged animal in the big wooden booth of Judge Older's courtroom. From across the room, he fixed me with that infamous *Life* magazine stare. I fidgeted on the hard wooden spectator bench as his laser-beam eyes bored into my skull. Was I next on his shit list? The intense hypnotic gaze lasted for what felt like an eternity, and in that timeless moment Charlie and I were of one mind. It was like a mini-acid flashback. Finally, he smiled and the clouds parted. Then he looked away and began to talk, slowly, sincerely, as if speaking one on one to everyone in attendance.

I could feel a powerful truth behind his words as he spoke of his childhood as an abandoned throwaway kid living by his wits in the underbelly of the Land of the Free, growing up in its brutal jails and institutions. Manson had been a lost, forgotten victim of the System; a bit of human refuse with a number instead of a name. And I sympathized, identifying with every word as his calm Southern drawl rang in my brain, clear as a temple bell.

"It's not *mah* responsibility. It's th' responsibility *yew* have toward yer children who ya neglect. Y'all say how bad and what evil killers yer own children are. Well, yer th' ones that *made* yer children th' way they are! I'm jis' a reflection of every one of *yew* people . . ."

And so he was. Charles Manson was like Iggy Pop's Forgotten Boy, "the one who searches to destroy." Manson was a cracked spookhouse mirror to the festering collective underbelly of America; a nightmarish reflection of the unwanted, unwashed, unloved Garbage People forgotten by the Great Society. The sincerity and simplicity of his long rambling discourse that day showed even a certain rare humility. There was a grim and moving fatality in his acceptance of his role as Monster: a scapegoat for larger and more universal wrongs. Seen in that light, his words were compelling on a deeper and infinitely more significant level. By the time his monologue came to an end, there was hardly a dry eye in the house— including mine.

It wouldn't do him any good, of course. He and his girls were all sentenced to die in the gas chamber at San Quentin. After California abolished the death penalty three years later, the sentences were commuted to life in prison—where Charles Manson and his surviving co-defendants remain to this day. One of the many counterculture conspiracy rumors making the rounds was that Manson was some kind of Manchurian

Candidate-style guinea pig for a top-secret CIA mind-control program; that he'd been "programmed" at Terminal Island—one of the prisons where MK-ULTRA experiments had been conducted. According to some speculation, the ensuing bloodbath was part of a complex government plot to discredit the anti-war movement by blaming the murders on a gang of drug-crazed hippies—thereby linking the Manson Family to the anti-war movement in public perception. Classic guilt by association.

Whatever the case, many of us felt a natural empathy for the Family kids as martyrs: outcasts victimized by the insane, murderous, hypocritical Establishment we despised in those emotionally charged and deeply polarized Vietnam years. We came to see them as innocent scapegoats, mainly because of what they represented to us. Perhaps it was that one nagging factor, more than anything else, that made so many people claim they'd been set up. Maybe they really had been set up in a sense, even if they *were* guilty of murder. Because at the end of the day they were just a bunch of unfortunate misdirected kids, runaways, outcasts, and losers from fucked-up dysfunctional families like our own; confused, alienated castaways from an insane, murderous, materialistic throw-away culture; throw-away people who'd simply been at the wrong place at a very wrong time with the wrong combination of toxic emotions and powerful drugs in their impressionable young heads. It could have been any one of us. Because, in a much deeper sense, they were our people. Garbage People. That's what Manson called them. And there were plenty of Garbage People wandering the streets of America back then, legions of the walking wounded; fucked-up teenaged refugees from an American Dream turned ugly.

In that sense, I believe Charles Manson—despite all his demented esoteric doubletalk and the ultra-violent tragedies he seems to have spawned—was a mad prophet of sorts: a living symbol of our spiritually crippled, deranged generation and time. Because he'd called it. We were the Garbage People; the garbage of an insane, unsustainable empire teetering on the brink of moral suicide. And our insatiable appetites for drugs and self-destruction were symptomatic of a greater malaise, a pervasive soul-sickness of our very time, place, and culture. In our desperate search for something real and authentic, for any kind of durable experience outside that monstrous ass-backward social structure and the confusing maze of lies and deception we navigated daily, we dumped all kinds of garbage into our systems, consuming truckloads of mind-altering chemicals like there was no tomorrow; because for us, on a very real and tangible level, there *wasn't* going to be any tomorrow. The straight world had its Vietnam War, its violent protests, political assassinations, and riots in the streets. But the Garbage People had their own insidious, dirty little war going on. And there were a lot of casualties, like my unfortunate cousin Malcolm; a widespread collateral damage of acid burnouts, suicides, overdoses, and ignoble, senseless, premature deaths.

By the time I turned eighteen—old enough to be sent to Vietnam to kill or die for the bullshit American Dream of a Great Society I despised—many of the people I'd grown up with had already lost the war and died by their own hands. What else did we have to aspire to?

68. HAVE A NICE DEATH

"I SEEN THE NEEDLE AND THE DAMAGE DONE, A LITTLE
PART OF IT IN EVERYONE. BUT EVERY JUNKIE'S LIKE A
SETTING SUN."

–NEIL YOUNG

JOURNAL ENTRY – *Hollywood: The weekend was another typical drunken blur; don't even feel like writing about it. I seem to have worn out what little energy I had, though I don't remember having much. All I really did the last few days was lie around wasted. At times I was feeling a lot of false energy, almost euphoric, but mostly I was so whacked out I wasn't even there. Woke up this morning in the same spot I passed out in last night, lying sideways on Kim Gordon's bed, friends snoring in the other room. I looked around, feeling kinda stupid. Where was I? What was I doing there? We're all just a bunch of broken dolls with a colossus of murderous insanity dangling from our earlobes. I drove home and crashed. Since getting up, I've done nothing but mope around this dirty little room feeling depressed, diseased. I wanted to go out and spend the day at the museum or something, revisit some happy old scene from the past, feel inspired, meet a mysterious young girl, whatever, but I never made it out of this hole. All I could do was sit around cursing my own lonesome lethargy. The most productive thing I did was wash my fucking socks in the bathroom sink, before puking all over them.*

JOURNAL ENTRY – HOLLYWOOD: *A few words on
ending it all: Yeah, I know, I know, tomorrow's another day, blah
blah. I've heard that same old song on so many sad and hopeless
yesterdays, and here I sit as a result today, still alive. Lucky me. Shit.
Sometimes suicide looks like a good way out; but I ain't gonna do
myself in over a pile of dirty socks and traffic tickets. Sure feel like
it sometimes, though. Things like that really have a way of putting
a big exclamation point on the Big Blues, just as chocolate chip ice
cream does with Sunday afternoon lover's bliss. Now I find the empty
ice-cream container of yesterday's loves sitting on my table, stinking
and molding like four-day-old rat meat vomited up by a cat. The
symbolic justice of such things reflects the ruined state of my soul
back to me: dirty ashtrays, empty bottles, crab lice, soiled linen, broken
boxes, broken dreams. It gets to a point when you're completely fed up
and disgusted with everything you see in the mirror, and the process of
change is as hard to come to as the decision to pull the plug on yourself.
I don't know. The easiest route for me, I guess, is to do it slowly
with a bottle or a bag of dope, the only way I know. Try to just keep
myself unconscious as much as I can. I know it won't work, though, not
without destroying everything I used to hold important. You can't beat the
system without paying somehow, but I just can't face the world without
drugs, it's too fucking scary—though probably not half as terrifying as
bum-tripping on bad acid or being drunk or stoned on dope all the time
just trying to numb out the memories of all the bad acid trips. Because
there are always these unwelcome epitomes when the veil falls away, no
matter how much drugs you do, and then you wake up screaming, not
knowing what happened to your shoes, your face, your bed, your soul, and
you realize you don't give a fuck. Then, there are those fleeting moments
of relief. When you're desperate, you'll clutch for straw dogs like a
drowning camel's back, man. Ah, fuck it! I'm doing myself in, but the
process is gradual, and I really don't know what else to do.*

"Toward the end of the Vietnam war," Cigano begins reading again,
"I was shooting a lot of heroin. At first, I told myself that being real
strung out would be a great way to dodge the dreaded Draft. But by the
time I turned eighteen, the war was already nearly over, so I had to find
other excuses."

"So you didn't have to go to Vietnam?" Jaco interrupts.

"Nope. Thank Christ." Cigano grins. "Even though the war was finally coming to an end, a lot of guys had been walking around with that shit looming over their heads for years. Turning eighteen was like a death sentence back then. Here, check out this next part . . ." He turns the page.

"Even not having to worry about getting sent to Vietnam anymore," he reads, "I kept doing my damndest to get myself killed right at home. One fine day, after getting chased through a ghetto alley by a gang of teenage gang-bangers with tire-irons and baseball bats, Paul and I were holed up in a dope pad with a bunch of other fiends, sitting around on dilapidated furniture, waiting in that blank uncomfortable junkie silence for The Man to show up."

His mind's eye squints into the glowing yellow realm of the past, seeing himself sitting in a dark dingy room in South Central. The Hood. Nobody speaks a word. A television is mumbling in a corner as details emerge; clumps of tin foil wrapped around broken antenna stubs; a fuzzy black-and-white image of a bombing raid on a Vietnamese village; the hated face of Richard Nixon talking some shit about freedom. *Freedom my dick, you lying murderer. Shit. Where's the guy with the dope, already?*

O   O   O

I sat in the airless gray limbo zone, nerves on fire, casting fleeting glances toward the door. All around me, a silent symphony of restless tapping feet and furtive junkie gestures; twitching, fidgeting fingers lighting cigarettes in the boob tube's flickering blue glow; windows covered in yellowed newspaper; overflowing ashtrays, burned-out black candle stubs on a tabletop littered with empty cans, candy wrappers, soda bottles. Everybody sitting around like ticking time bombs, watching the door, waiting.

Finally, a soft knock, and the chemistry of the room jumped like someone had hit a switch. A shadow moved across the darkness as an aging Negro slid inside and moved toward the cramped little kitchen. Junkies shuffled behind him, clustering around like pigeons in a park, glassine bags and balloons changing hands in a blur of crumpled bills.

I got my dope and found a spot on a threadbare sofa to get straight. I was waiting for Paul to bring some water from the kitchen when a pale kid with a ratty shred of beard sat down beside me and started preparing his fix on the table; a flash of light and a whiff of sulfur hit my nose as he held a trembling wad of matches under a carbon-blackened spoon. A wisp of sickly brown smoke rose from the bubbling amber sludge, dope boiling, needle dipping into a tiny wad of cotton like an alien metallic beak as precious golden liquid filled the thin plastic syringe. He pulled off his belt and tied off in a blur of single-minded focus. Squinting like a boy shooting marbles, he shot up into a tortured ditch of bruised, reddened tracks, a thin stream of blood sprouting, blossoming in the rig like a miniature red flower. As he shoved the plunger down to the hilt, Paul handed me a cloudy glass of water and I poured the dope into my bent-up spoon. Hearing a funny little grunt beside me, I glanced over at my neighbor just as he slumped to the floor, dead as a dirt-clod.

Paul and the others gathered round, talking in low frantic syllables of muted junkie panic. I reached over and grabbed the rest of the guy's stash, while they all picked through his pockets like a pack of vultures. Somebody produced a worn old carpet and laid it down by his dirty sneakers as I shot up half my bag and stashed the rest. I could feel the warm heroin comfort surging through my blood. The dope was good. Strong. No wonder he'd bought the ant-farm.

Surrendering to a comfortable numbness, I looked down at the unfortunate face at my feet. It seemed to be getting deader as they lifted his gray weight onto the rug. The owner of the pad, a wizened, tattooed Mexican named Flaco, folded the guy up in the carpet like a jumbo burrito. As I sat watching, the flat yellow circle of a happy face on his dirty white T-shirt seemed to be saying good-bye to the world with the ironic words:

HAVE A NICE DAY.

"Yeah," Paul mumbled, "have a nice death there, happy boy."

The party was over. He nudged me and we beat it out the door.

69. PRIMAL SCREAMS

"CAN WE OFFER HOPE? MAYBE, BUT AGAINST WHAT?"

-DR. ARTHUR JANOV

On a scruffy stretch of beach on the outskirts of Veracruz, Cigano and Jaco are sitting under a bamboo-and-straw *palapa*. Leaning back in a plastic chair on the dirty brown sand, the tattoo man picks at a plate of shrimp as he leafs through another one of his old diaries.

JOURNAL ENTRY – HOLLYWOOD: Since I last sat at this dusty old word-machine, I've been working. Hard, cheap, shitty manual labor, sometimes fifteen hours a day. It's only on weekends that I still stalk these empty streets of nowhere, looking for nothing. All the rest of the time, my life has a Legitimate Purpose. Working and working, then filling the time in between with more empty bouts of nothing, looking into this gummy old typewriter for the things that should be obvious to me by now but still remain a mystery. And now the System is dragging my ass through the grinder, taking my money, my time. First they revoke my license, and now they wanna put me in jail for my many dope-fiend transgressions. That's all I need right now. I've got four more court appearances to make this month alone. Meanwhile, Ellen Janov's out of the nuthouse and I been spending all the time I can with her, trying to have some happy moments in this miserable excuse for a life, navigating the twists and turns of a long depressing stinking river of shit. She's the only one who makes me feel alive anymore, even as I fall into a warm heroin bathtub with her and begin to die. I woke up this morning and she was gone. Then I found this little note she wrote for me, sitting on the table: This morning, I lay here and think wow, last night, last night, but last night is as far away as my worries seem today. My child, how do I wake you, take you? My body is waiting for your touch. How long must I wait? I finally get reached over to and don't think wow, last night or this morning. My skin merely gives in to you, and I can neither give nor take. But oh— your touch. *Reading her words, for some reason I wanted to cry.*

JOURNAL ENTRY - 1972: *Ellen just called. Truth is, I'd been waiting for her to call. She's got my head all messed up. She's so beautiful and tragic, I can't help but love her. But God, she's crazy. She told me she'd slashed her fucking wrist today. I said WHY? and she said she was bored and there wasn't anything to get high on. It doesn't seem real. I just refuse to believe it's true. How can someone so beautiful, so sweet, so smart, so amazing, and so good, how the fuck can one person be so self-destructive? Her family makes me wanna puke! They fuck her over all her life till she's so burnt-out at nineteen she has to be locked up, and then the self-righteous bastards still think they got the answers to her problems with their sadistic Beverly Hills hollering rituals? Gimme a fucking break! I hate that fucking prick Arthur Janov. It's like my Uncle Robert psychoanalyzing poor Malcolm. These money-grubbing rat-fuckers have used her as a guinea pig all her life. What do they think they can do for her now? A well-balanced wholesome family atmosphere? Primal Therapy, productive life schedule, whatever their latest delusional best of intentions may be, it ain't gonna work. How are they gonna help her when they're the ones who fucked her up to begin with? All they can do is destroy her even more. What can you do when you've got a mother who's a raging closet alcoholic with twenty backdoor muscle-boys creeping around, and your father charges neurotic rock stars half a nutsack to scream their fucking lungs out, then uses your bent mind to experiment his cockeyed therapeutic theories on before you've even reached the age of consent? She's too fucking smart for them, and too* *good to live among these morally corrupt pig-fuckers; who can blame her for not wanting to live? Poor Ellen. It's too fucking twisted and ugly for me to even think about. All I can do is love her and try to treat her like the princess she is and hope I can make her happy for a few stolen moments. What else is there? I can't reform her or wave some magic wand over her poor sick head to make her better; can't make her want to live in this fucked-up world anymore. Nobody can. Not after all the shit she's been fed. They stuck her in the nuthouse for a month. Now she's out and they're trying to keep her alive with Scotch Tape. I can't see what good that's gonna do. Shit, by the time she was eighteen she was all strung out on heroin like the rest of us. What did her father the great rock-star head doctor do? Stuck her in the bug farm to get her out of the way for a while, then puts her to work as a Primal Scream therapist charging celebrities up the rectum to be treated by a girl who's strung out on smack and just got out of the loony-bin and who's sitting at home right now, sawing away at her fucking wrists. Unbelievable.*

JOURNAL ENTRY – *Ellen came over and spent the night. She was still sleeping when I dragged my ass off to work shit-shoveling for the Man. I got back in the afternoon, and she was gone. I went over to my typewriter and found another little note from her:* Waiting. You must go away, while I see if it's okay, is it okay? All day I am there thinking, is it? Where is that man? Should I really be wondering, or has he gone to mope with another bottle someplace on the street to forget it? Well, maybe it's just one of those kind of flights. Two hours— no more . . . He comes! I smile. I can be a child. At last, I throw my arms on to the shoulders, I grab onto the chest, and kiss the face I've, well, yes, been waiting for. *I ran downstairs to the pay phone. I called and told her to come back. I had butterflies in my stomach as I sat waiting. I tried to write a poem for her:* My baby gave me a butterfly, like some ancient flower burning down through the ages. I know it will endure for as long as my eyes can see, my lips move, my body sweat. God, what an incredible thing I hold in my hands for this brief moment as it trembles, about to take flight. But I know it will endure, and for once I'm not afraid of it. What makes this thing tick? I don't really want to know or tear it up and destroy it to find out, just happy to know it's there for this night, and like all things, will pass, and endure forever. *Then today, a pounding at the door and Ellen's father came in with a bunch of his Primal Institute goons and took her away again. What could I say or do? She was a strung-out, weepy, dying mess. Guess she's on her way back to the nuthouse.*

With a haunted look, the tattoo man stops reading and stares out over the murky expanse of water. A gray pigeon lands on a wooden piling before him, silhouetted by the churning green Gulf, head cocked in dull concentration, puffing up its thousands of tiny shining feathers. Cigano studies the creature as a breeze blows through its multicolored plumage, sparkling like a million tiny jewels. It seems the most marvelous thing he has ever seen. *How can a stupid pigeon look so fucking beautiful?* As the bird flies off, he sighs. "Sometimes it all feels like a big long acid trip."

Jaco looks at him, waiting for him to go on. Explaining the only way he knows, Cigano begins to read again.

As the months slouched by, my little room grew into an empire of literary clutter: books and magazines piled up like Mayan pyramids; loose papers and journals spread across the bed, the floor, the desk, every horizontal surface; a sprawling civilization of dusty words, letters, concepts; avant-garde and Beat Generation literature, magazines, and newspapers: *Crawdaddy!, Evergreen, The Paris Review, Rolling Stone, The LA Free Press.* Coltrane's saxophone weaved through the air in dancing incantations, a mystical maze of wild geometrical vibrations beamed into this earthly plane through the sacred portal of my old Zenith record player. Dog-eared copies of *On the Road* and *Tropic of Cancer* lay atop piles of handwritten and typewritten poetry like royal seats of power. A neon *HOTEL* sign blinked and buzzed outside the dirty window. Eugene O'Neill's *The Iceman Cometh* sat propped open beside me as I sat hunched over my desk, fingers pounding away at my ancient thrift-store typewriter, writing, always writing; desperately spewing out the bilious ephemera of a myopic little existence onto the pages.

JOURNAL ENTRY – *Hollywood: With that Red White and Blue monkey of Vietnam off my back at last, it's time to get out and hustle again, find a job, whatever. At least the weather's been cool. I like the cold days, gives me a chance to put on the warm protective leather and wool; cover the bad old ugly scars and step out into the night. Old woolen scarves are to be wrapped around icy flesh in the dry dark city shadows, shooting for the stars without a pistol in my hand, without a needle in my arm, without a glance into the pit. Just a happy surrender to the void, where my feet find sanctuary in the dusty filth of my room. I like to sit here and write these letters to nobody, but it's depressing when the page runs out and I gotta stop writing and just exist again. Yeah, it's sad when the page runs out; like it was depressing when Ellen ran out to the bug farm. I dare not even think of when the drugs run out, the hope runs out, or when my life or someone else's life runs out again, like that kid in the dope pad the other day. I fear to look too hard at the war of our souls and my people dying all around me. Satisfaction and depression seem to come in quick flashes, seconds at a time, word by word. Even as I keep my fingers moving across the typewriter keys, I can feel the coming of something new, something bad, something weird, something ugly, something, nothing, life, death, whatever. I sat up all night with the radio on, waiting for a song to play that could move me from this listless stupor. It's easy to sit around waiting for the next catastrophe to move you like a firecracker blast under your ass. There are no answers that suit me and all my questions are foolish. I think it might be nice to have a television and watch it every so often, like a normal guy, not worrying about the rent or the money, just sit up and watch teevee and come up with great ideas and inspirations, never be at a loss, never have a page run out. These are childish things, I know, selfish things, not at all worthy of a young artist who should embrace his life and live it to the fullest. But the word "should" is the most depressing of all language. Gotta give myself a shove soon and hit the border, disappear to Mexico. Dress in fine tough Mexican leather and find a place where I'll be drugged by the tropical air and warm sea breezes. Dead things in the road won't feel so depressing there. Los Angeles is a stifling, soulless pit of cold, empty streets sprawling out to nowhere forever. Gotta get out. Can't stay. Too many unknown impossibilities to explore in the world. I just need to find a good leather jacket, a little cash, some clothes of strong denim, a small leather satchel, a pair of thin white cotton pants and a couple of lightweight shirts to hang loosely on my body in the tropics. I want to look good, feel good,* *try try try to do good with a holy survival routine; a switchblade knife, a passport, new friends, new music, new drugs and booze, moving down the road in boots of Spanish leather, yeah, dreaming of Brazil. I wanna travel light, though, not worry about where to put things when it's time to shed them all and stand naked on the shores of forever. I won't think of sharks or death or evolution then. One man, an island in this life I've come to love and hate in equal measure. Tomorrow I gotta make some calls, then push it. Will a stolen leather jacket, a passport, and a clean bill of health give me the freedom to come and go as I please? Ridiculous. And so I keep the fingers pounding at these keys now, 'cuz I don't want to run out of this page, no, just keep spitting it out, whatever comes next, Andy Warhol, sunrise breakfast windows, heroin relief. It's all a scream. I just don't want to see the end of a page, of a spree, of a sparkling summer sunrise, of a passionate fuck, of what have you. New beginnings are always scary.*

"New names and faces came and went," Cigano reads, "as my life became a hazy maze of fleeting drug-fueled transactions and sleazy subhuman bumps in the night; a fumbling nightmare parade of street girls slithering through my bed; anonymous zombie grunts in the dark . . ."

JOURNAL ENTRY – *Hollywood: I can't believe it's come to this, but here I am. Not even nineteen and resigned to hating the world on a beautiful Saturday afternoon—or so the radio tells me. I haven't left this hole for days. Wherever I go, I'm as welcome as a leper, all done in, drunk by noon, stumbling around feeling sorry for myself, waiting for morbid forces of darkness to surround me and protect me from the world and all its horrors as I tap on these pages through dark hours and days, collecting secondhand matchsticks, bouncing between cosmic consciousness and misery. I think of the people around me and I realize we're all lost lonely rats stuck in a big sticky jelly doughnut maze, reduced to slobbering junkies, like this corpse snoring in my bed. Sniveling junkie bitch whored out in Hollywood for Original Sin. A lot of funny chicks like this lost little Alice in Wonderland have been coming in for a crash landing on my sad old lonely mattress lately. What's that all about? Goddamn young cunt like this all dried up like a wasted old sponge. Like all these pathetic Hollywood bitches, she's spent too much time absorbing NOTHING. Her soul is a dry crusty old sponge. But she's been coming around here every day, tossing her* moans and sighs at me like scraps of moldy candy. She believes in me, she says, all my stale old junkie horseshit about running off to Mexico and Morocco and Brazil and all that; says she wants to go on the road with me. Soon as she left yesterday with a righteous talk from me about getting clean and straightening up, my bad old heroin karma NOW and all that, soon as she's out the door, yeah, I'm on the phone to the connection, getting ready to spend my last fifty on another little taste of death. And today she's back, scratching at the door like a stray cat. Her hair is a rat's nest of Camarillo Brillo. Trying to make it with her was like watching overripe slime slithering down a rubber hose. Soon as I got the dick into her flaccid drug-ravaged cunt, she passed out. What can I say? Cold fish? Frigid? Scared? Probably just traumatized from too many fuck-overs in her sterile flat-line reality, starting with Mommy and Daddy, just like poor tragic Ellen. I don't know. Just to come in a pussy was all right, I guess, especially after this latest long sexless junkie death march, but I think it's kinda nice when a chick is a little more responsive. Well, I came twice and she stayed dry as dirt through it all, snoring to wake the dead. Some Vaseline or even a tube of toothpaste woulda come in handy; except I haven't brushed my teeth or had sex in so long I'd have probably shot my load before two strokes. All this junk and all this nothing has made me a male counterpart of her useless carcass lying there in frigid tequila snores. It really is like fucking a corpse. Just pull down the panties and do whatever you want with it. Just don't expect it to do nothing back. A dried out old fuck-mummy. No blowjob even this time, getting my rocks off with a stone-cold-dead store mannequin. Store mannequin might make for a better fuck. Less trouble. Maybe not. With a chick, even a dried up sponge-cunt like this one, at least I know there's a soul in there somewhere. I think. But the truth of the matter is this: I dunno how to handle any fucking person anymore. Not when we're all surrounded like this by JUNK JUNK JUNK all the time, like a long walk-in-sit-down-wake-up-screaming nightmare. It really gets fucked up dealing with all kinds of other demented junkies. Sick or straight or loaded, it always gets sticky, even downright freaky, like with sponge-cunt here. How do I get rid of her? Throwing her out the window would make noise and bring unwanted attention. No good. What can I do? Yeah, I got myself into another fine mess, Ollie, and still I write, silently now, at two a.m. with a pen and paper, typewriter moldering away in the

corner, neighbors and all that, writing and killing time, soul rotting,
waiting for my connect to show up with the next little bag of oblivion.

○   ○   ○

"All through the long raging dope war," he reads, "I wrote every day, all day long. My only dubious salvation was that no matter what went down, even strung out as I was, I was always documenting it in writing. I lived by the formula that in order to create, I had to alter my perceptions however I could. That's how my literary heroes had worked, so who was I not to? I didn't know if my writing was any good. I always suspected it wasn't, that I was just kidding myself, but I was living it to the limit, milking that tragic bohemian lifestyle for all it was worth—just like my uncle Robert; and no matter how self-indulgent the method was, it gave me a vehicle and something to hope for; a reason to keep living. In that sense, the drugs and my daily writing practice may have literally saved my life; that and a real and compelling need to somehow find my way through the confusing matrix of existence."

With a weary shrug, he picks up another old journal and scans the words on the page. "What a sick little fuck I was, man! Seriously! Reading through all this old stuff," he sighs, "I dunno, man, sometimes it feels like I'm digging up somebody's fucking grave, y'know? Sometimes I wonder if this shit might be like cursed or something, like maybe I oughta just toss it all into the fucking sea and be rid of it . . ."

Jaco shrugs. Cigano stares off down the beach in silence.

70. THE DAMAGE DONE

"IN ORDER TO UNDERSTAND, I DESTROYED MYSELF."

—FERNANDO PESSOA

The Curse I thought I'd left behind with my family of origin was reconstructing itself now and infiltrating my new family of choice. As Dope walked among us like an invisible specter, overshadowing our every move, Richard O'Connell became the first real full-fledged junkie among us, the first domino in a crashing wave of drug-related calamities.

His best friend, Bruce Berry, was the first to topple. His tragic heroin overdose would later be immortalized in Neil Young's morbid rock ballad, *Tonight's the Night*. Bruce Berry's older brother Jan had propelled himself to fame and fortune in the early sixties as the Jan half of the musical duo Jan and Dean. Along with the Beach Boys, Jan and Dean defined the popular surf-music trend of the day. But it was their hit tune, *Dead Man's Curve*, that Berry would be remembered by—especially after wiping out his Stingray at the same deadly curve he'd immortalized in song and becoming a wheelchair-bound paraplegic. We used to go over to his place with Bruce and sit around smoking weed in the living room while poor Jan sat there drooling, surrounded by the framed gold records, photographs, and memorabilia of his defunct glamorous career.

Jan's younger brother had used his famous sibling's connections to get work as a roadie with Crosby, Stills, Nash, and Young. Soon after going on the road with the popular supergroup, he'd brought Richard along to work and travel the world with him. Back in town on a break from a European tour, where they'd gotten in over their heads with the plentiful backstage cocaine, they decided smack would be the best way to ease off from all the jittery blow. One morning, O'Connell went over to Bruce's place. It was winter, and the heater was blasting. He would later recount being kicked in the head by a horrible stench when he found his friend slumped over on the floor at a weird angle. Bruce had been dead for days already, but a stoned-out Richard, thinking he was just nodded out, shook his shoulder to wake him. When his finger sank into Bruce's rotting flesh, he let out a yelp and hauled ass out the door. Later, he told us it felt like dipping his hand into a plate of cold Jell-O.

After Bruce, others began to fall as the Curse stalked us like a rapacious hunter. Over the next years, people began dying off with such regularity and eerie precision, it left me with a vague sinking feeling of being somehow complicit in their deaths. The worst loss for me was the inevitable end of my sad, beautiful lover Ellen, who finally gave up the ghost in a fire at a Hollywood party. When I got the news, I winced, picturing her nodding out in a bathroom, applying lipstick to her chin, too stoned to notice when her so-called friends ran out like troop of rats, leaving her behind to die. Ellen's loss would haunt me for a long time.

Shortly after her death, I was bopping down Hollywood Boulevard in a comfortable heroin daze. It was one of those stupid meaningless holidays, Presidents' Day or some shit, when there's too many people on the street with nothing to do. I was on my way back to my room when I ran into Ellen's old boyfriend Chris. Without a word, he stomped over and punched me in the face. I didn't fight back. There was nothing to say or do. I just slithered off down the street sporting a bloody nose. I could identify with Chris's anger and pain. I felt I deserved it. It even lightened my burden of guilt for not having seen poor Ellen in the weeks before her death. All I wanted to do was hole up, stay high, and try to forget.

At that point I was so far gone, it didn't fully register for me that Ellen was really dead. Racked with shame and regret, shutting down and unable to face her loss, I would find myself talking and writing to her, as if trying to conjure her back from the grave.

JOURNAL ENTRY – HOLLYWOOD: *Yes, dear Ellen, like you, I've seen the sparkly side of life, and the dark underbelly too, and* *in this sweet cement death-house love spell I want to possess you and be possessed by you. I called this chick on the phone tonight, seeking some fumbling solace from these disjointed days and nights without you. But when I awoke at three in the morning after a fast futile grope session, the door was open and she was gone and so were you. All that lingered was the cloying stench of her rancid junkie perfume and her overcoat. I wonder if she'll call for it tomorrow, as you will undoubtedly call again one day in dry-mouthed madness, whispering into my heart, clamoring for the bits and pieces you left behind; all you will find is the sum total of me, the eternal abandoned land crab, seeking to possess a love I once spied through the watery regions of my solitude; the love you could never give, the love that no living creature could ever hope to give; a long and impossible eulogy for the inherited madness that started this dirty little ball of shit rolling, my life. No apology is necessary for the likes of us though, baby, so just forget it. I should have known better with this silly bitch tonight. I'd already smelled the sour stench of her stale junkie essence. I should have known better than to look for mercy where there can only be slithering, stinking impossibility. Nine o'clock, and we sat talking and drinking wine. She insisted on changing my radio music, the bitch, and so we did. We sat on the bed and drank. Then we began struggling with each other like a pair of mad insects, with no purpose but to merge our impossible separate longings. Ten o'clock, and our tepid fuck-lust was an old withered bag, dusty and cruddy and drowned, not even trying. We didn't even talk anymore, and by eleven o'clock I passed out. When I came to around midnight, she was gone like a pussy fart in the wind. At first, it was hard to grasp that it wasn't all another dream. Dreams are the only cohesive thing in my life now, dreams where I find you groping out of darkness with pale ghostly hands. I know it wasn't a dream tonight, though, and I even have her overcoat draped over my chair to prove it, all starched white and out-of-place-looking like a dead animal. So what is there to say now? Life is what I make it, and I think I can't make it without you. These fucking words are never enough. I should write about the time you told me, without the burden of words, that you didn't want any love, preferring death over it all, and what went down that night in my head as you sat filling colors into dead little paper spaces in my dream. It was quite an evening. I wouldn't have missed it for the world, baby. But for now I'm just happy to be here in my little self-made hell, while*

*you sit coloring those terribly small and dead little paper spaces with
your magic dead white fingers in my dreams, just as you did in my life.
That is why I will always love you, whoever you were.*

Some things you never get over. Ellen's death would be one of those
things for me, though at the time I was too numb and shell-shocked to
know it. Only years later would I finally acknowledge her loss. That's
when I remembered the words of a prominent member of the psychiatric community, writing about her megalomaniacal father's work:
"Arthur Janov is good at taking people apart, but not so good at putting
them back together."

Another close acquaintance would later comment, "You always felt
this strange sense of danger around Arthur." After growing up an experimental lab rat for her father's sinister psychiatric mumbo-jumbo, all the
king's horses and all the king's men could never put my unhappy little
friend back together again.

Ellen was soon followed to the grave by her star-crossed lover,
Chris. Another overdose. Coincidentally, he died at Arthur Janov's
house just a few months after her demise, while Richard O'Connell was shooting dope in the next room. Next on the deathwatch
was Steve Hartman, the Joker King. Our old pal was found in his
Laurel Canyon bathroom by O'Connell, convulsing and foaming at
the mouth like a rabid dog, dying of a heart-pounding speedball fix.
Others followed; and like a poor man's Grim Reaper, O'Connell's
knack for always being at the scene of every overdose was uncanny.
The Prince of Darkness—as he would be nicknamed—was always
around, somehow, each time the party turned deadly. As the list of
casualties grew, soon there weren't many friends left to mourn. Like
a morbid war correspondent, I kept writing as the Dirty Little War
tore through our world in a ceaseless dark tornado. And as my friends
dropped like ducks in a macabre burnt-out shooting gallery, I took
more and more drugs, a futile effort to kill the pain and shame of
being one of the surviving undead.

Cigano stops and hands some old journal pages to Jaco. "Here's
something I wrote about this guy Roger who got strung out real bad. His

wife had left him, and he'd been living on the street. I'd see him walking around Hollywood dressed in this ratty old poncho. Wasn't even a real poncho, just some dirty old Tijuana blanket he cut a hole in." Cigano shakes his head. "Dude looked like some kinda trash-picking junkie Clint Eastwood. One day I guess he got tired of being tired of living with this horrible dope habit. He went back to his family's place and hanged himself in the fucking garage."

JOURNAL ENTRY – HOLLYWOOD: *Feeling numb, living in fragments, my soul scattered like the stray possessions of a suicide in a dark garage. Yes, I live this way too, Roger, and I know what it is like. I'm very close to that jagged edge too, man. Always have been. I know the smell of a moldy wool blanket over the soul. Like you, I can feel the rough edge of sanity slipping away, and I too consort with the darkness that consumed you. It was probably cold out there in that mildewy old garage. I know you had your dreams smashed a hundred times and you just kept coming up for more. I know your woman must have been a bitch to live with, but she probably tried in her own fucked-up junkie way before she gave up and split. She could have been a simple pure soul who maybe just couldn't understand your confusion, couldn't live with your demons anymore. I didn't even know you that well, Roger, but I know the junk, that dark Other Woman who meant so much to the dark part of you. I can still see your face, your shy, crooked, elusive smile, of which I really knew nothing. You were just another junkie who seemed to live close to the edge like me. And then you fell to the demons, you fell long and hard. I always felt your plight in some strange way, and I could relate to it. I was in San Francisco, on the run from my own bad dope habit, fighting and crying and running and dying. Out of touch with my last thin fiber, I got to a pay phone and randomly dialed your number down in LA in search of a voice to sit the dope-sickness out with, just a voice like yours to sit the misery out with, and the lines got crossed and somehow in all the madness, in all the screaming howling flashing and wailing that seems to bring us all to our destinies like a rattling clattering old phantom trolley car, the lines got crossed from Los Angeles to San Francisco to East LA to Hell, nothing but crossed lines and busy signals and assorted recorded buzzings and bleepings and wailing spirit murmurings, and when the line was finally clear, a sad lonely little*

*voice came through and told me you had hanged yourself in the garage.
I pictured you strung up there under a bare forty-watt light bulb like
a dangling bag of nothing, dead, probably shit in your fucking pants.
I'd like to say I will wage war on such cowardice and everything that
your unholy defeat stood for, your slipping into the jaws of madness,
self-indulgence, weakness, suicide. I keep telling myself I know better
than to go and hang myself. Gimme a good old overdose any day. I'm
not looking for it; so don't get me wrong, Roger. I don't think I'm a
suicide like you. I'm not slipping any further than I allow myself to
slip for the all-important high, the rush, the junk, oh fuck it, you're
dead now, man, and I don't know what to do about it, ten-four, Roger,
over and out.*

Feeling dizzy, Cigano stops and shuts his eyes. His head is spinning as
unctuous yellow-gray pictures expand in his vision. A cold winter's day
in Los Angeles. He and Paul standing over a white marble tombstone,
friends and family gone after another funeral the two young addicts
didn't dare attend. They're drinking, smoking a joint, and pouring wine
from a bottle of Thunderbird over a freshly dug grave.

"You wanna like, say something, man?" Paul asks.

"Yeah, why not?" Jonathan holds up the joint. "Roger Martinez lived
twenty-two years in this shit-hole. Bon Voyage, brother."

"Yeah, see ya in Hell, homeboy." Paul grins. "Save me a seat, man."

Cigano sees his old friend hold the bottle out over the dirt and pour
some more wine out. Then he pulls out a can of black spray paint and
tags a crude skull and crossbones with X's for eyes onto the headstone.

The weary tattoo man opens his eyes and stares off down the deserted
stretch of beach. The sand seems to be made of millions of tiny bones,
like an endless graveyard stretching away into infinity.

71. SPEED

"ALL WRITERS ARE VAIN, SELFISH, AND LAZY. AND AT THE
BOTTOM OF THEIR MOTIVES, THERE LIES A MYSTERY."

—GEORGE ORWELL

Time stopped. Death was a constant companion. Somehow, I kept stumbling over to the old thrift-store typewriter sitting on a table by the window, a frowning stone idol commanding me to live another day. Like a tranced-out Pygmy headhunter, I paid daily homage to the cumbersome gray word machine as I kicked yet another heroin habit and tore off into the fast lane on a frantic magic carpet ride of crystal meth, cranking out reams of spun-out speedfreak rants.

JOURNAL ENTRY – HOLLYWOOD: Waking up from junkie oblivion into the piercing Benzedrine jitters of another day, the cord snaps. Fuck this, let me back in my test tube, my comforting nod-out nether-existence. After living so long in a daze of Pavlovian sensory deprivation, I feel like Nosferatu the Vampire, Life Eternal, frontal lobes disconnected, the line drawn so thin that Death seems to loom over my every movement. And still I cannot die, even from all the negative output of this miserable life. After my last dope fix, I resigned myself to dope-sickness again, so here I sit, facing down all the boogie-demons I been fighting for so long. As the life-giving liquid at the end of the dropper runs dry, at least there's always a cigarette around here somewhere. I dig under tables and piles of decrepit godknowswhat, a soot-faced coal miner in quest of the dried-out old cigarette roach. I wonder if I shouldn't secure my space in the bathroom shower (eccch, water! Shower curtain all slimy, dirty, stinking, filthy, old, wet drippy thing!). I ought to try and shave at least, run a washcloth over my aching carcass before the other roomers awaken and start to use the bathroom for their own hideous toiletries. I can already hear the doors squeaking open and slamming out there, heralding obnoxious morning sounds of chirping human activity rising above the tenor opera on my radio and the staccato tapping of this trusty rusty old clattering machine.

SPEED KILLS! was the ever-present slogan seen on bumper stickers and posters screaming from head-shop windows. Taking no heed, I dared it and all the other drugs to kill me. No such luck. I lived on, pounding away at the typewriter like a furious ape, spun out of my skull on meth.

JOURNAL ENTRY – HOLLYWOOD: *Speed Kills? Guess I'll find out. Meanwhile, the crank seems to be helping me focus. It's like some super-grainy magnified fly-fuck truth syrup. The focus is hard to live with, though. Like Edgar Allan's raven, it can drive you screaming into a twisted jungle of nightmare visions. Clarity, like beauty, seems to be in the eye of the beholder. Some people seem to find supercharged joy in it. They really baffle me, those sunny-side-up souls who live so happily in their quest for Truth, Justice and the American Way. I find it a truly horrible thing. Reality haunts me like an evil spirit and drives me right up against the walls of death and insanity, into oblivion and back again. The only thing you can do with Truth is try to shape it to your liking; that's the only way to live with it, but subtly; don't let it catch you in a lie, or it will become an angry adversary and drive you stark-screaming mad. A writer must live with clarity, of course. There's no other way, even if you gotta live in the clutches of a snarling ugly brute. You will have to work long and hard to tame the beast, or he will devour you and leave you standing in front of the Salvation Army Midnight Mission on a bitter cold night, wearing shit-caked trousers and talking to the pigeons. The truth don't stand for no bullshit; this has been a painful lesson to me, and still I sneak around looking for some way out. I guess that's why I'm sitting* *at this typewriter, cranked out of my skull, weeping and trembling, my second day off junk, all geeked up on speed at two in the morning. I hitched a ride home last night with some funny-faced hippie chick and within an hour I had her in my bed. She's from Burbank and thinks she'd like to be a witch or some shit and meet Mick Jagger and take a lot of downers, blah blah blah. She was pretty repulsive, but she had a kind face. Sometimes that's all it takes. I wonder where she'll be ten years from now. Me too, should I live that long. If I was Charlie Manson, I could take a goofy girl from Burbank (her name was Sunshine, for Chrissake) and turn her into a bloodthirsty killer. I feel kinda bad about giving her the crabs, like maybe I shoulda warned her or something, but it must be her lot in life. Whatever. Why feel guilty? I might wake up with the clap and it'd serve me right. I gotta get my shit together. I'm gone, my energy is waning, my cat hasn't been home for four days and I'm losing hope.*

Like a deranged puppet on a madman's string, I couldn't stop writing. Didn't matter what, I just kept churning out the words. I'd read somewhere that Kerouac had penned *On the Road* in one long speed-fueled marathon, feeding a roll of butcher paper through his typewriter and not stopping till the roll ran out or the bennies wore off or whatever. Uppers seemed like the ideal creative fuel for letting what was left of my brain run amok on paper, like a speedfreak hamster on a short-circuited electric treadmill.

○   ○   ○

Cigano rummages through his papers, holding them tight to his chest against the salty winds blowing in over the choppy Gulf. "I found a bunch of these old speed-freak short stories and poems in here. This is the kinda shit I was cranking out. No pun intended." He chuckles. "Some of it actually wasn't too awful, considering the deranged state I was in. Here, check out this one." He shoots Jaco a sheepish grin.

72. PISSING ON ICE

"ONE DAY I WILL FIND THE RIGHT WORDS, AND THEY WILL BE SIMPLE."

— JACK KEROUAC

RAINY WORLD – BY JONATHAN SHAW

"It's raining again today," someone said.

Raining, I thought. Yeah. Raining. Right. Raining P's and Q's all over the world. Cats & Dogs. Cadillacs and Spaghetti Westerns. Whatever. It wasn't at all the kind of day you'd expect any talk of rain. It must have been over a hundred degrees downtown and if it was raining anywhere, I sure as shit didn't think of it here in the surging heat of the day. I'd already set fire to my bathroom that afternoon, but that's another story. Wilshire Boulevard was glowing, an urban exoskeleton bathed in an apocalyptic red-hot mist, shimmering like a mirage from building to building all the way down the Miracle Mile.

As I stood waiting for the bus, every breath was a burning dry gasp of Moroccan desert dust.

"Armageddon . . ." I mumbled as the bus lumbered forward in the distance like a dinosaur emerging from the La Brea Tar Pits. "And some fucking idiot thinks it's raining . . . Well, maybe it is," I muttered as I handed the driver my two bits. "Maybe it is raining in Florida or Hong Kong or Madagascar."

The driver flashed me a glance, almost a grimace, as he handed me the ticket. I walked up the aisle and took an empty seat near the back. I sat by the window and waited, not thinking of rain as the bus rolled along the shimmering black asphalt. I looked out the window. People were scurrying about like flaming red rats in a burning house. It was quite a spectacle. The bus moved on. It seemed to be getting hotter as I sat there watching the world burn. It was making me kind of nervous. People got on and off, talking and reading their newspapers. Pretty soon the heat was unbearable.

FOOOF! A newspaper flared up in a man's hands right in front of me, as if a torch had been set to it. People just went about their business. The man continued to read his flaming paper, now just a smear of smoldering black embers. I looked out the window, then back to the man. His hair was on fire! I could hear it sizzle and pop and burn. The foul stench was overwhelming but he just sat there looking straight ahead. People sat in their seats making small talk as the bus grumbled down the avenue. It was getting hotter. I jumped up and pulled the cord. It fell off in my hand, burnt in half.

Hurrying to the door, I could smell burning flesh. Sweat drenched my body. As the bus pulled up to a stop, hissing like a giant boa constrictor, I pushed the exit button and glanced across the aisle. A chubby Mexican girl with long dark hair grinned at me and winked as her hair burst into flames! She was laughing, staring right at me, as the door flew open and I staggered out onto pavement.

I stood at the curb, watching the bus roll off. I could still hear her awful cackling rolling away as it turned a corner and disappeared. Then I felt the first drop. Rain. I looked around. It was dark as night. The streets were deserted, the slick damp sidewalk reflecting a shimmering greenish-blue light of a blinking neon BAR sign down the block.

I hurried over to the place, pulled my damp denim jacket up on my neck and pushed the big wooden door open. Inside, men in sweaty undershirts sat at tables. I took a seat at the bar and called for a double bourbon and a beer.

The bartender grinned. "Hot enough for ya?"

Ignoring him, I downed the whiskey as he sauntered off,

polishing a glass. There were two guys in suits at the other end
of the bar. They looked like salesmen. I watched as one guy
turned to the other with a cigarette.
   "Got a light?"
   "Sure." He reached into a briefcase, pulled out a big
blowtorch and aimed it at the other man's head. There was a big
whooooosh of flame.
   I looked down and drained my beer. I heard what was left of
the man with the cigarette say "Thanks, pal," as the flesh melted
off his skull like a candle.
   I bolted for the door and ran off down the street, into the
rainy world.

Cigano laughs, pulling out a brittle yellowed magazine with a
drawing of a pig in a cowboy hat on the cover. "Spun out as I was, I
even managed to get some of my whacked-out shit published. This one
wound up in a little literary journal."

PITTSBURGH ZOO – by Jonathan Shaw
The rains fell with blue force outside the aquarium. Down the street,
Jeff and Howard were driving at breakneck speed through Mrs.
Bender's living room, chasing a spider whose web danced like snow in
the attic.
   "I remember the old days when this hotel used to be fashionable,"
said someone.
   "Yeah," came the answer of a forlorn wind, toppling trees and
crew cuts in the night. "This old joint has sure seen better days, that's
the truth. When Eisenhower used to come and visit, boy, this place
really came to life."
   "Yeah, the good old Eisenhower days," someone said. "Those big
gala receptions, and all the young women would come cheer and fling
their Tampons after him like shiny red roses when they wheeled him to
the elevator in that big old bathtub."
   "Oh, my God, yes!" howled the wind. "That great red white and
blue bathtub of his, filled with his hairless white chest and Coca Cola
and air bubbles . . ."
   "And remember the somnambulant pilgrimages?" someone said.
"The newspapers tried to keep it hushed up, but everybody knew

there was something fishy going on. Late at night when everyone was sleeping, scores of housewives would slide out of bed and crawl out of their houses, sighing and moaning, dragging themselves along by their hands under the full moon, across the golf course toward the hotel. They were like zombies in silk negligees and leopard-skin panties and little red, white, and blue buttons pinned to their bleeding breasts that said 'I LIKE IKE . . .' Remember? And in the morning there would be that big trail of slime across the green, as though a giant snail had passed over it. Boy! That sure was something . . ."

"Yeah," sighed the forlorn wind, "I remember those days, but it all seems a little vague now. Sometimes I wish I had a foghorn inside to keep all these memories from colliding into each other all the time . . ."

"A foghorn in Pittsburgh?" the trees snapped back. Crewcut lads in suits and ties marched down the street carrying briefcases. "Good luck!" they all sneered.

In the morning, the newspapers shouted, "THREE TON SPIDER RUNS AMOK!" Some people couldn't believe it.

Back at the zoo, the fish cried until their white bellies floated on the water's surface like apples at a fair. Nobody came to see.

Cigano shakes his head. "Being off heroin, I was finally getting all my surreal visions down on paper. But I was so fucking hyperactive and crazed from all the speed, I could never finish anything I started. I ended up with dozens of these weird unfinished little prose poems and shit . . ."

DEAR SIRS – *please send me the newest edition of your novelty joke and general prank catalogue." That was how I began my letter, and, realizing there wasn't much more to say, how I ended it. I stuffed it into the envelope and mailed it. I'm waiting anxiously for a reply. I can't wait to find out if those little X-ray Specs really work. I've always imagined the possibilities of such things, of actually being afforded a glimpse into the greasy mechanisms of my neighbors' living arrangements. I'm sure they couldn't be more ridiculous than my own, but still I'd love to check it out. I'm quite bored here, you see. I want to be the first one on my block to leap tall buildings in a single bound or to build a radio transmitter under my bed and send out cryptic messages all over the world while I'm sleeping. I want to put itching powder in my foes' trousers and erect a giant penis-shaped police siren atop the*

*local church. I want to see the whole world go up in flames while I run
amok amidst the chaos conjured by my nifty Johnson-Smith Catalogue
atom bomb. I want to lie in wait in a dressing room at the Broadway
of Hollywood's lingerie department for a statuesque young housewife. I
want to harness her fine ass with a Cross Your Heart Bra and ride like
the Lone Ranger atop her quivering rump down the streets of Heaven.
All this and more. I hope that catalogue arrives soon. Hot damn. I'm
getting pretty bored sitting here trying to write my own.*

He looks up and shrugs. "Somehow, I got my foot in the door at
this short-lived offshoot of the *LA Free Press*, after a bunch of *Free Press*
staffers staged a mutiny and went off on their own. That's the first real
publication where I ever got any of this kinda shit published."

He opens his notebook and reads again. "The *Freep* was a local
counterculture weekly that ran cutting-edge articles by underground
icons like Abbie Hoffman, Ed Sanders, Timothy Leary, Allen Ginsberg,
William Kunstler, and Hunter Thompson: all the famous and infamous
cult heroes of the day. The paper was supported by ads in the back for
kinky sex, 'legal' drugs, draft lawyers, and V.D. clinics. After a flurry of
rejections, a couple of my pieces finally got picked up there. I was stoked
like a log-cabin conflagration. Not exactly *The Paris Review*, but that
twenty-dollar paycheck was like the jackpot at the end of the rainbow
for me. More importantly," he reads, "the *Free Press* ran a weekly column
by a writer I really dug. I'd never had a very high opinion of the literary
establishment as a whole, so coming across someone's work I could relate
to there was like striking gold."

JOURNAL ENTRY – *God only knows why I'd even want
to be a writer. Most writers' best efforts make my guts curl up like a
vat of deep-fried worms. Writers make me sick. When I try to picture
myself as a writer, I even make myself sick. Most popular literature
these days is a load of self-indulgent linguistic masturbation created by
ponderous, pedantic little shit-barnacles. I have a lot more respect for a
truck driver than most modern writers. The best compliment one could
pay a writer would be to say he writes like a truck driver. That's why
I like this guy's stuff in the* Freep, *cuz he writes like a fucking truck
driver. Really, just about all art makes me wanna retch my intestines
right out my blow-hole. I'm deranged, sure, but I really feel that art*

is in the smell of boiling cauliflower, the little daily tragedies and indignities that drive us mad. Art is not to be captured like crippled butterflies in the hands of overeducated fat-livered dilettante students of Literature. Fuck anyone who would bother to catalogue the fleeting details of this stinking cesspool of life and put them under a bland intellectual microscope. Art is not an intellectual pursuit. It's the old bum throwing up in the alley outside my window, not the beef-witted onion-eyed vision of some faggy Beverly Hills photographer who takes the bum's picture and sticks it up on some sterile white museum wall for a gang of overfed eggheads to stand around making tottering value judgments about its social relevance and such shit. Fuck that! Art is in the style, the act of making art; or in the non-act of simply being art. That's what I like about this guy's writing. It stinks of real life.

"My new favorite writer's work was unlike anything I'd ever come across," Cigano reads. "He wrote unvarnished ribald tales from the underbelly of a gritty urban landscape I knew. His work was a real inspiration. He was a real writer, not some college-educated milk-livered 'author' sitting in a stuffy book-lined den wearing an ascot, but a real-life local literary presence, an outlaw scribe whose work captured the brutal poetic essence of life on the edge with a cynical and elegant humanity."

He turns a page, clears his throat and resumes. "Paul and I would wait for the *Free Press* to come out every week and grab the first copies to hit the pavement. We were addicted to that column. Fuck Vietnam! To hell with government conspiracies, local rock shows, and the usual pretentious, predictable 'counterculture' spew. All we wanted now were new stories by our new hero. So when I saw my work appearing in the same birdcage-liners as his, I was really pissing on ice."

73. IN THE PRESENCE OF GENIUS

"THE WRITER IS THE FAUST OF MODERN SOCIETY, THE ONLY SURVIVING INDIVIDUALIST IN A MASS AGE. TO HIS ORTHODOX CONTEMPORARIES HE SEEMS A SEMI-MADMAN."

—BORIS PASTERNAK

On a mission to connect with this unsung genius, I pestered an older chick at the *Free Press* office to tell me where he lived. I got the vibe that she'd been over there for a bit of the old slap and grunt; maybe she was one of the hilarious floozies he wrote about! As she handed me a slip of paper with his address, I saw it was close to where I was staying: right off Hollywood and Western.

Late one afternoon, when I had just the right mix of liquor and drugs in my system, I conjured up the balls to walk over there.

Trudging the smoggy streets of Hollywood like a pilgrim on a holy quest, I came to a desolate stretch populated by heat-crazed winos and sweaty five-dollar whores lingering in the greasy shadows like demented clowns. A stench of piss and decay hung in the air. The beat-up neighborhood seemed to have sprung full-blown from one of his unvarnished tales. I stopped at a corner liquor store and got a couple of six-packs and a short-dog of bourbon; better not to go meet a living literary legend empty-handed. I walked up a cracked, weedy side street, past rows of rundown wooden houses. Rusty shopping carts and stripped-down cars sat on dirt-brown lawns littered with sun-bleached beer cans and liquor bottles. Looking at the paper in my hand, I turned into one of those ratty little alleys that the slumlords called "courtyards." All the way down on the right I spotted the anonymous gray bungalow. I walked up and peered in the window at a shadowy figure dressed in a wife-beater and boxer shorts. I could feel butterflies in my stomach—or maybe they were roaches.

Charles Bukowski was a bear of a man. Sitting in a cramped breakfast nook, his nicotine-stained fingers pounded away at an old Royal. Classical music was playing from a little plastic radio beside him. His scarred, oversized head seemed to move to the music like a prizefighter, in a motion so subtle only the spirits of his poetry could respond. Like a Peeping Tom, I watched as he stopped to fish a cigar stub from an overflowing ashtray surrounded by empty beer cans. He shoved the butt into his battered junkyard face and lit up. That was my chance. Now or never. Taking a deep breath, I turned and rapped on his door.

"Go'way!" The big man resumed banging at his typewriter.

Several more taps on the window got his attention.

Without looking up, he called out again in a weary W. C. Fields drawl. "Who ar-ya'whaddyawa-ant?"

"Hey, uh, sorry to bother you. I, uh, I write for the *Free Press* . . . ?"

He mumbled something and kept typing. I stood on the porch, waiting. Nothing. I addressed the window again. "I got some beers . . . and a bottle . . . ?"

He stopped and looked up like he was about to say something, then surveyed the empty cans surrounding his typewriter like little ghosts. He called out over his shoulder, "Yeah, aw'right, hold on." He clacked out a last line, grabbed a dirty towel, threw it over his typewriter, and rose.

I watched him step into a pair of slippers and slouch across the living room. Awkward as a schoolboy, I stood there, looking down at the dirty gray cement landing. Hallowed ground. No welcome mat. I shifted from foot to foot, holding the heavy beer like a temple offering. The box felt cold in the warm late-afternoon summer breeze as I breathed a scent of cat piss and night-blooming jasmine. Classical music blended with a baby's cries and a blaring Mexican television. What sounded like gunshots popped in the distance as the door flew open and Bukowski's big, battered face appeared before me. I was standing in the presence of Genius—and it looked like it was about to knock me flat on my ass. He reached into the box, extracting a can of beer. He cracked it open, then disappeared back into the shadowy apartment. I stood there, my eyes scanning the cracked cement, studying my brown leather boots, the frayed cuffs of my dirty jeans.

Finally, the weary voice drawled from inside. "Jeee-sus, kid. Whaddya just gonna stand around out there all night? C'ma-an, bring it in-siiiide . . ."

I brought it inside.

An hour later, we were still sitting, drinking at his beat-up coffee table, not saying much. Bukowski seemed to be drunk and feeling nasty. The empty whiskey bottle sat on his end like a captured queen in a chess match. A pile of my hyperactive speed-freak poetry lay between us, unread. As I reached into the empty box and cracked the last beer, feeling a little disappointed with my visit, Bukowski put his hand out and growled. "Hey, gimme that!"

I took a swig.

He sneered. "So-ooo, yer a writer, h-aah?"

I handed him the beer.

Bukowski looked me over with an evil grin. "Well, if yer a wri-iiter, man, what ya gotta do is write, get it? What ya don't gotta do is sit around talkin' about it. Ya just sit down and write. That's it, baby. But if ya got nothing to write about, yer just another bum with a ten-dollar typer and a lotta big talk and dog-shit fer bra-ains. And to be honest, you impress me as a sheltered little punk who needs t' get out and go do some fuckin' liv-iing."

"Who th' fuck you callin' a punk? Ya old fart!" I could hear my voice rising, already regretting it.

"You! Ya little cunt-lickin' fish-lipped momma's boy!! Punk!! Punk!! Puu-unn-nnk!!!"

"Motherfucker!" I rose up fast, knocking beer cans off the table.

"Yeeea-ahhh, that's right, baby, I fucked yer mother! And I'm gonna fuck you too, fish fucker!" He flew up and came at me like a rolling train.

I took a swing at him, connecting with rough unshaved skin. Not fazed, Bukowski clobbered me on the ear and I saw stars! He nailed me again, and I tasted blood. Pounding away at me like a demented ape, he was fast getting the upper hand. I crouched low and tried to head-butt him in his ample gut but he grabbed me like a bear and we wrestled, toppling over the table. It cracked and splintered as we fell to the floor in a spinning chaos of pages and empty beer cans. We kept duking it out, rolling around, pissed, crazed, gasping like some savage lumbering two-headed beast of old: an ugly, deformed, drunken puppet destroying everything in its path. Finally, breathing hard, bloody and sweating, we stopped.

Bukowski rose to his feet, cackling like a crazed monk. "Geez, kid! Ya fight like a girl I useta fuck in a toilet."

"Yeah? Was that before or after she shit in yer mouth?" I shot back.

"Shit? Hah! I shit bigger than you, baby! Look at my beautiful coffee table. You owe me fer that, ya little turd!"

Bruised and bloodied, I trudged back up to the corner liquor store, eager to make good my first debt to Charles Bukowski. I didn't know it then, but it wouldn't be my last. We sat on his floor drinking amidst the wreckage of our first encounter for the rest of the night, trading insults, reading poetry, and toasting to each other's speedy demise. Finally, the sun came up through his dirty windows, emerging like a punch-drunk sea monster from the smoggy depths of Charles Bukowski's doomed and beloved City of Angels.

74. EVERLASTING LOVE

"LOVE IS THE INFINITE IN THE HANDS OF POODLES."

–CÉLINE

Sitting at the beachside table peeling a shrimp from a plate, Jaco is staring at Cigano in awe. "I can't believe you met Bukowski! The man is a legend. It's incredible you knew him! Did you go see him again after that?"

"Yeah, man." Cigano grins. "That was just our first meeting. I used to go over there a lot. I got to know him pretty well. I guess he kinda took a liking to me. Bukowski's bark was worse than his bite. He was good to me, read my fucked-up poetry, even gave me encouragement in his own weird way. He turned me on to a lot of great writers too, Céline, Fante, stuff like that. We had some good talks. So many things he used to tell me about writing, living, whatever, I only remembered much later, long after he passed away . . ."

"So you stayed in contact with him over the years?"

"Nah . . ." Cigano shrugs, looking off down the deserted beach. "I didn't. I was living in Brazil when he died. Hadn't seen him in ages. It's one of my biggest regrets, that I let myself fall outta touch with Bukowski after knowing him before he got famous. It's no wonder, though." He lets out a deep sigh. "By the time I left town, I'd already lost touch with everybody and everything; lost touch with my own will to live."

"Why? What happened?"

"I just fell off the face of the earth and went down the tubes, man. I'm lucky to be alive after that shit." He shrugs. "The drugs started catching up, and I hit rock bottom. When I finally split, I never looked back . . . Till now." He sighs. "I been trying to piece all those happenings together here. It all started with this chick I fell in love with, and it was all downhill from there." He guffaws as he opens his notebook again and stares into the past.

○　　○　　○

I met her at a party in the Hollywood Hills. I was standing around drinking in a corner, all alone, when she came up and started talking to me. She had long, silky brown hair and translucent white skin like a pouty pre-Raphaelite angel. Tall and thin with delicate, intelligent features, Suzana was so perfect I couldn't believe she was real. Her face seemed to be made of porcelain. Her big green eyes bored right into my soul. She started telling me about her life, all these intimate details, with such sincerity it blew my mind.

I'd never met anyone like her. I was hooked. Then she just wandered off. My eyes followed her across the room as she flittered around talking with people. After what seemed like a long time, she came back and rubbed up against me like a cat. "That creepy guy over there keeps hitting on me." Her soft voice was breathing into my neck like a song as she slipped my arm around her waist. "Just pretend you're my boyfriend, okay?"

That was it. The moment our lips touched, her body started twitching like she'd been hit with an electrical charge. After the bothersome guy disappeared, we kept going at it. When we finally came up for air, she pulled me out the door. We went to my room and life would never be the same.

With Suzana, making love was a frenetic, lighthearted spiritual telepathy, unlike anything I'd known before, gazing into each other's eyes as we slowly, effortlessly brought each other to mad waves of screaming orgasms. Afterwards, we'd melt together in a magical sex stew. It was better than heroin. We stayed locked up in my room for a week, screwing like athletes and talking. It felt as if we'd known each other forever and had just met up again after a long, excruciating separation. I was nineteen and in love.

Suzana turned out to be the daughter of a famous actor; an old-time Hollywood celebrity of my parents' generation. Like Ellen and Stefani, she'd taken a walk on the wild side and never gone back. It was as if all my stoned-out writing had finally conjured a revival of a past that had never quite been with Ellen; like having my tragic lover back from the dead. But unlike Ellen, who'd never found any focus in her short unhappy life, Suzi was an artist, a painter. She was also a weekend junkie. Bingo! I'd met my Soul Mate.

Since my friends started dying, I'd become increasingly shut down. By the time Ellen had checked out, I was permanently shell-shocked. Even surrounded by people, I was always tortured by this deep sense of loneliness. With Suzana, that all went away. I wanted to get lost in her. All the feelings of alienation I'd harbored since childhood disappeared in a whirlwind of candlelight lovemaking as we snuggled on my little single mattress, drunk on each other's trembling caress; a long honeymoon stupor of hungry sex and late-night TV; cheap supermarket champagne and canned oysters with sour cream on Ritz crackers; aimless walks in the park; cherries and wildflowers, butterflies and breathless vows of eternal love. As we floated on air, light as turtledove feathers, dreaming an idyllic future together, I even swore off drugs. We were going to live Happily Ever After in a quaint shack in the hills, just Suzi and me and some cats; a new life of everlasting love, hungry sex, flying confetti, and colored balloons. High on that overpowering love-drug spell, I bought another old car, and off we went on nightly rides up the coast. We'd sit on the beach for hours, holding each other tight and gazing up at the stars.

JOURNAL ENTRY – HOLLYWOOD: *Used-car shopping. There must be some kind of evil conspiracy going on in the used-car lots of America. What dark purpose lurks behind the gay façade of multicolored banners blowing in the fresh wind of another bland, sunny California day? Who is the greed-infested demon with the no-bullshit smile and firm handshake? He is an expert confidence man, a merciless cold-blooded predator in a snappy sharkskin suit, an exemplary standard-bearer of the American Dream, the big glittering lie that took its first bite of my soul before I even knew I was alive. You never know how far to trust such a hype-merchant, with his malevolent powers of persuasion. Like a politician, a money-hungry, cash-guzzling tool of the Big Scam, his soul is full of worms. He'll screw you hard as*

Nixon. Some people have steady jobs and decent credit ratings, and are better equipped to play the game with success. They will slam the doors and kick the tires, maybe rev the engine and test the cigarette lighter, the radio, the windshield wipers, whatever. But always the dealer holds the cards. As he shuffles his loaded deck of Pink Slips and Red Tape and Credit Reports, you just gotta hope he slips up in the transaction and gives you a break. No such roll of happy dice for me. I left with a rattling old VW Beetle, another stinking, smoke-spewing jalopy. What else could I do?

JOURNAL ENTRY – HOLLYWOOD: *A gentle breeze surrounds the heart as another day unfolds with Suzana. A sweet cup of coffee and a chocolate bar may be all right, but not first thing in the morning, I tell her; no, I say, it's much better to experience that first cold slap of green life-wind to the face on an empty stomach, beckoning icy fingers to sunlight journeys. Warm melty sweet things can wait until day's end, to join with cuddly candy sleep. The stars will shine cool and bright over us then, I insist, and then we'll need the warmth, oh yes. So I talked her into another long walk. The great sprawling urban Shangri-La of MacArthur Park lay before us. As we walked beside the lake, we could snatch little bits of crazy conversation from other lives, like going fishing someplace quiet and waiting for the miracles to happen. Of course there are no fish in the lake. Only the bodies of bloody Mexican gang vendettas, rusty guns and knives at the bottom, but there are always stray encounters with the living who cast their reflections upon the water, and we know that one must learn to dream for life to unfold. Just ask the ones who live out there on the street among the debris and broken bottles and broken dreams; the old derelicts who shuffle back and forth over the cracked pavement talking to themselves. You can run out of money, friends, jobs, clothes, booze, warm weather, whatever, but it's when you run out of dreams that you're really finished. Skid row is full of failed dreamers, I told her, and so are the cold white mansions of Beverly Hills. It's only when a dream is shattered for good with no replacement that you hear a muffled cry and see a body leap from a rusty fire escape, or a penthouse balcony. That dirty old pavement is waiting for us all, rich and poor. One wrong move and we're all fucked. We dream and plan and plot and scheme to save our sad little lives, and nobody believes he'll be* *the next to go. And while this is the most basic truth in my life, Suzi and I walked along that weedy old litter-lined lake occupied with other things. Pleasant things. It was a beautiful day; at least I thought so, even though she complained of the cold. All in all, it was good. I did speculate that death isn't even the end of the dream, but just the doorway to another place where dreams are unnecessary and obsolete. By this token, I told her, death is the only freedom, but somehow most of us prefer illusions. She said never mind all that silly death talk, that I would live to be a hundred. I dunno what happens when one dies of old age, I said. I never tried it. Suzi tells me I think too much and try too hard to figure everything out. Yeah. She's probably right. What can I do?*

75. LIFE IN THE DOLLHOUSE

"ADDICTIVE RELATIONSHIPS, WITH THEIR EXCESSIVE
NEEDINESS AND DEMANDS ON OTHERS FOR EMOTIONAL
OR SEXUAL SALVATION, ARE LIKE CLOSED ENERGY
SYSTEMS . . . EACH PERSON HAS BECOME TOTALLY
DEPENDENT ON THE OTHER FOR A SENSE OF STABILITY. YET
THE 'STABILITY' DERIVED IN THIS WAY IS NOT AND CANNOT
BE STABLE."

–THE AUGUSTINE FELLOWSHIP

One afternoon, I came home with a surprise for Suzana. Bouncing down the hallway humming a little tune, a bouquet of wildflowers in my left hand and a cool bottle of cheap champagne sweating in the other, I tucked the bottle into my armpit and turned the key. "Bay-bee," I called.

The sound of a light moan hit me in the solar plexus and my heart froze like a baby cadaver. My sweet Suzana, my girl, my baby, my fucking angelic, soulful soul mate, was lying spread-eagled across the bed, her long brown hair flowing like spilt blood onto my quilt. The indelible image registered in my brain like a death sentence and my blood went cold. Carlos, the cross-eyed smack dealer from downstairs, was on top of her, his pants bunched up around his hairy brown ankles, feasting on her naked white porcelain carcass like a wild Mexican wolverine. His ugly brown pockmarked face looked up from the carnage with a befuddled glare as the champagne bottle slammed into the side of his head, bouncing off his ear. *BONK!* It didn't break, so I hit him again. Harder. *BONK!* As he struggled to his feet and stumbled across the room trying to pull his pants up, his taquito-shaped Mexican dick dangled before him like a guilty brown midget. *BONK! ARGGGHH! BONK! ARGGGAA! STOP! BONK! BONK! BONK! HELP! ARGGGAA!! STOP!!* Without mercy, I pummeled the purple-faced culprit's head, shoulders, and back. He scrambled for the door, cringing under the blows, crying out in pain and tearing shirtless and barefooted down the dirty red-carpeted hall.

Breathing hard, I glared at the scene of the crime. The wildflowers lay scattered over the floor like a flock of murdered bluebirds as I glowered into those dope-pinned eyes: eyes I'd stared into, hypnotized like a love-struck hamster, on nights of colored lights and dancing confetti balloons. Suzana was sitting up on the bed, covering her tits like a mother shielding the children's eyes from some unsavory horror.

"Get out!" I heard myself bark like an angry poodle.

"Please, baby . . ." She reached out for my arm.

"Get out, ya fuckin' bitch!" I spat, slapping her hand away. I raised the bottle. I wanted to clobber her like a baby seal. I could hear my voice again, as if coming from far away, spitting each word out like a rusty knife. **"Beat it!! Get! Out! Now! Go! Go! Go!"**

Crying and shaking, breathing in short bursts like an undernourished collie, she rose. I stood in a cold gray silence, watching her as she dressed. She seemed to be moving in some excruciating nightmare slow-motion as she fumbled with the buttons of her green silk shirt. I'd always loved that shirt; the way it outlined the contour of her perfect tits. I wanted to wake up from that foul nightmare of betrayal. I wanted to tell her to stop, to come back, to forget it, but I couldn't speak. Frozen into a statue of defeated pride, I watched as she picked up her purse and staggered out the door.

"Fuckin' bitch!" Muttering to myself, I looked around the room. My eyes came to rest on the painting she'd done for me after she'd first moved in: my portrait, made of thousands of colorful little dots of paint; a joyful confetti riot of playful love, passion, and hope. I felt sick. A greasy walrus was gobbling at my guts with cold, obscene, slobbering lips.

"Fuckin' bitch!" I stood there muttering as a slow red claw of rage rose from the senseless black pit of disgust where I knew my heart would never feel love again.

"Fuckin' bitch!" A primal death-wail flew from my throat and I hurled the bottle against the wall, watching in freeze-frame slow motion as it smashed into a million fragments of pink and green bubbling despair. In a final burst of blind, monkey-faced rage, I put my fist through the canvas, smashing my own hated image in the face again and again, beating my tortured knuckles against the wall till my hands were bloody and limp. I fell onto the bed, mouthing the hopeless words over and over again.

"Fuckin' bitch! Fuckin' bitch! Fuckin' bitch . . ."

Like my poor dead Ellen, Suzana was a broken doll. I'd just been her latest plaything, a weak substitute for a famous workaholic daddy's unavailable love. Blinded by drugs and lust-driven euphoria, I couldn't see the ominous signs that she was growing tired of being a blow-up fuck doll, a mirror for my own self-centered, narcissistic pipe dreams. Like Suzana, I was incapable of any real regard for the needs of another person. I was just toying with her, too. We were two lost souls playing house. Life in a dollhouse; a mindless, addictive little fuck fest, all dressed up as love; the closest a pair of broken toys like us could ever come to bonding with another human being.

Jaco frowns. "It's very sad, Jonathan Shaw."

The tattoo man shrugs and picks up a big blue book. "I been studying all this recovery literature, where it talks about selfishness. That's where it all starts with alkies and addicts, with a selfish mind-set. We either depend on people too much or we wanna dominate and control 'em. A real shit show . . ." He sighs and throws the book down on the table. "Story of my fuckin' life. The idea to write this book all started with me getting sober. Since then, it's been all about looking back over the roots of my addictions, trying to figure out just where I went wrong, y'know. Like they say, it's all about getting honest with yourself. And I've really come to believe that relationships are key, 'cuz they're like mirrors. Sometimes it's the most painful, messed-up ones that can do you the most good."

"How do you mean, Jonathan Shaw?"

"'Cuz they're like a roadmap to where *you're* out of balance, y'know? But that's only if you're willing to look and ready to change.

Until then, it's all just the same old shit, always playing the victim, blaming everyone and everything but yourself for your own fuckups and failures. That's how I lived for years, man, and not once did I ever stop to consider that my real problem in any relationship was always *me*. That kinda blindness turned out to be the fuel for the fucking horror show that was to come." With a trembling sigh, Cigano turns the page and continues reading his confession.

76. SKELETON BANQUET

"SELF-PITY IS ONE OF THE UNHAPPIEST AND CONSUMING DEFECTS THAT WE KNOW . . . IT IS A MAUDLIN FORM OF MARTYRDOM, WHICH WE CAN ILL AFFORD."

—BILL WILSON

In a mindless torrent of violent pain and rage, broken glass, broken dreams, broken promises, broken hearts, and broken lives, I was alone again. But being alone wasn't the same. It's like being sober after a long, consuming addiction. It's not like it was before. It can't be. There's an emptiness that doesn't go away. In the wink of a hermit crab's ass-crack, my girl and my best heroin connection were both gone. But the pain had taught me a harsh and unforgettable lesson: that falling in love is like being stricken with some deadly incurable malady, a soul-shattering affliction more devastating than any other addiction; an obsessive lie that kills you slowly, eating your soul from the inside and pecking out your eyes like an angry crow; blinding you and robbing you of all self-sufficiency or will to resist its fiendish demands.

After Suzana, I came to shun love like a plague, turning away from it as one recoils from a dangerous bully who kicks you down a long, sperm-slick ramp to Heartbreak Hotel; because when that piss-warm, fuzzy pink cloud of self-deception comes crashing to the ground, you better have a pink parachute, or it's going to hurt like nothing else. I didn't have anything to cushion my fall from grace. All I had was a merciless rage of maudlin despair, self-pity, self-hatred, and trampled pride. Those foul ingredients would come to a boil in a nightmare stew of heroin addiction, opening the gates of Hell.

> **JOURNAL ENTRY – HOLLYWOOD:** *She's gone. My brain is fused into a twisted black junkyard sculpture of pain. I want to rewind the horror movie of my life. I want her back. I'm beating myself bloody against invisible walls, so dark and cement-thick between us, my life reduced to a long, miserable, screaming wail, a pathetic existential lament she will never hear, never know, even if she existed. But she is nonexistent. Just another ghost. I may get over the disease of loving her, but it will leave its mark, just as other dark days and nights have conspired to make me the monster I am. I can feel this burning pain working me over like a gang of leather thugs, and I know the scars can't ever be erased. I don't regret it, though, even drowning in this raging shit-blood current of mocking, snickering devils. No regrets, because of what she stood for, what she meant to me: hopes, dreams, poetry, love, and all good children go to heaven. I'm trying like a snuffed star to keep something alive in my heart. I'd go right up on the fucking torture rack for it, but I'm like a lunatic on a hill trying to catch the wind with a butterfly net. That's what this thing called Hope is. I go to sleep and wake up the next morning and feed the cat when he comes around. I play with words and patterns in the air, but I'm sick to death with this pathetic need for her, for someone, anyone, anything to fill the empty space that is my heart. This isn't love, I know, it's just another dope habit. Worse. Shit. It would be easier to put a gun to my head and not need some goddamn bitch, not need anything or anybody. I'm living in Hell every minute with a big squirmy knot in my stomach, this big empty pit, not the kind you get from eating too many green apples, but the kind you get when you're a little kid watching his pet puppy, his best friend in the world of new life, get squashed under the wheels of a truck. This is how I live now, and still I hang on; because I tell myself I really had love for her, that she was more than some random fuck. Nothing touches this sadness. It's a big dirty bacon-fat blanket lying over me day and night. I cry and wail in the darkness and pray to angry sinister gods, trying to pretend that it was all just a nightmare and never really happened. But when you fall in love, it's like being with a sadistic lunatic doling out miserable little scraps of tenderness like stale Salvation Army biscuits. I don't wanna*

let my heart die in weakness and bitterness like some old grandmother festering away in a rest home in Arizona, waiting for death while the coyotes wail in the desert, but I can hear the voices of death from my window as I sit in this stinking shit-pond of despair, croaking like a crippled bullfrog. I've been alone all my life, and that doesn't bother me, but I'm scared of losing what I felt with her, 'cuz if that final glimmer of hope goes, I really can't see any sense in living. When we found each other in a gray deserted place, life was beautiful every day. It was us together who brought life and color like a carnival picnic to this horrible empty nothingness, and I was happy and willing to sing and dance and learn about the magic of love; and now I'm a pathetic loser sitting on a fucking anthill with a handful of flowers I picked for her, and now there is no her. Nothing. I can't see, can't taste, can't feel. Nothing nothing nothing, that's what my life is now, no matter what I do, and it only gets worse as the days pass like a long dreary drizzly funeral procession.

JOURNAL ENTRY – HOLLYWOOD: *She called this morning and I woke up out of delirium stupor, stumbled out into the hallway and grabbed for the cool black device like some hanging instrument of torture . . . Hello . . . I heard her voice far away, thinking: Could I have looked into her living eyes only a week ago? Could this static noise thing be her? I couldn't find words to say, feelings to feel. Nothing. Blank white nothing. She began to talk, slowly, casually speaking of this and that, but I was listening to a stranger and I wanted to scream. There's no one there, just me and this funny black handle that squawks and talks on about nothing while I stand here wanting to scream. Life is brutal and ugly and frightening. I look at the dark complicated circus of events over the years, and it's all shit. I'm resigned to standing alone in the world again, I tell myself. It's no big thing. I just got burned by love, like a beat bag of dope. Get over it and move on, man. But the withdrawal from this love drug is worse than kicking dope. Even a whole week later, it just keeps replaying over and over again, and it won't shut off. Only heroin dulls out the jagged edges, but I can't find anywhere to cop on this foul shitty night, so I sit and drink and drink and drink, waiting for the blessed click that will switch off the malevolent machinery of my brain.*

The Curse was at my throat with a bloodthirsty vengeance. Sitting all alone in that haunted room, I drank myself to sleep, night after night. I didn't know which I missed most, the girl or my dope connection— and just when I really needed to get high and stay high. I wanted to beat myself over the head with a hammer to stop the pain. But I knew there weren't enough drugs to put Humpty Dumpty back together again.

With Suzana gone, my final weak link to humanity was broken, kicked out of me for good. I proceeded to drink myself into a foggy quagmire of despair and brooding self-pity. When I came out of that miserable week-long blackout, I was driving my car through a red light at eighty miles an hour, going the wrong way down a one-way street.

I pulled to the side of the road, oozed out of the driver's seat and sat down on the curb, shaking, sobbing, holding my head in my hands like a rotten watermelon. Cars and trucks whizzed past in a bleak industrial wasteland of skeletal telephone poles and deserted gray warehouses. I had no idea where I was or how I'd ended up there in the middle of the night. Trembling, I reached in my pocket for a cigarette. Stuffed in the pack I found a balloon of heroin. Thank God!

I got back in the car and tore ass home to Hollywood with the blessed bag of dope, realizing I must have been out there copping, even though I didn't remember a thing. By the time I got to my empty room, I was shivering like a hooked flounder: my first case of full-on delirium tremens. Furtive bat-like shapes darted around in the periphery of my vision as I slammed the needle into a yearning vein. Then I grabbed a handful of pills and downed them with a big swig of vodka. Soon I was tumbling down into a warm, comfortable pit of oblivion.

When I came to the next day, it didn't take me long to see the error of my ways. I swore off alcohol and went on a straight heroin diet, a bloody intravenous skeleton banquet.

JOURNAL ENTRY – HOLLYWOOD: *Drowning in a rancid sea of blood and dope. Prideful mourning in endless night visions of damnation, living and dying in kinship with spirits of lost love and hope, in groveling, toxic echoes of loss. I remember again and again how we used to sit up drinking the wine of love till the sun came up and we didn't care. My spirit caught in a rock-tide whirlpool between hope and grief, I don't care about redemption. I seek only to embrace the darkness and suffering that was she, sad-eye* *love-starved siren, and the crippled strength I'm gathering with the loss of this woman, this dream, in this harsh look at grimy, stark, nothing reality. All I ask now is that my music sing the true blues through it all, that love may remain holy in my heart; that my heart may stay alive, even as the moths of dumb betrayal fly up out of my stinking unwashed clothes. I stir like a pile of dust in dull morning wind, coming out of another four-day heroin stupor, where I couldn't even dull the pain. I see the vision of what's to be, and it's all perfect. The illusions of this life are falling away from me in death and ending, shedding away like an old snakeskin dream as I crawl up intact again from shivery cold nowhere ocean depths. Ashes part and dissolve to make way for me again, what the changes of insane life have wrought with the loss of another love, another chapter, another dream, dying to move on to another place and flex my emaciated carcass in the sun; to travel and hover around the lonesome old planet like a satellite and not rest till I know why. This is the way of me and I can never hate a whore for snapping my brain back and showing me the truth of my own cluttered existence: that I, like the rest of those who love, can never be free of love's spiteful sting.*

In those dark lonely times, I spewed my soul's poison into my journals, embracing my sudden grim change of fortune. Fantasizing of far-off adventures and longing for exotic places in the sun, I wallowed in a crippling puddle of sniveling self-pity. Perversely reveling in my own tragic self-hatred with a morbid fervor, I filled page upon page of writing in a noxious litany of futile complaints. As the Curse of a Hundred Generations emerged from the shadows of my bombed-out brain, a full-fledged surrender to heroin addiction became my life, and a life force of its own.

JOURNAL ENTRY – HOLLYWOOD: Sold the car and spent all the money on dope. Lots of dope. Weeks go by. Strung out so bad now, I feel like a moldy bucket of dead man's turds. Living in a rusty delayed reaction to time and space; summer days and nights smothered in a long stuporous heroin nod, deleting all feeling, the good with the bad. No life. Just sopping up the dregs of this unholy misery and loss like a desperate deep-sea crab scrounging cobweb treasure chests of all deflated yesterdays; scavenging in dirty drawers for old dope-encrusted filthy cottons, feeding on fever, second-hand living, temporary death; that's all I can say of this junk-ridden nether-existence. And still sometimes the "I" comes to me in little random flashes through the blur. There's always that vicarious voyeur in me, a perverse little Peeping Tom watching the weeks pass like an old black-and-white movie reel. This is what makes me my own worst enemy: if I ever stumbled across anything good like I found with Suzi, I'd always try and keep it all to myself—though I'd gladly share my perceptions of ugliness with one and all, no qualms about that. Maybe that's why she fucked me over. Maybe that's why betrayal is all I've ever seen or known or done or been. Maybe that's why I've always felt such sympathy with the losers of this world like Paul. Because with them I can just be my dirty old self with no pretense, and maybe even hope for some sympathy in return. All support from up high or down low is always welcome to a junkie: send cards & letters, old shoes, cash dollars, drugs, whatever, care of the roof crumbling over my head. I'll always keep the door open so it can get in, even if I'm dead. All my friends are dead or in hiding. Everyone gone but Paul. Nobody left to hurt or betray me anymore, so now I have to hurt and betray myself. But when it hurts too much, I go for the good old junk lobotomy, an easier, kinder way to self-destruct. A real sure thing, this heroin-induced frontal-lobe job, while the wind blows warm and frantic outside, beating at the window and blowing the dirty curtains around. I listen to the glass wind chimes I bought with Suzi, still hanging there clinking against my deadened ears. Even my imagination has been killed off now, along with the pain. But it isn't really dead, just shifted, transposed against another blank surface, like a self-consuming microscopic demon. This is bullshit! I want my fucking money back! I'm not dead yet, goddammit, and my imagination is still in operation. I've just taken a brush and painted it all black. I've brushed over all of the poetry and good and righteous dreams in the process, killing time, killing myself, rolling around in this morbid limbo swamp. I don't know which way to turn. I've got myself boxed in an impossible cage, and I just can't turn the key, can't find a way out, sinking deeper and deeper into this savage depraved ugliness; can't live, can't die, losing all friends and all love, all hope and self-respect gone, and I just keep spinning down down down, until I can take that final dizzy plunge into death or life—whichever comes first.

JOURNAL ENTRY – HOLLYWOOD: *Finally went out for a walk just to get out of this clammy solitary cancer ward of cold sweats and tears for a while, seeking release from these creeping drooling walls and the hideous memories they whisper without respite. But as I walked the streets, I could feel the people staring at me like some unholy experimental laboratory ape released from his cage, trying to look all casual as he strolls down the sidewalk. I passed hot-dog stands and shop windows, but all I could see were slimy entrails and pig shit and blood, shredded fragments of what used to be human beings. Random snippets of conversations stabbed at my ears. "That boy had guts," some guy leaning against a wall guzzling a beer was saying, chatting with his friends after work. Guts. Yeah, I could see the blood and guts splattered all over the sidewalk, all over people's shoes. Someday those shoes will be empty, sitting on a dusty shelf for forty-nine cents in the Salvation Army store, and their feet will have turned to dust too, that's no lie. Don't you see? Don't you see, goddammit? You sit there drinking your piss-water beer and you go home and beat your fucking wife and eat some cold chicken out of the fridge and watch the television and go to bed. Do you have the nightmares when you sleep too? Do you ever stop and think that your feet will turn to dust, you fuckers?*

JOURNAL ENTRY – HOLLYWOOD: *When I got back from that bloody circus tightrope walk, I switched on all the lights and turned up the music on the radio loud as it could go and hoped the phone would ring out in the hallway. No calls came. I got up and turned off the music and lights. I stood by the window and cracked open a can of nuts I didn't want to eat. I walked down the hall to the bathroom and looked into the sink and thought about vomiting but I didn't. I walked back to my room and thought about Brazil and stared at my little picture postcard of Rio on the wall for a long time. This room is so empty; the bed is empty and the chairs are empty and the closet is empty and the world is empty. Shit. I walked around and around, waiting for something to happen. Nothing happened. I noticed there was dust everywhere, under the table and chair and all over the lampshade. I resumed my circular pace, a beat-up old circus tiger in a rusty cage, my eyes scanning the place like cold searchlights. Where* *is hope? Where is happiness? Under the chair, under the rug, in the bottom drawer? Behind the table? I got down on my hands and knees and looked under the bed. A bunch of old cigarette butts embedded in puffs of dust like decaying angel-hair Christmas ornaments. In that decrepit empire of dust, a sad reminder of my ungodly wretchedness: a tragic little pile of dead butterflies. Seriously. Dead butterflies in little clear plastic bags. I remembered when this love, now decayed and warped, only a fetid memory in a deadened mind, had placed them all along the windowsill with Suzi, and I remarked to her how beautiful they looked in the morning sun. They had long since fallen to take their place in the dust beneath my dying corners, like crippled skeletons. Like me. And now the morning sunrise is only a time when I moan out loud from my empty place of rest, like a vampire, a terminal cancer patient, my throbbing hand groping blind along dusty alleys of memory, hobbling along like a crippled spider in search of new drugs to spin its web of oblivion.*

77. THE HAMSTER WHEEL

"I SUSPECT THERE WILL NEVER BE A REQUIEM FOR A
DREAM, SIMPLY BECAUSE IT WILL DESTROY US BEFORE WE
HAVE THE OPPORTUNITY TO MOURN ITS PASSING."

-HUBERT SELBY JR.

Reading back in time, a stench of burning matches and rancid
junkie sweat fills Cigano's head as he conjures the image of his wretched,
dying junkie soul sinking down a murky bog of pitiful, incomprehensible
demoralization, one poisonous word at a time.

○ ○ ○

Sitting in my room, shirtless, gaunt, incoherent, suspended in empty space,
I looked down at the little hand-poked star tattooed on my arm. *When did I
get that? Can't remember. Whatever. Doesn't matter.* My head was throbbing with
a dull insistent ache. On the typewriter sat a leaden piece of paper, the
dusty blood-spattered remnants of a poem. I pulled it out and read:

> *The Cat People come as I sleep, gathering in shadows around my bed.*
> *I listen to the sound of purring as they eat my face.*

Reading the words again and again, they chilled me to my core. Did
I write that? Or was it Malcolm's tortured ghost, back from the grave to
torment me with dark insidious dead man's incantations? I could hear his

voice whispering like a phantom presence beside me, inside me. I knew I was done, circling the drain, almost dead. Like him.

Time was a bad hairpiece slipping off at the Grand Ball of Life as I sat suspended in that dark limbo zone. My body pounding with cotton fever, I stared for hours out the dirty window at a vista of dirt, rubble, and dust, stagnating in the city's smoggy air. A rusty hulk of a car lying in a bed of dry gray weeds out there was the perfect metaphor for my life, a dreary, vacuous self-portrait of an abandoned, burnt-out soul. I watched, as if from a distance, as months passed in a spell of empty, listless stupefaction. No middle ground, I was usually either unconscious or dope sick. Every few weeks I'd go cold turkey for a few days in order to lower my tolerance for the dope. Cleaning up for good was never an option. I spent most of my time just sitting in that ratty little room doing nothing.

My writing had long dried up like the weeds under my window. If I ever went out, it was only to hustle a fix, prowling the night like a vampire in search of a victim. The only victim was myself. Aside from hitting my mother up for increasingly frequent "loans" and peddling beat dope to weekend warriors out on the boulevard, the few interactions I had with other people were all centered around finding new hustles and ways and means to get the dope we needed to just get through another miserable junk-zombie day.

Besides Paul, who was equally strung out, I ran with a guy I'd gone to school with. School was out forever as Paul, Tony Fried, and I ran the streets like the damned, doing all the things junkies must do to keep from being sick. We lied, cheated, and stole like pirates, often from each other. No honor among junkies, the only rules were made by King Heroin, our common master. Tony Fried's father, Seymour Fried, had been Lenny Bruce's lawyer. We used to joke about his name, calling him See More Freed. Through Tony, I met Kitty Bruce, Lenny's daughter. We were all strung out bad, living and dying a day at a time with a crazed single-mindedness of purpose, an obsessive, creative junkie inventiveness and resignation bordering on genius: that singular dope-fiend survival instinct that enabled us to navigate a sleazy netherworld of hustles, scams, and desperate spastic brainstorms to feed the bloodthirsty monkeys on our backs.

Even in the shadowy nether-realm of heroin addiction, that old sense of coincidence continued to haunt my life: Paul's and Tony's fathers had studied at law school together, and now their sons were studying the laws of Hell together, as if all our twisted relationships to each other were written on some dark, sinister junkie star. When I was high, I would openly marvel at the strange confluence of circumstances that tied us all together. Later, I would learn that Kitty's father, Lenny Bruce, had also been close with my father.

○   ○   ○

Distracted by a random memory, Cigano's mind travels back to Artie's living room late one foggy winter's night. Fitting another piece into the puzzle, he stares at the words on the page, feeling as if he's looking down into a long, dark tunnel.

"Lenny Bruce." Artie reminisces. "We were very close. He was a good-hearted man. Lenny really meant well. But the poor guy was self-destructive."

"Well, he was a heroin addict." Cigano shrugs. "I know what that's like. It's funny you were friends with him. Back when I was all strung out, I used to run with his daughter, Kitty. Small world, huh?"

Artie ignores him and goes on. "Poor guy was really trying to kill himself. How he did it was just a matter of time and choice. But he chose it. Every day he chose. I tried to save him many times. Couldn't do it. I remember I got him to a doctor one time. He needed a fix bad. He was in terrible shape. I said, 'Jesus, Lenny, I don't wanna traffic in that kind of stuff, but if you need a phone number, I can call my doctor, maybe he can help you.' I called him right then. Nice man, that doctor. He's dead now, suicide. Anyway, I said, 'Listen, I'm sitting here with a guy named Lenny Bruce; you've heard of him?' He said 'Yeah.' I said, 'Well, he needs something. Can I send him over to see you?' He said sure. Lenny called me the next day and said, 'Thanks, man, that doctor was a nice guy.' Doctor gave him a shot. What are you gonna do for a junkie? You can't cure him. Just give him what he needs."

"Yep. That's all ya can do." Cigano lets out a weary sigh, wondering if the old man will ever hear a fucking word he says.

○   ○   ○

JOURNAL ENTRY – HOLLYWOOD:
Dealers I Have Known:

Yosh: *Chinaman. Korean or Japanese. Junkie. Moody. Deals from home in Koreatown where he lives with a fish-faced old mother who keeps the teevee chained to the radiator. Mom only speaks three words of English, "Yoshi no home," which get shriller and more agonized with each phone call. "Yoshi . . . NO . . . HO-OOME!!" Not bad dope, when you can find him. Got the connect from Tony Fried. Yosh's uncle was Lenny Bruce's dealer. Both dead now. Expired ghosts of Old Hollywood dope lore.*

Ray: *Gruff, paranoid old-timer. The eternal mystery man with no mystery worth uncovering. Another Tony Fried associate, sold smack to Lenny Bruce too once upon a time. Small fish now. Not very good bags, but reliable. Stable. Small old fish. Ambivalent old full-time junkie. A professional, he supports his own ancient habit and a grown-up daughter who lives with him. Daughter seems oblivious to his (and her) means of support. Had a wife who recently died of an overdose, according to Tony. Tough luck. Par for the course. Daughter has a nice obliging telephone voice. Ray is an elderly Negro of seemingly respectable character, with nebulous outside interests that keep him constantly busy, when not involved in his low-level dope business. Our relationship has been cordial, strictly peripheral and business-oriented. A one-bag dealer for the most part, at least where low-level hypes like me are concerned, though lately I smell bigger deals in the offing and good connections in the making. Many other single-bag customers for me as the Downtown Express picks up speed.*

Mari: *Garden-variety junkie. Fag. Garrulous. Some lingering signs of class left over from better days still shining through the murky haze of a nasty downward spiral. Nothing much in the dope hierarchy. The Sissy with the Golden Arm. Making it—barely. Venice street dealer. Very small fish. Ten-dollar bags of varying quality. Mexican tar hustled laboriously to a handful of pitiful losers who sell their food stamps for dope money. Real strung out, no big deals, no decent connections, no steady customers, probably saves old cottons. Gets kicks from flirting with danger. Bottom man, fall guy. Narked out and busted recently as a direct result of doing volume business with shady characters. Doing state time at Chino. Victim. Food for the System.*

Tiny: *Another bottom-feeding Venice junkie fag. Low level street* *dealer. Recently took over Mari's questionable business. Fat white-trash loser. False teeth come out for five-dollar blowjobs. Slimy denizen, low life, low rent, low IQ. No redeeming qualities. Gets four stepped-on Venice dimes for thirty and keeps one for himself. Sometimes burn artist. Definitely saves old cottons. Stumbles onto a good connection from time to time to support his jones. Always talking about kicking and saving his welfare checks for the big Sex Change Operation. Probably be dead in a year.*

Sammy: *Slick Persian businessman. Perfect gentleman. Always smiling. Non-addict. Many shadowy "associates." Probably mobbed-up. Never been ripped off. Makes prompt and efficient home deliveries in late-model Mercedes. One-stop shopping. Expensive leather briefcase filled with bags of good, strong Persian smack, Peruvian flake (cut and uncut), Colombian weed, a variety of pharmaceuticals, uppers, downers, and brand-new disposable insulin rigs. Delivers to rock stars up in the hills. Quality product. Makes the rounds of sleazy Hollywood buildings at regular intervals twice a day. Never late. Gets in the elevator and stops for transactions at each floor. Quick exchange in hallway. You better be there. No deals. No credit. No phone.*

Carlos: *Garden-variety Mexican street dealer. Cross-eyed weasel. Ugly pockmarked mug. Too friendly, you know the type. Prison tattoos. Junkie. Tracks all up and down neck and hands. Hustles beat dope on the boulevard. Decent dime bags for regulars when he's holding. Convenient. Gave credit. Lived downstairs. Fucked my old lady and got beat down. Never saw the dirty roach-fucking scumbag again.*

Flaco: *Another Mexican. Reliable. House dealer. Ray associate. Lives in dreary ghost-town shooting gallery full of rats and junkies and gangs. Hard to get to, but worth the hassle. Good bags and steady deliveries from Ray and others, when he's got a full house. Never leaves the pad, except to dispose of the occasional body. Bring your own rig and nod out at your own risk.*

Bernie: *(Affectionately known as Burn-ya or Burnout.) Strung-out beat-artist dirt merchant. Rock 'n' roll tragedy. Pawn-shop superstar. Dresses in black. Smells funny. From New Jersey. Sells from his pad a couple of buildings down, when not out burning weekend warriors with beat oregano lids with real seeds and stems for authenticity. Nice guy. Hustles stepped-on Mexican dope. Sometimes good for credit. Last resort.*

Laurie: Strung out like a lab rat. Part-time hooker. Part-time bartender. Part-time dope-runner. Full-time middleman. Personable. Pretty in a tore-up way. Likes speedballs. Likes to talk. Good connects. Have Rig, Will Travel. Good running partner, when not holed up with Beverly Hills sugar daddy. Soulful blowjobs and good conversation. UFO buff. Always wearing expensive designer clothes peppered with cigarette burns. Bad tracks. Bad skin. Bad luck. Sweet, generous nature. A good egg. Too good to live. Recently OD'd. RIP Laurie.

Dr. Harvey Rose: Script Doctor. Pharmacist's worst nightmare. Nice Jewish Boy gone wrong. Cy Devore bell-bottoms and mirrored Ray-Bans. Celebrity collector. Thriving Westside "Pain Clinic" with a line of hypes waiting on the sidewalk like hungry dogs salivating every morning at 7 a.m. Here comes Dr. Harvey in his shiny white Mercedes convertible. Fifty bucks a visit. Leave with a handful of scripts. No questions asked. A pro. Always good for a hundred nice water-soluble Dilaudid tabs, plus the usual codeines, uppers, downers, Quaaludes, and other assorted feel-good pills to move on the Boulevard. Recently busted. No more Pain Clinic. No more shiny Mercedes. No more Cy Devore. The best connection in the world, gone. Next?

As time dragged by, I came to know all the people I needed to know to keep my habit afloat. My favorite connection was this "hip" young Beverly Hills doctor who catered to rock stars and street-level hypes alike. I became a boutique dope fiend and the living was easy—till the cops raided the good doctor and hauled him off to jail; and there I was, stranded in Hell with my asshole in my hand, strung out like a rock star without a band.

JOURNAL ENTRY – HOLLYWOOD: *Dr. Harvey Rose, the junkie's best friend, finally got popped, and I'm out the best connection I ever had. Other script docs practice in Beverly Hills, or so they tell me. Just got a line on a new one today, some old croaker who's been pushing scripts to the rich and famous for years—used to be on Elvis Presley's payroll. The King supposedly sends him a new Cadillac every Christmas. But when I got there, the silvery-haired relic told me I'd have to shit in a little plastic container. I just looked at him, like what? Really? Moving in excruciating slow motion, he pulled out this little box, like one of those soup things they give you for Chinese* *leftovers. I couldn't believe my fucking eyes. It appeared I'd actually have to present him with a sample of my poor junkie dung. God, I'm thinking, is this old fart serious? He's really trying to find something WRONG with me so he can cure it and make me all healthy again? Well, that's his job, I guess, but the bitch of the thing is I can't just come right out and tell him the truth. After all, this is Beverly Hills. I could just see it now: "Listen, doc, there's nothing wrong with me!" Or maybe I should say "EVERYTHING's wrong with me. I just need some drugs, see, 'cuz I gotta get straight. I lied to you about the back pain! I just want the Dilaudid to get high and not be sick! Please have mercy, just shut up and write the goddamn script!" Bet that would go over real big! And they say honesty's the best policy? I'm already eying the locks on the Elvis doctor's cabinets, wondering how much dope he keeps in the office for "special" patients like The King. I was breaking out in a cold sweat by the time I got out of there.*

JOURNAL ENTRY – HOLLYWOOD: *Well, desperation being the Mother of Action, I did it. Not the rip-off, not yet, gotta come back at night for that. Paul says he's got a plan. Ah, good old Paul, the man with a plan. Meanwhile, I took the little Chinese food thing home and shit a sad little junkie rat pellet into the bucket. Gonna bring it back, get my script and stay the hell out of Beverly Hills. I've heard of Jack in the Box, but Crap in the Box?!*

Strung out to the gills and without a source to maintain our massive prescription opiate habits anymore, Paul and I started breaking into doctors' offices at night. We usually came up short. A handful of half-ass downers, some clean rigs; but we never hit the grand opiate jackpot. Too much risk for too little payoff; so I went back to supplementing my voracious appetite for self-destruction with parental "loans," shoplifting, and other petty larcenies. Eventually we found a decent connection and started running back and forth from the *barrio* to Hollywood with neat little bundles of good strong Mexican heroin. We stepped on the product hard, and then unloaded our half-beat bags on weekend warriors. But the more dope I did, the more I needed to keep the monkey fed. That's the real bitch about heroin addiction. It's a perpetual hamster wheel, a slow-spinning merry-go-round of restless low-grade misery.

78. STILL LIFE

"EVERY MAN HAS INSIDE HIMSELF A PARASITIC BEING WHO IS ACTING NOT AT ALL TO HIS ADVANTAGE."

—WILLIAM S. BURROUGHS

As the late-afternoon sun reflects over the choppy Gulf, Cigano looks back into the battered volume, conjuring an image of an emaciated junkie sitting in a dark room, a weak, befuddled Holocaust victim.

"I'd sit there for days on end," he reads, "staring into space, wondering how long it'd been since I'd last bathed, smelled, laughed, fucked, eaten, drunk, lived. How fucking long? Ravaged by drugs and the endless despair of that miserable junkie existence, time slunk through my atrophied little world like a pockmarked mugger. I shivered in cold sweats, languishing away in that burnt-out battlefield by a dirty window, looking out over the same blank view of nothing, the same dreary, smoggy wreckage.

The typewriter was long gone, swallowed up in a black hole of pawnshops and shuffling dope-fiend despair. Pages of scribbled ramblings lay forgotten on the desktop. My pallid hand reached across the desk drawer, rummaging through an abandoned slaughterhouse of blackened bent spoons, bottle caps, scraps of tinfoil, and filthy old blood-clogged works; a miniature wasteland of burnt-out matchbooks and empty pill bottles. Dusty, dried-out wads of cotton sat like tiny murdered ghosts atop sheets of blood-spattered poetry in that crumbling kingdom of failure."

Cigano stops and coughs, wincing at the memories, then reads on.

"Scavenging through sucked-out glassine bags and torn heroin balloons, I'd salvage enough residue for an impotent little fix. Blowing a dried-up fly from a blackened spoon, I cooked up and shot into the rancid gray meat of my arm. Then came the tired old ritual of cleaning my works from a glass of water, ignoring another dead fly floating on the surface; the gummy bitter taste on my mummified palate as the translucent appendage of my hand squirted a stream of pink water across the desk onto a dying cactus plant on the window ledge—the only other living thing in that shrunken limbo realm, bloody drops ricocheting off the carnivorous hell-plant in a maze of spattering trails across long-abandoned pages of writing. Like a wild-eyed mad scientist experimenting on bottom-feeding mutant urchins and crustaceans in my soul's sunless depths, I knew I was living under a death sentence. But I was powerless as a crotch-crab to curtail the nightmare."

JOURNAL ENTRY – HOLLYWOOD: Still life. I got these two little plants here. One mongrel California cactus, an alien-looking plant mascot spawn of Hell, drooping decrepit bloody tendrils over scattered pages of expired poetry. The other little plant I bought for a buck in a Mexican market in East LA one day when I was feeling almost alive. Like me, my little plant companions are junkies. I feed them by syringe. The cactus gets bloody water straight from the needle, along with whatever residue is left over after a fix; a junkie plant, it seems to be coming closer to me day by day. Or maybe I'm the one who's turning into a cactus, drooping and dripping my rancid lifeblood onto my writing. The other plant seems to be doing better. It gets the third or fourth cleansing squeeze from the needle: pure water almost. It would never survive the harsh opiate overload I lay on the cactus. This one sits beside my radio on the windowsill, getting a little sun and fresh air whenever I stumble over to let some light into this dump. The rest of the time it just sits there feeding on cigarette and opium-den incense smoke. I even sprinkle some marijuana seeds over its soil from time to time. It feels the mellow pot vibes. I sit between the two plants, feeding them both with the occasional stoned-out poem, some blood and a bit of cool jazz from the radio. The plant in the middle— me—exists somewhere in the center of plant life. Still life. It isn't easy being a plant, or a gardener, or a junkie. But these little writings are my humble offerings to the plant world: fertilizer from the shit of my life. Somehow, I am still able to hope sometimes, like if I can get off this fucking dog food, maybe the best is yet to come, taking dubious solace from the Eugene O'Neill quote tacked to my wall: "Why am I afraid to dance, I who love music and rhythm and grace and song and laughter? Why am I afraid to live, I who love life and the beauty of flesh and the living colors of the earth and sky and sea? Why am I afraid to love, I who love love?"

JOURNAL ENTRY – HOLLYWOOD: *Feeling like a sack of bleeding assholes. Fresh-cooked blood fermenting in the bathroom sink. Tea party in the neighbor's room down the hall. Blue veins rise and collapse beneath minuscule reflections of cold steel as metal and flesh meet. Gotta make this hit fast. Somebody wants the bathroom. No, not yet, missed the fucking vein, not yet, pull it out again. Now this junkie tea party is coagulating! Social diseases are spreading through cracks in the wall. GODDAMMIT, WHERE'S ALL THE TEASPOONS??!!?? The junkies are eating them! What? "Oh, yeah, be right out, just brushin' my teeth in here." WITH MY TEASPOON??? No no no no no. The toothbrush stands witness to all. Fuck it, let 'em ask the toothbrush, the bloody toilet seat, brush brush brush—puke, flush. Nice. Remember the Roto-Rooter jingle? "Call Roto-Rooter, that's the name, and away go troubles down the drain . . ." Fuck! What are they doing out there? WHAT ARE YOU DOING IN THERE? Communication breaks down, somebody's gonna call the cops! "He went out the window, officer, slithered right down the drain. The toothbrush is the only witness." So you think I'm sick, man? Granted, I've been in better spirits, but you oughta see yerself standing there in my mirror looking back at me while I sit here taking detailed notes of Hell, oh yes, so someday you may find yourself trying to decipher these pages like ancient Dead Sea Scrolls or some shit. You won't get very far, though, Future Boy, not until you learn that all is subject to interpretation, sick or healthy, whatever. Sons-a-bitches, trying to bust in here with a battering ram when the door was open already, and I'm just standing here, half-alive, looking down an empty drain. Room for one more. Like my grandma always said, that's the way the cookie crumbles. One day you're walking by the shore in rosy love stupor, and next thing, you're looking down an empty*

*drain. One thing's as good as the next, I guess, or maybe I'm just so
stoned I can't see past the fog in my brain. Been locked up in here
shooting dope for so long, I can shut my eyes and remember exactly
what the drain in the bathroom sink looks like. The brass ring says
Milwaukee Flush Valve Co. and the sink is one of those big old-style
porcelain jobs. As I look down into it about to puke, I can remember
all kinds of random shit. My mind is a septic tank overflowing
with memories; inconvenient bits and pieces of shit, like when you're
shaking hands with some guy in a suit and your mind hits you with
a wispy vision of a hit you missed that blew your arm up like Popeye
the Sailor. Or when you're fucking some sleazy cunt and right as
you're about to climax you think about shaking hands with some guy
in a suit, and all you're really doing is shooting bad dog-food dope
and sitting around a dusty old purgatory room, pounding at the keys
in your brain like a brain-damaged organ-grinder's monkey as your
life creeps down the drain like a crippled caterpillar.*

"I was all done in," Cigano reads. "Tore up from the floor up, beat up
from the feet up; living in a swirling limbo of spiritual nausea, yet obliged
by my diseased insatiable appetite for oblivion to just keep shuffling
through the bare motions of existing; a grim-faced remote-controlled
spook haunting a murky sub-world of self-annihilation. Invisible parasites
seemed to be feeding on my pitiful degradation as I poured my pain
and disgust into reams of Hell-fed automatic writing: a litany of ugly
static language from the tormented realms of the dead. The Curse was
the only thing keeping me alive anymore, like a cat toying with a small
animal before killing it off."

JOURNAL ENTRY – HOLLYWOOD: *Still life: Razor
blade and a book of matches atop a pile of blank white sheets of
paper. Does every eye see it the same? Tired old rush, tied off, tucked
in, and sucked away. Drop by drop. Away. Dried blood spots on
the walls, unique decoration, jazz writing, surreal hieroglyphics, no
more gimmicks. The Mexicans around here say it best in a song.
"No quiero nada . . ." Down on the street of the Saint Monica, Mr.
Cadillac pulls his double barrels, shotgun blast: BAM! BAM! Ten
bicycle writhers lying in the gutter, spewed asunder. Flash, thunder.
The occult bookstore on the greasy old boulevard stands monument*

to the moment, and a pizza joint blasphemes this crippled cradle of
sexless nostalgia with a sign: *HAD A PIECE LATELY?* Oh yeah,
and bicycles, bicycles, thousands, *MILLIONS* of bicycles. And rats.
Bicycles and rats, like a greasy combo sandwich. Like Count Dracula's
unfortunate junkie sidekick, Renfield, Malcolm lay on his hospital bed
for a week, delirious, raving of rats and bicycles, then he died, I say. I
was there, I saw it. Not Renfield, not bicycles and rats, not just then,
but I was there. I saw Malcolm die. Rat poison. Horrible. Well, not
so bad, really. I went out afterwards with O'Connell and had me a rat
and bicycle sandwich. Yeah, I've gotten used to it by now, a steady diet.
I never could stand the taste of pizza, the aftertaste of a hand-me-down
childhood, fairy-tale ending, even New York style. Silverfish, California,
"Oh yeah, that sure is a nice place to live!" they say, "No Neighbor Sam
to terrify your rat gardens there! It's just like Memory Lane, oh yes, such
a nice place, bla bla." But now let me finish. Poor boy had never ridden
a bicycle in his life, never flown a kite. But young Malcolm had his own
little designs, oh yes, all the little bottles of bacteria stacked up in mason
jars in a seedy old pigeon shed on a Manhattan rooftop, up above rows of
tenement buildings, and he lived in them all, up in Harlem, teeming with
junkies and winos and pigeons and rats and roaches and grease, bubbling
and mysterious, he controlled the whole sector there, man, the scene! And
he heard the Sunday Gospel music in his head. Oh yes! His brain circuits
were locked into the vibrations, and they crossed countries, gazing by
industrial moonlight into the murky bottles he collected up there, like a
little fucking god, *The Abnormal Child,* and he grew into the depths of
his microcosmic universe, and it grew into him, pulling his strings like
a cheap mechanical funhouse puppet, till one fine day little Malcolm
finally met his match. Yes. He beheld a row of gleaming perfect white
teeth, clicking away in a murky bottle, clicking and gleaming, perfect little
white incisors. That's how it all started, I say, and the clicking grew
and persisted in his head, louder and louder, distracting his thoughts at
the dinner table, and then the conventional prayers and incantations that
kept his fragile balance began to snap like worn-out underwear elastic,
and his manners grew dark and brooding. His family and friends cast
him out into the night. Madness blossomed. He bounded up the stairs
to the rooftop, clutching his jar of accursed teeth. He swallowed a bottle
of poison and his ghost fled off into the sea of teeming millions, emitting
strange radio waves. Furtive shadow-men in dark suits followed.

"Jesus!" Cigano shuts the book with a grimace. "It's like I was channeling Malcolm's tormented spirit." He shakes his head. "Reading this stuff now, I can see how haunted I really was by his death. I guess this was the only way I had to try and express all the horror I was feeling." He shrugs, looking up at his young confessor. "There but for the grace of God, man . . ." He sighs as he reaches over and opens another old journal.

79. THE EDGE

"THE EDGE. THERE IS NO HONEST WAY TO EXPLAIN IT,
BECAUSE THE ONLY PEOPLE WHO REALLY KNOW WHERE IT
IS ARE THE ONES WHO HAVE GONE OVER."

–HUNTER S. THOMPSON

JOURNAL ENTRY – HOLLYWOOD: *A minute ago, there were a couple of flies floating around in here. I think they were trying to fuck, but who can tell with bugs? They weren't those big shit-licking mothers you see; these little buggers were less obtrusive, like the ones that hover around the back doors of greasy taco joints on the boulevard. But they were bugging me anyway. With a lightning-quick movement, I ended their frantic little fly-fuck fiesta. Splat! Now there's five more floating around in here, and I grasp the futility of doing anything about it. They are far superior to me. Better equipped to live. They can fuck faster than I can kill. That's why they shall inherit the earth. They're waiting to eat my entrails, and they will win in the end. What can I do? But as long as my heart still beats, the little bastards won't get the chance. Not yet. Gotta keep going. Any minute now, a wasp or some other significant flying yellow-breasted cocksucker might come hurtling through the window and I'll have to take action again. But for now I'll just let all these shit-feeding mini-robots be. There's far too many of them lurking around for me to contend with. Already they've won. Look how they've distracted me from my writing. It's easy for me to get distracted, though, flies or no flies, mostly because most of the time*

I'd rather swallow a scorpian than have to face my miserable little life on paper—probably 'cause it makes me feel too much power over my own circumstances; and when your life's as beat as mine, who wants to admit that it's all your own doing?

JOURNAL ENTRY – *With my last few bucks, I got a new seventeen-dollar-a-week room in the back of another crappy old rooming house, after skipping out on the rent at the last place. Good-bye the plants. This new joint is one of the last spots in the neighborhood where I still haven't burned somebody, but it's a real hovel, engulfed on all sides by these ugly monolithic brick hell-pits inhabited by rusty old bums, winos, and dope-fiends. I did what I could to make my new room as "homey" as I could, but I only had enough cash for the cheapest, most uncomfortable space in the decrepit old joint, and then I couldn't get the fucking lights to work. First they would all blow out simultaneously when I tried to turn them on, and then, right around Christmas, it started to get real cold in here, and I had to walk up and down the stairs two hundred times a day to play with all the fuses, check the hot ones, the lights flashing on and off so fast, like acid flashback strobes, I might go blind. Finally, I got up the nerve to ask for a heater—electric, no less. Well, that was the beginning of the end. The circuits blew out every night at odd moments, and then the old cunt running the place got all stressed out and started yelling at me, saying I was a no-good dope addict and why didn't I ever leave my room or get a job? Shit, now the jig's up, and all I wanted was a heater and a few lights to read and write by and be able to crash in here without all my fucking clothes on. Now I'm fucked. Again. Now I have to deal with people: my worst nightmare. I would like to kill and maim and dismember anyone who tries to interfere with my writing or my dope. I try to come off like a nice quiet young man, but the heater and lights and radio all take a dump at once and then this hag starts calling me a dope fiend without the slightest provocation, threatening to call the cops, and I can't get any peace in this stinking, lousy dump for my fucking seventeen bucks. And I'm already three weeks behind on the rent. I'm gonna have to sneak out tonight and leave another heavy old typewriter behind. Fucking thing didn't work for shit anyway. Too much of my foul junkie blood sprayed all over the keys. I'm really getting tired of this shit.*

JOURNAL ENTRY – HOLLYWOOD: *The two detectives stand in the middle of my room like a pair of militant seals. It's the silent one I got my eye on. I'm not too worried about the other, with his pushy fast-talking intimidating mannerisms, cheap suit, and enigmatic threats, no doubt qualities borrowed from his silent partner: a form of emulation to the obvious brains of the team. I can see right through the pushy one, like a bad soap-opera actor, and I know I can handle whatever shit he dishes out. It's his partner that bothers me. He just stands there, silent as the man in the moon, all tight-lipped stoic bearing; all business, right down to his shiny leather shoes. Has a smile ever parted those straight-lined lizard lips? Yeah, it's in that one that I sense the danger, the cold-blooded killer. The talkative cop goes on and on with his boisterous, garrulous speech and threatening little cop gestures, but even as I pretend to listen to his bullshit, I'm watching the silent one out of the corner of my eye. He's watching me too in his inscrutable cop way. He has the brand of the assassin on him, the heartless executioner. I know they're trying to get me to rat out Mr. Big. What a scream! Far as I'm concerned, they can both go take a dump. I ain't no fucking snitch. But I gotta play along. Not much choice. This will all be over soon. I'm already feeling the Sickness creeping up my gut like a rusty nail. It's too early in the day to lose my shit and blow it. Even I've got enough sense to know that would only trigger a human time bomb like that silent psycho-sphinx in the corner. Guys like that love to see guys like me twitching and sweating blood, just for fun. Too early in the morning and I sure don't wanna be dope-sick sitting in the pokey. I still gotta get out to cop. Stay cool. Junkie pad or not, this is a quiet place, just a little sanctuary for a miserable low-level hype. Nothing for these guys in here. They're trolling for bigger fish. I am small fish. So I just sit quietly, playing my role as a small-fish junkie, which isn't much of a stretch, as I watch these second-rate narcs going through their tired little intimidation act. Soon it will be done. They won't find any hidden guns or bodies in here as they lift my table askew and run their unwelcome pig knuckles through my notebooks. They'll just get bored and hand me their official cop business cards. I know the drill. They'll tell me to call if I happen to think of something. Dream on. Soon they'll be on their way, on the prowl for bigger fish to fry.*

After the dope squad started coming around, I knew it was just a matter of time before I'd go out of that rat-hole in handcuffs. They had me on their list. Maybe I was just an insignificant dope fiend, but sooner or later they'd have to make their monthly junkie quota. The clock was ticking. I skipped out on the rent one night and cleared out of Hollywood.

JOURNAL ENTRY – Downtown Los Angeles:

I snap out of a warm comfortable heroin nod to terrible sounds flying like fists at my head, bang bam slam, crumbling the doors, earthquake turbulence rocking the walls, noise swinging from the chandelier like King Kong from the fucking Empire State Building, and I'm caught like an invisible ghost in a barroom brawl of noise in a very bad Western movie. I look around for the source of the confusion, but the television is silent. This is the movie, the very bad shoot-em-up movie of bad ugly life in the shadows of downtown LA. What the fuck am I doing here? Babies crying, kids screaming and fighting, a mad-woman junkie hag yelling and stomping around, bitching, moaning and groaning, trying to exterminate the whole fucking planet, clamoring for attention, wham bam slam, clang, bang, yaddata yaddata yaddayayadda, filthy worthless degenerate human excrement. I'm in her fucking HOUSE, she yells, screeching above the rumble of mindless violence that is her miserable existence, and I'm trapped in this dried-up junkie cunt's private pit of Hell here, because it's cold and rainy out and she knows it, she knows I got nowhere else to go and she's bitching, challenging, belching and farting horrible noises from her rotten toothless junkie blow-hole, that this is HER house. This is what drives people to murder. She doesn't know that part, that the knife is in my pocket as my hand slips into my jacket like a lizard, and now it's in my grip, my fingers closing around the blade in an impatient fist, and her throat is blossoming like a ripe apple before my startled vision. I've never felt so much revulsion for this horrible life, never felt so close to snapping the final cord and going right over the fucking edge. I wanna hang her entrails from the chandelier like Christmas ornaments. Fucking Manson Family's got nothing on me. The pressure mounts and mounts and the rain is coming down in filthy buckets of frozen piss water and I'm trapped in here with this screaming cunt of a dope-sick harpy, and the knife is in my hand and, yes, I'm finally losing my mind.

Wherever I went, I was as welcome as a turd in a punchbowl at a party. For me, the party was over. After sleeping in downtown doorways for weeks, I finally crawled back to Hollywood and hustled up enough cash for another room. Whatever money I got went right up my arm, but, between scams, hustles, ripoffs, and the usual humiliating "loans" from my mother, somehow I managed to pay the rent. A junkie needs a place, like a rat needs a dark crevice to hide in, and I didn't dare get kicked out on my ass in the winter cold.

Often, I couldn't pay for the room and still keep the monkey sated. It was murder. My game was shot. I would sit in that dank little space for days on end, dope-sick and delirious, moaning and writhing around on the bed in a cold clammy muddle of shot nerves, shooting up the germ-infested dope residue from dried-out cottons at the bottom of a dusty drawer.

Cotton fever was even worse than being dope-sick. I'd lie there shaking like a sick Chihuahua shitting razor blades, feeling Malcolm's cold phantom breath whispering beneath the creaking floorboards. Close to copping the big dirt nap and powerless as an overturned cockroach to pull myself out, some feeble little spark of life kept me going somehow, dreaming a vague and distant dream.

Cigano's vision drops into another dim chamber of memory, and then he is there again, seeing, feeling, and smelling it all. Taking a seat at a table, the emaciated young junkie pops a red heroin balloon from his mouth. His hands tremble as he pours the powder out into a spoon, spilling some onto the dirty tabletop. He scoops it up with a finger and licks it, his gut twitching at the familiar bitter taste. He fills a syringe from a glass and squirts a few drops into the spoon. Lighting a cluster of Pep Boys matches, he holds them under the blackened metal, watching like a dog at feeding time as the muddy sludge comes to a boil. He pinches a scrap of filter from a butt in the overflowing ashtray, drops it in and dips the needle into the soggy cotton, bending it sideways to draw up the precious amber liquid. Tying off above his elbow with a cracked leather belt, he pumps his fist till a scarred, blackened vein rises. After a few trembling stabs, a thin column of blood sprouts in the rig. He pushes the plunger down. Holding his breath, he draws it back till it fills with blood. He depresses the plunger again and tastes the warm surge of relief coursing through his body. Smiling, he draws water into the rig and squirts a thin pink jet onto the ratty carpet, then tosses it back in the drawer. He fishes through the ashtray, finds a butt, and lights up.

He sits back, smoking, feeling peaceful. Bolstered by the sudden absence of acute suffering, he stares at a postcard of Rio de Janeiro tacked to the wall. He gets up and shuffles over to his little record player, a humble survivor too worthless for the voracious pawnshop monsters to have swallowed. Flipping through a stack of albums, his last worthless possessions, he sits on the floor staring at the familiar cover. *Black Orpheus*, the Brazilian Bossa Nova soundtrack to his favorite film, the story of Orpheus, set in the vibrant hillside slums of Rio de Janeiro. He thinks of the movie he used to drag Suzana to. He closes his eyes, nodding off, picturing himself and his long-lost sweetheart holding hands in the dark sanctuary of the two-dollar movie theater at the ass end of the boulevard.

Reading on, Cigano can see it all playing out, a nightmare vision from another life: a young junkie placing a threadbare disk on the turntable, a cigarette dangling from bluish lips. The music begins a scratchy prelude to his demise as the tattoo man stares at the page.

"Dreaming of long-gone hazy summer nights with Suzana," he reads, "the theme was tragic love. Love and tragedy, hand in hand. My life was a long melodramatic movie, a hopeless, loveless, sordid little tragedy; and there I was, playing my tragic part, just like in a movie, wallowing in it to the bitter end, with a perverse satisfaction of maudlin self-pity that only a junkie or skid-row wino could ever possibly enjoy. Wilfred Wormus on smack, a nostalgic soundtrack playing in his head, dreaming sensuous Bossa Nova dreams of a faraway life of warmth and comfort. I coughed, and my bones seemed to rattle around like dirt clods in a mummy's dried-out hollow chest cavity . . ."

Cigano envisions himself sinking into a deep opiate reverie, nodding off, going down, down, as the languid soporific sounds of the Bossa Nova fill his head with a sensual perfume, conjuring verdant visions of a distant tropical paradise. Happy dream images play across the screen of his heroin fantasy, slow-dancing across a fuzzy Technicolor landscape. A shimmering vision of Rio de Janeiro emerges, sparkling and vibrating, blinking on and off, on and off. He can see himself running along a beach under the sun, sliding into the water and over the edge of time as the movie reel of his life fades to black.

ta-fit . . . ta-fit . . . ta-fit . . . ta-fit . . .

The needle skips at the end of the record.

Nobody hears.

A silent ash drops to the floor as the cigarette burns out between young Jonathan's cold, cement-gray fingers.

80. WAKE-UP CALL

"A GOOD SCARE IS WORTH MORE TO A MAN THAN
GOOD ADVICE."

—E.W. HOWE

I came back to life protesting, growling like a disturbed wildcat, sputtering, spitting, cursing, as Paul held me up under the cold shower spray soaking my filthy clothes, dousing my lethal heroin torpor. He slapped me hard across the face, again and again, yelling at me, shaking me, shouting my name, commanding me to live as he propped me up there like a blow-up fuck doll. I could taste the sour remnants of cocaine on my palate from the shot he'd hit me up with before dragging my inert carcass into the wet moldy indignity of the bathroom.

"Turn that fuckin' water off, goddammit! Fuck!" I shouted, cursing my only friend for bringing me back to suffer another day in Hell.

After that near-fatal overdose, something snapped in me. I realized that if Paul hadn't happened to stop by with a bag of coke that day, I'd have been gone: another blue hunk of dead meat on a cold metal slab in the County Morgue, sporting a toe-tag like Malcolm and all the others. That brief visit to death's waiting room finally got my attention and woke me up, just long enough to make one last try for life. Begrudgingly, I made a decision to curtail the madness and get off the dog food once and for all.

O   O   O

"Dog food?"

"Yeah, man," Cigano looks up at Jaco. "That's what we called the shit. Dog food was like our nickname for dope. Heroin. Smack. I think it was some kinda Pavlovian reference." He chuckles. "Like we knew what we were up against. This was back in the day," he explains, "before they had these fancy rehab places for junkies and drunks, before recovery from 'substance abuse' became big business. Back then if ya wanted to kick a dope habit, you were pretty much on your own. Here, listen to this."

Cigano turns the page. "A part of me still wanted to live, at least long enough to make it to Rio. Ever since seeing *Black Orpheus*, that was my only dream. So I decided to go cold turkey. It wasn't a tough decision, given my options. I'd already burned every bridge a dope-fiend could burn. What did I have to lose?

The first day was bloody murder. Paul lent me twenty bucks to get this old short-circuited electric typewriter out of hock. My idea was to write my way through one last heroin withdrawal, then get the hell out of town before I could get myself strung out again."

JOURNAL ENTRY – HOLLYWOOD: *So this is it. The big dope kick, Day One. Broken down like a garbage truck with four flat tires, kicking this monster habit, trying to get my weak carcass nourished by gorging myself with candy and swallowing gallons of sweet yogurt with the same fucking spoon I used to cook the dog food in. I hate this shit, hate it here, hate it everywhere. Hate myself, hate being dopeless, hate feeling useless. Weak as a sick poodle, I sit in front of this broken electric typewriter like a stunted grunting monkey, pounding away at a mechanical garbage machine just to keep from jumping out of my fucking skin. I wanna stab myself in the eyes! Nothing helps. The words are useless as cold, rusty buckets of pig shit. Writing is pig shit; this isn't for me, but I'm not ready to sentence myself to death yet. So here I sit, boxed into a world I hate, lying around in a pathetic dope-sick heap, a slug-sucking parasite existing for tomorrow and hating every goddamned minute of this wretched miserable today. Feels like I've been juggling little balls of shit forever. Somewhere along the line, I lost my balance and the balls all tumbled down and crumbled into this horror hell of musty dust and decay. The nuthouses and the streets are full of crazy, godless, loveless, directionless losers like me.*

I need to write it all down here, need to document every excruciating detail of this squirming stomach-flipping misery. The goddamn buzzing of this fucking infernal machine is driving me nuts. The lights in this room are too bright. And, like an overgrown Kafka cockroach, I can't stand the light; it shows too many scars and too much ugliness, and there goes the horrible noise of this fucking electric typewriter again, defective from sitting on a pawn-shop shelf. Like me. Defective, short-circuited, broken, destroyed! FUCK FUCK FUCK JESUS CHRIST SHUT THE FUCK UP I CAN'T THINK!! THIS FUCKING NOISE IS DRIVING ME BUGFUCK BATSHIT CRAZY!!

JOURNAL ENTRY – HOLLYWOOD: *Day Two. I wanna stab a needle into my arm so bad. I wanna poke a fucking knife right into my eyeball and drive it into my skull to shut up the fucking noise in my head. Maybe then I could just cease to exist. That would be the ticket, but I'm too fucking selfish to die. I have to make it through this fucking kick somehow, gotta find another day to kill, just hang on for another day, while all the normal folks are sitting in their rooms down the hall with their televisions and card games and pizza and beer. God, it makes me sick, all of it. But this is my only hope, so I just gotta live through it till I can get straight and decide on something, anything, some way out of this stinking roach-shit maze. I'm trying to put the juggling balls back into the air. I feel like a quivering heap of molding clay, all naked and weak, sloshing around in the dirt. This is what it's all come to, stuck in a crappy little room, lying on my back like a crippled worm, trying to get those goddamn shitty little juggling balls back together again and rise back to my feet so I can start the whole damn clown show all over again.*

JOURNAL ENTRY – HOLLYWOOD: *Day Two. It's a fucking mystery to me why I'd even wanna put myself through this again, and not just cop an overdose and die like everybody else. Why bother? It's all just pain and suffering and lies and betrayal and murder. And I am a coward. That is probably the only fucking reason I'd wanna live through this torture. I might as well just shove that needle into my arm and fade away like all the others. But no, I am an American, goddammit, and no matter how hard I try to escape*

my shit-brained cultural programming, I'm stuck with this ridiculous "Will to Live," along with all the other crummy little mechanisms and gears and workings and the Grand Madness of this Great Society, America. Living in this pigshit-shoveling world has driven me to drugs. Ha! Now, how's that for some fucking hypocrisy? Shit, I spend more than a hundred American dollars in one day—equal to the means of survival for a whole family of decent, hard-working, honest, God-fearing human beings for a year in some other part of the world—and I piss it away in ONE FUCKING DAY just to keep a heroin habit sated in this Great Society of America. That is some kind of rotten soul sickness, a demented self-perpetuating virus. And I hate myself for it. What a monster I am in the world! I can't live with the guilt and frustration heaped on top of all the self-hate I'm already drowning in, just for existing in the first place. So what do I do? I turn around and spend another hundred dollars, piss away another hundred goddamned fucking American dollars, piss away another dozen decent human lives in one fucking bang, one shot, one cowardly little pop in the arm. And all for NOTHING. Just to exist for another day like a slug in the cracks of this Great Society of America, while the planes fly over the planet dropping bombs on babies. And what do I do to try and make it better? I sit around a dark clammy little room for an eternity, pissing away my fucking life, killing myself slowly, day by day, which is the worst fucking bloodsucking sin and baseness of all, considering all the starving shuffling shit-shoveling masses of the world: people who would rather be a stray dog in America than a human being eating dogshit in the third-world sewer they live in. Yes, I am the Great Monster. The Devil is in me and I know it. Every minute of my life I know it: I am the Great Beast, Moloch, the Motherfucking Devil himself. The Plague. The Curse. The Scourge of Humanity. Every day of my life I must be aware of this as an American, whether I'm a slobbering bottom-feeding junkie, or sitting down to breakfast with a copy of The Wall Street Journal. *Shit shit shit. I know the choice is down to me now, right here and right fucking now, and I can choose as I please. That's the rules of the game here in the good ol' Land of the Free. So for another day, I will sit here and sweat out this horrid heroin heartache and try try try to squeeze this fucking dog food out of my soul, like pushing dead rats out a dead man's ass, and just hope it gets a little easier tomorrow.*

Closing his eyes, the tattoo man sees himself rolling around on a dirty mattress, drowning in a fetid mire of toxic sweat. Cringing under merciless nightmare visions of pounding grinding machines, he shivers. He shudders. He whimpers like a puppy in the rain. Hours crawl by like tiny red spiders of delirium as the machinery closes in around him in a cacophony of angry incoherent voices, shouting, cursing, accusing. His nerves are on fire as a stifling chaos of tangled bedsheets knots up around his throat and he senses a dark reptilian shadow closing in: the Jabberwock sinks its claws into him, choking the life out of his weak, drug-ravaged carcass.

"*Agghhhh!!*" He flies up from the mattress, a demented Jack-in-the-box of pain. Tears roll down his face, burning like acid sizzling into tormented flesh. Moaning like a dying sea lion, he reaches over the side of the bed. The floor is rolling around like a tipsy lifeboat bobbing in a sickly sea of bloody fish entrails. He grabs for the wine bottle. With a weak burst of effort, he hoists it to his parched lips and gulps down a mouthful of the stale red horror, then projectile-vomits a gushing crimson stain across the bed. A blood-red vision widens and spreads across Cigano's mind, coloring his memory, as the gates of Hell swing open.

"Never again, never again!" he hears the desperate junkie croak. *"Oh, God, I swear I'm gettin' outta here and I'm never coming back, never again, never again! Never again! Never again!"* The hellish mantra eases young Jonathan into a mutilated delirious stupor, which for now must pass for sleep.

Cigano takes a long, deep breath and continues. "The kick was worse than I'd feared. With nothing but some cheap wine, Valium, and weed to take the edge off, it was a season in Hell. Finally I had to stop writing because of the stomach cramps and shaking, the shivering, the vomiting and diarrhea. Then it got even worse. But what I still didn't know was that living through heroin withdrawal would be the easy part. The worst part of it is the other part; the part they never tell you about; that hideous, insidious curse that snuffs out addicts and alcoholics like smelly thrift-store candles."

With a sad smile, he flips the page. "Because it's not the drugs that get you in the end. What really kills you is the relentless psychic torture of just being who you are *without* drugs; the restless irritable torture of living in your own skin; the torment of being in this shitty world with all its excruciating little daily indignities; the perpetual horror of being aware. Of being clean. Of being. It's only *after* you put down the drugs that your mental landscape really turns to shit. But I still didn't know that. I still had a big wide world waiting for me; a tangled, unexplored, mysterious roadmap crisscrossed with exciting, enticing new bridges just waiting to be burned."

"The minute I got off that bed of nails," he reads, "I left town without looking back. And from that day on, I ran the world like a condemned man, burning up a hundred dead-end roads to nowhere with an urgency I'd never known, running the planet like a rat on a fiery treadmill. Running like the damned. Running from the Devil with a flaming red pitchfork of Hellfire stabbing at my ass. Running from the Curse.

"Like most addicts, I'd been a runner all my life. As a child, I'd run to fantasy. Later, I'd run to liquor and drugs, then to a woman's tender caresses. But no matter how fast or how far I ever ran, I'd never be free from the prison of myself. Even as I traveled the Seven Seas, I would always end up right back where I started. Face to face with the Curse."

The tattoo man looks up at his young listener. A salty ocean breeze rattles the palm trees as a ship moving out to sea blasts its long, mournful horn.

81. KEY TO THE HIGHWAY

"THE GREAT HOME OF THE SOUL IS THE OPEN ROAD."

— D.H. LAWRENCE

JOURNAL ENTRY – HOLLYWOOD: *Day 6 off dope.
I gotta get out of this fucking country quick now before it all starts
up again. What else am I gonna do? My whole life here has
been a long throbbing toothache. My eyes have stared upon
America's dead listless shadows too long. Her angry rednecks
have whipped my ass with picks and axes and taxes and cops and
the jackhammers of her dreary pre-fab plastic fantastic failure.
So this is the Big Adios, America, old friend. May you keep a
tight asshole, and may the bombs of your dead not explode in
your face; you'll find a million new ways of staying blind and
stupid, just don't take me with you. I don't know where I'll end
up next, but a big part of me is already gone, always was. I'm
just the baggage to be shipped behind. So behind I'll go, like a
rabid dog with a throbbing red dick, ready for action. Your doors
are all closed to me now, America. I've overstayed my welcome.
Your sad-faced soulful Negroes smoke pot and drink cheap gin
in blinking neon backstreet bars and greasy alleys, and may the
good and soulful among you bebop on till the cows come home.
The cows gotta come home sometime, but this one's going out
to pasture. So good-bye, America, so long, happy trails, see ya
way out west, old partner. I'll be peeking into the erotic delights
behind your curtains from time to time, ya kin bet yer boots. Only*

this time I won't be standing outside in the rain waiting for your dirty old downtown buses or sleeping in doorways or all-night sleaze dens, waiting for your evaporating dancing girls. This time, I'll be ridin' high in the saddle, trotting off into the sunset while you tend to your own dirty backyard. Louie Louie, oh baby now, me gotta go go go eat cream cheese wrapped in blankets like sleeping babes while your people fester away in cockroach rooms on the corner, down the block, across the street, in the nuthouse, whatever, wherever. I am out. The anarchist opens your door a crack and peers in for a moment. With shaking hands, he pulls the bomb from his ratty overcoat and tosses it in. You are dissolved for a moment, America, with your Academy Awards and Superbowl Sundays, but everything with you is fleeting and futile, even your demise. I can't bear the disappointment of your great Second Comings, your meaningless distractions and heartless destructions. My thoughts are bombs which never explode; volatile, dangerous even, yes, but essentially worthless. Who cares? Nothing matters. Nothing left behind. Nothing to lose. I'm already gone.

Cigano looks up and sighs. "Even knowing that staying on would be a death sentence for me, making the decision to leave for good was an act of pure desperation. I was totally fed up with my fucked-up junkie life, y'know, but I just couldn't fully see my part in it. I was so fucking blind, everything around me seemed to be the cause of all my problems. That's how an addict's brain works, man. Denial. And it ain't a fucking river in Egypt, man. I always thought if I could just get away from the scene of my own crimes, everything would be better. And for a while, it kinda was, I guess."

Silence. Jaco watches him, waiting for him to go on.

The tattoo man shrugs. "That's the funny thing about looking for external cures for internal maladies, bro. It takes a while to catch up, but sooner or later it does, and then there's no escape. Eventually, ya gotta face the truth, or it just keeps coming back, in one form or another. Anyway, I packed a little overnight bag and got the fuck out."

He stares out over the Gulf's choppy brown waters, thinking back, time-traveling. "I'll always remember the day I split. That shit's tattooed on my brain forever. Been writing about it here." He picks up his book again, conjuring the time and place like an old black-and-white movie in his head.

O   O   O

Daytime. The Big Day. Still feeling kind of shaky, and pallid as a haggard old ghost, I was doing better. The monster dope kick was over. Weary and weathered beyond our combined years, Paul and I were sitting, like a pair of old men, in a cramped little corner greasy spoon. The air smelled of stale cigarette smoke and fried eggs. Mexican music was playing on a jukebox. My little plastic thrift-shop valise sat on the sagging ass-worn vinyl seat beside me. Almost a week off heroin; a trace of color had crept back into my face.

I regarded my friend's pasty, somnambulant visage across the fake-wood Formica tabletop, then turned and glanced out the window at the smoggy scenery. It all seemed unreal, ethereal, faraway. I looked over at Paul again. His dark eyes were pinned back at a comfortable half-mast as he contemplated a glazed jelly donut in his hand, peering from the donut to me and back to the donut. In agonizing slow-dope-motion, he opened his mouth to take a bite, then stopped. As if not to waste the effort, he started talking in a high-pitched, heroin-muddled croak.

"So yer finally off the dog food, Jon. Good job, man." He regarded his donut again. As if to delay the unpleasant task of eating it, he looked up at me and spoke again. "How ya feelin'?"

"Like stepped-in dogshit." I forced a weak smile, feeling a lot worse than dogshit.

"Yeah, well, th' worst is over now. Ya look all right."

"You look a lot better, man," I ventured. "I wish I had a little taste . . ."

"No, ya don't!" Paul snapped at me like a concerned turtle, shaking his uneaten donut for emphasis. "Just think about it, man."

I managed a sad little nod. "Yeah, I know, brother. I just wanna little hit. One last time, y'know, one for the road . . . You holding?"

"Ferget it," Paul grunted, before nodding off again.

Silence. Mexican music. Traffic.

I reached over and fished a good-sized butt out of the black plastic ashtray. I wiped a pinkish lipstick smear from the filter and lit a match. A smell of sulfur hit my nostrils, conjuring the familiar scent of boiling heroin in a spoon. I winced and stubbed out the smoke. Eyeing the donut inching southward in my friend's hand, suddenly it hit me. I was feeling hunger! A first in a long time. My mind flashed back over the last couple of years: subsisting on a subhuman diet of heroin, downers, cheap wine, cigarettes, some ginger ale, the occasional Kit Kat bar, maybe a bag of potato chips once in a while. That was about it for nourishment as far back as I could remember. Hamster food. And like a giant rodent, I'd drop a rock-hard little rat pellet or two out my ass once a week or so. Life on dog food. Suddenly I was craving real human food! The smell of greasy bacon, fried eggs and donuts was making my mouth water. Everything felt new and different. Life was unfolding around me like some exotic new flower garden. A trapped insect of excitement stirred in my gut. But I was still feeling kind of scared and shaky too. I looked up and saw Paul's stoned out eyes peering at me across the table.

"So yer rilly gonna beat it all th' way to Brazil, huh?"

"That's the idea." I shrugged.

My friend cracked a devilish grin. "Ya got some big fuckin' balls, Jon. Don't they got, like, headhunters an' shit down there?"

"I dunno, don't think so, bro." I smiled weakly. "Hope not, but, hey, whatever the fuck they got, can't be any worse than this shithole." I gestured out the window at the dirty old boulevard.

"How ya gonna get there? It's a long ways, ain't it?"

"Yeah, well, I'm in no big rush. You know. Just start hitchhiking south, I guess, see what happens. Whatever. I'll get there."

"Ya got some big balls, Jon. Fuckin' bowling balls ya got there, man." Paul grinned, then started to nod out again.

"Well, what do I got to lose?" I mumbled, not really expecting an answer.

Silence.

I sat back and stared out the window. Through the smoggy afternoon haze I watched the freeway entrance across the street, an endless, colorless river of cars and trucks, as I replayed the last few hours in my mind: the uncomfortable, too-long hug my mother gave me that morning. I shuddered with a familiar revulsion, recalling the cool red lipstick stain the old lady had planted on my cheek like a brand. But I had the six hundred bucks I "borrowed" from her stashed in my boot. And this time it wasn't going up my fucking arm. It would take me a long way away from all that shit.

I remembered the book I swiped from the newsstand on the corner while waiting for Paul: *Mexico and Central America on Five Dollars a Day*, replaying the words *Mexico and Central America*, in my head as that restless insect began to stir again. I thought about *On the Road*, how the story ended in Mexico; how those final chapters had always been my favorite part of the book as I'd read through it over and over, unconsciously formulating my escape.

I smiled to myself, anticipating the upcoming adventure, my new life on the road in Mexico. *Mexico and Central America on Five Dollars a Day. Yeah!* In my head, I could hear the Little Walter song that had been stuck in my brain for days. *I gots de key to de highway. Believe it's time to go. I'm gonna leave ya runnin', baby. Walkin's much too slow.*

Coming up out of his heroin trance, Paul set his donut down on the table and took off his "lucky" ring. He looked at it, then shoved it across to me with a crooked grin.

"Fer good luck, man," he croaked, picking up the donut again.

I turned the silver star ring over in my hand. I'd always liked that ring. I tried it on. A perfect fit. I smiled. "Hey, thanks, brother."

My friend winked back, then began his slow nod again, his chin drooping south for the count.

Silence.

I sat gazing out the window. Same old smoggy scene. Little Walter playing in my head. *I gots de key to de Highway.* I could feel that restless bug stirring. Paul was gone, far away in a deep nod.

I reached over and took the donut from his weak grasp. I turned it over in my hand, examining it like some weird alien life form. I took a timid bite. Then another. *Wow! Who knew a fucking jelly donut could ever taste so fucking good?* I thought about going to the counter to get another one, but decided not to. I stood up and grabbed my little vinyl bag from the seat. Now or never. *Believe it's time to go. Gonna leave ya runnin', baby. Walkin's way too slow.*

When de moon peep over de mountain, I'll be on my way. I'm gonna roam dat highway till de break o' day.

Still chewing the doughnut, I slung the bag over my shoulder and stepped out into a smoggy wasteland of dirty brown palms and hazy power lines. I sprinted across the street to the freeway entrance without looking back.

○   ○   ○

The tattoo man closes his book and sits back, staring out over the choppy brown waters of the Gulf. Finally, he looks over at Jaco and sighs. "That's about all I've got written for this thing so far."

"It's a lot."

"There's a whole lot more, brother."

"So you're going to keep working on it?"

Cigano nods absently, looking out over the water.

Silence.

"What happened after you got to Mexico?"

"All kinda stuff, man." Cigano shrugs. "I bummed around for months, hitchhiking around the country, before I finally got to Veracruz almost a year after I left LA. Then I kinda just settled in here. Stayed in this same hotel for a long time, before I finally got work on a ship to South America."

"So, how long did it take you to get to Rio?"

"Quite a while, man. Coupla years, I guess. I jumped ship at the mouth of the Amazon, then made my way down to Rio overland, hitching rides, staying in a lot of different places along the way. I lived on the road in Brazil for a long time. Lotta crazy stories . . ."

"So you're going to keep writing."

Cigano gives his young confessor a funny look.

"Like about all those travels?" Jaco prods.

"Already got 'em all written down, brother." The tattoo man takes a long, deep breath and points a finger to the side of his head. "Right in here." He grins and falls silent again.

Staring out over the water, surfing the waves of his memory, Cigano pictures an old tattoo design he saw as a kid, peering on tiptoes in the window of an old tattoo parlor: a sailing ship riding the high seas, with a flowing banner and the mysterious words: "Homeward Bound."

The glowing talisman drifts across his mind's vision now, just as a young boy's imagination once drifted away on a sea of hazy yellow nicotine-stained images, conjuring dreams of far-off adventures in exotic faraway lands.

Cigano smiles, remembering the day, a long time ago, when his destiny set sail on that high-masted sailing ship, cutting through a sea of paint and ink, sailing away forever, with no final destination or port of call.

Shaking his head, the tattoo man picks up a pen, opens his notebook to a blank page, and starts writing the next chapter.

POSTSCRIPT

While some of the characters in this book are fictional composite personalities, many of them are actual people. Some, like myself, still walk among the living. Most of them, however, have long ago crossed over into the mysterious lands of the Great Beyond.

If you happen to believe in prayer, dear reader, please take a moment to pray for their eternal souls. And please petition whatever Higher Powers you may be on speaking terms with to show their suffering spirits the same mercy and charity you would ask for yourself and your loved ones.

For my part, I will continue, God willing, to tell their stories in upcoming installments of this ongoing book series, always in the sincere hope that my humble efforts might lend some ease and comfort to their challenging disincarnate pilgrimage into the light.

AFTERWORD

TRUE ARTIST

BY ALESSANDRA DE BENEDETTI

Just as it's difficult to discuss modern jazz without Artie Shaw's name coming up, it's nearly impossible to talk of modern tattooing without conjuring the name of the legendary jazzman's unlikely offspring, Jonathan.

A traveler of the Seven Seas, tattooist to Johnny Depp and celebrities galore, confidant to the rich and famous, the dark and infamous, and the original inspiration—alongside Keith Richards—for Depp's famous pirate Jack Sparrow, Jonathan Shaw has been a lowbrow cultural icon for decades, wearing many hats: Underground entrepreneur. Gonzo journalist. Producer. Director. Poet. Novelist. Screenwriter. Painter. Creator. Curator and collector of lowbrow art and memorabilia. Low-life. Underworld celebrity. Wheeler. Dealer. Hustler. Healer. Psychic. Psycho. Pirate and pimp. Roving reporter. Contributor and editor-in-chief to cutting-edge art culture publications. And, last but not least, the eccentric, eclectic, world-famous founder, owner, and operator of the legendary avant-garde New York City landmark, Fun City Tattoo Studio. While Jonathan has long left Fun City and the tattoo scene behind for new challenges on happier horizons as a full-time writer, his legacy is forever carved into New York City's collective conscience—not to mention a thriving tattoo culture he begrudgingly admits to having spawned.

When I first met Jonathan Shaw, he spoke to me about such diverse topics as the spirit world, exorcism, metaphysics, science, anthropology, history, political conspiracy, quantum physics, art, literature, and God; everything, in fact, *but* tattooing. He talked for hours, describing with disarming openness his fifty-something years of hard living, sex, drugs, and rock & roll, burning up the road to Hell. Stories of pain and suffering. Experience, strength, and hope. Fame and fortune. Success, failure and ruin. Pitiful, incomprehensible demoralization. Major-league insanity, eventually giving way to his many hard-earned years of solid recovery from alcoholism and drug addiction, the curses of a long and colorful life.

"There's a lotta water gone under that bridge, sailor. Shit, man, I was in Baghdad when you were in Dad's bag." He winked at me through a cloud of cigarette smoke, the ever-present cheap filterless Mexican cigarette dangling from his lips, dancing as he talked, his gold teeth flashing in the smoggy shadows of another Hollywood night in exile from his home in Rio de Janeiro. "My motto used to be: *'Live fast, die young, and leave a pretty corpse.'* Well, it's too late for all that now, so I guess all I can do is just keep living the best I can. But, hey, I got no regrets. Every day above ground's a good day for me." He threw back his head and laughed out loud.

This statement seems to underscore a newfound peace and simplicity after a long absence from the world of tattooing, a world he was once passionately involved with. After a week-long nighttime montage of motorcycle rides between Hollywood coffee shops and late-night taco stands, I was beginning to understand the essence of the man sitting in front of me: Jonathan Shaw, the infamous cult figure, lowbrow author and underground journalist; a walking, talking, living encyclopedia, embodying vast experience and knowledge of all my budding interests; the enigmatic tattoo master who, over the last three decades, spawned an industry—before disappearing into thin air; the outlaw visionary who I would soon find myself consorting with on much deeper levels.

As his longtime editor, part-time personal assistant, and full-time sounding board, I have to say that Jonathan is not an easy being to keep up with. Still as demanding of quality from those he works with as he has always been of himself, he's forever pushing the envelope—often to his own consternation. A true artist, an old-school craftsman and one-man creative enterprise, he's a perfectionist who breaks balls to get things done. And he does get things done. Naturally. After all, he is the

Captain; he calls the shots and that's that; he's been there and done that for decades in all of his various endeavors and incarnations.

On a recent trip to New York, freshly clad in a brand-new sleeve and back piece from JS (one of his last major tattoo works), I got to hear many firsthand accounts of some of his more colorful personality traits. Traits that, happily, I have never seen myself. His old character: the control freak, the boss-man, the ne'er-do-well playboy, coked-up drunk and junkie—the world-class asshole; the trend-setting artist and dangerous maniac who carried two pistols and a ball-peen hammer in his many pockets, which he wouldn't hesitate to use on any poor devil who stepped out of line as he conducted his nefarious outlaw business with thieves, derelicts, outcasts, criminals, and other dregs of society. JS was always out there, making it happen in an aggressive, edgy, authentic way, among bloody, bone-breaking rumbles, gunplay, chaos, and good old garden-variety drunken punch-ups.

Most of the people I talked to were decorated in Jonathan's surreal abstract black and gray neo-tribal work. All of them made it abundantly clear that he was boldly pioneering the style long before it reached a mass-market phenomenon to become the meat-and-potatoes, status-quo staple of today's tattoo industry. That was, to my understanding, around the time when the Captain finally abandoned ship, the beginning of the end of an era, an era in which tattooing was still edgy and antisocial and, well . . . hip.

JS, like the song goes, was "Country When Country Wasn't Cool." And, talking to him, I got the impression that he'd known for years that he'd somehow created a monster. Continuing to go through the motions after losing his fervor for tattooing, he described himself like a ghost haunting a house long after its death. Ghosts are haunted, too, by memories and regrets about their previous lives.

With a sigh, he shrugs. "What can I tell ya? If I had it all to do over again today, I'd do a lot of things different. I was an insane person back in those days, simple as that, a pissed-off alcoholic who couldn't drink anymore and didn't give a fuck about my own life or anybody else's. What they call a 'dry drunk,' restless, irritable, a ticking time bomb. In a word: miserable. People didn't even have to do anything most of the time to piss me off. I was already pissed off. I just came that way. Unfortunately, I was in the position where I came into contact with a whole lot of really irritating people." He breaks out a sheepish, gold-toothed grin. "Bad news. Guess I might owe a few apologies here and there . . ."

After years of white-knuckled abstinence from booze and drugs, predictably, he eventually relapsed and began another steady descent into a slow, drug-addled alcoholic suicide. But divine intervention was at hand. Just after the apocalyptic events of September 11, he had something of a spiritual awakening. Realizing once and for all that he was tired of living a life he'd come to hate, being a "brand name" with diminishing returns, Jonathan Shaw soured on being a parody of himself, chasing his tail for money and acclaim. The tattoo world had finally lost all sparkle or appeal to an artistic spirit in desperate need of redemption. The time had come to begin working in earnest on his many long-neglected literary projects.

Long story short: he sobered up. Then, after one last swan-song tattoo tour of Yakuza family business in Japan, without fanfare or comment, he quietly retired from tattooing. He was heard to remark to a friend at the time: "Old tattooers are kinda like old tattoos. They never die. They just sorta faa-aade away."

A lot of the stories I heard about his "dry drunken" years tattooing in New York City seemed blown far out of proportion, like long-held urban myths: incredible, cinematic anecdotes of a mysterious gun-packing psychopath who would go off on anybody for just about any reason—or no reason at all. Strangely, though, most of these lurid accounts ended in breathless, almost reverent accolades. "What a great artist!" was a common theme heard from friends and detractors alike.

Alfred Albrizio, owner of another legendary downtown business, the landmark C'est Magnifique jewelry store, a fixture on Macdougal Street for decades, was a close friend on the scene back in the early days of Jonathan's World Famous Fun City Tattoo. He recounts the time when a local wannabe tattooist, who'd managed to build up a prosperous clientele by operating in Jonathan's shadow, one day fizzled out and quit after a short, lackluster career.

According to Alfred: "Jonny was kind of offended this guy didn't bother to tell him he was going out of business, maybe give him some referrals and so on, especially after he'd been generous to the guy with his time and experience. Tattooing was an old-school, underground thing in the city back then, real shady and competitive. Nobody ever told nobody their trade secrets. And Jonathan had been good to the guy, gave him a lot of good advice and so on. He never said nothing about it, though; he just went and called the phone company, pretending to be the guy. Ha! He had the guy's old number transferred over to Fun City, so whenever customers called, Jonny or one of his workers would tell 'em, 'Yeah, sure, so-and-so just stepped out for a minute. We're at a new location. Come on over and we'll take care of you.'

"Jonny was always pulling funny shit like that!" Alfred laughed. "The other guy found out about it and yelled at Jonathan's wife on the street. Real tough guy. I guess he didn't have the balls to face JS in person. He's lucky to still be alive and not crippled, I'll tell ya, the way JS used to carry on. Thank the good Lord he's got religion now."

Another old friend and Fun City customer, Vinnie Sorentino, got a faraway look in his eye, remembering the enigmatic tattooist. "It's true, he used to have a pretty bad temper. But it was usually well-placed. His victims always had it coming, one way or another. A lot of people thought he was just a straight-up lunatic. But he was really a pretty crafty businessman. He just had his own whacked-out code of honor. JS was a product of the streets; a Gypsy, y'know; he always had a million crazy tricks and scams going on. Nobody could keep up with him, though, as an artist. He was always way ahead of his time, but at the same time he was a real balls-out, no-bullshit, old-school tattoo man, not some egghead, college educated, art-fag artiste like ya got around here nowadays. We miss him, hot temper, blunt objects and all. New York won't be the same without Shaw."

I listened to these bizarre, disquieting tales, all chillingly alike. Story after creepy story of dirty tricks, bloody beatings, death threats, rumbles, hostile takeovers, urban piracy, and all sorts of shady underworld dementia, all taking place in a decrepit nether-landscape: a burned-out, pre-Giuliani, thug-controlled Lower East Side operating on the same streets I grew up on, decades before I was born. It sounded like something out of *Gangs of New York*. I was confused and amused by these epic accounts. It seemed that my soft-spoken friend and kindly mentor Jonathan, the kitten-loving, girl-chasing, hopelessly romantic, generous-beyond-measure dude I'd come to know and love, had been the stuff of legends back in the day.

"Teddy Roosevelt said, 'Speak softly and carry a big stick,' right?" says a longtime friend, Hollywood screenwriter Kenneth Shiffrin. With him, Jonathan wrote a screenplay, along with Hubert Selby Jr., based on his ongoing *Scab Vendor* memoir series. "Well, Jonathan used to speak loudly and carry a really big stick too. But he has a big heart. And he's really a much nicer dude now. No doubt about that."

Even today, mellowed down, chilled out, living a new incarnation as a sober, reflective man of letters who spends a good deal of his time trying to help and inspire other people, Jonathan, hard as he tries, is still just not terribly tactful. Suffice it to say he doesn't suffer fools gladly. No doubt a tricky personality trait for a tattoo artist to have possessed and still survived, even thrived, in a world of raging egos, frantic greed, undisguised vanity, and ugly, unprincipled ambition. Truth is, he's much better suited to being a solitary writer than a tattoo artist in constant contact with John Q. Public. As he himself has allowed repeatedly, Jonathan is not much of a "people person." But in his well-documented New York tattoo persona he had been, by all accounts, a real hard-ass, albeit a colorful one. That's the Jonathan Shaw who was once described in a blurb for his first novel, *Narcisa—Our Lady of Ashes*, as "the great nightmare anti-hero of the new age" by rock legend Iggy Pop. Why am I not surprised? Perhaps because I know him personally to be one of the most eccentric and unpredictable human beings I've ever met.

On a recent trip together to his home base in Rio de Janeiro, we schmoozed at high-society cocktail parties with one of his many weirdly diverse groups of friends: movie directors, captains of industry, architects, artists, and musicians. Then, a heart-stopping motorcycle ride later, bobbing and weaving through road-warrior traffic and midnight military police roadblocks, we were hanging out in a teeming, decrepit shanty-town-world of foul-smelling third-world favelas, eating *feijoada* with hairy cooked pork snouts peeking out through bowls of beans while coked-up, gun-toting twelve-year-old drug-soldiers and pregnant teenage whores crowded around Jonathan, shooting the shit and gawking at his full body-suit of tattoos.

This exemplifies that same weird duality that always made him stand out from the herd: a singular cross-pollination of diverse worlds and unlikely cultural orientations. Grinning crookedly at his own off-color jokes, flashing his diamond-studded gold teeth, putting out his hand with the dollar sign tattooed on his palm. Jonathan was always more than just a tattoo artist, more than even a living legend. He's a bloody pirate! He's been around the world a hundred times and has enough stories to tell for days on end, speaking with uncanny authority on subjects ranging from art and literature to the Hidden Hand in global politics; from philosophy and anthropology to obscure underworld history, to the occult.

In his penthouse office and home away from home in a landmark gothic building overlooking Hollywood's glittering lights, hanging above his desk where I worked for years, editing his literary efforts while he was off writing and traveling the world, are framed portraits of him drawn by old friends: well-known artists like R. Crumb, Joe Coleman, Robert Williams, and Johnny Depp. The Depp portrait bears a portentous inscription:

"To my brother JS – Captain Jack the Pirate."

Oh, my God! Jonathan was the original Captain Jack! So *that's* where Johnny Depp got so much of that character from: the gold teeth, that cynical, mischievous half-drunk swagger. I knew I'd seen all that somewhere before. "You know, you remind me of someone," I'd told Jonathan when we first met. But it wasn't until I read that inscription (penned many years ago, before Captain Jack the Pirate was a gleam in a Hollywood screenwriter's eye) that it all clicked into focus.

Still, it's just another brief episode in Jonathan's long, colorful life. He likes to reminisce about the old New York, reminding me that I never experienced its glory days; that by the time I was born, I had missed the '70s and '80s completely, spending most of the '90s learning how to ride a bike and write in cursive. He talks about his original tattoo studio just off the Bowery—years before the acclaimed Fun City—in an innocuous basement on a shabby street peopled with beggars, drunks, and junkies. The Bowery. That name conjured up images for me. The birthplace of Electric Tattooing, and the end of the line for armies of lost souls—including Jonathan's own grandfather, "an alcoholic Lithuanian Gypsy who died in the gutter before I was born," as Jonathan describes his unlucky progenitor. It's weirdly prophetic that Jonathan would have conducted his own shady business in the shadows of the Bowery two generations later, as if he'd been led back to the scene of ancestral crimes by some bizarre DNA strand.

"It was a really dodgy, dangerous underground scene down there," says Luke Miller, a customer and helper at the original Bowery location. "I used to answer the phones, wrangle customers for them, stuff like that," he tells. "It was crazy. Super secretive. That's the way Jonathan wanted things. This was before cell phones. We used to tell people to go to the corner and call us from a pay phone. Nobody knew where the place actually was." He laughs. "After the secret call, JS or one of us would walk up there and check them out from across the street. If they looked all right, we'd go up and introduce ourselves, then walk 'em back over to the studio. The place was real low-key, just a boarded-up little storefront, no sign, nothing to indicate a tattoo shop in there. It was a violent, hardcore environment to do business. He used to get all kinds of death threats and stuff, mostly from other tattoo artists over in Jersey and other places. I guess they didn't like the idea of competition from some upstart Brazilian Gypsy tattoo guy running a busy illegal shop right in their backyard. Jonathan was pretty paranoid back then. I guess he had good reason to be. He didn't even go out for smokes without packing at least one gun."

Jonathan laughs about it today. "Yeah, well, like Lenny Bruce said, 'I may have been paranoid, but there really *were* people out to get me.'"

Characteristically, he persisted, slowly, stealthily building an underground art empire in the shadows of the great city, working from an anonymous basement studio covered from floor to ceiling in original antique tattoo-design flash sheets. These were priceless folk-art archives collected over years of travel and adventure in his insatiable hunger for scraps of knowledge and obscure tattoo history. An antique wooden case above his work area displayed real South American shrunken heads. The walls were covered with pictures, exotic mementos, original artwork and paintings by friends and frequent visitors, underground art icons like Robert Crumb, Joe Coleman, Robert Williams, S. Clay Wilson, and Kim Deitch. These artists were Jonathan's true peers, since he never really felt at home among other tattooists—save for a select few, such as tattoo legend Filip Leu, who often worked from the secretive appointment-only studio, tattooing side by side with Jonathan. Influential old-time New York hipsters like Jim Jarmusch, Dee Dee Ramone, Vincent Gallo, John "Bloodclot" Joseph, Steve Bonge, Clayton Patterson, Jonas Mekas, Ronnie Cutrone, Carlo McCormick, Larry "Ratso" Sloman, Lydia Lunch, Jean-Michel Basquiat, and Kembra Pfahler would stop by to hang out. The Maysles brothers, film-makers of *Gimme Shelter* fame, filmed the proceedings, while Pulitzer Prize-winning artist Art Spiegelman sat in a corner sketching a portrait of Jonathan at work for the cover of *The New Yorker* magazine.

What? A tattoo artist on the cover of the stately old *New Yorker*? All in a day's work for Jonathan Shaw. The paintings that once hung in that fabled studio now decorate his homes in Hollywood and Rio de Janeiro. Paintings that I gawk at in amazement, because I know they really belong in a museum. But his houses, like the shops he used to run, are a lot more like museums than homes, filled with rare, eclectic works of art and littered with random tchotchkes from around the world.

"Jonathan was always a step ahead of the rest; he intuitively knew what was cutting edge, way before it ever became popular," says Clayton Patterson, Gonzo historian and president of the seminal but now-defunct New York Tattoo Society. "But he was never what you'd call kitsch. The culture he cultivated was completely uncommon. All of Jonathan's art collection, including his own paintings and tattoo works, are testimonials and souvenirs from a lifetime of exploration, all showing some side of his very special weirdness and coolness."

As graffiti artist Angel Ortiz took Keith Haring's crawling baby and barking dog and made them into pop art by filling them in with bright colors, Jonathan did something similar with traditional "tribal" art. By adding his own original design spin of color, finesse, obscurity, flavor, and creativity, he made each piece individual and unique, something that would be enthusiastically embraced by an American counterculture always craving something novel and fresh. The difference between Angel Ortiz and Jonathan Shaw, though, is that Ortiz did not have the wherewithal to sustain the spotlight, nor the inspiration and savvy to continue to grow as an artist, remaining stuck in the familiar realms of his brief success. No one-trick pony, Jonathan did, and has continued to evolve and grow creatively. And that represents another aspect of his artistic success: his innate ability to float like a butterfly and sting like a bee, to adapt and excel in everything he ever put his hand to in whatever field of endeavor.

He spent decades traveling the world, working alone by appointment, as well as alongside other notorious tattoo legends like Spider Webb, Crazy Ace, Zeke Owen, Bob Shaw, Colonel Todd, Gil Montie, and Filip Leu. Then, in the mid-'80s, Jonathan Shaw's World Famous Fun City Tattoo was born, flaunting—for the first time ever—an archaic law banning the practice within the city of New York. Spawned out of the original clandestine Bowery basement location, it landed one day like a flying saucer at 94 St. Mark's Place, smack dab in an astonished public eye, blowing minds and turning heads. Tattooing was still illegal in New York City. The bold new studio emerged as New York City's first legitimate walk-in tattoo shop since the decades-long official prohibition was enacted in the early 1960's.

Fun City Tattoo became the impetus for the legalization of tattooing in New York City, eventually becoming "the" East Coast landmark tattoo parlor, synonymous with the highest standards of tattooing the world over. The same antique flash from around the world covered the walls. Other décor: classic handwritten signs like "If assholes could fly, this place would be an airport," and the rusty meat cleaver that hung under a plaque reading *TATTOO REMOVER*. A pistol was duct-taped under Jonathan's chair—just in case. A dead fly was crucified on the wall with a tattoo needle by tattoo legend Zeke Owen, and it stayed there for years. You could not sit in the place for an hour without learning volumes about tattoo lore, just by looking at the walls. And if you spent weeks or months in there and thought you had seen everything, you could walk in one day and suddenly notice something completely new.

"Jonathan drilled tattoo history into us all day long," says Elvis Crocker, one of the scores of seasoned tattoo artists who worked at Fun City over the years. "I'm so grateful for that now."

The studio wasn't just a prominent landmark because of its well-earned reputation in the trade, but also a bold testament to the Lower East Side's own oddball collective personality. The first time I set foot in there, I remember being overwhelmed, and not just because I was a stoned-out fourteen-year-old punk rocker, but because I couldn't believe how much stuff was everywhere. It was astonishing! By all accounts, Jonathan loved that place like a baby. He made it, watched it grow, and when it passed its prime, beginning a slow, steady descent into decadence—largely marked by his increasing disinterest and absence from the scene—he let it go gracefully, selling out to an ambitious local operator, even as St. Mark's Place not-so-gracefully suffered its own gentrified, globalized transformation into a youth-oriented version of Fifth Avenue.

Today, like the neighborhood, the shop is different: clean and sterile, devoid of much of its old air of mystery and danger, reflecting a "safe" and sanitary new New York, stripped of its once-terrible and fantastic aura of history, mystery, and tradition. Gone are the walls and ceilings oozing the deranged mystique of its former owner and his colorful cronies. The place retains only the notorious Fun City name now to distinguish it from the dozens of other neat, modern, cookie-cutter tattoo places that sprang up like a crop of plastic mushrooms in the creeping wake of respectability and post-Giuliani homogenization.

"In all fairness to the new kids on the block," Jonathan explains with a grin, "Fun City had really degenerated into a filthy, morally bankrupt, toxic old shit-hole over the years. Kinda like me; a nasty old dinosaur." He chuckles sheepishly. "Toward the end, I was just too soul-sick and burnt-out on liquor and drugs to even give a shit. My heart wasn't in the thing anymore. I ended up with a bunch of crack-heads and junkies running the joint while I kept my distance from the scene. I was already gone, living back in South America getting sober, and the place just sorta went to rats and ruin. Oh, well." He shrugs. "The people who bought it off me did a big fancy renovation there, spent a shitload of daddy's dough fixing it up. They just pulled the wicked old plant out by its roots and built a whole new shop in its place. All that remained was the name. The old Fun City was long dead and gone. Good riddance, I figured. One of the guys who used to work for me ended up buying it from them later. Last I saw, he was doing a really good job blending the old school with the new, turning it into a really nice environment with a deep respect for tradition, but more in keeping with modern times."

"Working under Jonathan back then was really cool and immersed me with some of the best artists in the industry" says Steve Pedone, Fun City's current owner. "There was definitely a wild cast of characters, but I couldn't have asked for a better place to start."

After a long, reflective silence, Jonathan laughs, not without irony. "Yeah, well, tattooing has become a respectable gig nowadays, ya know. No place in the modern 'tattoo industry' for a crusty old dump like that. Whatever, I'm just glad to be done with the whole nasty mess. By the time I sold the place and split from tattooing, it was like waking up from some long, terrible, bloody nightmare. Getting out was a relief. Done. Next?"

Before the Lower East Side of Manhattan underwent the mass urban "yuppification" Jonathan describes, it was essentially a small tight-knit community where Fun City Tattoo played its own unique role. Everyone on the block knew the notorious tattoo man well and always had his back. He did business with everyone. The cops would drive by as he stood in the middle of the street with his size-twelve motorcycle boot on someone's face and wave to him without stopping. Everyone was on his side. I listened to another day-in-the-life account where Jonathan had gotten into a bloody rumble with some bridge-and-tunnel "jimooks" because some guy had been harassing one of his girlfriends, and a gang of Dominican drug dealers on the corner jumped in to help him settle the beef. Business as usual on St. Mark's Place. There was drama every day on that street. I was able to see a little of it firsthand myself, having spent half of my teenage years lurking in front of Tompkins Square Park. There was always a whole vibe over at Fun City, kids hanging around outside drinking beer, smoking, laughing, breaking bottles, and talking shit. Everyone seemed to get along, though, living harmoniously in a splendidly dysfunctional downtown ecosystem of artists, freaks, and weirdos.

Jonathan knew those mean streets well and respected them equally. But when people wanted to fuck with him, he was ready. Shaking his head, he reminisces. "Yeah, man, over there, if ya fucked around, ya laid around real fast. We had bloodstains all over the walls in that shop, and most of it wasn't from tattooing." More than a few times he is said to have pulled baseball bats, sawed-off shotguns, and other blunt objects, gleefully inflicting insult and injury on would-be tough guys who came in with attitude. As I've learned, Jonathan Shaw meant business. He'd even had a peephole on the diamond-plate-armored front door of the original Bowery studio specially fitted so the barrel of his AK-47 could fit through it.

Like so many visionary artists, Jonathan's binge drinking, massive drug habits, and unrestrained fast-lane lifestyle eventually took its toll, shuttling him out of a mundane world he didn't relate to and burying him alive in a hellish parallel dimension of bloody warring fragments and surreal nightmare visions, all raging away in his own battle-scarred, increasingly deranged mind. St. Mark's Place had become like a Vietnam minefield. No limbs went missing there, though. They were just marked indelibly by complex, angry-looking tattoo marks: weird dreamlike hieroglyphics of an underworld landscape that Jonathan's singular perspective personified for a whole generation of New Yorkers.

Through it all, Jonathan always maintained his own special brand of streetwise diplomacy, a certain something that might best be summed up by a sign, a half-hearted reminder to himself, perhaps, that hung above his work station, among the clutter:

TACT—THE ABILITY TO TELL A MAN TO GO TO HELL AND MAKE HIM FEEL HAPPY TO BE ON HIS WAY.

"He was really fucking nuts, and I don't mean that lightly. He just didn't give a fuck. I think Jonathan was basically always more afraid of living a half-assed life of quiet desperation than he was to die," says longtime friend Billy Leroy, an antique dealer, kick-boxer, reality show star, actor, and outlaw biker, referring to an incident that occurred when some big drunk guy changed his mind about getting a tattoo. After paying up front, the would-be bully backed out, demanding a refund after Jonathan already spent time working up a design. According to Billy, who was there at the time, "He told the guy there were these carrier pigeons at the window and that the birds flew over to a place in Brooklyn with all the shop's money, so he couldn't give him his money back. Carrier pigeons? Where'd he come up with that?! He just stood up and looked this big bruiser right in the eye and turned out his empty pockets like he didn't have a penny to his name. What balls! The look on his face, you hadda be there! The guy just shrugged and walked out scratching his head. Played by the master. Carrier pigeons! Shit, JS probably had a grand tucked in his boot. What a beautiful maniac." Billy laughs.

As Fun City became "the" staple NYC tattoo parlor in the early '90s, it began to grow an even bigger name for itself. "Jonathan ruled that shop with an iron fist," says Marcus Epstein, who wears one of the last great full-body pieces that Jonathan completed before retiring. The master's swan song was an innovative neo-tribal style masterpiece that won every award going at tattoo conventions all over the world. "He used to say to me, 'Damn it, Marcus, I wish you could just drop your arm off, then come back and pick it up in the morning.' Later, after he got sober, he told me he was massively strung out on heroin the whole time he was doing all that brilliant work on me. How he managed to pull off that quality of tattooing stoned out of his mind seems to defy the laws of nature. But there it was. He was a genius. Nothing could stop that. And we were working five nights a week for months."

Fun City was well-named. It was a notorious Bohemian gathering place and hectic underground Mecca packed to the rafters with all the crazed flora and fauna of the still-vibrant counterculture neighborhood: beautiful losers, visionaries, street thugs, cops, mobsters, artists, tourists, bikers, hipsters, high rollers, stock brokers, artists, junkies, strippers, and movie stars. Long days and late nights were just a part of Fun City's surreal everyday dynamics. It stayed open until four a.m. or later, depending on street traffic, visiting friends, hot chicks, the combination of liquor and drugs flowing through Jonathan's veins, or the number of Hells Angels bikes lined up out front. Over time, the clientele got larger and more demanding, eventually growing into a wild feeding frenzy of major proportions. The spot became a timeless twenty-four-hour netherworld time warp of vital art and local flavor. Busy all the time now, Jonathan was right in his element, casually banging out pieces that would end up changing the tattoo world forever, without even realizing it. His combination of old-school technique (taught to him directly by the old-time tattoo masters, tattoo legends like Bob Shaw and Colonel Todd), blended nicely with an innovative neo-tribal primitive graffiti spin, producing his ever-present colorful abstract neo-cubist style. His growing body of groundbreaking tattoo work was turning heads all over town, putting him in charge as a true leader in what by then had evolved into a fledgling industry. And with this trailblazing work, he was also building a more demanding, sophisticated, and affluent clientele. By the mid-'90s, he had become the world's *Numero Uno* celebrity tattoo artist.

"You could tell the difference right away between his work and anyone else's," said a heavily tattooed guy I talked to in Tompkins Square Park. "Just the way he dragged his tattoo needles across the skin, it was a whole different technique. Nobody around here had ever seen that kind of thing before. I've been tattooed by a lot of different people over the years, but Shaw really had a special touch."

And that "special touch" let him create unique works of art, employing a traditional technique that was unusually old-school and simplistic for such intricate masterpieces. He puts ink in with a heavy hand, and I do mean heavy. It stays. JS makes three-hundred-pound tough guys cry, just to say he did. And despite his cold-blooded bedside manner, those of us who have been tattooed by him reap big benefits. They never need a touchup. You can't tell if a tattoo is ten months or ten years old. Musician, and longtime friend of Jonathan's, Ricky Beck knows from experience. Over dinner recently, I asked him about his first tattoo. He lifted his sleeve to reveal a colorful, intricate piece by Jonathan. Over twenty years old, the thing looked like it had been done a month ago. Then he pointed to a fuzzy blue mark on his upper arm, laughing. "See that dot there? That's really my first tattoo. Jonathan did it back in 1982. I asked him 'Does that hurt?' while he was tattooing my friend. We were all coked up and drinking hard. He didn't say nothin'. All of a sudden he just picks up another tattoo gun and stabs me with the fuckin' needle. He goes: 'Well, tough guy, whaddya think? Did *that* hurt?'"

This kind of unorthodox weirdness went on throughout his entire career, I would learn as I pieced together the fuzzy shadow of the old Jonathan Shaw. Secretive bordering on paranoid, as protective of his craft secrets as the old-timers who schooled him, he became like one of the Mulberry Street wiseguys he tattooed. Jonathan never liked to be asked too many questions about his business. So it was particularly ironic when, in the mid-'90s, he made his first appearance on the David Letterman Show: the first and only tattooist ever to do so at the time. And so, he began building another kind of reputation, now not only in the insular tattoo community, but suddenly in the general public eye. As Fun City's advertisement said, it was "Where the Tattoo Elite Meet," and this was fast becoming the stuff of legend. The names "Fun City" and "Jonathan Shaw" were known in the celebrity crowd as the Where and Who to go to for tattoo work. But, to his consternation, he was coming to be known publicly more for his high-profile clientele than for his actual tattoo skills. All of a sudden, the very taboo mystique that had once enticed the entertainment world was becoming a sort of fly in the shaman's ointment.

Sucking his teeth with a wry shrug, Jonathan reminisces. "It wasn't what I wanted when I first started tattooing. Never, man! I mean, yeah, the business was good and all that, but then it all just started getting kinda stupid, ya know. Hordes of all these real squaresville types coming in from all over the place, and they weren't even coming for the quality of the work anymore, but just because I was the guy who tattooed all these famous people. It coulda been anybody, for all they cared. The good old herd mentality. Most of these fuckers didn't know enough about tattooing to care, they just wanted the status of that whole 'I got tattooed by the famous guy who did so-and-so's shit.'"

"So and so" indeed: Iggy Pop, Johnny Depp, The Cure, Shane MacGowan, Dee Dee Ramone, Marilyn Manson, Jim Jarmusch, Johnny Winter, Kate Moss, Orlando Bloom, Kathy Acker, Tupac Shakur and all his bitches. The VIP list goes on. Even Vanilla Ice was lining up for an appointment, much to Shaw's embarrassment. Everyone who was anyone—or thought they were—was clamoring for ink from the Master. While fellow tattoo pioneer Ed Hardy was tapping into the fine art world on the West Coast, JS was doing the same in New York. But Jonathan was also creating a durable personal myth with his own colorful, weirdo, edgy flare.

In 1991, he curated a high profile exhibition of tattoo flash art at New York's cutting edge Psychedelic Solution Gallery. One of the first mainstream tattoo-related public events, the show was a huge success. Jonathan laughs. "We were totally shocked and unprepared for the kind of crowds it drew. They had to set up police barricades around the whole block to keep order on the night of the opening. It was insane. The press came out in droves, newspapers, TV, the works. That's when I first began to see the kind of power this stuff had to bring people out of the woodwork. Up till then, the whole thing was still pretty underground. The next show I did was about a year later on the West Coast, at this big gallery in Hollywood. Same thundering crowds, same mad interest. You had all these big movie stars and rock stars lining up to gawk at the artwork. After that, it all just kinda snowballed into a scene."

Jonathan became one of the first tattooists to successfully cross the fine-art line with a high-profile style, and all in public view, as he continued working tirelessly to legitimize the art through the numerous gallery shows he subsequently curated and/or participated in as a painter. There were also the scores of TV, MTV, radio, and news media appearances he made, both locally and internationally. Jonathan Shaw was always in the spotlight, later taking it to the next level yet again - this time with his very own magazine, *International Tattoo Art*.

After cutting his teeth as a regular contributor to *Outlaw Biker*, a motorcycle mag with a section devoted to tattooing, and being the creative driving force behind the short-lived, seminal *Art Alternatives* (predecessor and original role-model for today's highly successful *Juxtapoz* magazine), Jonathan was approached by market-conscious rival publishers with the idea of starting a brand-new publication, one that would be dedicated exclusively to tattoo art. He snapped at the bait, and so it was that *International Tattoo Art* magazine was founded in 1991, christened with an article by Jonathan Shaw, founder and managing editor. With worldwide distribution, it was the perfect opportunity to raise the bar another notch for tattooing, and right at the height of its new novelty status with an increasingly receptive public. Jonathan ran with it in style, engineering a magazine that was the very first of its kind. His brainchild and obsessive new creative project, *ITA* took the common grassroots tattoo-rag format and elevated it to the level of a legitimate art magazine, changing forever the way the public would perceive tattooing. To that end, *ITA* focused greatly on tattoo history, ensuring that priceless folklore, information, and archives were not kept hidden away to be hoarded by a few elitist folk-art collectors. *ITA* created and maintained the highest standards for the emerging worldwide tattoo industry by showcasing world-class works of art. These included many of Jonathan's own revolutionary pieces: his neo-tribal work and detailed abstract back pieces, his first-of-a-kind tattoos of world-class underground art paintings, copied immaculately in loving tribute to his old friends and art peers. Each tattoo looked just like the oil painting from which it was derived. All this had been totally unseen before his time, much to the chagrin of the growing legions of Jonathan's increasingly envious competitors. Via his in-depth interviews with legendary artists from around the world, some of the art world's most respected players—household names today, like Joe Coleman and Robert Williams—were first introduced to a tattoo audience. Through Jonathan's groundbreaking historical articles, the long-neglected exposure he felt was due to his own tattoo heroes, mentors, and old friends was now a reality. Legendary tattooists like Bob Shaw, Jack Dracula, Coney Island Freddy, Colonel Todd, Crazy Ace, Japan's Horiyoshi and the Leu Family, to name just a few, were finally getting their props. Jonathan had brought tattoos into the mainstream by creating a magazine that was centered in tattoo culture and packed with vital information and history in every issue. A whole generation of new tattooists came up weaned on Jonathan's sophisticated, cutting-edge articles and editorials. And he was cool. Mysterious and attractive, well-spoken with a hip, bad-boy charisma, he was an A-list mover and shaker who knew everybody worth knowing. Essentially, he was propelling himself beyond the confines of his own neo-celebrity status, something unheard of at the time. A superstar tattoo artist? No way! Yes, way.

"JS took the role of being a tattoo artist to a whole new level," says Clay Decker of True Tattoo in Hollywood, one of the now-famous Kat Von D's early mentors. "He was completely tapped into all these different worlds, and long, long before anyone else, especially after he started the magazine. Jonathan paved the runway for all these so-called 'celebrity tattoo artists' to glide in and take a bow."

Jonathan laughs. "Oh, man, when that fuckin' rag hit the newsstands, the haters came out of the woodwork like a swarm of locusts. I remember when I was first breaking into the business, Bob Shaw always warned me, 'These tattoo people are like a bunch of jealous old whores.' I didn't know what he was talking about at the time but I sure found out after I started the magazine. Suddenly everybody in the tattoo business wanted to be my best friend. Most of 'em wanted to knife me in the back at the same time."

Indisputably, when Jonathan was running *ITA*, it was at its best. It personified not only a vibe and esthetic that people were into, but, more important, perhaps, the essence of Jonathan Shaw himself: his coolness and sophistication, his dark sense of humor, his ruggedness, his outspoken opinion and no-bullshit outlook. All that along with a neo-traditional view of tattooing and underground culture across the board. Knowing full well that he was kicking up the level at which tattoo culture would be held forevermore, he painstakingly compiled every piece of information for every issue, personally. At a time when the art form was still largely frowned upon and misunderstood, Jonathan Shaw raised the standard higher than most had ever thought to push it before. To do so, he made his classic big demands on contributors. He wanted research, humor, detail, depth, drama, and art. And he got it.

"*ITA* proposes to edify, educate, and entertain its readers," he stated in the first edition's Editor's Note. In the hundreds of pieces he wrote for subsequent issues, he always gave the reader a feeling of intimate familiarity with his interview subjects, putting you in a place and time so accurately described and well documented that it was almost eerie. An accomplished and well-read writer, Jonathan lovingly devoted his vision and talent to detail, poetic phrase,and description. Many of his articles in *ITA* are the only accurate pieces of written history on many legendary tattoo figures. Needless to say, *ITA* was a contribution beyond measure to the art form, and Jonathan finally gained well-deserved—if short-lasting—worldwide respect for it. That was despite a growing feeling of sour grapes from within the tattoo community.

He shakes his head sadly and reflects. "Even though I lived and breathed tattooing back then, on some levels there was always this perverse part of me that never let me feel I fit in with the crowd. Any crowd. It was no different with the so-called tattoo world I suddenly found myself in the center of. And it would eventually be my undoing, especially where the magazine work was concerned."

It's an inherent reality that he was born into a level of sophistication that set him apart in any crowd. Jonathan's mother, Doris Dowling, was a glamorous Hollywood film star. His father was Artie Shaw, the legendary jazzman and bandleader. But his mother was an alcoholic, and Artie left her when Jonathan was just a baby. As a teenager, Jonathan rebelled against his parents' American Dream values, dodging school and sticking to the streets, later traveling the world for years as a merchant sailor, bartender, and jack-of-all-trades. Nonetheless, a certain artful maturity of vision and taste must have been tattooed into his DNA, always shining through whatever he created in every area of his schizophrenic, multi-faceted world.

"Yeah." He shrugs. "I was pretty much orphaned by the violent alcoholism in my family of origin, so I was kinda raised by wolves, running the streets of Hollywood and New York City, hitchhiking around the country, getting high and living on the edge. Eventually, I took off on the road. I wound up living in Mexico and South America, and never really looked back. I was pretty much on my own from about the age of twelve, so my real family and school were always the streets, bikers, beatniks, winos, weirdos, druggies, hustlers, criminals, and whores. Those good people taught me the art of survival. I didn't come to tattooing so much for the art as I did because of the outsider lifestyle that surrounded the whole deal. For me, the artistic part came later. Much later. Eventually, it all just jumbled together and took over my life, like some kinda fucked-up Frankenstein creation."

Nonetheless, Jonathan seems to have been raised with an inherent affinity for the finer things in life, his rough-hewn personal grace and charm tempered by a very real, streetwise worldview. Sometimes, when I pester him and ask stupid questions, he looks up from whatever he's doing and snarls like a medieval warlord, scaring me half to death. Yet when he walks into the realm of high society, he is somehow immediately respected and accepted as an equal. Jonathan Shaw simply carries an aura of tarnished nobility, some invisible "something" that people in positions of power and prestige seem to smell on him like an exotic cologne—even as he scavenges their fancy buffet tables like he hasn't eaten in weeks.

Maybe his ability to pull this off comes from the rare success he has enjoyed in a diverse multitude of fields. As a writer, he hung out with Charles Bukowski, their first meeting ending in a drunken punch-up, hilariously recounted in the pages of this first volume of his ongoing *Scab Vendor* saga. As a tattoo artist, he apprenticed with tattoo legend Bob Shaw, who taught him the basics of the craft and much respect for the game over countless hours and months of practice on drunken sailors up and down the fabled tattoo factory of the Long Beach Pike. As a screen-writer, he collaborated with the great Hubert Selby Jr. As an aspiring independent filmmaker, he was coached and encouraged by the likes of

Johnny Depp and Jim Jarmusch. As an actor, he played the part of a stereotypical tattooed thug in a feature-length Hollywood movie, sharing a scene with none other than Clint Eastwood. As a lifelong biker, he is old friends with many respected Hells Angels. As an editor, he founded and ran the first widely recognized top-shelf tattoo magazine. The list goes on and on. A "Renaissance Lowlife," as he was dubbed by legendary New York author Larry "Ratso" Sloman, Jonathan has an uncanny capacity to carry the most intense levels of perfectionism and sophistication into whatever he chooses to do.

But it was with his innovative, trendsetting, abstract freehand tattoo work that Jonathan Shaw would eventually change the face of popular modern art. When I first came to him for a tattoo, he was already long retired. I used my dubious feminine charms to persuade him to tattoo me—even though I still had no idea what the hell I wanted. That ended up working in my favor. He told me it would have to be the "artist's choice" if he was going to do it. It was his way or the highway. I consented. I just wanted something beautiful and flowing. And I got it, beyond my wildest expectations. Like me, over the decades legions of clients came to Jonathan with nothing specific in mind, only a blank canvas of skin for him to do his bold, original work on. It was easy for me to see why he became so famous for his ability to casually bang out masterpieces, right off the top of his head.

Jonathan Shaw is also notorious for his nomadic lifestyle and his mysterious disappearing acts, which have been going on for the last forty years. He is an enigmatic, spontaneous creature of many faces, a real-life, low-life Indiana Jones, speaking several languages fluently despite his lack of any formal education. Whenever I see someone who knows Jonathan, they always seem to ask "How is he? *Where* is he?" Every time. They name a list of cities and countries he may currently be inhabiting. For decades, as a resourceful, functional maniac forever seeking a geographic cure for his own baffling restlessness, whenever he grew tired of wherever he was living, he would simply "vaporize," then effortlessly build a whole new world for himself elsewhere; only to destroy it and move on again. This rootless Gypsy lifestyle went on *ad infinitum* until eventually Jonathan came to see himself like a dog chasing its tail, always seeking the next place of imagined sanctuary and never finding it. After many years of frantic travel, finally he found the road itself to be his only real home; more, perhaps, than any of the homes he built, then fled from like a fugitive. Maybe it's the

Romany blood in him—being the grandson of a Lithuanian Gypsy on his mother's side. Whatever its roots, this practice has earned him a multitude of homes, pretty much anywhere in the world he happens to be. This all started back in the '70s, when he jumped ship in an Amazon port town in Brazil and began hitchhiking his way across South America. Making crude tattoos for money to survive, he eventually ended up in Rio de Janeiro, the one place in the world he truly considers his spiritual home; and where he is still known by many only as "Cigano" (Gypsy). Maybe that's because, to this day, he still comes and goes so often. But Rio is not the only place he has laid down deep roots. The product of a lifetime of travels, Jonathan literally has odd home bases all over the world, peopled with thriving tribes of friends and family, history and memory. He's equally at home in Bangkok, Buenos Aires, Bombay, Mexico City, Veracruz, Asunción, Porto Alegre, New York, Los Angeles, New Orleans, Miami, Paris, Tokyo, Rio de Janeiro, and a dozen other places. And like an actor on the stage of his own strange, confusing life, it seems he gets to be all the things he is, different sides of a shattered, multifaceted personality naturally coming out to play in all these divergent settings.

During the course of his travels, Jonathan met and studied with tattoo masters from far-flung cultures and traditions. After tattooing in Mexico, Brazil, California, Texas, and New Orleans, he eventually ended up in New York, the city of his birth. Having grown tired of working on sailors in sleazy port towns, he concluded that New York would be a new challenge—one he was born for. His first stint in the Big Apple found him teamed up with old friend and early mentor Spider Webb. He worked side by side with the legendary "Webbo" for years in a midtown Manhattan studio before going off on his own.

Jonathan smiles widely at the memories. "Boy, it was never a dull moment working with old Spider. What a guy! I fucking love that man! He taught me stuff nobody else coulda." He laughs, shaking his head. "We both liked liquor and drugs, and pretty girls. Wooo! We were like a pair of outlaw rock stars without a band, living in this surreal, no-limits world of underground art. It was like Andy Warhol meets *Easy Rider* on DMT. Warhol actually showed up there one time. It was a magical, anything-goes kinda creative situation, y'know? Dinkins was mayor. New York was like in that movie *The Warriors*. This was all back in the day when Times Square was still Times Square, not fucking Disneyland. We worked in this big loft upstairs from a whorehouse. Man, it was total mayhem."

This was all way before mass-marketed tattoo equipment was readily available. It required real perseverance and determination to break into the game. The handful of professional tattooers in the world back then were a secretive lot: closedmouthed, inbred, and fiercely protective of their mysterious "trade secrets." But persistent to the bone, Jonathan did learn. The hard way. And to this day he carries that old-school way to all who come around him. In keeping with his reverence for tradition, Jonathan has, over the decades, had major tattoo history carved onto his own body. With Ed Hardy's only full-scale black-and-gray oriental dragon back-pieces, done back in the late '70s, a chest-piece by famed underground cartoonist-turned-tattooist Greg Irons, and a miscellaneous collection from legendary artists like Bob Shaw, Crazy Ace, Coney Island Freddy, Zeke Owen, Filip Leu, Spider Webb, and even Johnny Depp, his body is a colorful road map of his many diverse lives, adventures, friendships, love affairs, and dreams, all etched into his skin over countless journeys around the world.

Maybe because Jonathan was taught by the original masters of old-school tattooing, he always ran his business like they had, keeping it painstakingly traditional, authentic, and down-to-earth. He tried to teach all those who worked for him the meaning of respect, carrying on those old-time carny codes of honor, credos that barely survive in today's tattoo world.

"Yeah! He's a real two-fisted, old-school tattoo man," Baba, of Vintage Tattoo in Los Angeles, says of Jonathan. "He learned the tricks of the trade straight from the old-timers, and he has always honored them, all through his career. Old school is who he is, where he comes from, what he does."

"He's exactly what he says he is, which is rare," says punk-rock icon Howie Pyro. "He's an old-school tattoo gangster with true respect for those roots, not some newfangled goon trying to play Picasso."

And Jonathan was always an astute hustler when it came to the business. By all accounts, he really knew how to sell a tattoo. His over-the-top personality and dark charisma were always a gift in the tattoo shops he worked in before going off on his own. "If ya can't dazzle 'em with brilliance, baffle 'em with bullshit," Bob Shaw once told him. And he mastered that trick of the trade, the whole show-business, carnival aspect of the game. With his slicked-back hair, gold teeth, and gold Rolex, he always looked his best when he went out to meet the public. He possesses the mysterious qualities of any good salesman: that special magnetism that makes people nervous and at the same time excited for whatever's in store. Jonathan was notorious for making customers wait outside for outrageously long periods of time. No one was ever allowed backstage while he set up—even if he was just sitting inside drinking and bullshitting with friends, rock stars, maybe some neighborhood kids, or the guys who worked for him. People knew his tattoos were worth the wait. Jonathan always knew how to keep 'em smiling and keep 'em coming back for more. And although his contributions to tattooing over the most important decades of its evolution have been immeasurable, from his point of view he was just in the right place at the right time, making a buck doing what he liked, and sharing his love for it with the world. For his efforts, he won all sorts of industry awards over the years, most of them recognizing his trademark freehand work. When asked about the accolades, though, he just scowls and waves his hand dismissively. "It's a lot of nonsense, man. Smoke and mirrors. Cheap tricks to impress the thundering herds of 'tattoo fans.' Award-winning this, award-winning that. Shit, man, those fucking trophies were the first thing to hit the dumpster when I sold the shop."

That statement seems to paraphrase his view of the emerging tattoo industry: a lot of meaningless garbage. A jaded view, but one he has certainly earned. Without a doubt, he has a great deal more respect for those who came before him than for many of those who emerged in his wake. Jonathan always saw himself as a craftsman rather than an entertainer. In today's industrialized post-Shaw tattoo world, however, the two have collided, often with surreal results—as seen on TV. Like a handful of other old-school veterans, Jonathan watched, with a somewhat amused, often perplexed, attitude, the humble craft that crawled its way out of the old low-rent bucket shops on the Bowery explode into a worldwide "industry." "Industry!? Really?" He howls with laughter. "Jeez! Some people take this whole thing a little too serious, doncha think? I mean, c'mon, man, all these big-name scab slingers ain't exactly curing cancer, y'know! Seriously. Let's face it, for a lot of these new folks, it's all about the cash and prizes, right?"

He makes a good point. Sadly, in an increasingly globalized, homogenized, media-driven marketplace, tattooing has become a fast track to easy money for many who seem to care little about its real history and essence. To many tattoo artists of Jonathan's generation, this trend seems incomprehensible. And, as much as he tries to downplay any lasting bitterness, that aspect of its evolution clearly disgusts him—even as it may be argued that he was among the first to steer the art form in that direction. In his defense, however, history will prove that if he unwittingly unleashed a monster by helping to legitimize tattooing, Jonathan was always working to promote the art itself, rather than merely exploiting it for personal gain. Nonetheless, a faceless media machine soon discovered and milked tattoo culture in a big way, eventually converting the once-venerable and ancient art into a trendy fast-food phenomenon— and usually without giving anything back. TV has turned tattooing into little more than another facile commercial commodity in the public eye, a source of prime-time ratings, something hip and groovy and young, while neglecting its true potential and ignoring the subject's uncharted depths. The art of tattooing, for all the great technological and artistic advances it's achieved in its long-awaited renaissance, has likewise been cheapened and largely degraded to the level of sitcom culture, catering to a formulaic bottom line. And the focus has rarely been on any of its true pioneers. Joe Dante, a downtown Manhattan resident who was on the scene back in the day, had this to say: "We lived a much more interesting life on the Lower East Side during the '80s and '90s than any of those supposed 'Reality Stars.' Real reality never makes it to the boob tube. The more 'reality' shows they make, the less real they get. The things that went down at Fun City before tattooing got legalized was the stuff of legend. You just can't make that kinda shit up!"

Ironically, right before the advent of the current wave of tattoo-based "reality" shows, Jonathan was approached by a producer for a first shot at the television market. Just having gotten out of tattooing, however, he was committed to his newfound freedom and happiness, living a simpler life in South America, traveling and writing books. Without thinking twice, he turned the offer down flat. When I ask him how come he missed the boat, he scoffs. "Missed *what* boat? Are you kidding? I didn't wanna be on that fucking boat. For me, it was like being offered a luxury stateroom on the *Titanic*. No way was I gonna waste any more of my life pandering to the lowest common denominator of public taste. The public is a shit-eating monster. Just look at what they're putting out in the media these days! And the fuckers just eat it up! It's pathetic. Shit, man, that's why I quit tattooing in the first place, to get away from public taste. Let somebody else do that shit."

I had to wonder how many times JS used to roll his eyes when some dumb chick would come in asking for a ladybug on her hip, really small so her mom wouldn't see it. Or some lame-ass hair-moussed goon asking for a tattoo of a Looney Toons character. When I got my first tattoo, I remember I wanted it real, real low, so my parents wouldn't see it. The artist—if one could call him that—didn't roll his eyes. He didn't even check my ID (good thing, 'cause I was only thirteen). He obviously didn't give a shit about the art. He wanted the cash. He took my money, slapped on the stencil and did the thing in about twenty seconds. I guess the joke's on me, though, since I'm the one stuck with a blurry, scarred-up, lopsided star that looks like a crippled spider sitting in the middle of my crotch. As a relative newcomer to the world of tattoo myself, I'm really glad to have gotten a glimpse of its radical transformation, if not firsthand, then through the eyes of someone who has been there and done it all.

Tattoo artists like Jonathan are a rarity nowadays, a dying breed. He came in with the old school and is a direct link to those who fought a bloody, unpopular battle to clear the runway for future generations. Jonathan Shaw is a living witness to tattooing coming of age, and then turning into the worldwide cultural phenomenon it is today. And like a true survivor, he lived it to the fullest and got out intact, with no regrets. Despite his cynical cracks about the burgeoning "industry," he was right at the forefront of modern tattooing's most important technological, ideological, and artistic advances. And, whether he likes to admit it or not, his contributions were a huge impetus for much of that growth. He was one of the first high-profile artists who always kept tattooing original and artful, while others were working just as hard to contribute to its mediocrity. And through his writing, he has helped keep its artistic soul alive—no small accomplishment in a time when unprincipled greed is taking over the world, the youth, the arts, and the quality of human endeavors in general. With the growth of international tattoo conventions to fuel the fire, the tattoo world has become a ready-made cash cow for new generations of hacks to jump into. It seems to be a sign of the times. Just look at what's become of rock & roll, unrecognizable today from the badass outlaw grassroots art form it once was. For better or worse, it's thanks largely to Jonathan Shaw's decades of hard work and dedication that we now have the glossy tattoo magazine, the explosion of "tribal" tattoos, the tattoo-oriented reality shows, and acceptance of the craft the world over—a world in which every other young person seems to be wearing one or more.

Since retiring from full-time tattooing in 2001, Jonathan has mostly split his time between his homes in Rio de Janeiro and Hollywood, where he continues working on a number of literary and tattoo-related projects. Those include the next several volumes of this meticulously detailed, blow-by-blow personal memoir; several books of poetry and fiction; screenplays; and, last but not least, a magnificent coffee-table art book and accompanying traveling gallery show of the huge collection of antique tattoo design sheets he amassed over his decades working with the old-school tattoo masters.

In 2010, on a visit to New York City, Jonathan Shaw once again made headline news. This time it was for being arrested while cleaning out a storage locker containing the remnants of the life he'd long left behind there. Under pressure by a publicity-hungry New York District Attorney, he was indicted by a Grand Jury and charged with eighty-nine felony counts of illegal weapons possession. Released from jail on a quarter-million-dollar bail and facing the rest of his life in prison, Jonathan had his Brazilian passport confiscated, pending the outcome of an ensuing four-year legal battle. Like the cat with nine lives, Jonathan was cleared of all charges in 2014. With a smile on his face and a prayer of gratitude in his heart, he moved back to Brazil to continue his writing. The rest is history.

No matter where he goes from here, Jonathan's artistic legacy will always remain fresh. His work lives on forever, tattooed on hearts and minds around the world. He is a revolutionary. His contributions have changed Western pop culture. His knowledge, skill, and ideology have been passed on to emerging generations of upcoming artists, many of whom are likewise committed to maintaining tattooing's sacred traditions. The doors of the future of tattooing that Jonathan Shaw first kicked open are open today for good.

And with that began a new chapter in his long, crazy, multifaceted creative life: an unarmed one-man pirate attack on the world of letters. With one widely acclaimed, non-tattoo-related work of fiction under his belt, Jonathan Shaw, the writer, has labored over a lifetime on the book you're holding in your hands. In its pages, he takes the reader deep, not only into the recesses of his extraordinary mind and life, but also into the strange and magical process of memoir-writing itself. If truth is indeed stranger than fiction, then, like his old friend and literary mentor Charles Bukowski once told him, much of the contents of this book would have to be lived before it could be written. In that sense, *Scab Vendor: Confessions of a Tattoo Artist* is much more than a fascinating memoir of a popular artist's creative evolution. It is a multicolored, cinematic, modern-day Odyssey, written in blood, ink, and tears—a multifaceted, visionary road map to the journey of the human soul.

THANK YOU!

First, I must give major thanks to God, and secondly to my dear brother-by-another-mother, Johnny Depp, for his invaluable encouragement and support. From the day JD first read the original rough outlines of the *Scab Vendor* book series (in the form of a screenplay written at his kind suggestion) and told me of his wish to make this ongoing saga into a movie, the spark of hope he lit in my heart was often the only light guiding me through the daunting process of bringing this especially challenging, and often painful, first volume to completion. Over the years, he has selflessly shared his home, heart, and patronage with a struggling writer. Johnny is a modern-day Medici, an old-school benefactor to the underground, the underdog, and the dispossessed. For those angelic, soulful qualities, and for his loyal friendship, vision, generosity, love, and undying belief in my humble efforts, I am eternally in his debt.

It would be almost impossible to express the depths of my gratitude to the great American artist, Robert Crumb, not only for his generosity in gifting us with the amazing cover art for this book, but also for his inspired editorial advice to me during the writing process, and lastly, for his courageous overall contribution to our culture. His dedication over the decades has served as a guiding light of inspiration to generations of artists like myself.

Big thanks must also be expressed here to Todd Bottorff, Stephanie Beard, Jon O'Neal, Maddie Cothren, and Caroline Herd of Turner Publishing for their diligent efforts in the production, promotion, and publication of this first volume of the *Scab Vendor* series. Without their hard work and persistent efforts, this book would still be but an intention.

Another deep tip of the Cigano hat goes out to the late, great American writer, my dear friend Dan Fante, whose support and example has been a constant inspiration. My fair colleagues, Lydia Lunch and the superlative English author, Chris Campion, are also at the top of my gratitude list for their invaluable encouragement. Heartfelt thanks also to the great American film director, Orson Oblowitz, for putting me together with a real literary agent who cares, the persistent and attentive Mark Gottlieb of Trident Media. And a special shout out to three of my closest and dearest old friends and brother artists, the great visionary painter, Joe Coleman, the legendary filmmaker, Jim Jarmusch, and our badass spiritual godfather and muse, Iggy Pop. Without these guys' loyal friendship, inspiration, example, encouragement and support, this journey wouldn't be half the fun.

Especially, I wish to bestow loving kudos upon my dear friend and longtime editorial consultant, Alessandra De Benedetti—who wrote the book's marathon afterword—for her loyalty, patience, and indispensable input and advice through the long, daunting task of bringing this work to life.

Special posthumous thanks also to the iconic American authors Charles Bukowski and Hubert Selby Jr., who both took time from their brilliant careers to share generous wisdom and advice with an unknown writer. They are both unforgettable examples of how this whole deal works.

Last, but certainly not least, an expression of eternal gratitude to my brilliant muse and partner, the kind and beautiful Genevieve Altamirano—to whom this book is lovingly dedicated.

There are many other good people, entities, and institutions to whom I owe a deep debt of thanks as well, for their help, inspiration, and guidance. Many of them have been with me constantly throughout the process of bringing this book to life. Other supporters came along later in the game, kindly offering advice and moral sustenance. Others have simply lent a quick suggestion or a kind word along the way. Still others, whose names and contributions have been misplaced in the anonymous mist of my own forgetfulness, will nonetheless linger forever, deep in my heart of gratitude.

Principally, I would also like to thank:

Aaron Finnin, Adult Children of Alcoholics, Al-Anon Family Groups, Alcoholics Anonymous, Alex Bregyan, Alex Orbison, Alfred Albrizio, Amy Fields, Ana Paula Mendes, The Augustine Fellowship, Anisa Irwin, Ariel Electron, Baba Austin, Bara Byrns, Basil Pologianis, Bill Leroy, Billy Shire, Bob Anderson and Primetime Recovery, Bruce Paly, Captain Kirk McFadden, Carlo McCormick, CEFLURGEM, Ceu do Mar, Cheyenne Crowe, China Kong, Chris Davis, Chris Garver, Chris Lohnes, Christa and Samantha Fuller, Christi Dembrowski, Christian Jurgensen, Christine Natanael, Clayton Patterson, Cynthia Lou, Dan Depp, Dave Ores, Debbie Harry, Denis Fahey, Eduardo Rabasa, Enrique Aular, Eugene Hutz, Familia Vacite and the União Cigana do Brasil, e toda a Familia de Juramidam, Gibson Hayes, Heidi Day, Herbert Reichert, Hidalgo Neira, Howie Pyro, Ida Maria, Isaac Baruch, Izara García Rodriguez, Izzy Zay, Jake Reiss, Jason Black, Jeff Ward, Jerome Ali, Jerry Stahl, Jim Kiriakakis, Joe Ryan, John Bloodclot, John Jardine, John Joseph, Johnny Brenner, Johnny Carco, Jorge Flores-Oliver, Jose Angel Baez Albarracin, Julia Cameron, Justin Clark, Justin and Brigitte Smith, Kelly Cutrone, Kembra Pfahler, Kenneth Shiffrin, Kortez, Kyle Tonniges, Lance Gold, Legs McNeil, Leon Ichaso, Leslie Westbrook, Lia Fanelli, Lisa Douglas, Lizzy Cline, Lluisa Matarrodona, Lucas de Barros, Luiz Alfaya, Luiz Segatto, Luke Miller, Madrinha Nonata, Mãe Iansá, Mariana Thomé, Matthew Bishop, Mayra Dias Gomes, Meredith Miller, Mestre Ireneu, Michelle Cushing, Michelle Delio, Miguel Flippowitch, Nick Wong, Noah Levine, Nuria Ocaña, Oliver Peck, Padrinho Paulo Roberto de Souza, Padrinho Sebastião, Paí Ogum. Patacori Ogunyé!! Saravá meu Paí!! Paloma Butcher, Pascal Perich, Paul Gerard, Ceu dos Anjos, Paul Williams, Paulo Lins, Pavlo Pushkar, Peter Antico, Peter Kuhn, Philip Sitbon, Ratso Sloman, Richard O'Connell, Rob Pistella, Robert and Suzanne Williams, Ron Turner, Rosemary Hochschild, Salete Andrade, Salvador Preciado, Sami Yaffa, Santa Sara, Seu Tranca-rua, Snake Eyes, Stacey Richman, Stefani Kong-Uhler, The Stern General Iboga, Steve Bonge, Steve Jones, Steve Mora, Steve Wiener, Tanya Mayberry, Tessa Hughes-Freeland, Theo and Andrez Castilho, todo o povo da floresta, Toiskallio Kaisu-Maria, Tomas Diaz, Tonico Monteiro de Carvalho, Tony Fried, Vera Perrone, Victoria Talbot, Vovó Catarina de Angola, Walter Gregory, Wayne Henlis, Whitney Ward, Zoe Romero Miranda.

AUTHOR BIO

Jonathan Shaw may be best known for his long, star-studded career as a world renowned, globetrotting tattoo master. But after embarking on a decades-long hiatus from the skin trade, he has worked exclusively as a full-time writer. Since establishing himself as an outlaw literary cult figure, Shaw has published several critically acclaimed works of fiction and memoir, as well as a popular series of lushly illustrated museum quality art books on tattoo history. His work has been featured in countless international publications, translated into several languages, and optioned for film by Leonardo DiCaprio. A new line of designer fashion clothing featuring Jonathan Shaw's unique, innovative tattoo-related artwork and personal brand is currently being launched worldwide.

When not traveling the world, he splits his time between homes in Rio de Janeiro, New York City, and Los Angeles—where a feature length documentary film about his life and times is currently in production.

His motto: "Comforting the disturbed and disturbing the comfortable —since 1953"

For readings, book signing events, speaking engagements, and exclusive tattoo appointments, Jonathan Shaw can be reached at: jsfuncity@gmail.com

Photo credit: Larnce Gold

CPSIA information can be obtained
at www.ICGtesting.com
Printed in the USA
LVHW091515060619
620401LV00009B/185/P